Europe's Rich Fabric

AF837725

Throughout human history luxury textiles have been used as a marker of importance, power and distinction. Yet, as the essays in this collection make clear, the term 'luxury' is one that can be fraught with difficulties for historians. Focusing upon the consumption, commercialisation and production of luxury textiles in Italy and the Low Countries during the late medieval and early modern periods, this volume offers a fascinating exploration of the varied and subtle ways that luxury could be interpreted and understood in the past. Beginning with the consumption of luxury textiles, it takes the reader on a journey back from the market place, to the commercialisation of rich fabrics by an international network of traders, before arriving at the workshop to explore the Italian and Burgundian world of production of damasks, silks and tapestries.

The first part of the volume deals with the consumption of luxury textiles, through an investigation of courtly purchases, as well as urban and clerical markets, before the chapters in part two move on to explore the commercialisation of luxury textiles by merchants who facilitated their trade from the cities of Lucca, Florence and Venice. The third part then focusses upon manufacture, encouraging consideration of the concept of luxury during this period through the Italian silk industry and the production of high-quality woollens in the Low Countries. Graeme Small draws the various themes of the volume together in a conclusion that suggests profitable future avenues of research into this important subject.

Bart Lambert *is a Lecturer in the History of Renaissance and Reformation Europe at Durham University. His research interests focus on the history of international trade and banking in late medieval Europe and the history of immigration in England during the Later Middle Ages.*

Katherine Anne Wilson *works as a Senior Lecturer in Medieval History at the University of Chester. She is a specialist in the history of tapestry production and consumption, cultural history, material culture and gift-exchange relations in the Burgundian Dominions.*

Europe's Rich Fabric

The Consumption, Commercialisation, and Production of Luxury Textiles in Italy, the Low Countries and Neighbouring Territories (Fourteenth–Sixteenth Centuries)

Edited by

Bart Lambert
Durham University, UK

Katherine Anne Wilson
University of Chester, UK

Routledge
Taylor & Francis Group
LONDON AND NEW YORK

First Published 2016 by Ashgate Publisher

2 Park Square, Milton Park, Abingdon, Oxfordshire OX14 4RN
52 Vanderbilt Avenue, New York, NY 10017

Routledge is an imprint of the Taylor & Francis Group, an informa business

First issued in paperback 2019

Copyright © Bart Lambert and Katherine Anne Wilson 2016

Bart Lambert and Katherine Anne Wilson have asserted their right under the Copyright, Designs and Patents Act, 1988, to be identified as the editors of this work.

All rights reserved. No part of this book may be reprinted or reproduced or utilised in any form or by any electronic, mechanical, or other means, now known or hereafter invented, including photocopying and recording, or in any information storage or retrieval system, without permission in writing from the publishers.

Notice:
Product or corporate names may be trademarks or registered trademarks, and are used only for identification and explanation without intent to infringe.

British Library Cataloguing in Publication Data
A catalogue record for this book is available from the British Library

The Library of Congress has cataloged the printed edition as follows:
Europe's Rich Fabric: The Consumption, Commercialisation, and Production of Luxury Textiles in Italy, the Low Countries and Neighbouring Territories (Fourteenth–Sixteenth Centuries) / Edited by Bart Lambert and Katherine Anne Wilson.
pages cm
Includes bibliographical references and index.
1. Textile industry – Europe – History – To 1500. 2. Textile industry – Europe – History – 16th century. 3. Luxury goods industry – Europe – History – To 1500. 4. Luxury goods industry – Europe – History – 16th century. 5. Textile fabrics – Social aspects – Europe – History – To 1500. 6. Textile fabrics – Social aspects – Europe – History – 16th century. I. Lambert, Bart, editor. II. Wilson, Katherine Anne, editor.
HD9940.A2E82 2015
338.4'767700940902–dc23 2015015380

ISBN: 978-1-4094-4442-8 (hbk)
ISBN: 978-0-367-87913-6 (pbk)

Contents

List of Tables, Figures and Plates *vii*
Notes on Contributors *xiii*
Preface *xvii*

Introduction: Luxury Textiles in Italy, the Low Countries and Neighbouring Territories (Fourteenth to Sixteenth Centuries): A Conceptual Investigation 1
Bart Lambert and Katherine Anne Wilson

PART I: CONSUMPTION OF LUXURY TEXTILES

1 'In the chamber, in the garde robe, in the chapel, in a chest': The Possession and Uses of Luxury Textiles. The Case of Later Medieval Dijon 11
Katherine Anne Wilson

2 'O per honore, o per commodo mio': Displaying Textiles at the Gonzaga Court (Fifteenth–Sixteenth Centuries) 35
Christina Antenhofer

3 Between Mass and 'Mystère': The *Life of Saint Remigius* and the Ceremonial Function of Choir Tapestries 69
Laura Weigert

PART II: COMMERCIALISATION OF LUXURY TEXTILES

4 'Se fist riche par draps de soye' The Intertwinement of Italian Financial Interests and Luxury Trade at the Burgundian Court (1384–1481) 91
Bart Lambert

5 Florence, Nuremberg and Beyond: Italian Silks in Central Europe during the Renaissance 107
Francesco Guidi-Bruscoli

6 Trading Silks and Tapestries in Sixteenth-Century Antwerp 131
Jeroen Puttevils

PART III: PRODUCTION OF LUXURY TEXTILES

7 The Move to Quality Cloth. Luxury Textiles, Labour Markets and Middle Class Identity in a Medieval Textile City. Mechelen in the Late Thirteenth and Early Fourteenth Centuries 159
Peter Stabel

8 Woollen Luxury Cloth in Late Medieval Italy 181
Franco Franceschi

9 A Luxury Industry: The Production of Italian Silks 1400–1600 205
Luca Molà

Centres, Peripheries and the Performative Textile: By Way of Conclusion *235*
Graeme Small

Index *241*

List of Tables, Figures and Plates

Tables

2.1	Detailed list of cloths.	45
2.2	List of cloths.	45
2.3	List of textiles taken by the physician, Magistro Bernardo.	46
2.4	Expenses for gold and silver threads, enamels and minor silk cloths.	47
5.1	Raw silk sent from Calabria to Florence, on behalf of the Olivieri of Nuremberg (Sept–Nov 1545).	112
5.2	Florentine silks sent to Nuremberg (21 July 1544–6 June 1545).	116
5.3	German cloths sold to Florentine *setaioli* on behalf of the Olivieri of Nuremberg (Feb 1545–Mar 1546).	118
5.4	Sales of silks and purchases of raw silk and German cloths by Florentine *setaioli* (1544–46).	122
6.1	Tapestry exports based on toll records, mid sixteenth century.	135
6.2	Share of Netherlandish tapestry production centres in the export to Iberia in 1553 (January 1–June 30 1533).	135
8.1	Composition of the costs of some fine and medium quality cloths (1396–end fifteenth century).	198

Figures

1.1	Map of Dijon 1574. Edouard Bredin. Archives Municipales de Dijon, cote 4, Fi 956. Used with permission of the archives.	16

2.1 Barbara of Brandenburg, *Letter to Margareta of Bayern-München*, 1478, Archivio di Stato di Mantova, AG b. 2103bis c. 545. Used with permission of the Archivio di Stato di Mantova and the Ministero dei Beni e delle Attività Culturali e del Turismo. 54
4.1 Statue representing Dino Rapondi, erected by Philip the Good in the ducal Sainte Chapelle in Dijon, Bibliothèque nationale de France, Bibliothèque de l'Arsenal, ms. 3901, c. 22. 96
6.1 Prices of textiles available on the Antwerp market in 1575. 138
6.2 Price quotations of organzina silk in the Van der Molen letters, 1538–1544. 144

List of Colour Plates

The plates fall between pages 112–113

1 Andrea Mantegna, *The Encounter*, Camera degli Sposi, West Wall, Palazzo Ducale, Castello San Giorgio, Mantua. Used with permission of the Archivio di Stato di Mantova and the Ministero dei Beni e delle Attività Culturali e del Turismo.
2 Andrea Mantegna, *The Court*, Camera degli Sposi, North Wall, Palazzo Ducale, Castello San Giorgio, Mantua. Used with permission of the Archivio di Stato di Mantova and the Ministero dei Beni e delle Attività Culturali e del Turismo.
3 Simon von Taisten, *Mary's Death and the Donors Leonhard von Görz and Paula Gonzaga*, Chapel Schloss Bruck, Lienz. Used with permission of the Museum Schloss Bruck.
4 Simon von Taisten, *The Miracle of the Cross of St. Elisabeth of Thüringen* (detail), Museum der Stadt Lienz, Schloss Bruck, Lienz. Inv. Used with permission of the Museum Schloss Bruck.
5 Portrait of Robert de Lenoncourt, Panel 10 of the *Life of Saint Remigius*, Reims, Musée de Saint Remi (detail). Copyright Camara StudioDVL, Reims, France.
6 *Lives of Piat and Eleutherius* (detail), Tournai, Notre-Dame Cathedral. Copyright KIK-IRPA, Brussels.
7 *Life of Saint Anathoile of Salins* (detail), Paris, Louvre (photo: RMN).
8 Interior of La Chaise-Dieu (photo: Chaise-Dieu).
9 Panel 3 of the *Life of Saint Remigius*, Reims, Musée de Saint Remi. Copyright Camara StudioDVL, Reims, France.
10 Panel 8 of the *Life of Saint Remigius*, Reims, Musée de Saint Remi. Copyright Camara StudioDVL, Reims, France.
11 Detail of panel 8 of the *Life of Saint Remigius*, Reims, Musée de Saint Remi. Copyright Camara StudioDVL, Reims, France.

12 Panel 9 of the *Life of Saint Remigius*, Reims, Musée de Saint Remi. Copyright Camara StudioDVL, Reims, France.
13 Panel 10 of the *Life of Saint Remigius*, Reims, Musée de Saint Remi. Copyright Camara StudioDVL, Reims, France.
14 Chasuble with embroidered scene of the Passion, Genoese velvet embroidered with dyed silk and gold thread, c.1530, Maagdenhuis, Antwerp. Copyright KIK-IRPA, Brussels
15 Large leaf verdure with Hercules killing the Stymphalian birds, Wool & silk, 1541–1560, Provinciebestuur Oost–Vlaanderen, Ghent. Copyright KIK-IRPA, Brussels.
16 The Mechelen cloth hall in the first half of the 19th century Jan-Baptist De Noter, *Mechelen Cloth Hall*, Collection Schoeffer, City Archives Mechelen. Copyright City Archives Mechelen-www.beeldbankmechelen.be.
17 Sandro Botticelli, *Portrait of a Young Man*, 1485, Private Collection.
18 Domenico Ghirlandaio, *Stories of Saint Francis (detail)*, 1485, Santa Trinita, Sassetti Chapel, Florence. Used with permission of the Ministero dei Beni e delle Attività Culturali e del Turismo.
19 School of Agnolo Gaddi, *Stories of Saint Nicholas (detail)*, circa 1385, Santa Croce, Castellani Chapel, Florence. Used with permission of the Fondo Edifici di Culto, Ministero dell' Interno.

Notes on Contributors

Dr Christina Antenhofer (University of Innsbruck)

Christina Antenhofer is associate professor of medieval history at the Department of History and European Ethnology of the University of Innsbruck. She has been visiting professor at the University of New Orleans. She works on political communication in Italian Renaissance city states and has devoted particular attention to the role played by textiles in this process. She has published the book *Briefe zwischen Süd und Nord. Die Hochzeit und Ehe von Paula de Gonzaga und Leonhard von Görz im Spiegel der fürstlichen Kommunikation (1473–1500)* (Innsbruck, 2007), and various articles, including 'From Local Signori to European High Nobility. The Gonzaga Family Networks in the 15th Century', in *Transregional and Transnational Families in Europe and Beyond: Experiences Since the Middle Ages* edited by Christopher H. Johnson, David W. Sabean, Simon Teuscher and Francesca Trivellato, 55–74 (New York, 2010), and 'Letters across the borders. Strategies of Communication in an Italian-German Renaissance Correspondence', in *Women's Letters Across Europe 1400–1700. Form and Persuasion*, edited by Jane Couchman and Ann Crabb, 103–122 (Aldershot, 2005). Recently she has co-edited with Axel Behne, Daniela Ferrari, Jürgen Herold and Peter Rückert the letters of Barbara Gonzaga, *Barbara Gonzaga: Die Briefe/Le Lettere (1455–1508)* (Stuttgart, 2013).

Professor Franco Franceschi (University of Siena)

A former fellow of the Istituto Italiano per gli Studi Storici in Naples and the Harvard University Center for Italian Renaissance Studies in Florence, Franco Franceschi is professor of medieval history at the University of Siena. He is the author of numerous articles and books on the history of labour and guilds, economic policies, the transmission of knowledge and the mentality of productive classes in Italy between the thirteenth and the sixteenth centuries, including *Oltre il 'Tumulto'. I lavoratori fiorentini dell'Arte della Lana fra Tre e Quattrocento* (Florence, 1993), *« … E seremo tutti ricchi». Lavoro, mobilità sociale e conflitti nelle città dell'Italia medievale* (Pisa, 2012) and, with I. Taddei, *Le città italiane nel Medioevo. XII-XIV secolo* (Bologna, 2012). With S. Cohn, M. Fantoni and F. Ricciardelli, he edited *Late Medieval and Early Modern Ritual: Studies in Italian Urban Culture* (Turnhout, 2013).

Dr Francesco Guidi-Bruscoli (University of Florence)
Francesco Guidi-Bruscoli teaches economic history at the Università di Firenze and is Senior Research Fellow of the History Department of Queen Mary University of London, where he led the Borromei Bank Research Project together with Professor Jim Bolton. His research interests focus on the activities of Italian merchant bankers from the fourteenth to the sixteenth centuries, covering the production of and the trade in Florentine silks. Francesco Guidi-Bruscoli is the author of *Bartolomeo Marchionni, «homem de grossa fazenda» (ca. 1450–1530). Un mercante fiorentino a Lisbona e l'impero portoghese,* (Florence, 2014), *Papal Banking in Renaissance Rome: Benvenuto Olivieri and Paul III, 1534–1549* (Aldershot, 2007), *Benvenuto Olivieri, i 'mercatores' fiorentini e la Camera apostolica nella Roma di Paolo III Farnese (1534–1549)* (Florence, 2000), 'When did Antwerp replace Bruges as the commercial and financial centre of north-western Europe? The evidence of the Borromei ledger for 1438', *The Economic History Review* 61 (2008): 360–379, with J.L. Bolton, and 'Drappi di seta e tele di lino tra Firenze e Norimberga nella prima metà del Cinquecento', *Archivio Storico Italiano* 159 (2001): 359–394.

Dr Bart Lambert (Durham University)
Bart Lambert is a lecturer in the history of Renaissance and Reformation Europe at Durham University. He worked as a research assistant on the AHRC-funded 'England's Immigrants 1300–1550' project at the University of York and on the Belgian Science Policy Project 'City and society in the Low Countries, 1200–1800: space, knowledge, social capital' at Ghent University. His research focuses on international trade and banking in the late medieval Low Countries, Italy and England and the history of immigration in England during the Later Middle Ages and early modern period. His publications include *The Duke, the City and their Banker. The Rapondi family and the formation of the Burgundian state (1385–1430)* (Turnhout, 2006), on the silk trade in late medieval Bruges, and 'Pouvoir et argent. La fiscalité d'État et la consommation du crédit des ducs de Bourgogne (1384–1506)', *Revue du Nord* 91 (2009): 35–59 with Jelle Haemers.

Professor Luca Molà (European University Institute, Florence)
Luca Molà is the Chair in Early Modern History of Europe at the European University Institute in Fiesole (Florence). He is a former lecturer at the University of Warwick, where he was director of the Centre for the History of

Innovation and Creativity (CHIC). Luca Molà has published extensively on the history of the Italian Renaissance, on the economic and social history of Europe in the early modern period, particularly the production and commercialisation of luxury textiles, and on the first age of globalisation. His main publications include *The Silk Industry of Renaissance Venice* (Baltimore, 2000), *La comunità dei lucchesi a Venezia: Immigrazione e industria della seta nel tardo Medioevo* (Venice, 1994) and *La seta in Italia dal Medioevo al Seicento. Dal baco al drappo,* edited with Reinhold C. Mueller and Claudio Zanier (Venice, 2000), as well as numerous articles on luxury textiles in renowned international reviews.

Dr Jeroen Puttevils (University of Antwerp)
Jeroen Puttevils is a postdoctoral researcher of the Research Foundation Flanders (FWO) and a member of the Centre for Urban History at Antwerp University. He was a Fulbright Scholar in 2013 at the University of Pennsylvania in Philadelphia. Among his other work, he has undertaken research on the Van der Molen, a merchant family working as commission agents for Italian firms in the Antwerp silk trade from the middle of the sixteenth century. He has published *Merchants and Trading in the Sixteenth Century: The Golden Age of Antwerp* (London, 2015) and 'Klein gewin brengt rijkdom in: de Zuid-Nederlandse handelaars in de export naar Italië in de jaren 1540', *Tijdschrift voor sociale en economische geschiedenis* 6 (2009): 26–52. His current work focuses on lotteries and economic culture in the fifteenth and sixteenth-century Low Countries.

Professor Graeme Small (Durham University)
Graeme Small is chair of medieval history at Durham University. He works on international court culture, the prosopographical study of elites, the process of state formation, the history of propaganda, textual reception and codicological analysis. He is also a member of the academic advisory panel for the publication of the Burrell Collection tapestry catalogue. Among many other publications, Graeme Small is the author of *Court and Civic Society in the Burgundian Low Countries c.1420–1520* (Manchester, 2007) with Andrew Brown, *Later Medieval France* (Basingstoke, 2009), 'Of Burgundian Dukes, Counts, Saints and Kings (14 C.E–c.1520)', in *The Ideology of Burgundy: The Promotion of National Consciousness, 1364–1565*, edited by Jonathan D. Boulton and Jan R. Veenstra, 151–194 (Leiden, 2006).

Professor Peter Stabel (University of Antwerp)
Peter Stabel is professor of history at Antwerp University and a member of the Centre for Urban History. He has undertaken extensive research on textile history and the economic, social and urban history of the Low Countries in the late medieval and early modern period. He is the author of 'For mutual benefit? Court and city in the Burgundian Low Countries', In *The Court as a*

Stage: England and the Low Countries in the Later Middle Ages, edited by Steven Gunn and Antheun Janse, 101–117 (Woodbridge, 2006) and *Dwarfs among giants: the Flemish urban network in the late Middle Ages* (Antwerp, 1997) and the editor of *Buyers and sellers: retail circuits and practices in medieval and early modern Europe* (Turnhout, 2006), with B. Blondé, J. Stobart and I. Van Damme and *International trade in the Low Countries (14th–16th centuries): merchants, organization, infrastructure* (Antwerp, 2000), with B. Blondé and A. Greve. Currently he is finishing a monograph on economic change, luxuries and guilds in late medieval Bruges. His current research projects include work on medieval labour markets and on market organisation and power relations in the cities of Western Europe and the Islamic world.

Professor Laura Weigert (Rutgers School of Arts and Sciences)
After teaching at the Université de Nantes and Reed College, Laura Weigert was appointed associate professor of Northern Renaissance art at Rutgers University (New Brunswick, NJ) in 2006. Her research focuses on the interaction between visual images and their architectural and ritual settings in the fifteenth and sixteenth centuries and includes the study of textiles, manuscript illumination, prints and panel painting. She is the author of *Weaving Sacred Stories: French Choir Tapestries and the Performance of Clerical Identity* (Ithaca, 2004), *Judith et Holopherne* (Desclée de Brouwer, 2003), with Marc de Launay and Catherine Lépront and 'Chambres d'Amour: Courtly Tapestries and the Texturing of Space', *Oxford Art Journal* 31 (2008): 317–336. Her next book, *The Arts of Performance and the Making of Medieval Theater in France,* is forthcoming.

Dr Katherine Anne Wilson (University of Chester)
Katherine Anne Wilson is senior lecturer in medieval history at the University of Chester. A former lecturer in medieval history at the University of York, her research seeks to understand the relationship between social and cultural change, and shifting patterns in the use of material culture in the Burgundian Dominions during the Later Middle Ages. Her main publications in this area are: 'The household inventory as urban 'theatre' in late medieval Burgundy', *Social History* 40 (2015) : 335–359, 'Paris, Arras et la cour: Les tapissiers de Philip le Hardi et Jean sans Peur, ducs de Bourgogne', *Revue du Nord* 389 (2011): 11–31, 'A Complex Product. Tapestry of the Burgundian Dominions, c. 1363–1500', in *La cour de Bourgogne et l'Europe,* edited by Torsten Hiltman, Frank Viltart and Werner Paravicini, 317–331 (Ostfildern, 2013) and 'Political tapestries of Philip the Bold and John the Fearless, dukes of Burgundy', in *Visual exports/imports: New Research on Medieval and Renaissance art and culture,* edited by Emily Jane Anderson and Jill Farquhar, 145–158 (Cambridge, 2012). Currently she is working on a project titled 'Urban society, consumer revolution and the Burgundian court'.

Preface

This book is the result of several workshops, conferences and discussions among a group of historians and art historians in 2010 and 2011 held at the University of St Andrews, Ghent University and the European University Institute in Florence. Debate centred around the issue that from the fourteenth to the sixteenth centuries luxury textiles including damasks, silks, velvets and luxury woollens frequently formed a part of the trade between the two greatest areas of luxury textile production, Italy and the Low Countries. The discussions also recognised that these textiles were of great importance to the economies of these areas and were owned by an increasing variety of consumers. The participants acknowledged that while elements of their history have been the subject of past and current research, work that attempted to cover the consumption, commercialisation and production of luxury textiles during the Later Middle Ages and early modern period in an integrated way was still lacking. This book, an outcome of the work and discussions of these workshops, seeks to go some way towards stressing the interdependency of Italy, the Low Countries and their neighbouring territories in manufacture, marketing and consumption.

The editors would like to thank all the contributors of the workshop at St Andrews in 2010, the session at the Urban History Conference in Ghent in 2010 and the workshop at the European University Institute in 2011. The funding and organisation that was made available by these institutions enabled important themes and discussions to be developed over time. We would also like to thank Professor Martha Howell of Columbia University, who generously gave up her time at the Urban History Conference in Ghent in 2010 to chair the session and to provide essential comments on the themes of the workshop and on the format of this book. The colour plate section in this volume was made possible thanks to the financial support of the Belgian

Science Policy IAP VII project 'City and Society in the Low Countries (c. 1200–1850). The "condition urbaine": between resilience and vulnerability'. Finally we would like to extend our thanks to all those individuals and institutions that kindly provided permission to publish the images for our volume.

Introduction
Luxury Textiles in Italy, the Low Countries and Neighbouring Territories (Fourteenth to Sixteenth Centuries): A Conceptual Investigation

Bart Lambert and Katherine Anne Wilson

Describing the city of Bruges in 1438, the Castilian nobleman Pero Tafur was moved to pronounce that 'Without doubt, the goddess luxury has great power there, but it is not a place for poor men, who would be badly received'.[1] Clearly, part of the power of the goddess luxury lay in the ability of the concept to evolve over time, yet luxury's malleability and the multiple connotations it carries, make clear that it is a term that has to be carefully considered by all who use it in their work. Furthermore, as the term is used to describe the textiles under examination in this volume it deserves some detailed thought.

Originally from the Latin *luxuria*, the term in its basic sense denotes excess, extravagance and magnificence. While these facets remain inherent to our modern usage of the term and understanding of the concept, there is no shortage of recent works emphasising the problematic usage of luxury both as a concept and as a term of description. As Christopher Dyer points out, the first issue lies in its shifts in meaning over time and thus its inability to 'be strictly and easily defined'.[2] The second issue arises in the use of the concept of luxury by individuals from the classical to the modern period to describe actions or desired actions of individuals, groups or polities. Jan de Vries underlines luxury as 'an essential prop upholding the established order,

1 Pero Tafur, *Travels and Adventures*, trans.Malcom Letts (London: Routledge, 2005), 200.

2 Christopher Dyer, 'Luxury Goods in Medieval England', in *Commercial Activity, Markets and Entrepreneurs in the Middle Ages. Essays in Honour of Richard Britnell*, ed. Ben Dodds et al. (Woodbridge: Boydell and Brewer, 2011), 217.

yet at the same time ... universally fraught with moral danger'.[3] For Marina Belozerskaya, the concept is 'charged and politicised' and 'has forever been a subject of contention'.[4] The final issue lies in the modern attachment of the term luxury to an object. It is commonplace when writing on broadcloths, silks and tapestries to state that they are 'luxuries' or 'luxury textiles'. But what exactly made them a luxury and did contemporaries regard them as a luxury?[5] Reflecting on objects described within probate inventories, Anton Schuurman notes that it is essential that such terms, if they are to be used, are properly defined and explain which criteria they use to distinguish between basic and 'luxury' goods.[6]

A brief historical consideration of the concept of luxury is useful to consider the potential pitfalls historians face when using the term due to its inability to be 'strictly and easily defined' and the multiplicity of associations it can carry as a result. For Aristotle great expenditure on texts and jewels was essential and befitting to those of appropriate status.[7] But luxury also held negative connotations. As Jan de Vries notes 'Only a thin line separated the noble patron of the arts from the vain, prideful self-aggrandiser; the refined pallet merged effortlessly with gluttony; the admiration of a fine garment easily turned to lust'.[8] For many medieval commentators this boundary, more often than not, was frequently transgressed. In Chaucer's eyes both gluttony and lust were connected to luxury: 'The holy writ take I to witnesse that luxurie is in wyn and dronkenesse' and 'If he be ploungid in fowle and unclene luxuries, he is witholden in the fowle delices of the fowle sowe'.[9] While Chaucer's negative view of luxury had long been espoused by churchmen such as Bernard of Clairvaux (1090–1153) who criticised the adornment of churches as a corrupting influence that lead the faithful away from God, the concept of luxury was not universally condemned. For medieval users of the

[3] Jan de Vries, 'Luxury in the Dutch Golden Age in Theory and Practice', in *Luxury in the Eighteenth Century. Debates, Desires and Delectable Goods*, ed. Maxine Berg et al. (New York: Palgrave Macmillan, 2003), 41.

[4] Marina Belozerskaya, *Luxury Arts of the Renaissance* (Los Angeles: J. Paul Getty Museum, 2005), 1.

[5] Christopher Berry, *The Idea of Luxury: A Conceptual and Historical Investigation* (Cambridge: Cambridge University Press, 1994), 4–5, 32. He argues that the values needed to make an object a luxury are values assigned to the product to increase consumption and also the difficulty of acquisition.

[6] Anton Schuurman, 'Probate Inventories: Research Issues, Problems and Results', in *Probate Inventories. A new source for the historical study of wealth, material culture and agricultural development*, ed. Ad van der Woude et al. (Utrecht: HES Publishers, 1980), 25.

[7] Maxine Berg and Elizabeth Eger, 'The Rise and Fall of Luxury Debates', in *Luxury in the Eighteenth Century. Debates, Desires and Delectable Goods*, ed. Maxine Berg et al. (New York: Palgrave Macmillan, 2003), 8. They note that Aristotle, in *Book IV of the Nicomachean Ethics*, developed the concept of 'liberalita', as a virtue with an objective of moral beauty in contrast to the vices of prodigality and avarice.

[8] De Vries, 'Luxury in the Dutch Golden Age', 42.

[9] Sherman M. Kuhn, ed., *Middle English Dictionary* (Michigan: University of Michigan Press, 1998), 1318.

concept it could still embody the positive connotations ascribed by classical thinkers. Adornment and expenditure were deemed necessary to furnish places of worship through which one could also honour God as suggested by Bishop Suger (1081–1153).[10] As the Middle Ages progressed, these tensions may have become ever more acute. The effect of a transformation in consumer goods and spending in the later fourteenth and fifteenth centuries saw not only a shift in the relationship between people and their possessions, but another alteration in the concept of luxury.[11] In Samuel Cohn's assessment, the humanist thinkers of Italy in the fifteenth century saw clear benefits in riches accumulated by a household.[12] These assets and possessions could act as instruments in the struggle for virtue, and their wealth could have the benefit of strengthening the body politic as a whole.[13] But the use value, the exchange value of an object and accumulation for its own sake were not yet celebrated in the fourteenth, fifteenth and sixteenth centuries. The benefits of luxury were to be seen in the utility of wealth, the splendour of objects and the people and places of status they could elevate, but its drawbacks were clear, abundant and to the fore of the medieval understanding and usage of the term.

It took the social and economic transitions of the seventeenth and eighteenth centuries to foreground the positives and benefits of luxury both as a concept and as a term of description. The association of luxury with corruption and vice faded, and was replaced by the positive connotations of production, trade and commodities.[14] Luxury was re-conceptualised as a public benefit by Bernard Mandeville, David Hume and Adam Smith who all associated luxury with positive economic gain.[15] In their view, it helped to oil the wheels of commercial prosperity and as a result the 'cost' aspect of the concept of luxury, which is pre-eminent in the modern usage of the term, is a legacy of the seventeenth and eighteenth centuries. However, it took until the early twentieth century for the word 'luxury' to be used in an adjectival form. Despite the cost aspect of luxury still being pre-eminent in its twentieth and twenty-first century usage, it is now more multi-dimensional than its earlier conceptualisations in that it also embodies symbolic value and quality. These continual shifts in meaning and the multiple associations that can be made when the word is used as a term of description, may lead us to ask: how useful is the term at all for describing textiles consumed, commercialised and

10 Belozerskaya, *Luxury Arts of the Renaissance*, 1.

11 Maryanne Kowaleski, 'A consumer economy', in *A social history of England: 1200–1500* ed. Rosemary Horrox et al. (Cambridge: Cambridge University Press, 2006), 239.

12 Sam Cohn, 'Renaissance attachment to things: material culture in last wills and testaments', *The Economic History Review* 65 (2012), 30–32.

13 Cohn, 'Renaissance attachment to things', 30–32.

14 Berg and Eger, 'The Rise and Fall of Luxury Debates', 7.

15 Berg and Eger, 'The Rise and Fall of Luxury Debates', 10–11.

manufactured in Italy, the Low Countries and their neighbouring territories from the fourteenth to the sixteenth centuries?

Thankfully, the concept of a textile is far less fluid. The term 'textile' denotes weaving, woven fabric and cloth.[16] The textiles that form the focus of this volume, broadcloths, silks and tapestry can be categorised under this heading. While tapestry has at times been separated from other textiles, and considered an art object in its own right (although more frequently downgraded by the nineteenth-century classification of the textile as a decorative art rather than as a fine art) Peter Stabel and Wolfgang Brassart have argued that while it can carry visual programmes and agendas, nonetheless it was also part of an increased diversification towards high quality textiles that occurred in the Low Countries during the fourteenth century, described by Brassart as *luxustextilien*.[17] Of course, the term textile encompasses a huge variety of forms and types produced during the two hundred years covered by this volume. Therefore this volume proposes to consider what made textiles a luxury in order to allow the contributors to examine and explore a range of textiles from broadcloths, tapestry through to a wide variety of silk and silk products.

When the term 'luxury textile' is used in this volume it is in a modern sense. The term luxury is not found in connection with the textiles under examination in this volume during the fourteenth to the sixteenth centuries. When broadcloths, silks and tapestry are described by household, narrative or travel accounts of the fourteenth and fifteenth centuries, the terms most commonly connected with these objects are 'costly' or 'large'. These terms can reflect and refer to the production processes used to manufacture the objects described. As the chapter by Katherine Anne Wilson in this volume explores, the terminology used in the descriptions of the silks and tapestry possessed by the inhabitants of Dijon still carried associations with their original places of manufacture or reflected the production processes used in the manufacture of the textiles. Importantly, the terms also often allude to the difficulty of acquisition of the object described and the perceived 'exclusivity' of the textile under discussion, especially when it is associated with an exotic place of manufacture.

The volume proposes to consider whether, from the fourteenth to the sixteenth centuries, these broadcloths, silks and tapestry constituted a luxury in its modern sense. In order to use the concept fruitfully, it will split luxury into three major components. First it will address the symbolic value of the textiles, exploring their use and perception as markers of distinction by their commissioners, owners and viewers across different layers of society.

16 Guy de Poerck, *La draperie Médiévale en Flandre et en Artois. Technique et terminologie* (De Tempel: Bruges, 1951).

17 Peter Stabel, 'Guilds in late medieval Flanders: myths and realities of guild life in an export-orientated environment', *Journal of Medieval History* 30 (2004), 8; Wolfgang Brassart, *Tapisserien und Politik an den Europäischen Höfen* (Berlin, 1992), 10.

Secondly, the volume will investigate their economic value: how they were commercialised and distributed and how their prices were determined by both the intermediaries who negotiated their sale and the customers who purchased them. Finally, it will discuss the quality of the broadcloths, silks and tapestry under consideration and the ways in which this was guaranteed during their production process. The contributors will seek to explore these questions by looking at the late medieval and early modern Low Countries, Italy and, to a lesser extent, their neighbouring territories. The geographical scope will allow them to adequately cover some of these textiles' most important areas of consumption, their centres of production and the channels of commercialisation that connected them. At the same time, it will demonstrate how geographical boundaries or regional centres affected definitions of what was a luxury. After all, Christopher Dyer reminded us that what might be considered as fashionable in the North, may well not be so in the South.[18]

Unlike other volumes, this work will choose to invert the usual order of things and will begin by addressing the consumption of luxury textiles, then their commercialisation, and finally their production. The rationale for such a structure is more than simply a desire for novelty. The first reason lies in the fact that the finished product of silks and tapestries is the form that we are most often directly confronted with, whether this be in contemporary accounts of their use, in visual programmes from the period, or in textiles preserved and venerated in present day museum collections around the world. The second reason is that by beginning with consumption, it allows the volume to present a dialectical concept of the relationship between manufacture and consumption, especially in a later medieval and early modern world where, as our chapters prove, manufacture of these types of textiles were driven in large part by changes in the perception, taste and fashion of consumers.

In the first section of the book, dealing with the symbolic value that was given to luxury textiles through their consumption, Katherine Anne Wilson explores who were the owners of silks and tapestry in later medieval Dijon as well as the spaces in which they were used. Christina Antenhofer discusses what kind of social meanings were connected to textiles displayed at the fifteenth and sixteenth-century Gonzaga court in Mantua and which political implications should be deduced from these performances. In her study, Laura Weigert describes the reception and ceremonial function of an individual tapestry within the setting of the abbey church choir for which it was made, during the fifteenth and sixteenth centuries. The volume's section dedicated to commercialisation and the textiles' economic value equally consists of three chapters. Bart Lambert provides new insights into the relationship between the Italian intermediaries who supplied silk products and the Burgundian

18 Dyer, 'Luxury Goods in Medieval England', 217–238.

court, one of the most conspicuous centres of luxury textile consumption in fifteenth-century Europe. Francesco Guidi-Bruscoli draws on understudied letters, accounts and receipts to examine the export of Florentine fabrics to a more peripheral market, that of sixteenth-century Central Europe. Through a study of an Antwerp merchant company, Jeroen Puttevils analyses the impact of the expanding consumer market for silks and tapestries in the sixteenth-century Low Countries on the supply, demand and the marketing of these goods. In the final section, treating the production and quality of luxury textiles, Peter Stabel investigates the effects that the transition of the cloth manufacture into a luxury industry in the late thirteenth and early fourteenth-century Low Countries had on the identity of its workers. Franco Franceschi deals with the chronology of the development of high-quality cloth production on the other side of the continent, in late medieval Italy. A parallel paper on the characteristics of the Italian silk industry between 1400 and 1600, written by Luca Molà, finishes the volume. Luxury textiles were objects that crossed geographical boundaries and created interdependent connections between territories and individuals. It is through the themes of consumption, commercialisation and production that our volume will explore these dynamics.

Bibliography

Belozerskaya, Marina. *Luxury Arts of the Renaissance.* Los Angeles: J. Paul Getty Museum, 2005.

Berg, Maxine, and Eger, Elizabeth. 'The Rise and Fall of Luxury Debates'. In *The Rise and Fall of Luxury Debates, Desires and Delectable Goods* edited by Maxine Berg and Elizabeth Eger, 7–27. London: Palgrave Macmillan, 2003.

Berry, Christopher. *The Idea of Luxury: A Conceptual and Historical Investigation.* Cambridge: Cambridge University Press, 1994.

Brassart, Wolfgang. *Tapisserien und Politik an den Europäischen Höfen.* Berlin, 1992.

Cohn, Samuel. 'Renaissance attachment to things: material culture in last wills and testaments', *The Economic History Review* 65 (2012): 984–1004.

De Poerck, Guy. *La draperie Médiévale en Flandre et en Artois. Technique et terminologie.* De Tempel: Bruges, 1951.

De Vries, Jan, 'Luxury in the Dutch Golden Age in Theory and Practice'. In *Luxury in the Eighteenth Century. Debates, Desires and Delectable Goods* edited by Maxine Berg and Elizabeth Eger, 7–27. New York: Palgrave Macmillan, 2003.

Dyer, Christopher. 'Luxury Goods in Medieval England'. In *Commercial Activity, Markets and Entrepreneurs in the Middle Ages. Essays in Honour of Richard Britnell,* edited by Raquel Soeiro de Brito, Ben Dodds and Christian Liddy, 217–238. Woodbridge: Boydell and Brewer, 2011.

Kowaleski, Maryanne. 'A consumer economy'. In *A social history of England: 1200–1500,* edited by Rosemary Horrox and William Mark Ormrod, 238–259. Cambridge: Cambridge University Press, 2006.

Sherman M. Kuhn, ed., *Middle English Dictionary.* Michigan: University of Michigan Press, 1998.

Schuurman, Anton. 'Probate Inventories: Research Issues, Problems and Results'. In *Probate Inventories. A new source for the historical study of wealth, material culture and agricultural development,* edited by Ad van der Woude and Anton Schuurman, 19-31. Utrecht: HES Publishers, 1980.

Stabel, Peter. 'Guilds in late medieval Flanders: myths and realities of guild life in an export-orientated environment', *Journal of Medieval History* 30 (2004): 187–212.

Tafur, Pero. *Travels and Adventures,* trans., Malcom Letts. London: Routledge, 2005.

PART I
Consumption of Luxury Textiles

1

'In the chamber, in the garde robe, in the chapel, in a chest': The Possession and Uses of Luxury Textiles. The Case of Later Medieval Dijon

Katherine Anne Wilson

Three examples of inventories surviving in the collection of the *marie de Dijon* and dating from the end of the fourteenth century serve to remind us of the range of luxury textiles that were possessed by wealthy urban inhabitants in the Later Middle Ages and the variety of uses to which they could be put.[1] The first, from 1392 and of the mercer Etienne Marchant, details over a thousand objects destined for sale to customers of Dijon as well as his and his wife's personal possessions.[2] Included among these were several ounces of different coloured silks and robes of cameline.[3] The second, from 1395, records the possessions of Regnault Chevalier, tailor to the duke of Burgundy.[4] Among his household objects we find several houppelandes of green, black and white satin, a cloth of gold worked with the image of My Lord, and a cushion of silk.[5] The third inventory, from 1434 and of Jaquote Martin, bourgeois of Dijon, documents a black and red silk pillow of satin and seven old squares of tapestry.[6] The Dijon inventories are part of a much wider corpus of sources from the Later Middle Ages that include references to luxury textiles. References to silks and tapestry have been used to illustrate broader transformations that occurred in later medieval European consumer demand, particularly increased demand

1 Archives départementales de la Côte-d'Or, series B II/356. Hereafter referred to as ADCO.

2 ADCO, BII 365, Cote 1 pièce IV.

3 A mixture of wool, angora and silk.

4 ADCO, BII 356, Cote 2 pièce III.

5 Houppelandes were large overgarments of different lengths worn by men and women. The inventory and a plan of Chevalier's house can be found in Françoise Piponnier, 'Maisons du XIVe au milieu du XVIe siècle: notices, 48–55, 61', in *Cent maisons médiévales en France (du XIIe au milieu du XVIe siècle). Un corpus et une esquisse*, ed. Yves Esquieu et al. (Paris: CNRS, 1998), 324–326.

6 ADCO, BII 356, Cote 17 pièce XI.

for a greater range of material goods. For England, Wendy Child's assessment of English custom accounts during the fourteenth century has demonstrated that a wider market for silks, brocades and velvets was opening up.[7] Crossing to mainland Europe, a similar market for silks and tapestry appears evident. In the Low Countries we begin to see a wider range of silk and tapestry products materialising in testaments and inventories of urban inhabitants, as covers for household furnishings such as bench covers, cushions and beds and also as accessories for clothing.[8] While tapestry production had been a recognised speciality of these territories from the fourteenth century onwards, these lands also witnessed a move to the production of imitation silks in the later fifteenth and sixteenth centuries.[9] Françoise Piponnier has pointed to a wider availability of silk products in later medieval France, again from furnishings to belt embellishments, while tapestry producers and merchants were both resident and operating from Paris from at least the end of the thirteenth century, and production of silks was established in Tours by the end of the fifteenth century and then in Lyon by the sixteenth.[10] Given that the majority of silks were still produced and exported by Italy during the fourteenth and fifteenth centuries, the variety of silk products found in Italy, from silk clothing and furnishings to silk embellishments for small purses and belts, is perhaps unsurprising.[11] Tapestry products were evident in greater numbers there too, again as cushions, bench covers, and bed and wall hangings, and several Italian rulers such as the Gonzaga in Mantua sought to

---

7 Wendy Childs, 'Cloth of Gold and Gold Thread: Luxury Imports to England in the Fourteenth Century', in *War Government and Aristocracy in the British Isles*, ed. Christopher Given-Wilson, et al. (Woodbridge: Boydell Press, 2008), 279.

8 Patrick Chorley, 'The 'draperies légères' of Lille, Arras, Tournai, Valenciennes: New Materials for New Markets?', in *Drapery Production in the late Medieval Low Countries: Markets and Strategies for Survival. 14th to 16th Centuries*, ed. Marc Boone et al. (Leuven: Leuven University Press, 1993), 151–165; Julie De Groot and Peter Stabel, 'The domestic interior in mid 15th century Bruges. Between representation and material reality', (Unpublished paper); Peter Stabel, ' "Le gout pour l'Orient". Demand cosmopolite et objets de luxe à Bruges à la fin du Moyen Âge', *Histoire Urbaine* 30 (2011): 21–39; Isis Sturtewagen, 'The fabric of everyday life: clothing oneself and one's home in 15th and 16th century Bruges', (Paper presented at the 11th International Conference on Urban History, Prague, 29 August–1 September 2012).

9 Katherine Anne Wilson, 'Tapestry in the Burgundian Dominions. A complex object', in *La cour de Bourgogne et l'Europe. Le rayonnement et les limites d'un modèle culturel*, ed. Werner Parvacini (Ostfildern: Jan Thorbecke Verlag, 2013), 317–332; and the chapter by Jeroen Puttevils in this volume, 'Trading Silks and Tapestries in Sixteenth-Century Antwerp'.

10 Françoise Piponnier, 'Usages et diffusion de la soie en France à la fin du Moyen Age', in *La Seta in Europa sec. XIII–XX. Atti della 'Ventiquattresima Settimana di Studi', 4–9 maggio 1992*, ed. Simonetta Cavaciocchi (Firenze: Le Monnier, 1993), 785–800; René de Lespinasse and Françoise Bonnardot, *Les métiers et corporations de la ville de Paris. XIIIe siècle, le Livre des métiers d'Étienne Boileau* (Paris, 1879). In 1277 *tapissiers sarrasnois* are mentioned, in 1292 *tapissiers*, 1295 *tapissiers nostrez* and then *tapissiers hautelisse* in 1302. Also see, Anne-Marie Piuz, 'La soie, le luxe et le pouvoir dans les doctrines françaises (XVIe–XVIIIes.)', in *La Seta in Europa sec. XIII–XX. Atti della 'Ventiquattresima Settimana di Studi', 4–9 maggio 1992*, ed. Simonetta Cavaciocchi (Firenze: Le Monnier, 1993), 818.

11 Susan Mosher-Stuard, *Gilding the Market: Luxury and Fashion in Fourteenth-Century Italy* (Pennsylvania: University of Pennsylvania Press, 2006).

acquire tapestry weavers from the Low Countries during the fifteenth, and into the sixteenth, century.[12]

While the growth in silks and tapestry available for a wider consumer base across Western Europe is relatively well documented, there has been relatively little exploration of the possession and use of these high-quality textiles. Françoise Piponnier's work, while including many examples of silks from the Dijon inventories, is broad in its scope, designed to guide the reader through wider changes in silk use and ownership in France. Furthermore, Piponnier's other work on the Dijon inventories, which includes extremely valuable work on cloth merchant's inventories, residential spaces recorded by the inventories, clothing and ceramic ownership, has never been brought together, nor does it completely set the evidence from the inventories in the context of Dijon as a commercial or consumer centre, or fully explore the biographies of individuals recorded by these documents.[13] To understand patterns of consumption it is necessary to consider discrete centres, single consumers and their careers, and investigate whether these 'luxury' textiles were in fact considered as a luxury by later medieval consumers and what implications this has for the growing attraction of consumers to these products during the fourteenth and fifteenth centuries.

The silks and tapestry of the inhabitants of the town of Dijon represent a significant opportunity to examine the possession and use of 'luxury' textiles. Several thousand inventories survive for Dijon and its surrounding area from the final years of the fourteenth century to the end of the eighteenth century.[14] The worth of the collection has been highlighted on more than one occasion over the past thirty years, but little recent work has been undertaken on these documents.[15] While inventories have well-documented limitations as a historical source, in that many may omit a complete list of an individual's possessions, fail to give valuations for the objects described, or tend predominantly to reflect the middling or upper ranks of society, they

12 Hillie Smit, 'Flemish Tapestry Weavers in Italy c.1420–1520. A survey and analysis of the activity in various cities', in *Flemish Tapestry Weavers Abroad. Emigration and the Founding of Manufactories in Europe*, ed. Guy Delmarcel (Leuven: Leuven University Press, 2002), 113–130.

13 See, Françoise Piponnier, 'Linge de maison et linge de corps au Moyen Age d'après le inventaires bourguignons', *Ethnologie française* 16 (1986): 239–248; Françoise Piponnier, 'Vivre noblement en Bourgogne au XIVe siècle', *Mélanges d'archéologie et d'histoire médiévales en l'honneur de Michel de Boüard* (Genève–Paris, 1982), 309–317; Françoise Piponnier, 'Dénominations et fonctions des espaces dans l'habitation dijonnaise XIVe–XVe siècle', in *Cadres de vie et manières d'habiter XIIe–XVIe siècle (VIIIe Congrès international de la Société d'archéologie médiévale)*, ed. Danièle Alexandre–Bidon et al. (Caen: Paris, 2001), 109–116.

14 The potential of these collections was first highlighted in Anton Schuurman, 'Probate Inventories: Research Issues, Problems and Results', in *Probate Inventories. A new source for the historical study of wealth, material culture and agricultural development*, ed. Ad van der Woude et al. (Utrecht: HES Publishers, 1980), 19–32.

15 Céline Vandeuren-David, 'L'apport des inventaires après décès dans la connaissance de la parure civile à Dijon (1383–1403)', in *La Vie matérielle au moyen âge. L'apport des sources littéraires, normatives et de la pratique ; Actes du colloque international de Louvain-la-Neuve, 3–5 octobre 1996*, ed. Emmanuelle Rassart-Eeckhout et al. (Louvain-la-Neuve, 1997), 261–276.

nevertheless remain a valuable tool for examining the possession and use of objects. In the case of the Dijon inventories, the clerk frequently records the rooms and then lists the objects of each room. At times, monetary values assigned to possessions by assessors and witnesses are recorded, and occasionally some of the rooms or objects are given personal descriptions. Finally, the inventories can be set in the context of the extensive work undertaken by Pierre Geoffroy, Henri Dubois and Thierry Dutour among others, on the notables of the town in the thirteenth and fourteenth centuries from the collections of notarial documents, tax records and household accounts of the dukes of Burgundy, which facilitates a reconstruction of Dijon commercial life and society as a context for the possession and use of luxury textiles.[16]

Four methods of investigation are proposed by this chapter to begin unpicking the possession and use of luxury textiles of the inhabitants of later medieval Dijon. First, Dijon will be considered as a centre of retail and luxury activity, a place where silks and tapestries could be traded, purchased, possessed, displayed and re-used. Second, the biographies of some of the owners of silks and tapestry in Dijon will be outlined. Third, the spaces silks and tapestries were used, and the ways in which they might have been distinguished from other objects listed alongside them in the inventories by their use, position or terminology, will be explored. Finally, a problematic issue will be addressed – *why* silks and tapestry were possessed and used by these inhabitants and if they were considered to be a 'luxury'. Christopher Dyer has suggested that luxury objects may be defined by the fact that they 'conferred status on those who used them, brought people of similar standing together, and excluded those who did not belong'.[17] In light of his definition, do the Dijon references to these textiles and the spaces in which they were used in any way suggest that these items were valued through the quality of the product or through their symbolic value, contributing to the perception of the textile as a luxury object?

Where: Dijon as a Commercial Centre

The town of Dijon in the Later Middle Ages is commonly described in terms of its relationship to the dukes of Burgundy, and during the rule of Philip the

---

16 Pierre Geoffroy, 'Commerce et marchands à Dijon au XVe siècle', *Annales de Bourgogne* 25 (1953): 166. Henri Dubois, 'Marchands dijonnais aux foires se Chalon-sur-Saône à la fin du Moyen Âge. Essai de prosopographie', *Publication du Centre Européen d'études Bourguignonnes (XIVe–XVIes)* 27 (1987): 63–79 and Thierry Dutour, *Une société de l'honneur. Les notables et leur monde à Dijon à la fin du Moyen Âge* (Paris: 1998).

17 Christopher Dyer, 'Luxury Goods in Medieval England', in *Commercial Activity, Markets and Entrepreneurs in the Middle Ages. Essays in Honour of Richard Britnell*, ed. Ben Dodds et al. (Woodbridge: Boydell and Brewer, 2011), 219.

Bold (1363–1404) as one of the centres for Burgundian administration.[18] When the terms 'commercial' or 'consumer centre' are applied to Dijon, these are applied to early modern Dijon, under the control of the French crown. James Farr has done much to rehabilitate sixteenth and seventeenth century Dijon as a centre worthy of the attentions of French urban historians.[19] His vision of a thriving centre of commerce and consumption can also be convincingly applied to later medieval Dijon. Instead of the neglected provincial centre of the Burgundian dukes, Dijon can be reimagined as a hub of retail activity, a place where a variety of luxury textiles were possessed, benefiting from its dual role as a regional centre and from its close links with the Burgundian household. Henri Dubois's description of the town as a 'place of passage' neatly encapsulates its geographical situation on a major trade route North (Paris and the centres of the Low Countries) from the East and South (Germany and Italy).[20] The producers and retailers of the centre were able to tap into a populous town and hinterland. Dijon had an estimated population of around 11,000 in 1390, increasing to about 12,000 by 1450.[21] In the bailiwick of Dijon, which covered a large area outside of the town, some further 32,000 people resided.[22] Several surviving cartularies and guild ordinances from Dijon dating from the thirteenth to the sixteenth century add further to the depiction of the town as a hub of retail and consumption, which incorporated a wide range of occupations.[23] Christopher Dyer identifies 'luxury' trades of towns in that they satisfied demand at the upper end of a consumer's budget[24] and among the bakers, weavers, tanners, and grocers of Dijon we also find embroiderers, goldsmiths, tapestry, parchment, glove, robe, and doublet makers as well as fabricators of silk and toile caps.[25] In its other role, as a centre for Burgundian administration, Dijon provided opportunities for the elite families of the town to enter into lucrative careers with the Burgundian household, as suppliers of wine, textiles and food or by holding fixed positions within the ducal household itself, a fact underlined by the work of Thierry Dutour, Henri Dubois and Pierre Geoffroy.[26] The residences of many of these elite Dijonnais familes, who served both the Burgundian court and the town as aldermen or

18 Richard Vaughan, *Philip the Good. The Apogee of Burgundian Power* (Woodbridge: Boydell, 2002), 241.

19 James Farr, 'Consumers, commerce and the craftsmen of Dijon: The changing social and economic structure of a provincial capital, 1450–1750', in *Cities and Social Change in Early Modern France*, ed. Philip Benedict (London: Routledge, 1989), 134–173, and James Farr, *Hands of Honor: artisans and their world in Dijon, 1550–1650* (Ithaca: Cornell University Press, 1988).

20 Geoffroy, 'Commerce et marchands', 166.

21 Vaughan, *Philip the Good*, 239.

22 Vaughan, *Philip the Good*, 239.

23 Albert Chapuis, *Les anciennes corporations Dijonnaises: Règlements, statuts et ordonnances* (Dijon, 1906).

24 Dyer, 'Luxury Goods', 229.

25 Chapuis, *Les anciennes corporations*, 7–8.

26 Dubois, 'Marchands dijonnais', 63–79, Geoffroy, 'Commerce et marchands', 161–181, Dutour, *Une société de l'honneur*.

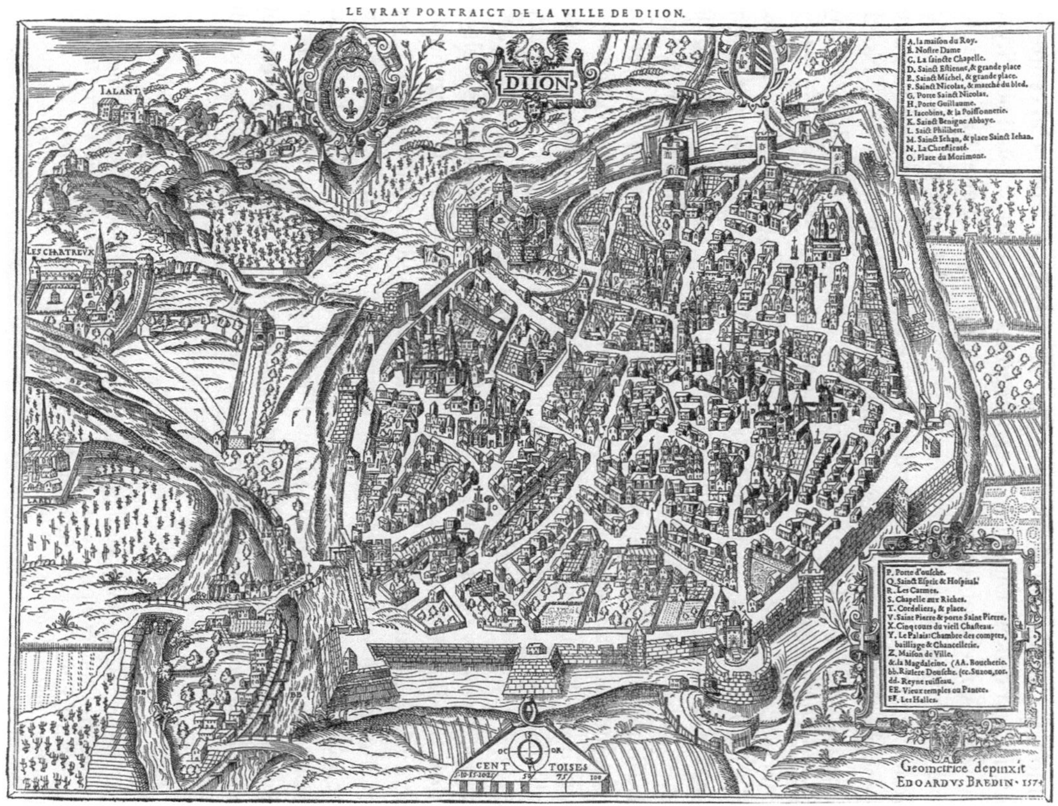

Figure 1.1: Map of Dijon 1574. Edouard Bredin. Archives Municipales de Dijon, cote 4, Fi 956.

mayors, were generally located in the most exclusive district of the town in the parish of Notre Dame, only a stone's throw from the ducal palace.[27]

Purchasing and retailing opportunities for the inhabitants of the town were to be found at local and regional markets. Locally produced goods were sold and bought in markets around the town, at the Bourg, Proudhon road, the square of Saint-Jean and close to its major religious centres, at the churches of Notre Dame, Saint-Michel and the cemetery of Saint-Etienne (see Figure 1.1).[28] Dijon also hosted bi-annual three-day winter and summer fairs.[29] For the more enterprising Dijonnais, retailing and purchasing opportunities were pursued at the larger fair of Chalon-sur-Saône some 60 km away.[30] The fair was a meeting place for regional and international merchants, attracting merchants not only from Dijon, but also from further afield in France, the Low Countries and Italy.[31]

The dual role of Dijon as a regional and Burgundian administrative centre supplied Dijon with a variety of consumers, and, more particularly for our chapter, consumers interested in purchasing silks and tapestry. Several Dijon elites were recorded as supplying silks to the elite end of the consumer base, the Burgundian household and local nobility throughout the fourteenth and fifteenth centuries. In 1374 Jean Bernart, mercer of Dijon, supplied five ounces and three quarters of blue silk for a belt with a clasp of gold for Philip the Bold. In 1377 another Dijon mercer, Ami Bernart, was paid nine francs for an ell and three quarters of a cloth of silk that had been bought from him by another Dijon inhabitant, Regnault Chevalier the ducal tailor, whose possessions opened this chapter.[32] Moving into the fifteenth century we find that in 1424, Jean de Courbeton was paid 165 *francs*, 15 *sols*, 10 *deniers tournois* for 20 ells of vermillion damask for duke Philip the Good, while in 1428 and 1444 Etienne Chambellan was paid by the Burgundian household for the sale of cloths of silk.[33] However, it is far rarer to find mercers or merchants of Dijon involved in the supply of tapestry to the Burgundian court in the ducal accounts, though this is not unsurprising given that the major tapestry-producing centres that supplied the Burgundian household were almost exclusively situated in the northern centres of Paris, Arras and Tournai during the fourteenth and fifteenth centuries. Dijon itself has no real record of an active

---

27 Dominique Viaux, 'Fortunes Immobilières à Dijon au commencement du 15e siècle', *Annales de Bourgogne* 66 (1994): 65–80.

28 Emile Collette, *Les foires et marchés à Dijon* (Dijon, 1905), 38.

29 Collette, *Les foires*, 46.

30 Dubois, 'Marchands dijonnais', 63–79; Geoffroy, 'Commerce et marchands', 161–181.

31 Paul Toussaint, *Les foires de Chalon-sur-Saône des origins au XVI siècle* (Dijon, 1910); Henri Dubois, *Les foires de Chalon et le commerce dans la vallée de la Saône à la fin du Moyen Age (vers 1280–vers 1430)* (Paris: Sorbonne, 1976).

32 Bernard Prost, *Inventaires mobiliers et extraits des comptes des ducs de Bourgogne de la maison de Valois (1363–1477)* vol. 1 (Paris, 1908–1913), 606.

33 Geoffroy, 'Commerce et marchands', 169,173.

tapestry industry before 1531 and it was not until 1676 that formal regulations were set for tapestry weavers.[34] The odd individuals we find reference to who hold the title 'tapissier' seem to be involved in many other commercial activities, and are assigned a string of professional categories when they are mentioned in municipal or ducal accounts. For example, Dutour notes that Jean de Paris, who was active in the latter half of the fourteenth century, was described as a marshal, saddler, tapestry maker and seller of pelts in the ducal accounts.[35] Demoingin de Rolampont, another Dijonnais, appears to have been occasionally involved in the repair and upkeep of the ducal tapestries, supplying threads of repair and canvas to line tapestry, pavilions and textile chambers from 1388 to 1400. His multiple professional categories in the ducal accounts included armourer, cover maker, maker of chasubles, and repairer of chambers and tapestry.[36]

Yet, the inventories of Dijon reinforce that later medieval Dijon mercers and merchants were not only reliant on custom from the ducal household. Several mercers' inventories give a glimpse into the commercial potential for individuals with a ready stock of consumable goods. One thousand and nine objects are mentioned in the 1392 inventory of the mercer Etienne Marchant, and 741 for the 1394 inventory of the mercer Jean Maul Meu.[37] Their stock ranges from rings, hatpins and bells for purses and clothes to gloves, hats, rosaries, belts, threads and skins. Although silks make up but a small part of the stock accounted for in their inventories, it does give an insight into the potential for possession of silk by a wider section of the later medieval population of Dijon. Several ounces of silk appear in the workshop of Etienne Marchant and silk is recorded as included in a number of belts and purses in the stock of Jean Maul Meu.[38] Etienne Marchant was also the owner of several silk garments, including several coats and robes of cameline which are recorded alongside other dresses and mantels for both Marchant and his wife in the upstairs front chamber of their residence.

Who Owned Luxury Textiles?

Even a cursory examination of the inventories for later medieval Dijon confirms that a range of individuals were able to own pieces of silks and tapestry in a wide variety of forms. Françoise Piponnier's work on silks, heavily based on her survey of the Dijon inventories from the fourteenth and fifteenth centuries, is emphatic that ownership of silks was not only

[34] Chapuis, *Les anciennes corporations*, 490–494.
[35] Dutour, *Une société de l'honneur*, 92.
[36] Prost, *Inventaires mobiliers*, vol. 1, 155.
[37] Vandeuren-David, 'L'apport des inventaires après décès', 273, 274.
[38] ADCO, BII 356, Cote 1, pièce IV and Cote 2, pièce II.

reserved for Dijon aristocracy or for the Burgundian entourage, but included doctors, apothecaries, clerks and artisans.[39] A detailed investigation of inventories recording silks and tapestry over fifty years, ranging from 1395 to 1445, including those highlighted by Piponnier, only serves to reinforce the point. For the inventories that identify a professional category, a range of wealthy urban individuals appear as owners of silks and tapestry, including Burgundian court officials and servants, merchants and artisans whose careers can be reconstructed. Four detailed examples of individuals who have luxury textiles recorded among their possessions serve to illuminate the potential owners of luxury textiles in later medieval Dijon.

The frequently cited 1395 inventory of Regnault Chevalier, 'tailor to the duke', is one of the earliest examples from the collection of the *mairie de Dijon* to document the ownership of luxury textiles, both as clothing and as furnishings.[40] The inventory records the possessions of the 24 rooms of his extensive residence, which comprises a garde robe, six chambers, a large salle, a workshop, galleries and a chapel around a courtyard, and underlines that he was an individual of some means.[41] In his lower chambers we find beds complete with hangings and feather cushions as well as tables. In his garde robe and chapel references to silk textiles are to be found. Several houppelandes (an outer garment of clothing) of green, black and white satin along with a purse of black satin are recorded in the garde robe.[42] In the chapel, three chasubles of gold cloth, a cloth of gold worked with the image of Christ and a cushion of silk are listed. The textiles of the chapel are recorded alongside an 'image of my lady' in white alabaster and goblets of silver. The professional category 'tailor to the duke' ascribed to him by the 1395 inventory is also used alongside the term *valet de chambre* to Philip the Bold in accounts of Burgundian expenditure where Regnault Chevalier appears frequently from 1367 to 1395.[43] These accounts reveal that he was paid to turn purchases of luxury textiles into wearable garments. Red velvets, sendals of azure and red and ribbons of gold of damask were transformed by Regnault Chevalier into houpellandes, mantles and robes to be worn by the duke, his wife Margaret of Flanders and his daughter the countess of Nevers.[44] In 1386 he was entrusted with the making of four short coats with sleeves for the duke from two ells of alexandrine velvet purchased at 45 francs each which

39 Piponnier, 'Usages et diffusion de la soie', 793.

40 ADCO, BII, 356, Cote 2 pièce III.

41 Piponnier, 'Maisons du XIVe au milieu du XVIe siècle', 324–326.

42 ADCO, BII, 356, Cote 2 pièce III. It had a long full body and flaring sleeves, worn by both men and women in Europe in the Later Middle Ages. It could potentially be lined with fur or other materials and embroidered.

43 Prost, *Inventaires* mobiliers, vols 1 and 2.

44 Prost, *Inventaires mobiliers*, 236, ADCO, B1435, f. 52.

had been supplied by Dino Rapondi, the Burgundian household's principal supplier of luxury textiles.[45]

In a later inventory, identified as dating from 1397, a number of luxury textiles are described for the Sauvegrain family.[46] The objects listed as belonging to the first chambers record houpellandes of black silk and undergarments of red silk. Silks and velvets also appear as a component in the furnishings of a bed. The ceiling and backing to the bed are described as two pieces of serge worked with silk and the bed is finished with a cover of black velvet. As the Sauvegrain family have been well documented by the prosopographical investigations of Dijon notables by Henri Dubois and Thierry Dutour, it is clear that like other elite families they were concerned with their social ascendancy.[47] Dutour notes that although Jean Sauvegrain first arrived in Dijon without any previous ties, he quickly established himself in the commercial networks of the town by making an advantageous match to the daughter of a cloth merchant, who brought to the marriage a large dowry.[48] Thus, Jean Sauvegrain integrated himself into the commercial and political life of Dijon, successful in the wool and wine trade and the owner of several properties.[49] In 1385 he made his entrance into the government of the town as an alderman.[50] His political and commercial career was no doubt enhanced by positions he was able to attain at the Burgundian court, described as *valet de chambre* and *ecuyer de cuisine* in the ducal accounts dating to 1366 and 1372.[51] His responsibilities for the Burgundian household included transporting hunting dogs of Philip the Bold to Burgundy in 1374, overseeing the purchase of collars for the same dogs in 1377, and also as acting as the middleman in the delivery of green cloth from a Dijonnais 'merchant of cloth' which was to be transformed into seven outfits for both 'large and small' dogs in 1377.[52] Ennobled in 1377 as the lord of Vesvrottes, he accompanied the future John the Fearless on the ill-starred crusade to Nicopolis in 1396, the only misjudgement of Jean's career.[53]

The objects described in the 1434 inventory of the goldsmith Jean Villain illuminates both his professional and personal life.[54] Like Regnault Chevalier

45 Prost, *Inventaires mobiliers*, ADCO, B1466, f.22. For a detailed analysis of the Rapondi family see, Bart Lambert, *The City, the Duke and their Banker. The Rapondi Family and the Formation of the Burgundian State (1384–1430)* (Turnhout: Brepols, 2006).

46 ADCO, BII, 356, Cote 2 pièce 13. There is no date on the cover, but it has been dated by the archivist to 1397.

47 Dubois, 'Marchands Dijonnais', 63–79.

48 Dutour, 'Une société de l'honneur', 460.

49 Dutour, 'Une société de l'honneur', 460. Dutour notes a transaction where he is recorded making a purchase of wool for 1500 francs in 1384 and in 1387 as the proprietor of a house rented to a Jew named Moussey de Turcey.

50 Dutour, 'Une société de l'honneur', 460.

51 Prost, *Inventaires mobiliers*, 328.

52 Prost, *Inventaires mobiliers*, 538. The dogs are described as *levriers*, which are dogs with an elongated and pointed snout that can run very fast, such as greyhounds and lurchers.

53 Prost notes that it was on that crusade that he possibly died, given that the first Sauvegrain inventory is dated from 1397.

54 ADCO, BII, 356, Cote 17, pièce VI.

and Jean Sauvegrain, he held the position of *valet de chambre* and goldsmith to the duke of Burgundy; he was awarded a pension of 20 francs in 1412.[55] He was still active in ducal employ in 1433: an account records that Jean Villain 'goldsmith and resident of Dijon' was to be paid for making 12 cups of silver and 6 fleeces made from gold. The cups were to be given to the men at arms 'who had fought in the siege before the town of Avalon' and the gold fleeces were destined for knights of the order of the Golden Fleece.[56] Given his profession and position in the ducal household, it is perhaps unsurprising that the preamble to his inventory records his residence as located on the *rue des forges* which conveniently placed Jean Villain in the key parish of Notre Dame, a road directly adjacent to the ducal palace.[57] The first chamber of his residence is stacked full of the products of his profession: rings of gold, goblets and cups of silver abound. Tissues of silks in white, blue, green and red are also present in the inventory, listed alongside a mitre embroidered with gold thread under the heading 'other jewels'. Among his personal possessions, silk taffeta is listed by the inventory as part of the furnishing of a bed in an upstairs room.

Links to the Burgundian household are not the only means to identify the possessors of silk and tapestry in later medieval Dijon. The 1412 inventory of Jean Poissenot and description of his professional category as *epicer* gives little hint of his eventful career in town politics.[58] Among the possessions listed in some 16 rooms of his residence, we find two pieces of black sendal, a chest of oak with two cushions of red velvet worked with swans of gold and other cushions of red sendal and velvet. As a wealthy resident of Dijon with the ability to loan money to both the town and Philip the Bold, duke of Burgundy, in 1364 and 1372, he was mayor from 1364 to 1366, 1370 to 1371, and 1395 to 1396 as well as alderman and auditor of accounts for the town.[59] Recorded in the service of the Burgundian dukes, he and two other individuals were sent by Philip the Bold in 1370 to negotiate with the French king.[60] In 1405–6, he supplied the Burgundian household at the residence of Artois with spiced wine and oranges.[61] In 1364 he took centre stage in a contested mayoral election, as one of two mayors elected by opposing parties.[62] Although fortunate enough to retain his seat until 1366, he was replaced in the same year by his rival of 1364, Monnot de Beaune.[63] The reasons for this turbulent

55 Léon Laborde, *Les ducs de Bourgogne: Études sur les lettres, les arts et l'industrie pendant le XVe siècle et plus particulièrement dans les Pays-bas et le duché de Bourgogne*, vols 1 and 2 (Paris, 1851).
56 Laborde, *Les ducs de Bourgogne*, 337, 338.
57 ADCO, BII, 356, Cote 17, pièce VI.
58 ADCO, BII, 356, Cote 6, pièce V.
59 Dutour, 'Une société de l'honneur', 178.
60 Dutour, 'Une société de l'honneur', 178.
61 Laborde, *Les ducs de Bourgogne*, 18.
62 Dutour, 'Une société de l'honneur', 132.
63 Dutour, 'Une société de l'honneur', 132.

event in the municipal rule of Dijon remain unclear.[64] According to Dutour's detailed assessment of the situation, tempting though it may be to ascribe the conflict to the unwelcome imposition of taxes by the Burgundian duke, or their efforts to place their key servants into positions of municipal power, it may well be that the mayoral dispute simply reflected a rivalry between two prominent and increasingly powerful individuals in the town.[65]

For the individuals for whom we cannot yet reconstruct detailed careers in town or court, the preamble to the inventory and the objects listed therein frequently reveal further information on their occupations or the specific area of the town they lived or worked in. The 1425 inventory of Jean de la Croix describes him as a *patissier*, resident in the *grant rue de la boucherie*.[66] His residence included a workshop and a chamber specifically dedicated for his valets.[67] He was not the only owner of silks and tapestry to live in an area of town described by a trade. The preamble to the 1438 inventory of Henri Maistre, merchant, records his residence in the *rue drapperie*.[68] The contents of the workshop of his residence, which comprised a large and extremely valuable amount of cloth, a loom, shearing scissors and various dyes, cements his professional identification as a cloth merchant.[69] Hugenot Alerdot, recorded as a tanner by his 1439 inventory, records the objects found in his hotel and also in his workshop on the *rue de pont* on 'the tannery' of Dijon, the name given to an island on the river Ouche, which was a separate quarter outside the walls of Dijon reserved for tanners because of the smell created by their manufacturing processes.[70] However, for several of the inventories that record silk and tapestry, little information on the individual is given. Some only comprise a list of goods, such as the inventory of Girart de Grant Val, chamberlain to the king and the duke of Burgundy, and the inventory of Margot de Troyes in 1438.[71] Inventories of women or those that include the names of wives, often fail to name the individual, instead linking them to their husbands by the term 'wife', as in the inventory of 'Jean Martin and his wife' in 1434.[72]

64 Dutour, 'Une société de l'honneur', 177–178.

65 Dutour, 'Une société de l'honneur', 178.

66 ADCO, BII 356, Cote 13, pièce VI.

67 The term 'valet' used in the inventory can refer to the helper of a master craftsman, possibly an unskilled servant or journeyman.

68 ADCO, BII 356, Cote 19, pièce XIX.

69 Piponnier, 'Dénominations et fonctions des espaces', 237–238.

70 Piponnier, 'Dénominations et fonctions des espaces', 114; ADCO, BII 356, Cote 20, pièce XXII.

71 ADCO BII 356, Cote 6, pièce XXVIII and Cote 19, pièce IV.

72 ADCO BII 356, Cote 17, pièce XI, XII.

What and Where: What Silks and Tapestries Appear in the Inventories and Where are they Recorded?

Moving on from the investigation of the careers and occupations of some of the individuals who possessed silks and tapestry, it is necessary to turn to examine exactly what types of luxury textiles were recorded in their inventories. From inventories taken from 1395 to 1445, three main types of silk and tapestry emerge.[73] First, silks could be used as clothing and dress accessories. The 1397 inventory of Jean Sauvegrain records several items of silk clothing, ranging from a cloak of camelot embellished with silver buttons, to a tunic of red silk.[74] Similarly, the 1431 inventory of Nicholas Giret, saddler, listed a figured pourpoint of old satin and the 1438 inventory of Etienne Marchant, mercer, listed coats and houpellandes of cameline.[75] Belts, boxes, purses and pins also appear either being made from silk, or embellished by silk. The inventory of the tanner Hugenot Alerdot, compiled in 1439, records an old purse of 'cloth of silk' adorned with pearls and silver buttons.[76] Another purse, this time of 'old silk' is found in the possessions of Jean Martin and his wife in 1434.[77] Gold cloth and buttons of silver are also used to embellish the purses listed in the 1398 inventory of one Jehannote, wife of Etiennot Lemoutardier, the apothecary.[78] The 1421 inventory of Pierre Sancenot, bourgeois, records a small box adorned with cloth of gold and with silver buttons.[79]

While tapestry is absent from clothing and dress accessories, both silks and tapestries appear as household furnishings. Silks seem to be commonly used as covers for pillows or cushions. Among the possessions of Jean de la Croix, *patissier*, two cushions of silk vermeil are listed in 1425. In 1403 the inventory of Lady Julienne, widow of Henry Lebevrier, records a cushion of down covered with cloth of silk while Nicolas Giret, a saddler, has a small cushion of sendal listed in his inventory of 1431.[80] As Françoise Piponnier rightly points out, silk hangings, curtains or covers are far more rare and usually reserved for the wealthy.[81] The 1395 inventory of Regnault Chevalier, our ducal tailor, and the 1403 inventory of Lady Julienne, widow of Henry Lebevrier, both possess curtains of silk.[82] The tanner Hugenot Alerdot also owned a cover of 'old' silk.[83] Tapestry, perhaps given its more durable nature, is listed in the inventories as wall hangings, general covers or bench covers.

---

73 Piponnier, 'Usages et diffusion de la soie', 792.
74 ADCO BII 356, Cote 2, pièce XIII.
75 ADCO BII 356, Cote 16, pièce XIII and Cote 1, pièce IV.
76 ADCO BII 356, Cote 20, pièce XXII.
77 ADCO BII 356, Cote 17, pièce XI, XII.
78 ADCO BII 365, Cote 2, pièce XII.
79 ADCO BII 356, Cote 11, pièce XVII.
80 ADCO BII 356, Cote 13, pièce XIII, Cote 3, pièce XXIII.
81 Piponnier, 'Usages et diffusion de soie', 792.
82 ADCO, BII 356, Cote 2, pièce III and Cote 3 pièce XXIII.
83 ADCO BII 356, Cote 20, pièce XXII.

Squares of tapestry are regularly described. The 1434 inventory of Valentin de Cerremonde lists two squares of tapestry, the inventory of Hugenot Alerdot four.[84] Henry Maistre, a cloth merchant, had five old covers of tapestry recorded in his inventory of 1438.[85]

Different types of silks were recorded as being used for religious purposes or for personal devotion in the Dijon inventories, also noted by Piponnier.[86] Chasubles of silk appear in the chapel of Regnault Chevalier in 1395 and that of Jean Pourcelot in 1431.[87] Silks used for baptism are recorded in the inventories of Pierre Sancenot, bourgeois, in 1421 and of Jean Martin and his wife in 1434.[88] Another inventory, from 1413, records a book of hours covered in 'cloth of silk' with two small clasps.[89] Finally, there are several types of silks that cannot be so neatly categorised into distinct types. In the inventory of the goldsmith Jean Villain in 1434 we find several 'tissues of silk' in a variety of colours, without any indication of where or what they are used for.[90] Listed among the possessions of Jean Martin and his wife in the same year, we find a 'quantity' of thread of silk.[91]

As Piponnier has noted, the most common terms used to describe the silks listed in the Dijon inventories tend to be sendal, satin, damask, velvet and simply the term 'silk'.[92] By her estimate sendal is the most common, while references to cloth of gold remain extremely rare.[93] For the textile of tapestry, *tapisserie* is the most common descriptor to be used, which can refer to more than one piece of the textile. Far less common is the term *hautelice*. One cloth of *drap de hautelice* 'where there are twelve months of the year' is listed among the possessions of Lady Julienne in 1403.[94] Colour is rarely recorded when descriptions of tapestry are given, but silks are listed within a wide range of shades. Piponnier points out that red was the most common colour, although the language chosen by the assessors to describe the colours of the object in front of them perhaps did little justice to the great variation in tones.[95] One of the most common terms used to describe the colour of silk, *rouge*, is extremely vague and could encompass a range of different reds that existed including vermeil, sanguine and cramoisy.[96] Several silks in the later medieval inventories are described as vermeil, suggesting they were of

84 ADCO BII 356, Cote 17, pièce X and Cote 20, pièce XXII.
85 ADCO BII 356, Cote 19, pièce XIX.
86 Piponnier, 'Usages et diffusion de la soie', 786–788, 790–791.
87 ADCO BII 356, Cote 2, pièce III and Cote 16, pièce XII.
88 ADCO BII 356, Cote 11, pièce and Cote 17, pièce XI, XII.
89 ADCO BII 365, Cote 6, pièce XXVI.
90 ADCO BII 356, Cote 17, pièce VI.
91 ADCO BII 356, Cote 17, pièce XI, XII.
92 Piponnier, 'Usages et diffusion de la soie', 792.
93 Piponnier, 'Usages et diffusion de la soie', 792.
94 ADCO BII 356, Cote 3, pièce XXIII.
95 Piponnier, 'Usages et diffusion de la soie', 793.
96 Kurt Zangger, *Contribution à la terminologie des tissues en ancient français, attestés dans des texts français, provençaux, italiens, espagnols, allemandes et latins* (Bienn, 1945), 88–89.

a dark red colour, such as the robes of sendal vermeil and damask vermeil recorded in the 1438 inventory of Richard du Chancey, confessor of the duke of Burgundy.[97] Silks are also listed in the inventories in the colours of white, green, blue, often noted in the inventories as *pers*, suggesting a shade of dark blue, and less frequently as black, yellow and lavender.[98]

However, simply listing the types of silks found in the Dijon inventories can only take us so far in an understanding of their use and in their potential to act as a 'luxury' item for their possessors. Their use, their ability to act as a 'luxury', is intimately connected to the spaces in which the textiles are recorded, the other objects that surround and are listed around them, and the terms used to describe the textiles. Henri Lefevbre's influential idea that 'space produced in a certain manner serves as a tool of thought and action' and that space could act as a means of control, domination and power, has encouraged a reflection on the agency possessed by the individuals who constructed or furnished spaces, but has also given more weight to the agency possessed by the groups or 'ensembles' of objects presented and arranged within these spaces.[99] The principal spaces in which silks and tapestry are listed in the inventories of later medieval Dijon are used as the title of this chapter, 'in a chamber, in a garde robe, in a chapel, in a chest' and the 'ensemble' of objects grouped or listed within these spaces are fundamental in understanding their use or their potential to act as a 'luxury'.

Chambers are a space in which silks and tapestries are habitually listed in the Dijon inventories.[100] The most frequent room description given in the Dijon inventories, they acted as multi-functional spaces, both private and public, as a place to sleep, eat, cook or receive visitors. Multi-functionality is demonstrated by the chamber listed in the inventory of Jean Suivard in 1412.[101] His chamber included a bed, hangings, a cushion of red sendal, goblets, a table, as well as pots and other implements for cooking. Piponnier notes that some of the chambers in the Dijon inventories are given more precise designations to their use in that the clerk records the name of the principal inhabitant of the room, or that it was a chamber where a particular individual slept.[102] In the 1397 inventory of the Sauvegrain family, we find a chamber specifically linked to Jean Sauvegrain, and also in the inventory of that of the tanner Hugenot Alerdot in 1439.[103] The inventory taken in 1421 of Thierry Chastellan describes the upstairs front chamber as where 'the said mister

97 ADCO BII 356, Cote 19, pièce III.

98 Piponnier, 'Usages et diffusion de la soie', 793.

99 Henri Lefebvre, *The Production of Space* (Cambridge: Cambridge University Press, 1992), 132, and Bruno Latour, *Reassembling the Social. An Introduction to Actor-Network-Theory* (Oxford: Oxford University Press, 2007).

100 Piponnier, 'Dénominations et fonctions des espaces', 110.

101 ADCO BII 356, Cote 6, pièce IV.

102 Piponnier, 'Dénominations et fonctions des espaces', 110–111.

103 ADCO BII 356, Cote 2, pièce XIII and Cote 20, pièce XXII.

Thierry slept'.[104] In these chambers, silks and tapestry are often listed among a variety of objects that principally include a bed, hangings or covers for the bed and cushions, as well as implements for the fireplace, a table, chairs, benches and frequently chests. Less commonly, we find silks and tapestries included in *salles*. Piponnier notes that *salles*, a term generally reserved for the description of a large room used for receiving visitors, tended to be limited to the houses of the wealthy.[105] 'In the upstairs front *salle* at the front on the road', of the residence of Henri Maistre on the *rue drapperie*, listed among several cloths, some for hanging on the wall, toile, curtains, shearing scissors, wool and a table, we find 12 squares of tapestry and one cover of tapestry.[106] In the lower large *salle* of Richard de Chancey, confessor of the duke, several of his robes, including those of sendal and damask, are listed. His *sale* also incorporated a large bed, furnished with hangings, cushions, and a cover of serge of tapestry as well as ceiling and backing of tapestry.[107] A smaller bed, also with hangings and backing of tapestry, was also listed alongside old squares of tapestry that included images of people.

Chests and armoires also play a prominent role as a place for the storage of silks.[108] Using the Sauvegrain inventory as an example, silks are listed in a number of chests, even before the principal rooms of the residence are described. In one of the first chests to be recorded we find ceilings and backings possibly for beds or chairs embellished with silk and some of red camelot. In the second chest, various items of clothing are listed including those of silk. In the third chest, yet more apparel is found, again including clothing of silk. Yet, silks and tapestry are also listed in chests and armoires that are described by the inventory as being part of the furnishings of a room. Returning to the chamber that is designated as belonging to Jean Sauvegrain, we find an armoire described as situated close to the chimney of the chamber, full of cushions of silk, two covers, a collar of silver embellished with tissue of silks and another large collar of silk.[109] In the same chamber another chest is recorded, this time described by the clerk as in close proximity to the large bed. Among its contents, half an ell of black silk, and three cushions of red, green and lavender silk are included.

Another space where silks and tapestries are listed in the Dijon inventories, is in garde robes. A garde robe could be a large chest or separate compartment of a chamber and usually functioned as a storage place for precious or

104 ADCO BII 356, Cote 11, pièce XVI.
105 Piponnier, 'Dénominations et fonctions des espaces', 112.
106 ADCO BII 356, Cote 19, pièce XIX.
107 ADCO BII 356, Cote 19, pièce III.
108 Piponnier, 'Dénominations et fonctions des espaces', 111.
109 ADCO BII 356, Cote 2, pièce XIII. The covers are described as *tapis*.

personal objects.[110] In Piponnier's study of the different denominations given to spaces in the Dijon residences, garde robes appear less frequently. In the 1395 inventory of the ducal tailor Regnault Chevalier, silks used for various items of clothes, as cushions, as covers and for a pavilion, are recorded among the contents of his garde robe.[111] A pourpoint of silk is included alongside other items of clothing in the 'garde robe of the said chamber' in the inventory of Pierre Sancenot in 1421.[112]

Finally, silks and tapestries can be found listed in spaces described by the clerks as chapels. Chapels, like garde robes tend to be reserved for the wealthiest inhabitants of Dijon. The contents of Regnault Chevalier's chapel have already attracted interest, mainly because of the variety and richness of the goods listed, including a number of silk items.[113] Among the alabaster image of Mary and a tableau of Mary and St John the Baptist, noted as being 'under the altar', are cups and goblets of silver, a tableau of My Lady, several linen cloths, two chasubles, one of cloth of gold which bears the motto of Philip the Bold, duke of Burgundy (1384–1404), '*I am waiting*', a cloth of gold for putting on the altar, a cushion of silk and a chamber for the chapel.[114] The detail is exceptional, and the scene is set for mass and the taking of communion. Another space where we find silks is in the garret of the tower of the residence of Jean Villain, goldsmith, in a 1434 record that lists cushions of silk. Yet, the spaces where silks and tapestry were recorded can only take us so far in why these textiles were sought out by our inhabitants of Dijon.

Why?

The first associated meaning of silks and tapestry, and a reason why individuals sought to possess these textiles, lay in the fact that these textiles were 'both rare and widely available'.[115] As the introduction to this volume has made clear, the difficulty of acquisition, either real or perceived, is a key factor that contributes to the consideration of an object as a 'luxury'. Both silks and tapestry carried this associated meaning. Silks had traditionally been the preserve of only the very wealthy, first manufactured and limited to the Byzantine realm before being adopted by the nobility of Western Europe, and

110 Definition of *garderobe* as given by Godefroy, *Dictionnaire de l'ancienne langue française et de tous ses dialects du IXe au XV siècle* (Paris 1880–1902), vol. 4, 225. Either a 'Pièce, chambre où sont rangés les vetements' or a 'Coffre de grandes dimensions, armoire où sont rangés les vêtements, le linge et les objets précieuses'.

111 ADCO BII 356, Cote 2, pièce III.

112 ADCO BII 356, Cote 11, pièce XVII.

113 Piponnier, 'Dénominations et fonctions des espaces', 112, 113.

114 Noted in the inventory as 'y me tarde'.

115 Robin Fleming, 'Acquiring, flaunting and destroying silk in late Anglo-Saxon England', *Early Medieval Europe* 15 (2007):128.

woven there from the twelfth century onwards.[116] Tapestry had a rather more complicated genesis, but tapestry weaving on a high loom is also considered a European importation from the East, and before the Later Middle Ages seems to have been mainly confined to the upper echelons of the nobility.[117] Associations and hints of the Eastern origins of silks still clung to the silks described in our Dijon inventories of the fourteenth and fifteenth centuries, revealed by the terminology assigned by the assessors of the objects. Terms of description were important markers of luxury to those who sought to possess silks and tapestry, signifying the inherent quality of the product and its distinction from other textiles. As Maxine Berg and Elizabeth Eger have emphasised, Eastern and oriental imports were part of the classical, Western definition of luxury.[118]

The term camelot as used in the inventories of Jean Sauvegrain and Jean Villain was related to its Asia Minor origins where it had originally been woven with silk, using fine cashmere or Armenian goat hair in India, Tibet and China.[119] Sendal, one of the commonest terms of description for silks in the Dijon inventories, related to its origins of manufacture in the orient, while the term damask, listed in the inventories of Jean Sauvegrain, Richard du Chancey and Dame Julienne, was named after its original place of manufacture, Damascus, renowned for its rich silk textiles throughout the medieval period.[120] The term satin also had an association with an exotic origin, originally manufactured in Alexandria.[121] Although it is unlikely that any of the silks listed in the possessions of our Dijonnais originated from these far-flung areas, given that the production of these textiles was by the Later Middle Ages well established in Italy and were beginning to be produced in France and the Low Countries, their exotic associations established through the terms of description still mattered to those who possessed them, and to those who sought to possess them. The terms used to describe *hautelice* or *tapisserie* also carried associations of high quality and of scarcity. The term *hautelice*, used in examples like the large cover of *hautelice* depicting twelve months of the year, listed among the possessions of Dame Julienne in 1403, was predominantly used for the description of high quality textiles. In the accounts of the Burgundian dukes from the same period, cloths of *hautelice* are

116 Anna Muthesius, 'Silk in the medieval world', in *The Cambridge history of western textiles*, ed. David Jenkins (Cambridge: Cambridge University Press, 2003), 325–327.

117 Guy Delmarcel, *Flemish Tapestries* (London: Thames and Hudson, 1999), 16.

118 Maxine Berg and Elizabeth Eger, 'The Rise and Fall of Luxury Debates', in *The Rise and Fall of Luxury Debates, Desires and Delectable Goods*, ed. Maxine Berg et al. (London: Palgrave Macmillan, 2003), 8.

119 Zangger, *Contribution à la terminologie des tissues*, 38–39, and Gay, *Glossaire archéologique*, vol. 1, 262.

120 For sendal see, Zangger, *Contribution à la terminologie des tissues*, 42–45, Victor Gay, *Glossaire Archéologique du Moyen Âge et de la Renaissance* (Paris, 1887–1928), vol. 1, 295–297; and for damask see, Gay, *Glossaire Archéologique*, vol. 1, 535–538.

121 Gay, *Glossaire Archéologique*, vol. 2, 328–330, and Zangger, *Contribution à la terminologie des tissues*, 99–101.

among some of the textiles that are purchased for hundreds and thousands of francs, with the inclusion of detailed visual programmes and gold and silver threads.[122] The term *tapisserie* carried associations with production outside Europe, and had been linked in the twelfth, thirteenth and fourteenth centuries with the term *sarrasnoise*, a word used to denote either the origin or imitation of an oriental style.[123] These exotic associations, which established silks and tapestry as rare and difficult to acquire, were qualities that could be transferred to the possessor whenever the silks or tapestry were used or worn. Silks and tapestry may well have been owned by more people than ever before, and appeared in more forms than ever before, but these textiles had lost none of their power to be associated with status, wealth or the ability of an individual owner to tap into wider trade and commercial networks. It was these associations that would have mattered greatly to possessors of silks and tapestry like Regnault Chevalier, Jean Villain, Jean Sauvegrain, and Jean Poissenot.

A sense of how these silks and tapestries may have mattered to their possessors can be derived from one of the contexts we commonly find them in, chests and armoires. Their storage in this context suggests a desire to restrict their use and prolong their life. On the one hand, there was clearly a practical motivation behind the storage of silks and tapestry in chests. Textiles were less durable than wooden chairs, tables, iron chests and metal utensils, more prone to damage from light, fire, moths and the general wear and tear of everyday life. On the other hand, placement in a chest suggests the need to protect and preserve. That impulse to protect and preserve was bound up with an individual's perception of how valuable an item was to that person. Two examples of silks associated with the ritual of baptism provide an interesting case study in light of the above considerations. The first example comes from the objects listed as belonging to Jean Martin and his wife in 1434.[124] In a chest, listed in an upstairs chamber located at the front of their residence, we find a piece of white silk for baptism wrapped in another piece of green silk. The second example is also listed in a chest, in an upstairs chamber, and is described as a piece of linen for baptising children, together with a piece of silk in the residence of Pierre Sancenot in 1421.[125] In the case of the first example, it seems as if some care has been taken in the storage of this textile, carefully wrapped to preserve not only the textile, but also its association with a particular moment of life. It is stored with other items of silk, including an old purse and a pillow of satin half black and half red in colour. Tapestry can also be found in a similar protective and preservational context. In another

122 Katherine Anne Wilson, *Courtly and Urban Tapestries of the Burgundian Dominions* (Forthcoming, Brepols).

123 Gay, *Glossaire Archéologique*, vol. 2, 328. The use of the term *sarrasnoise* more or less disappears as we move into the fifteenth century.

124 ADCO BII 356, Cote 17, pièce XI, XII.

125 ADCO BII 356, Cote 11, pièce XVII.

chest of Pierre Sancenot among a list of clothes, linen and cushions, we find described five old squares of tapestry and a green cloth as well as a cloth of toile painted with images.[126] Silks and tapestry also appear in armoires, such as the four squares of *tapis* ornamented with birds found alongside collars and cushions of silk in the armoire described in the inventory of Jean Sauvegrain, as do the four purses of silk in the armoire of Pierre Sancenot. Observing silks and tapestries in these contexts allows us to reflect that there must have been deliberate choices made about when they were used and how they were displayed. These choices may well have been important when the audience for the silks and tapestries were predominantly individuals of neighbourhood networks and peers. While we cannot know exactly how the rooms were reconstructed and how the silks and tapestries interacted with the other objects listed in each residence, we do know that the inventories were often witnessed by neighbours and friends and certain objects were valued by expert assessors. For example, in 1431 the cups, rings and belt bells of silver in the inventory of Nicholas Giret, saddler, were valued by the goldsmith Jean Villain, before his own inventory was compiled in 1434.[127] As Christina Antenhofer has illustrated in her contribution to this volume, opinion of your peers mattered when it came to the display and assessment of personal possessions.

Conclusion

Investigation of the different forms of silks and tapestry, and the contexts of their use, emphasises that these textiles functioned in a variety of settings in a multiplicity of forms, silks in particular. Both textiles could be important props and possessions of everyday life. They were cushions for beds and chairs, bed and bench covers, wall and bed hangings. They were the fabrics that clothed and embellished individuals and they were textiles appropriate for use in religious and devotional settings as chasubles, baptismal silks or, as in the reference found in the inventory of Dame Julienne, as relic purses.[128] Anna Muthesius reminds us that silks were rarely thrown away, they were reused, and given the descriptor 'old', a term which is frequently attached to silks and tapestry in the Dijon inventories.[129] There is no simple answer why silks and tapestry were owned and used in later medieval Dijon. But by considering the context of their use, this chapter argues that as a textile often displayed in prominent and personal *chambres* and *salles* of Dijon, protected and preserved, and described through terms emphasising their exotic associations, they

126 ADCO BII 356, Cote 11, pièce XVII.
127 ADCO BII 356, Cote 16, pièce XIII.
128 ADCO BII 356, Cote 3, pièce XXIII.
129 Muthesius, 'Silk in the medieval world', 325–354.

were considered a luxury by contemporaries and this is an important part of understanding the decision to purchase and use them in greater numbers in the Later Middle Ages.

Bibliography

Manuscript Sources

Archives départementales de la Côte-d'Or, series B II/356.

Published Sources

Berg, Maxine, and Eger, Elizabeth. 'The Rise and Fall of Luxury Debates'. In *The Rise and Fall of Luxury Debates, Desires and Delectable Goods* edited by Maxine Berg and Elizabeth Eger, 7–27. London: Palgrave Macmillan, 2003.

Chapuis, Albert. *Les anciennes corporations dijonnaises : règlements, statuts et ordonnances.* Dijon, 1906.

Childs, Wendy. 'Cloth of Gold and Gold Thread: Luxury Imports to England in the Fourteenth Century'. In *War Government and Aristocracy in the British Isles* edited by Christopher Given-Wilson, 267–286. Woodbridge: Boydell Press, 2008.

Chorley, Patrick. 'The 'draperies légères' of Lille, Arras, Tournai, Valenciennes: New Materials for New Markets?'. In *Drapery Production in the late Medieval Low Countries: Markets and Strategies for Survival (14th to 16th Centuries) (Proceedings of the Colloquium Ghent, April 28th, 1992)* edited by Marc Boone and Walter Prevenier, 151–165. Leuven: Leuven University Press, 1993.

De Groot, Julie and Stabel, Peter. 'The domestic interior in mid 15th century Bruges. Between representation and material reality' Unpublished paper.

De Lespinasse, René and Bonnardot, Françoise. *Les métiers et corporations de la ville de Paris. XIIIe siècle, le Livre des métiers d'Étienne Boileau.* Paris, 1879.

Delmarcel, Guy. *Flemish Tapestries.* Thames and Hudson: London, 1999.

Dubois, Henri. *Les foires de Chalon et le commerce dans la vallée de la Saône à la fin du Moyen Age (vers 1280–vers 1430).* Paris: Sorbonne, 1976.

Dubois, Henri. 'Marchands dijonnais aux foires de Chalon-sur-Saône à la fin du Moyen Âge. Essai de prosopographie', *Publication du Centre Européen d'études Bourguignonnes (XIVe–XVIes)* 27 (1987): 63–79.

Dutour, Thierry. *Une société de l'honneur. Les notables et leur monde à Dijon à la fin du Moyen Âge.* Paris, 1998.

Dyer, Christopher. 'Luxury Goods in Medieval England'. In *Commercial Activity, Markets and Entrepreneurs in the Middle Ages. Essays in Honour of Richard Britnell,* edited by Soeiro de Raquel, Ben Dodds and Christian Liddy, 217–238. Woodbridge: Boydell and Brewer, 2011.

Farr, James *Hands of Honor: artisans and their world in Dijon, 1550–1650.* Ithaca: Cornell University Press, 1988.

Farr, James. 'Consumers, commerce and the craftsmen of Dijon: The changing social and economic structure of a provincial capital, 1450–1750'. In *Cities and Social Change in Early Modern France,* edited by Philip Benedict, 134–173. London: Routledge, 1989.

Fleming, Robin. 'Acquiring, flaunting and destroying silk in late Anglo-Saxon England', *Early Medieval Europe,* 15 (2007): 127–158.

Gay, Victor. *Glossaire Archéologique du Moyen Âge et de la Renaissance.* Paris, 1887–1928.

Geoffroy, Pierre. 'Commerce et marchands à Dijon au XVe siècle', *Annales de Bourgogne* 25 (1953): 161–181.

Laborde, Léon. *Les ducs de Bourgogne: Études sur les lettres, les arts et l'industrie pendant le xve siècle et plus particulièrement dans les Pays-bas et le duché de Bourgogne.* vols 1 and 2 Paris, 1851.

Lambert, Bart. *The City, the Duke and their Banker. The Rapondi Family and the Formation of the Burgundian State (1384–1430).* Turnhout: Brepols, 2006.

Lefebvre, Henri. *The Production of Space.* Cambridge: Cambridge University Press, 1992.

Mosher-Stuard, Susan. *Gilding the Market: Luxury and Fashion in Fourteenth-century Italy*. Pennsylvania: University of Pennsylvania Press, 2006.

Piponnier, Françoise. 'Vivre noblement en Bourgogne au XIVe siècle'. *Mélanges d'archéologie et d'histoire médiévales en l'honneur de Michel de Boüard,* 309–317. Genève–Paris, 1982.

Piponnier, Françoise. 'Linge de maison et linge de corps au Moyen Age d'après le inventaires Bourguignons'. *Ethnologie française* 16 (1986): 239–248.

Piponnier, Françoise. 'Usages et diffusion de la soie en France à la fin du Moyen Age'. In *La Seta in Europa sec. XIII–XX. Atti della 'Ventiquattresima Settimana di Studi', 4–9 maggio 1992*, edited by Simonetta Cavaciocchi, 785–800. Firenze: Le Monnier, 1993.

Piponnier, Françoise. 'Maisons du XIVe au milieu du XVIe siècle: notices, 48–55, 61'. In *Cent maisons médiévales en France (du XIIe au milieu du XVIe siècle). Un corpus et une esquisse,* edited by Yves Esquieu and Jean-Marie Pesez, 314–326, 345–347. Paris: CNRS, 1998.

Piponnier, Françoise. 'Dénominations et fonctions des espaces dans l'habitation dijonnaise XIVe–XVe siècle'. In *Cadres de vie et manières d'habiter XIIe–XVIe siècle (VIIIe Congrès international de la Société d'archéologie médiévale)*, edited by Danièle Alexandre-Bidon, Françoise Piponnier, Jean-Michel Poisson, 109–116. Caen: Paris, 2001.

Piuz, Anne-Marie. 'La soie, le luxe et le pouvoir dans les doctrines françaises (XVIe–XVIIIes.)'. In *La Seta in Europa sec. XIII–XX. Atti della 'Ventiquattresima Settimana di Studi', 4–9 maggio 1992*, edited by Simonetta Cavaciocchi, 817–837. Firenze : Le Monnier, 1993.

Prost, Bernard. *Inventaires mobiliers et extraits des comptes des ducs de Bourgogne de la maison de Valois (1363–1477).* Vol 1 and 2, Paris, 1908–1913.

Puttevils, Jeroen. 'Trading silks and tapestries in sixteenth century Antwerp'. In *Europe's Rich Fabric. The Consumption, Commercialisation, and Production of Luxury Textiles in Italy, the Low Countries and Neighbouring Territories (Fourteenth–Sixteenth Centuries)* edited by Bart Lambert and Katherine Anne Wilson, 131–155. Aldershot, Ashgate, 2016.

Schuurman, Anton. 'Probate Inventories: Research Issues, Problems and Results'. In *Probate Inventories. A new source for the historical study of wealth, material culture and agricultural development*, edited by Ad van der Woude and Anton Schuurman, 19–32. Utrecht: HES Publishers, 1980.

Smit, Hillie. 'Flemish Tapestry Weavers in Italy c.1420–1520. A survey and analysis of the activity in various cities'. In *Flemish Tapestry Weavers Abroad. Emigration and the Founding of Manufactories in Europe,* edited by Guy Delmarcel, 113–130. Leuven: Leuven University Press, 2002.

Stabel, Peter. 'Le gout pour l'Orient'. Demand cosmopolite et objets de luxe à Bruges à la fin du Moyen Âge'. *Histoire Urbaine* 30 (2011): 21–39.

Sturtewagen, Isis. 'The fabric of everyday life: clothing oneself and one's home in 15th and 16th century Bruges'. Paper presented at the 11th International Conference on Urban History, Prague, August 29–September 1, 2012.

Toussaint, Paul. *Les foires de Chalon-sur-Saône des origins au XVI siècle*. Dijon, 1910.

Vandeuren-David, Céline. 'L'apport des inventaires après décès dans la connaissance de la parure civile à Dijon (1383–1403)'. In *La Vie matérielle au moyen âge. L'apport des sources littéraires, normatives et de la pratique; Actes du colloque international de Louvain-la Neuve, 3–5 octobre 1996*, edited by Emmanuelle Rassart-Eeckhout, Jean-Pierre Sosson, Claude Thiry and Tania van Hemelryck, 261–276. Louvain-la-Neuve, 1997.

Vaughan, Richard. *Philip the Good. The Apogee of Burgundian Power*. Woodbridge: Boydell, 2002.

Viaux, Dominique. 'Fortunes Immobilières à Dijon au commencement du 15e siècle', *Annales de Bourgogne* 66 (1994): 65–80.

Wilson, Katherine Anne. 'Tapestry in the Burgundian Dominions. A complex object'. In *La cour de Bourgogne et l'Europe. Le rayonnement et les limites d'un modèle culturel* edited by Werner Parvacini, 317–332. Ostfildern: Jan Thorbecke Verlag, 2013.

Wilson, Katherine Anne. *Courtly and Urban Tapestries of the Burgundian Dominions*. Forthcoming, Brepols.

Zangger, Kurt. *Contribution à la terminologie des tissues en ancient français, attestés dans des texts français, provençaux, italiens, espagnols, allemandes et latins*. Bienn, 1945.

2

'O per honore, o per commodo mio': Displaying Textiles at the Gonzaga Court (Fifteenth–Sixteenth Centuries)

Christina Antenhofer

> To this I respond that if you mean by *camera principale* the one which is at the head of the *saletta*, I am determined that also the ceiling [*solaro*][1] has to be rendered beautifully following the judgment of *signor Giuliano* no matter how much it costs, because it has to be decorated with the most beautiful tapestries you can find since any honourable person who will come to court or speak to me will have to stay there; but if the room is not the one I am saying I wish that you make yourself understood well beforehand because I do not have money to spend if it is not for things which are necessary, either for my honour or my convenience.[2]

The letter that cardinal Ercole Gonzaga wrote to Bernardino Pia in 1558 giving him instructions on the arrangement of *arazzi* in his palace in Rome is interesting from several points of view. First, we get an impression of the highly organised process of interior decoration in Renaissance Italy, which included 'supervisors' responsible for watching and organising the decoration process

1 *Solaro* or *solaio* designates a horizontal structure dividing different floors and thus forming the ceiling of the lower ones and the floor of the upper ones. It can also designate the attic. See Salvatore Battaglia, *Grande dizionario della lingua italiana* (vols 1–21, Torino: Unione Tipografico Ed.Torinese, 1961–2002), vol. 19, 296 and 299.

2 'A questo vi rispondo che se per camera principale voi intendete quella che è in capo alla saletta, son risoluto che, dovendo andare ornata delle più belle tapezzarie che mi truovi et affermarsi in essa ogni persona honorata che venga per corteggiare o per parlarmi, si faccia anco bello il solaro a giudicio del signor Giuliano et costi ciò che vuole; ma se la camera non è quella che dico io, disidero che vi facciate prima ben intendere perché io non ho danari da spendere, se non in cose che sieno necessarie, o per honore, o per commodo mio'. Ercole Gonzaga answers Bernardino Pia concerning the arrangement of *arazzi* in his palace in Rome, 11 August 1558, Archivio di Stato di Mantova (ASMn) registro (r.) 6514 carte (cc.) 16–17, edited by Clifford M. Brown and Anna Maria Lorenzoni, 'Ricordi dell'archivio', in *Gli arazzi dei Gonzaga nel Rinascimento*, ed. Guy Delmarcel (Milano: Skira, 2010), 242–3, n. 38. All the translations are by Christina Antenhofer.

while constantly keeping in touch with the princes as an 'ordering party'. Second, we get a sense of the active involvement of princes, an involvement not only directed by an appreciation for the fine arts. Rather, we get a sense of their highly pragmatic and political use of decoration as Ercole neatly puts it in his letter: 'I do not have money to spend if it is not for things which are necessary, either for my honour or for my convenience'. In addition, we get a distinct impression of the function of the Renaissance palace as a highly performative place that worked on different levels. For example, how best to decorate a room depended on where it was situated and what its function was. The best and finest decoration was reserved for the principal hall. Its purpose was to be shown to 'honourable guests' who came to *corteggiare*, to court the prince or to speak to him. The description of the room as a place to receive visitors beautifully illustrates the double semantics of a potential visit. People coming for courtship were equally courted by the prince who spent his money in an apparently lavish way to impress flatterers.[3]

The concept of performativity as a reciprocal act involving the prince performing his richness and splendour and the public spectating, applauding, and commenting will be the focus of this chapter when dealing with the act of displaying luxury textiles as a political act. Following Cohen and Cohen's study of the circulation of 'charismatic objects' in Italian Renaissance towns,[4] four central forms of social interactions and exchanges can be observed. First is a common enjoyment and admiration of the objects, which Cohen and Cohen call 'a form of communion',[5] where the patron shows his invited guests the precious objects he possesses. Second are the 'social dynamics' that are linked to the objects. These include the buying and selling, gift giving, loaning, using them as a form of credit or even stealing the objects. Third, a form of interaction and bonding via objects is created by the desire to protect (or destroy) these fragile objects. Finally, the objects entail actions of *stimare* (estimate and esteem) by guests, rivals and the emerging community of *connoisseurs* who can either appreciate the exposed objects or despise them.[6]

The approach of Cohen and Cohen, which consists of deciphering different social actions in the process of representation via luxury goods, is fruitful and more precise than merely talking about communication via objects or representation. Trying to identify specific forms of social interaction provides a deeper understanding of the social interdependence between patrons, artists, merchants, customers, public and the objects involved. In this study of the Gonzaga luxury textiles, the focus on the social actions connected with the

---

3 On the arrangement of the Renaissance house and palazzo see the articles in the catalogue: Marta Ajmar-Wollheim, Flora Dennis and Elizabeth Miller, *At home in Renaissance Italy* (London: V&A Publishing, 2006).

4 Thomas V. Cohen and Elizabeth S. Cohen, 'Postscript: charismatic things and social transaction in Renaissance Italy', *Urban History* 37 (2010): 474–82; here 479–81.

5 Cohen and Cohen, 'Postscript', 479.

6 Cohen and Cohen, 'Postscript', 479–81.

objects and the people involved will be the methodological guiding line leading to four central questions for our chapter. In terms of documenting and buying textiles, what kind of sources record luxury textiles at the Gonzaga court and who were the people involved in buying or producing them? In addition, what were the occasions for displaying cloths? The issue of display then leads us to consider the semantics of textiles. What kind of social meanings were connected to textiles and which political implications can be deduced from the actions and forms of communication linked to the displaying of textiles? Finally, we must examine the audience of this performance. Who were the people to whom the cloths were displayed and what part did they play?

Why Study Gonzaga Luxury Textiles?

Studying the Gonzaga court as a case study for the purchasing and display of luxury textiles is attractive from several points of view. Starting from a rather modest background, the family established themselves as one of the leading Italian dynasties of the sixteenth century – together with the Medici, Este, Farnese and Savoy.[7] Moreover, they became the Italian dynasty that intermarried most frequently with the Habsburg dynasty.[8] As their territory was rather small compared to other dynasties, more or less limited to the city of Mantua and its surroundings, and because of their humble background and usurped status of power over Mantua, they seem to have adopted an aggressive strategy of art patronage in order to push the family into the highest ranks of European aristocracy.[9] Gonzaga patronage is most visibly reflected by their vast palace in Mantua, one of the biggest Renaissance *palazzi* covering an entire quarter of the city. Their history as patrons of the arts has above all been marked by the outstanding figure of Isabella d'Este (*1474 †1539), who had a huge impact on the Gonzaga generations to follow. Nonetheless, it was already in the middle of the fifteenth century, at the court of Ludovico II, that the Gonzaga made the decisive move into becoming patrons of art utilising the presence of such outstanding artists as Leon Battista Alberti and Andrea Mantegna, later to be followed by the presence of Giulio Romano under Federico II in the sixteenth century.[10] Despite their impressive history

---

7 See Angelantonio Spagnoletti, *Le dinastie italiane nella prima età moderna* (Bologna: Il Mulino, 2003), 168–9.

8 Paula Sutter Fichtner, 'Dynastic Marriage in Sixteenth-Century Habsburg Diplomacy and Statecraft. An Interdisciplinary Approach', *The American Historical Review* 81/2 (1976): 243–265; Christina Antenhofer, 'From Local *Signori* to European High Nobility: The Gonzaga Family Networks in the Fifteenth Century', in *Transregional and Transnational Families in Europe and Beyond: Experiences Since the Middle Ages*, ed. Christopher H. Johnson, et al. (New York - Oxford: Berghahn Books, 2011), 55–74.

9 See on this family strategy Antenhofer, 'Local Signori'.

10 Arturo Calzona, *Il principe architetto. Atti del convegno internazionale Mantova, 21–23 ottobre 1999* (Centro Studi L. B. Alberti Ingenium 4) (Firenze: Olschki, 2002); Cesare

as patrons of the arts, studies on the Gonzaga have remained behind the great amount of research on the Medici family; focus was most frequently directed exclusively towards Isabella d'Este. Yet, from the 1990s more interest has been turned towards the Gonzaga, resulting in several comprehensive studies on the family and their art patronage.[11] Along with leading scholars in the field, the main Mantuan institutions – namely the *Archivio di Stato di Mantova*, the *Palazzo Ducale* and the *Palazzo Te* – produce new research with voluminous editions of primary sources from the archives as well as major exhibitions accompanied by catalogues that provide important essays as well as material from the archives.[12]

Fortunately, the archives of the Gonzaga provide historians with a large number of documents, because the Gonzaga (succeeded by the sideline of the Gonzaga-Nevers in 1627) dominated Mantua from 1328 until 1708, allowing almost 400 years of uninterrupted domination. In addition, from their early days, the Gonzaga family was engaged in an extensive correspondence practice that makes Mantua one of the primary areas for research on letters and letter writing. The correspondence includes various strands of communication – among family members but also between a range of people from the court, including artists and others.[13] When studying properties and their interiors,

---

Mozzarelli, Robert Oresko and Leandro Ventura, *La corte di Mantova nell'età di Andrea Mantegna; 1450–1550/The Court of the Gonzaga in the Age of Mantegna; 1450–1550, Atti del convegno (Londra, 6–8 marzo 1992; Mantova, 28 marzo 1992)* (Europa delle Corti. Centro studi sulle società di antico regime. Biblioteca del Cinquecento 75) (Roma: Bulzoni, 1997). For an exhaustive bibliography on the Gonzaga see Raffaele Tamalio, *La memoria dei Gonzaga. Repertorio bibliografico Gonzaghesco 1473–1999* (Biblioteca di bibliografia italiana CLVIII) (Firenze: Olschki, 1999).

11 For example, Arturo Calzona, *La rotonda e il palatium di Matilde* (Parma: Università degli Studi di Parma, 1991); Marina Romani, *Una città in forma di palazzo. Potere signorile e forma urbana nella Mantova medievale e moderna* (Quaderni di Cheiron 1) (Mantova: Publi Paolini, 1995); Filippo Trevisani, ed., *Andrea Mantegna e i Gonzaga. Rinascimento nel Castello di San Giorgio* (Milano: Electa, 2006); Ebba Severidt, *Familie, Verwandtschaft und Karriere bei den Gonzaga: Struktur und Funktion von Familie und Verwandtschaft bei den Gonzaga und ihren deutschen Verwandten (1444–1519)* (Leinfelden – Echterdingen: DRW, 2002); Molly Bourne, *Francesco II Gonzaga. The soldier-prince as patron* (Biblioteca del Cinquecento 138) (Roma: Bulzoni, 2008); Clifford M. Brown, Guy Delmarcel and Anna Maria Lorenzoni, *Tapestries for the courts of Federico II, Ercole, and Ferrante Gonzaga, 1522–63* (Seattle and London: College Art Association in association with University of Washington Press, 1996); David S. Chambers and Jane Martineau, eds., *Splendours of the Gonzaga: Catalogue, exhibition, 4. nov. 1981 – 31 jan.1982* (London: V&A Museum, 1981).

12 See the edition of the ambassador's letter from Milan to Mantua (1450–1500) comprising 16 volumes: Franca Leverotti, ed., *Carteggio degli oratori mantovani alla corte sforzesca* (1450–1500) (Pubblicazioni degli archivi di stato) (16 vols, Roma: Ministero per i Beni e le Attività Culturali, 1999ff).

13 For a quick overview on the stocks of correspondence in the archives see Alessandro Luzio, *L'Archivio Gonzaga di Mantova. La corrispondenza familiare, amministrativa e diplomatica* (Pubblicazioni della R. Accademia Virgiliana di Mantova. Serie 1, Monumenta, vol. 2) (Verona, 1922; Reprint Mantova: Grassi, 1993). On the working of the Gonzaga chancery in the fifteenth century see Isabella Lazzarini, *Fra un principe e altri stati. Relazioni di potere e forme di servizio a Mantova nell'età di Ludovico Gonzaga* (Istituto storico italiano per il Medioevo/ nuovi studi storici 32) (Roma: Nella sede dell'Istituto, 1996). For a current edition of the correspondence around one Gonzaga daughter see Christina Antenhofer et al, eds. *Barbara*

it is productive to examine inventories or account books. These sources list objects as well as provide an overview of expenses and acquisitions which can give historians an idea of the way in which items were used, what kind of actions were linked to them and some insights into their performative aspects. Yet, it is also vital to utilise narrative sources such as letters or reports of chroniclers in order to place these objects back into their daily settings.

This chapter focuses on the following major archival editions and studies in order to explore the Gonzaga's display and use of luxury textiles from the fifteenth to sixteenth centuries. The biggest edition concerning correspondence, repertories and inventories that give insights in the artistic collections of the Gonzaga is the series *Le collezioni Gonzaga* comprising twelve volumes covering the sixteenth and seventeenth centuries.[14] For the period covered by this chapter, I will rely on the edition of the comprehensive series of Gonzaga inventories compiled in 1540–1542, edited by Daniela Ferrari.[15] The creation of this inventory as a major dynastic act of *memoria* above all directed by duchess Margherita Paleologa has been closely studied in the unpublished PhD thesis by Martha Sue Ahrendt.[16] Further insight into Gonzaga properties of the fifteenth century is based on belongings and correspondence concerning the two daughters of Ludovico II, Paula and Barbara Gonzaga, as well as their bridal trousseaus.[17] A further comparative study of the specifically female use of material culture is offered by the unpublished PhD thesis of Sarah Bercusson, who focuses on female networks based on material culture comparing three Habsburg sisters married to the Este, Gonzaga and Medici court in sixteenth century.[18] Finally, the preeminent luxury textiles, namely precious tapestries, were presented in a comprehensive exhibition accompanied by a rich catalogue in 2010, which offers a detailed

Gonzaga: Die Briefe/Le Lettere (1455–1508). Edition und Kommentar deutsch/italienisch (Stuttgart: Kohlhammer, 2013).

14 http://www.silvanaeditoriale.it/catalogo/categoria.asp?id=43 [accessed 14 June 2011].

15 Daniela Ferrari, ed., *Le collezioni Gonzaga. L'inventario dei beni del 1540–1542* (Fonti, repertori e studi per la storia di Mantova. Collana del centro internazionale d'arte e di cultura di Palazzo Te 1) (Milano: Silvana Editoriale Spa, 2003). The second big programme of compiling an inventory of the Gonzaga collections took place a century later, in 1626–1627, and it is edited in the same series: Raffaella Morselli, *Le collezioni Gonzaga. L'elenco dei beni del 1626–1627* (Fonti, repertori e studi per la storia di Mantova. Collana del centro internazionale d'arte e di cultura di Palazzo Te 2) (Milano: Silvana Editoriale Spa, 2000).

16 Martha Sue Ahrendt, 'The Cultural Legacy and Patronal Stewardship of Margherita Paleologa (1510–1566), Duchess of Mantua and Marchesa of Montferrat', (PhD diss., Washington University, Saint Louis, Missouri, 2002).

17 Christina Antenhofer, *Briefe zwischen Süd und Nord. Die Hochzeit und Ehe von Paula de Gonzaga und Leonhard von Görz im Spiegel der fürstlichen Kommunikation* (1473–1500) (Schlern-Schriften 336) (Innsbruck: Wagner, 2007); Peter Rückert, ed., *Von Mantua nach Württemberg: Barbara Gonzaga und ihr Hof. Begleitbuch zur Ausstellung* (Stuttgart: Kohlhammer, 2012). The belongings of their brother cardinal Francesco have been studied by David S. Chambers, *A Renaissance Cardinal and His Worldly Goods. The Will and Inventory of Francesco Gonzaga (1444–83)* (Warburg Institute Surveys and Texts 20) (London: Warburg Institute, 1992).

18 Sarah Jemima Bercusson, *Gift-Giving, Consumption and the Female Court in Sixteenth-Century Italy* (PhD thesis, London Queen Mary College, University of London, 2009).

study of tapestries from the fifteenth to the seventeenth centuries and also a rich documentation of archival material such as letters, extracts from account books, inventories and wills that help to reconstruct the primary functions and uses of these textile masterpieces.[19]

What Kind of Textiles? Studying Gonzaga Inventories

Documenting Textiles

The enormous undertaking of compiling a general inventory of the Gonzaga belongings, an undertaking that covered the space of two years – namely from August 1540 until October 1542 – was motivated by the death of Federico II Gonzaga in 1540.[20] His widow, Margherita Paleologa, together with his brother, cardinal Ercole Gonzaga, gave the order to compile the document in order to get an overview of the belongings of the 'city, the State and the duchy of Mantua' as well as of the 'belongings of the marchesato del Monferrato', palaces and mansions including a detailed list of objects, documents of the archives as well as lists of incomes, expenses, debits and credits.[21] The first impression when studying the inventory is a sense of getting lost in the list of belongings. In fact the notaries themselves did not obey their pre-established order and worked their way through the belongings without following a chronological or typological order in listing goods.[22] However, the textiles that are the focus of interest here were functionally separated from the rest of the belongings already in the organisation of the ducal household which comprised the textiles in the *Guardaroba di Corte*.[23] According to the division of the court between male and female, the *Guardaroba* of the duke and the duchess were separated and supervised by different people. In the outline of the organisation of the inventory we read a section concerning textiles stating: 'The tapestries, paraments, beds with the corresponding fitments of which are responsible Nicolò Capilupi, head of the *Guardaroba ducale* or *Drapperia*, and Eleonora Bandelli for the part of the wardrobe which regards the duchess

[19] Guy Delmarcel, ed., *Gli arazzi dei Gonzaga nel Rinascimento* (Milano: Skira, 2010). The catalogue is based on the English book: Brown, Delmarcel and Lorenzoni, *Tapestries*.

[20] Daniela Ferrari, 'Introduction', in *Le collezioni Gonzaga. L'inventario dei beni del 1540–1542* (Fonti, repertori e studi per la storia di Mantova. Collana del centro internazionale d'arte e di cultura di Palazzo Te 1) (Milano: Silvana Editoriale Spa, 2003), 9–27; Ahrendt, 'Legacy'.

[21] Ferrari, 'Introduction', 9–10.

[22] Ferrari, 'Introduction', 11.

[23] Ferrari, 'Introduction', 17–21. For the organisation of the Gonzaga household see Guido Guerzoni, 'La corte gonzaghesca in età moderna. Struttura, ordini e funzioni', in *I Gonzaga. Moneta Arte Storia*, ed. Silvana Balbi de Caro (Milano: Electa, 1995), 90–96.

Margherita Paleologo'.[24] Luxury textiles made of silk and gold are singled out from the more general listing of Gonzaga textiles. The general entry on paraments is followed later by the entry 'the paraments in silk and gold which are consigned to Giovanni Colla, *maestro di camera* of the duchess'.[25] As Ferrari demonstrates, the pragmatic order in which the notaries proceeded followed the spatial organisation of the court, including the *Guardaroba di Corte* and the 'Guardaroba della marchesa Isabella d'Este e del duca Federico',[26] that is the belongings of the recently deceased duke and duchess Isabella who had died only one year earlier leaving an impressive patronage to be administered by her daughter-in-law Margherita. According to Ferrari, the *Guardaroba di Corte* alone occupies roughly the seventh part of the whole inventory.[27]

Taking a closer look at what kind of textiles are mentioned we get a real insight into the place textiles occupied at court as detailed lists of bed and table cloths dominate. However, this inventory does not mention a great number of dresses;[28] rather it notes undergarments, some jackets (*giacche*) and outergarments (*sopravesti*, such as *giupponi* and *zornee*) which are mentioned in the section of the *armeria* and may thus have been kept there along with armour.[29] Ferrari singles out four groups of textiles that can be found in the section on the *Guardaroba di Corte*, including the *camicie*, which served a hygienic function. Changing the *camicie* often helped to keep the body clean in times of reluctance to use water.[30] As such, they were stored together with the bed linens. The *camicie* varied in cuts and materials, the most luxurious

---

[24] 'le tappezzerie, i paramenti, i letti con i relativi arredi di cui sono responsabili Nicolò Capilupi, superiore della Guardaroba ducale o Drapperia, ed Eleonora Bandelli per la parte della Guardaroba riguardante la duchessa Margherita Paleologo;' Ferrari, 'Introduction', 10. Ahrendt has shown in her thesis that it was in fact Margherita who was responsible in the end for supervising both the male and the female *Guardaroba*. The organisation of the *Guardaroba* was subject to several rearrangements which Ahrendt convincingly interprets as female acts of power in the court. Thus, the responsibility of the supervision of the textiles in general seems to have been in the hands of the duchess, at least in this generation of Gonzaga. However, the key role Margherita played in the organisation and structuring of all the Gonzaga belongings may have been due to her role as widow and mother of minors (see Ahrendt, 'Legacy', 141–146).

[25] Ferrari, 'Introduction', 10; 'i paramenti in seta e oro affidati a Giovanni Colla, maestro di camera della duchessa'.

[26] Ferrari, 'Introduction', 11.

[27] Ferrari, 'Introduction', 17.

[28] This is of course not the case for the inventory of the bride's trousseau, which will be studied later.

[29] Ferrari, 'Introduction', 17-18. Inventories seem to have been compiled in a very pragmatic way, registering the content of rooms and places. This becomes obvious in Ferrari's introduction, where she claimed that the notaries did not really follow the order they had originally planned. The same results from Ahrendt's studying of the same huge inventorying process. The order that can be detected in the inventories thus seems to result primarily from the way the objects had been stored at court. See Ahrendt, 'Legacy', 126–182.

[30] See Ferrari, 'Introduction', 18; Sara F. Matthews Grieco, 'The Body, Appearance, and Sexuality', in *A History of Women in the West. 3. Renaissance and Enlightenment Paradoxes*, eds. Natalie Zemon Davis and Arlette Farge (Cambridge, MA - London: Belknap Press of Harvard University Press, 1994), 46–84.

being made of silk. Linen, pillowslips, tablecloths, table napkins, pillows, and covers for benches, forming the second group, were decorated in different styles of embroidery. The real luxury textiles were to be found in the section concerning wall covers. Practically any part of the interior could be, and was, covered by textiles, beginning with the walls but also including the doors.[31] Ferrari above all mentions the *spalliere*, small and long 'straps' either made of textiles or out of leather; they were used to cover the walls of the dining room, initially to enable people to sit on the benches and lean on these tapestries with their shoulders (*spalle*), hence their name.[32] These *spalliere* were made of a variety of fabrics, such as damask, silk, brocade, velvet, sateen and wool. A basic distinction between these textiles was further made establishing whether they were *a figure*, meaning displaying paintings, or *a imprese*, that is representing the coat of arms or the famous emblems of the Gonzaga family, which were much loved by them. Moreover, textiles could be *a verdura*, the term the sources applied for the now so called *millefleurs* decoration, or depict *fregi* (friezes). Lighter colours and textiles were used for summer decoration, darker and heavier for winter.[33] According to Ferrari, the most precious *arazzi* were probably displayed only on special occasions, a point that will be discussed further in this chapter. The final section of the inventory includes the textiles used for the bed, especially bed canopies (*cortinaggi per il letto* o *sparvieri*).

The entries include detailed descriptions of the textiles – material, colour, embroidery, shape and measures – yet limited information on the provenance of the cloths. The only clear indications to provenance in the entries concerning the contents of the *Guardaroba* are the following: *tela todescha* (German linen); *pignolato todescho* (German *pignolato*);[34] *tela nostrana* (local linen); *renso nostrano* (local *renso*); *tela fatta in casa* (homemade linen); *tela / renso / fodra da lion* (linen / renso / cover of Lion); *scarlato fiorentino* (Florentine scarlet); *sarza / tela de Fiandra* (sarza / tela from Flanders); *tela de sancto gallo* (linen of Sancto Gallo); *tela / terliso da monacho* (linen / terliso from Munich); *terliso da frisengo* (terliso from Freising). Starting with the listing of *tovaglie* (tablecloths) we get many references to *renso de Fiandra*, although all referred to *renso* for tablecloths or napkins.[35] Another entry mentions blankets of the kind that came from Venice; another a *renso* of Spain.[36]

31 As has been stated before, the mentioning of the Gonzaga wall tapestries in inventories has been very well documented in the catalogue: Delmarcel, *Arazzi*.

32 Ferrari, 'Introduction', 18.

33 Ferrari, 'Introduction', 18.

34 *Pignolato* designates a cloth of linen and hemp used to cover mattresses. See Ferrari, *Collezioni*, 436.

35 Ferrari, *Collezioni*, 235–6. Entries 5650 und 5651 mention 'sarza morella de Fiandra', 271.

36 All mentioned entries, see Ferrari, *Collezioni*, 188–271 and the index of materials ibid. 382-396.

Buying Textiles

According to Ferrari, the expenses of the *Drapperia* were enormous. In the trade accounts of the court from 1554, 1,500 ducats are mentioned, while for simply maintaining the fabrics 4,000 ducats were spent.[37] The high value of the textiles also becomes clear from the fact that textiles along with jewels and silvers formed the most precious entries of inventories,[38] in that they were used in the place of money as part of dowries.[39] The comprehensive term of *Brautschatz* or *bridal trousseau* does not appear in the contemporary sources; instead they refer to single items, usually comprising jewels, textiles and silvers as demonstrated by the following excerpt:

> Moreover the before mentioned illustrious lord margrave promised and promises that at the time when the before mentioned lord count will take lady Paula with him he will let him give 10,000 florins from the Rhine in jewels, silvers, clothes and tapestries, decorations, utensils and other necessary things for the use of the before mentioned Paula, in the way that these jewels, silver, clothes, tapestries, decorations, utensils and other necessary things make up the sum of the mentioned 10,000 florins from the Rhine.[40]

The high value of the textiles, especially wall tapestries is also apparent from the fact that they were used as assurances for loans, similar to jewels, in times of financial hardship to raise money.[41] Of course, the way these textiles were purchased varied according to what kind of textiles they were. The purchase of precious *arazzi* was organised in a very professional way, as the Gonzaga were competing with the leading collectors of tapestries, in the *botteghe* of Brussels and other Flemish tapestry stores.[42] However, they also had tapestries and other textiles manufactured in Mantua. Using this evidence, it is possible to trace individuals from the court purchasing materials such as silk or threads

37 Ferrari, 'Introduction', 19; she refers to Archivio di Stato di Mantova (ASMn) Archivio Gonzaga (AG) busta (b.) 401 carta (c.) 325r.

38 Juan Luis González García, 'Charles V and the Habsburgs' Inventories. Changing Patrimony as Dynastic Cult in Early Modern Europe', *RIHA Journal* 0012 (11 November 2010), http://www.riha-journal.org/articles/2010/gonzalez-garcia-charles-v-and-the-habsburgs-inventories [accessed 20 March 2012].

39 Evelyn Welch, 'Women in Debt. Financing Female Authority in Renaissance Italy', in *Donne di potere nel Rinascimento*, eds. Letizia Arcangeli and Susanna Peyronel (I libri di viella 85) (Roma: Viella, 2008), 45–65; Antenhofer, *Briefe*, 151–172.

40 'Item promisit et promittit prefatus illustris dominus marchio tempore quo prefatus dominus comes ipsam dominam Paulam traducet eidem consignari facere in iocalibus argentis vestibus tapezariis ornamentis utensilibus et aliis necessariis pro usu prefate domine Paule florenos decem mille Renenses ita quod iocalia ipsa argentum vestes tapezarie ornamenta utensilia et alia necessaria ascendant ad summam dictorum florenorum decem millium Renensium [ut] supra'. Extract from the wedding contract of Paula Gonzaga: ASMn AG b. 219 c. 4 original; copy of 7 November 1491 ASMn AG b. 219 c. 5. Edited in: Antenhofer, *Briefe*, 156–8.

41 Clifford M. Brown, introduction to *Gli arazzi dei Gonzaga nel Rinascimento*, ed. Guy Delmarcel (Milano: Skira, 2010), 21–31; here 22; for the jewels: Welch, 'Women'.

42 Guy Delmarcel, 'Prefazione', in *Gli arazzi dei Gonzaga nel Rinascimento*, ed. Guy Delmarcel (Milano: Skira, 2010), 13–6.

of gold and silver in Italian cities such as Venice or Florence.[43] In 1539, the Flemish *arazziere* Nicola Karcher, who had been working in Ferrara from 1536, moved to Mantua to work there, thanks to the close kinship bonds between the courts of Ferrara and Mantua.[44]

The active involvement of women in the purchase of textiles becomes evident when studying Gonzaga daughters who married abroad:[45] as did other Italian princesses, they maintained imports of special goods from their native courts and 'countries'. In the case of Paula Gonzaga (*1464 †1496), two shopping lists have survived that document the kind of textiles as well as gold and silver threads she bought. Her purchases were made via individuals from her court who on one occasion went to Mantua, and on the other to Milan.[46]

The first shopping list dates from 13 October 1483 and concerns textiles for Paula;[47] Nicolo Mayolino, a Gonzaga *familiaro*, had been commissioned by the margrave of Mantua to source textiles in Milan and then hand them over to Paula's *familiaro*, Filipo da Parma, who would bring them to her court in Lienz in today's Eastern Tyrol. Five years after her marriage, the list documents how the familiar bonds – overshadowed by severe conflicts concerning the unpaid dowry of Paula – continued to work on a level of social interactions through the purchasing of textiles. The account begins with an entry giving the date and the people involved in the purchasing of textiles. The entry clearly shows how the textiles passed through several hands and that they were bought by commission of the margrave of Mantua, Federico Gonzaga, for his sister Paula, who had asked for the textiles.

> Today 13 October 1483
>
> Cloths of silk taken in Milan from Nicolo Mayolino in the name of the illustrious lady Paula, countess of Gorizia, by me, Filipo da Parma, which Zacharia da Pissa has had given to me with commission of the illustrious lord the margrave of Mantua.[48]

The entry is then followed by a detailed list of different cloths indicating the amount and the prize, including the following items (see Table 2.1).

---

[43] Nello Forti Grazzini, '1. Annunciazione', in *Gli arazzi dei Gonzaga nel Rinascimento*, ed. Guy Delmarcel (Milano: Skira, 2010), 36–45; here 39.

[44] In 1545 Nicola Karcher and Giovanni Rost, another Flemish tapestry weaver, were then called to Firenze to work for Cosimo I de Medici; Delmarcel, 'Prefazione', 15–16.

[45] For other examples see Bercusson, 'Gift-Giving'.

[46] Edited in: Antenhofer, *Briefe*, 192–6; I have studied these two bills ibid.

[47] Tiroler Landesarchiv Innsbruck (TLA) Sigmundiana (Sigm.) 16.31; edited in Antenhofer, *Briefe*, 192–4.

[48] 'Adi 13 octobre 1483. Drappa de seda tolto in Milano da Nicolo Mayolino in nome / di la ill(ustre) d(omina) P(aula) contessa de Goricia per me Filipo da Parma li quali / me fece dare Zacharia da Pissa de comissione de lo ill(ustre) s(ignor) d(omino) / lo marchixo di Manta'. Antenhofer, *Briefe*, 192.

Table 2.1 Detailed list of cloths

veluto refigurato cremesino	(crimson figured velvet)
raso cremesino	(crimson raso)
veluto lioneto	(ginger velvet)
dalmascho zaldo	(yellow damask)
veluto lioneto	(ginger velvet)
veluto nigro	(black velvet)
dalmascho nigro	(black damask)
oro filato mita subtille mita grosso	(gold threads, half of them subtle, half of them thick)
seda turchina	(turquoise silk)
seda nigra	(black silk)

The costs of textiles purchased amounted to 100 ducats of Milanese money.[49] This list of luxury textiles and gold threads was followed by a list of *panno de lana*, woollen cloths, including white, ginger and scarlet cloths, amounting to 24 ducats, purchased from Gabriel, merchant citizen of Milan.[50] The list is superseded by another that included the following items (see Table 2.2).

Table 2.2 List of cloths

panno d'oro cremesino	(crimson gold cloth)
dalmascho nigro	(black damask)
valise per mette li drappi	(cases to put the cloths in)
(ter)lisso[1] *per involtare il panno lioneto*	(terlisso to wrap the ginger cloth)

Note: [1] *Terlisso* is a particularly tough type of cloth of hemp, cotton or jute, Ferrari, *Collezioni*, 442.

After carefully accounting all the costs and the money Filipo had already been given by Paula, Filipo goes on to list textiles and other things that had been taken by the physician, Magistro Bernardo, in Mantua for Paula during the Lenten season, which included the items below (see Table 2.3).

49 'E le sottscripte (libre) 450 fano duc(ati) 100 (a libre) 4 s(oldi) 10 de moneta milanisa'. Quot. according to Antenhofer, *Briefe*, 193.

50 'Le sottscripte (libre) 109 e s(oldi) 12 fano duc(ati) 24 (e libre) 3 s(oldi) 2 (a libre) 4 (e soldi) 10 per duc(atum)'. Quot. according to Antenhofer, *Briefe*, 193.

Table 2.3 List of textiles taken by the physician, Magistro Bernardo

zanbeloto cremesino[1]	(crimson camelot)
zaffrano	(saffron)
raso cremesino	(crimson raso)
scarlato	(scarlet cloth)
dalmascho nigro	(black damask)
panno morello	(black-brown cloth)

Note: [1] *Giambellotto* (in the regional Mantuan version *zambellotto*), also *cammellotto* or *ciambellotto* is a heavy cloth defined in different ways; according to Battaglia it is made of goatskin or camelskin. See: Battaglia, *Dizionario*, vol. 6, 764. Sandtner, on the other hand, explains it as a heavy silk used for coats: see Claudia Sandtner, 'Zum Brautschatz der Antonia Visconti: Kleidung, Stoffe und Schmuck', in *Antonia Visconti (+ 1405): Ein Schatz im Hause Württemberg. Begleitbuch und Katalog zur Ausstellung des Landesarchivs Baden-Württemberg – Hauptstaatsarchiv Stuttgart*, ed. Peter Rückert, (Stuttgart: Landesarchiv Baden-Württemberg – Hauptstaatsarchiv, 2005), 72–7, here 73. The Dizionario De Mauro explains it as a woollen cloth, most often made of camel hair (De Mauro. Il dizionario della lingua italiana, Paravia 2000, edition on CD-Rom).

The next *familiaro* mentioned in the list is Cristoforo, who frequently circulated between the Gonzaga court and the courts of the daughters who had married German princes delivering letters and goods. Cristoforo gave Filipo money from Paula to buy black velvet. Finally, Filipo mentions some black velvet he had to buy for Paula's husband, count Leonhard of Görz. Filipo's account is interesting not only for the kind of textiles it mentions. The account is a highly intriguing document that illustrates how the purchase of textiles was realised through several *familiari* from different courts, which even included a physician. Moreover, it documents the different cities people frequented to buy textiles, in this case the cities of Mantua and Milan.[51] Purchasing cloths was organised through *familiari* who were sent to the related court where they organised the purchase via *familiari* from the local court. However, the transaction had to be commissioned by the head of the local court, which in this case was Paula's brother Federico Gonzaga.

The second shopping list (see Table 2.4), which has no date, explicitly refers to expenses that had been made for Paula alone, concerning gold threads and gold and silver of different kinds as well as minor silk cloths, which all had been purchased in or near Mantua.[52]

---

51 Evelyn Welch has studied similar ways of purchasing goods via *familiari* at the court of Paola Malatesta Gonzaga: see Evelyn Welch, 'The Art of Expenditure: The Court of Paola Malatesta Gonzaga in Fifteenth-Century Mantua', *Renaissance Studies* 16, no. 3 (2002): 306–317.

52 TLA Sigm. 4a.29.014; edited in Antenhofer, *Briefe*, 196.

Table 2.4 Expenses for gold and silver enamels and minor silk cloths

Purchase made for the most illustrious Madonna Paula[1]			
First for six ounces of gold threads which have been brought by Cristophoro[2]	duc(ati) 6	(libre) –	s(oldi) 1
For eight ounces of gold and silver of different kinds amounts[3]	duc(ati) 1	(libre) –	s(oldi) 14
For six ounces of silver in gilding of various kind of enamels[4]	duc(ati) 5	(libre) 3	s(oldi) 10
For three ounces of gold threads which brought Zoannes de Toblach[5]	duc(ati) 3	(libre) –	s(oldi) –
For the changing of 80 ducats at 1 soldo per ducatum[6]	duc(ati) –	(libre) 4	s(oldi) –
For expenses made at different times like to go to Mantua, to Ferrara, to Gonzaga, to Marmarolo and other places[7]	duc(ati) 4	(libre) –	s(oldi) –
To Gasper Todescho for the writing of her highness[8]	duc(ati) 2	(libre) –	s(oldi) –
For six small cloths of silk for her highness[9]	duc(ati) –	(libre) 2	s(oldi) 5
For the Turkish horse that fell ill at Trento[10]	duc(ati) 1	(libre) –	s(oldi) –
	duc(ati) 24		s(oldi) 23
Moreover Dorothea[11] the niece of Antonia got married and I gave her as donation ten ducats which is[12]	duc(ati) 10	(libre) –	s(oldi) –

Notes

[1] 'Spesa facta per la illustrissima madonna Paula'.
[2] 'Primo per onzi sei de oro filato li quali portò Cristophoro'.
[3] 'Per onzi octo de oro et argento de più sorte monta'.
[4] 'Per onzi sei de argento in dorato de smalti de più sorte'.
[5] 'Per onzi tre de oro filato el quale portò Zoan(nes) de Toblach'.
[6] 'Per cambio de duc(ati) 80 a s(oldo) 1 per duc(atum)'.
[7] 'Per spesi facti in più volte como per andar a Mantua a Ferrara a Gonzaga a Marmarolo et in altri loci'.
[8] 'A Gasper Todescho per la scripta de la sua s(ignoria)'.
[9] 'Per drapeselli sei de setta per la sua s(ignoria)'.
[10] 'Per el cavalo turcho el quale stette amalatto a Trento'.
[11] The source first gave the name 'Magdalena' which was then cancelled and the name 'Dorathea' written above.
[12] 'Item maridata la Dorathea nepota dela Antonia (et?) datogli in dotto duc. dece (videlicet)'.

The above account is in form of a small script that even gives details that occurred to the *familiaro* during his travels and the way in which he had to deal with sudden and unexpected events, if the horse fell ill, or if a marriage took place and donations had to be given. Finally, we gain an insight into how he had to travel around small places of the Mantuan territory in order to organise all the purchases he had been commissioned to make.

Occasions for Displaying Textiles

Decorating Rooms

As stressed by the quotation opening this chapter, textiles served two basic functions at the court. First, they served pragmatic purposes, what Ercole Gonzaga had called 'il mio commodo'. However, whenever we are dealing with luxury textiles there is a second function we have to bear in mind above all. Textiles were used to display the honour of the house; thus, occasions for displaying cloths played a vital part in understanding how these textiles were actually brought into 'action', and were raised to the attention of a broader public. A second distinction that needs to be made is the one between daily methods of representation and special occasions. Daily representation becomes most obvious in the permanent decoration of rooms with textiles, or with textiles that could be changed according to season. Special occasions for displaying textiles consisted of visits from important guests and big events and feasts; most important among these were weddings and coronations.[53] As is evident from the inventory described above, a major function of textiles was to almost entirely cover rooms. Textiles thus formed a second 'skin' of the house, they constituted mobile furniture that could be changed and transported.[54] An excellent description of the abundance of textiles in a residence is provided by a description of the choice of textiles made by cardinal Ippolito d'Este for his palazzo in Rome in 1539.[55]

> The cardinals accompanied him home where the door was decorated as it is usual, the interior as follows: the first hall is all over decorated with beautiful tapestries, and there is a table on the long side where twenty people can sit and eat; the antechamber, that is the one of the *parament*, is equally decorated, the antechamber then, is of *parament* in crimson velvet and brocade and since he did not like the part uncovered where the chimney is, he wanted that the one is displayed by putting over the windows and the chimney the same frieze of gold and velvet with golden and silk fringe. And between the chimney and the windows he has put the textiles that are necessary. In this room there is a beautiful bed of crimson velvet, with textile embroideries of gold and silk; the room where he sleeps is arranged with red violet[56] *raso*, with certain lace of gold and silver, which is broad three finger, and his bed with a board covered with crimson velvet with golden fringe which I have had made. In these last two rooms there are eight velvet chairs … ; at the door of the *salotto* and at the door

[53] Brown, 'Introduction', 21–31.

[54] Delmarcel, 'Prefazione', 13.

[55] ASMn b. 1909, cc. 256–7; Nino Sernini informs Ercole Gonzaga on the choice of textiles made by cardinal Ippolito d'Este to serve as a model for the decoration of the *palazzo* of Ercole Gonzaga in Rome, 31 October 1539. Edited in Brown and Lorenzoni, 'Ricordi', 227, n. 8.

[56] *Pavonazzo* probably derives from *pavone* (peacock) and refers to the iridescence and brilliancy of its feathers, usually indicating a red violet colour, see *pavonaceo* and *pavonazzo* in Battaglia, *Dizionario*, vol. 12, 876.

of the room [camora][57] of the *parament* there are scarlet *portiere* embroidered by velvet of the same colour, which have been realized very beautifully, but at the second night one was burnt half, since some people had come to make a certain *moresca*[58], and they did not know how to fix the fire, however this will be adjusted. At the door of the antechamber and of the room there are *portiere* of velvet embroidered in gold, which have been realised in a very beautiful and gracious way, and there is no thing that is more beautiful … .[59]

A visible impression of the way a room adorned in this way could have looked is represented by the *Castello San Giorgio* in Mantua in the famous *Camera depincta*. The room was entirely painted by Andrea Mantegna (*about 1430/31 †1506) (see colour plates 1 and 2), yet only two walls are covered with frescoes, while the others show painted wall coverings and seem to mirror a view of a room decorated partly with tapestries *a figure*, and partly with textiles.[60]

This room, which Ludovico II Gonzaga had painted between 1465 and 1474, is a good example of early use of tapestries at the court of the Gonzaga, and it is precisely the generation of Ludovico (*1412 †1478) and his wife Barbara of

---

57 Here and in the following lines *camora* seems to be used in the sense of *camera*, meaning 'room', see the example of *anticamora*, which certainly means *anticamera*.

58 The *moresca* is a dance with Arab origins that was introduced in Spain by the Moors and diffused in Europe from the fifteenth to the sixteenth centuries, see Battaglia, *Dizionario*, vol. 10, 899.

59 'Li cardinali [vennero a (…) compagnarlo] a casa, dov'era la porta ornata secondo l'usanza, di dentro (…) a questo modo: la sala prima è tutta parata di bellissime tapezzerie, dove per lo lungo è una tavola che vi mangiano accomodatamente venti persone; l'anticamera, cioè quella del paramento, è pure aparata del medesimo modo, l'anticamera poi, di quel paramento di velluto cremesi et broccato [et non] gli essendo piaciuto quella parte dove è il camino scoperta, ha voluto che del medesimo s'appare tirando sopra le fenestre et il camino il medesimo fregio d'oro et di velluto con le sue francie pur d'oro et di seta. Et fra il camino e le fenestre vi sono messi li teli che vi bisognono. In questa stanza vi è un bel letto di velluto cremesi, con racami tessuti d'oro et di seta; la camera dove dorme è parata di raso pavonazzo, con certe trine larghe tre dita, d'oro et d'argento, et il letto del medesimo con una tavoletta coperta di velluto cremesi con le francette d'oro che l'ho fatta fare io. In queste due ultime stanze stanno otto sedie di velluto (…); a la porta dil salotto et a quella di la camora dil paramento stanno portiere di scarlatto racamate di velluto del medesimo colore, le quali sono riuscite molto belle, ma la seconda sera se ne abrusciò mezzo una, che vennero certi a fare certa moresca, né si seppe come si ataccassse [!] il fuoco, pure si remediarà. Alla porta di l'anticamora et de la camora vi sono le portiere di velluto racamate d'oro, che sono riuscite bellissime et vaghe, né v'è cosa più bella'. Quot. according to Brown and Lorenzoni, 'Ricordi', 227, n. 8.

60 For the camera see Rodolfo Signorini, *La più bella camera del mondo. La Camera Dipinta di Andrea Mantegna detta 'degli sposi'* (Mantova: MP, 2002); Rodolfo Signorini, *Opus hoc tenue. La camera dipinta di Andrea Mantegna. Lettura storica iconografica iconologia* (Parma: Artegrafica Silva, 1985); Christina Antenhofer, 'Der Fürst kommuniziert. Die *Camera Picta* des Andrea Mantegna', in *Bildmagie und Brunnensturz. Visuelle Kommunikation von der klassischen Antike bis zur aktuellen medialen Kriegsberichterstattung*, ed. Elisabeth Walde (Innsbruck – Wien – Bozen: Studienverlag, 2009), 217–37; Christina Antenhofer, 'Meeting the Prince between the City and the Family: The Resignification of Castello San Giorgio in Mantua (14th–16th Centuries)', in *The Key to Power? The Culture of Access in Early Modern Courts, 1400–1700*, ed. Sebastiaan Derks and Dries Raeymaekers (Leiden–Boston: Brill, forthcoming). 'Epilogo', in *Gli arazzi dei Gonzaga nel Rinascimento*, ed. Guy Delmarcel (Milano: Skira, 2010), 265–6.

Brandenburg (*1422 †1481) that is regarded as a first high point of the collection of tapestries. However, only one surviving tapestry is now dated to the Gonzaga of the fifteenth century.[61] Beautiful though it may be, the painted room also demonstrates a concern for saving money, since it was much cheaper to have a room painted imitating precious materials such as marbles and textiles, than actually using these materials. On the other hand, if the room had been decorated with tapestries, the walls without frescoes would have probably been left undecorated, again in order not to waste money.[62] This room, which was used to welcome guests and impress them with the rich decoration, also functioned as a bedroom and is frequently referred to as Ludovico's room. Although some doubts remain about the actual use of the room, it is obvious from the suspension devices still visible that a bed was placed in the south-east corner of the room.[63] The double function of bedroom and audience room reinforces the representational function the bed and its expensive coverings might have, and it is a beautiful example of the interplay of private and public functions of a room, since only the most exclusive guests would be allowed to see the room of the prince.[64] Another occasion for displaying the bed was when women were visited after they had given birth.[65] The impression that decorated walls and palaces left on the guests who saw them is expressed in the words of the

61 See Grazzini, 'Annunciazione', 36–45. For more tapestries see the inventory of their daughter Paula, edited in Maria Kollreider, 'Madonna Paola Gonzaga und ihr Brautschatz', in *Lienzer Buch. Beiträge zur Heimatkunde von Lienz und Umgebung*, ed. Raimund von Klebelsberg (Schlern-Schriften 98) (Innsbruck: Wagner, 1952), 137–48.

62 See, for example, Brown and Lorenzoni, 'Ricordi', 243, n. 38: 'Io non credo che si sia fatto questo errore di smaltare di fresco le camere mie ove si sono fatti li fregi, dalli detti fregi in giù, perché oltre che la spesa sarebbe stata buttata via andando tutti quei muri coperti di tapezzarie, sotto le quali non importa che'l muro sia bianco o nero, ne nascerebbe questo inconveniente che tutte quelle stanze per la humidità delle smaltature sarebbono inhabitabile per un gran pezzo'. (I do not think that they made the mistake to plaster my rooms where the friezes have been applied, below the friezes, because the expense would have been wasted since all the rooms will be covered by tapestries, under which it does not import if the walls are white or black; moreover this would produce the inconvenience that because of the humidity resulting from all the plasterings all these rooms would be inhabitable for a long time.)

63 Signorini, *Opus*, 248–52.

64 On this creation of a semi-public space, see Antenhofer, 'Meeting the Prince'.

65 See Susanne Kress, 'Frauenzimmer der Florentiner Renaissance und ihre Ausstattung: Eine erste Spurensuche', in *Das Frauenzimmer. Die Frau bei Hofe in Spätmittelalter und Früher Neuzeit*, eds. Jan Hirschbiegel and Werner Paravicini (Residenzenforschung 11) (Ostfildern: Thorbecke, 2000), 91–113, here 102; Ajmar-Wollheim, Dennis and Miller, *At home*; Norbert Elias, *Die höfische Gesellschaft. Untersuchungen zur Soziologie des Königtums und der höfischen Aristokratie* (Suhrkamp Taschenbuch Wissenschaft 423) (Frankfurt a. M.: Suhrkamp, 1989 [1969]); Johan Huizinga, *Herbst des Mittelalters: Studien über Lebens– und Geistesformen des 14. und 15. Jahrhunderts in Frankreich und in den Niederlanden*. 12th ed. Ed. Kurt Köster (Kröners Taschenausgabe 204) (Stuttgart: Kröner, 2006 [1941]), 69-70. For the political role of the royal bed, see the 'lit de justice', 'lit funèbre' in: Ernst H. Kantorowicz, *The King's Two Bodies. A Study in Mediaeval Political Theology* (Princeton: Princeton University Press, 1997 [1957]), 414–5.

Venetian ambassador Giovanni da Mulla, at the end of the sixteenth century, who described the Gonzaga palace worthy to be the palace of a king, 'richly decorated with *paramenti* of walls in great number, of finest *arazzi* as well as of silk and gold'.[66]

Special Occasions for Displaying Textiles: Visits of Kings, Coronations, Weddings

The most precious tapestries and wall hangings were reserved for special occasions. They were used to decorate the palace but also other parts of the cities on the occasion of feasts, important visits, religious processions and above all for weddings. Brown and Lorenzoni edited several documents from the *Archivio di Stato di Mantova (ASMn)* that prove this use of the Gonzaga tapestry collections.[67] In the *libri contabili* (account books) we read several entries from the 1540s that demonstrate how cardinal Ercole lent some of his tapestries to the Dome of Mantua, so the church might be decorated for the Feast of *Corpus Domini*. The account reads, 'To the tapestries of the most illustrious Lord to ornate the church on the day of the Feast of Corpus Christi'.[68]

In 1574 Guglielmo Gonzaga received some suggestions from Teodoro di San Giorgio on what tapestries to choose to decorate the rooms for the expected visit of Henry III of France. He suggested besides large numbers of 'paramenti di tessuto e corame' (paraments of textile and leather) two series of *arazzi* with figurative subjects, namely the *Puttini* commissioned by cardinal Ercole to be placed in the *Camerone de' Capitani* and specifies another series of 'tapezzaria di Fiandra' that belonged to Cesare Gonzaga and had been chosen for the *Sala Grande*.[69]

Although according to Brown the collections of tapestries of Federico II consisted in great part only of *paramenti* made of textiles and not of *arazzi figurative*, the richness of the collection was recognised in the famous quote that, on the occasion of the visit of Emperor Charles V in 1530, Federico was able to decorate the whole 'Castello da cima in fondo' (from top to bottom) with *arazzi*. Among his treasures was a *paramento d'arazzo* made of gold, silver and silk estimated to be worth more than eighteen thousand ducats.[70] On the occasion of the coronation of Vincenzo Gonzaga on 22 September 1587, the gothic façade of the cathedral of Mantua was decorated with the famous series of *arazzi* showing the *Atti degli Apostoli*.[71] However, most of the sources

66 'riccamente addobbato di paramenti di muro in gran numero, così di finissima razzeria, come di seda ed oro'; quoted in Ferrari, introduction,19–20. She quotes Bertelli.

67 Brown and Lorenzoni, 'Ricordi', 223–63.

68 Brown and Lorenzoni, 'Ricordi', 230, n. 11. 'Alli tappezarie del signore Illustrissimo per fare apparare la Giesa il dì dil Corpo di Cristo'. According to Brown, Ercole did so every year for the Feast of *Corpus Domini*. Brown, 'Introduction', 30.

69 Brown and Lorenzoni, 'Ricordi', 251, n. 56.

70 Brown, 'Introduction', 25.

71 Brown and Lorenzoni, 'Ricordi', 253, n. 62.

refer to *arazzi* being displayed or lent for the occasions of weddings.[72] The description of the wall covers (*paramenti*) being exposed in the *Palazzo Vescovile* on the occasion of the wedding of Francesco III and Caterina d'Austria in October 1549 not only gives an impression of the rich decoration of the palace especially arranged for the wedding, but it also shows the interest that guests showed in these decorations. Their interest is demonstrated by the literary source written to commemorate the wedding:

> They all withdrew into some rooms decorated with finest and most beautiful textiles of gold and silver and of silk of different colours, fabricated masterfully, in which you could discern many different and realistic animals, trees, fruits and flowers, like the *great Parasio* and the *ingenious Fidias*, the first in fabric, the other in marble, only hardly they could have been realised more likely to the mastery of nature.[73]

On the occasion of Vincenzo Gonzaga's first marriage with Margherita Farnese in 1581, paraments of the collection by Ercole Gonzaga were chosen to decorate the rooms. Two letters by Federico Donato provide further insights in the way the tapestries were chosen according to the different rooms.[74]

> In the room of the coat of arms I have had put the old *Tobbia*[75] which are however beautiful and appropriate for this room. The other rooms have tapestries with figures and woods, which have been taken out, and the most gracious ones have been put in the third room where meals will be taken. Then I have had prepared five more rooms in the apartment which has been of the ladies of our most serene Lady, and the last room I have had ornated with the tapestry of the *Fortuna*.[76]

It is interesting to note, that the same *arazzi* were used three years later when Vincenzo celebrated his second wedding with Eleonora de' Medici,

---

72 See also Brown, 'Introduction', 28.

73 'Si ritirorno [!] tutti insieme in alcune camere tappezzate di finissimi et bellissimi drappi d'oro, d'argento et di seta di piú colori, maestrevolmente contesti, ne i quali tanti diversi animali, alberi, frutti et fiori al vero conformi dentro vi si scorgeano, che'l gran Parasio et l'ingegnoso Fidia, l'uno in tela et l'altro in marmo a gran pena gli havrebbe potuti piú alla maestra natura verisimili dimostrare'. *L'Entrata della Serenissima et Illustrissima Signora Caterina d'Austria Sposa del Eccellentissimo Duca di Mantova (…) nella detta sua Città con l'ordine di Tornei, Giostre, Banchetti, Comedie, Musiche, et altri sontuosi apparecchi fatti per la venuta sua,* Mantova, ottobre 1549, Mantova, novembre 1549, 5v–6; quot. in Brown and Lorenzoni, 'Ricordi', 238–9, n. 29.

74 Brown and Lorenzoni, 'Ricordi', 252, n. 59.

75 This refers to the *arazzi* showing the 'Storie di Tobia' [histories of Tobia], Brown and Lorenzoni, 'Ricordi', 252, n. 59.

76 'Nella camera delle armi ho fatto mettere li Tobbia vecchi, che sono però belli et proprii a detta camera. Le altre stantie hano tapezarie a figure et boscaie, tolti fuori et li più vaghi si son messi nella terza camera ove si mangierà. Poi ho fatto preparar 5 altre camere nell'appartamento che era delle done di Madama Serenissima, et la camera ultima ho fornita della tapezzaria de Fortuna'. (9 October 1580; Brown and Lorenzoni interpret the displaying of these arazzi to honour the bride, although she arrived only in March 1581 in Mantua). Quot. according to Brown and Lorenzoni, 'Ricordi', 252, n. 59.

after having divorced his first wife with the accusation that she was physically inapt for the marriage act.[77]

The Bridal Trousseau

However, it was not only because of the precious wall decorations that weddings were the number one occasion for displaying textiles. According to Claude Lévi-Strauss[78] weddings were one of the biggest occasions of gift exchange, where a wide range of objects circulated around the bride and groom, the most visible form taken by the bridal trousseau. The 1478 inventory of the bride's treasure of Ludovico II's daughter Paula Gonzaga is a representative example.[79] Since it was modelled upon her sister Barbara's bride's trousseau and it was used to arrange that of her niece Chiara – all of these marriages taking place between 1474 and 1481 – the inventory can be looked at as a model of a bride's treasure in the Gonzaga family of this generation. In the case of Paula Gonzaga we have ample evidence of the way her bridal treasure was put together and who was involved through the correspondence in the Gonzaga family (see Figure 2.1). In fact, it was her mother Barbara of Brandenburg who asked her daughter-in-law Margareta of Bayern-München, the marchioness in charge, to bring her the little book with the *cose* that had been put together for her daughter Barbara on her marriage so she could compare them with those she had prepared for Paula. She argued, that this was necessary since the bride's treasure would be displayed openly in the *Castello San Giorgio*. Thus, we can conclude that an audience might seek to compare whether both daughters were treated in the same way.

> Moreover we would like you to send us our little book of the things that had been given to Barbara our daughter because now we have to compare the things we have for Paula with those. Therefore by God see that you can send it to us ... : As soon as the messenger whom we are waiting for will have arrived if the count [of Görz] has accepted the arrangement we will go to San Giorgio and the *castello* in order to pack and display the things of Paula and then we would like you to send one or more of your people to see them.[80]

[77] Brown and Lorenzoni, 'Ricordi', 252, n. 60. On the divorce of Margherita see Giuseppe Coniglio, *I Gonzaga* (Grandi famiglie 13) (Varese: Dall'Oglio, 1967), 346–7; Christina Antenhofer, 'Familien-Körper. Die Organisation der Körper in adeligen Familien', in *Körper er-fassen. Körpererfahrungen, Körpervorstellungen, Körperkonzepte*, eds. Kordula Schnegg and Elisabeth Grabner-Niel (Innsbruck–Wien–Bozen: Studienverlag, 2010), 113–133.

[78] Claude Lévi-Strauss, *Les structures élémentaires de la parenté* (Paris: Presses Universitaires de France, 1949).

[79] I have analysed this bride's treasure extensively in my PhD thesis: Antenhofer, *Briefe*, 159–172.

[80] 'Preterea haressemo caro ce mandasti quel nostro libretto de le cose se desero ala Barbara nostra fiola perchè adesso ce accadaria scontrare le cose habiamo per la Paula cum quelle. Sichè per Dio vedetu de mandarcelo [...] Como sia venuto el messo qual aspectamo sel signor conte harà acceptato il partito nui se transferiremo in continenti a San Zorzo et in castello per incassare et far la monstra dele robbe de la predicta Paula et alhora havemo caro

Unlike the rather general Gonzaga inventory examined at the beginning of this chapter, Paula's inventory details her clothes and considerable space is dedicated to the meticulous description of the precious dresses.

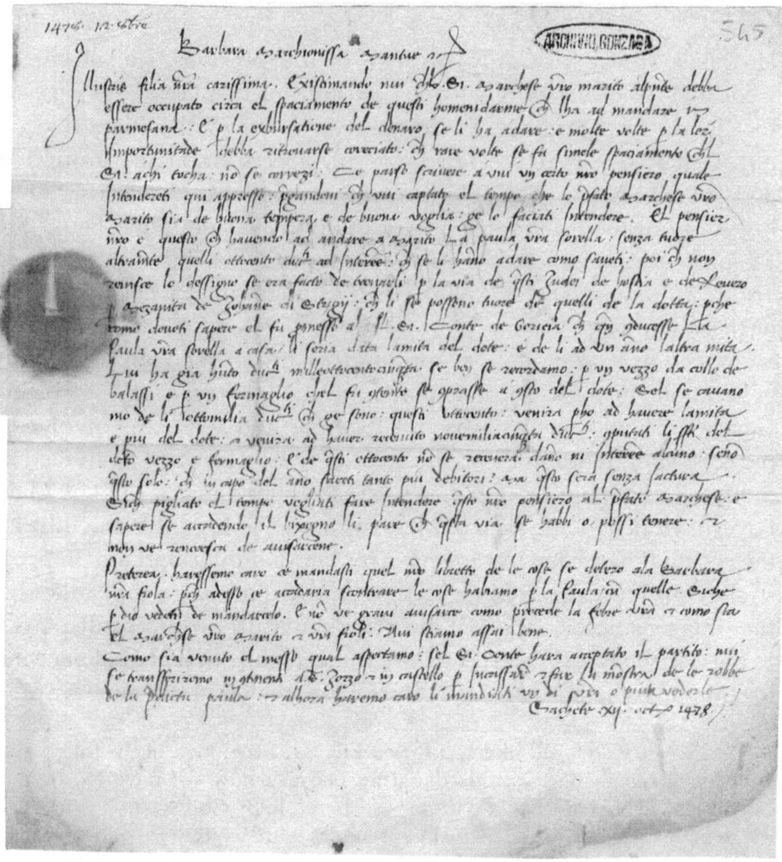

Figure 2.1: Barbara of Brandenburg, *Letter to Margareta of Bayern-München*, 1478, Archivio di Stato di Mantova, AG b. 2103bis c. 545. Used with permission of the Archivio di Stato di Mantova and the Ministero dei Beni e delle Attività Culturali e del Turismo.

Moreover a long golden white dress with open sleeves, lined with silver brown cloth and the bodice[81] of the dress is with *Schilher*.[82] Moreover a golden green dress with open sleeves, lined with golden red cloth and the bodice is with

li mandiati un di vostri o più a vederle'. ASMn AG b. 2103bis c. 545; 12 October 1478, Barbara of Brandenburg writes to Margareta of Bayern-München. Edited in Antenhofer, *Briefe*, 162.

[81] The German *bust* means according to Kollreider the fringe of the dress (Kollreider, 'Paola', 141, note 21) yet it could also indicate the bodice of the dress, since German *Büste* still indicates a bust.

[82] In German: *Schillertaft*, a kind of (iridescent) taffeta.

> brown sendal. Moreover a golden red dress with tight sleeves, embroidered with pearls on the trimming and on the sleeves, lined with green sendal … . Moreover a dress with liver coloured sateen with tight sleeves. It is embroidered with pearls and rubies. There are 450 pearls and twelve rubies. It is lined with ermine fur.[83]

The precious dresses (*Lang Röckh*) were mentioned first. They were made of fabrics such as velvet, sateen and damask and decorated with pearls, rubies, furs, gold and silver. The coats (*Mantll*) are made of sateen and damask and we also read of one white silk coat with golden fringe. Most of them include furs as decoration and to keep warm during winter. It is even possible to identify the yellow dress with pearls on the devotional portrait of Paula showing her in the court chapel of *Schloß Bruck* in Lienz. The description goes on to include *Uber Rockh* (upper dresses) and the *Unndter Rockh* (under dresses), similarly precious garments. The sleeves are mentioned in a separate section followed by shawls, stomachers and, finally, girdles. The following section goes on to list precious textiles in the section of 'bed decoration' (*Pett Zier*). Here we read about a bed curtain made of golden fabric with a baldachin, three curtains of taffeta (*Zendl*) and golden borders, another curtain of green feathers (*plůmen*)[84] with its baldachin, four more white curtains made of linen, a tent made of linen with a golden green 'coat' to be put on top of the tent. Also included are two large tapestries, a good fine tapestry of mediocre quality, four foreign tapestries (*de strana*), a curtain for the door with figures, four bench covers with figures, two more bench covers with flowers, two large wall tapestries with green flowers, a bench cover with flowers and coat of arms, a bench cover with flowers and animals, two wall tapestries with figures, several cushions, covers and cushions for the carriages and harnesses for the horses. The section on textiles closes with underwear and textiles for the home.[85]

In the section concerning linens, we are even given indications on the provenance of the textiles. A distinction is made between linen from the Rhine and linen from St Gallen. Other regional and geographic indications refer to the way fabrics are cut, such as chemises made in the Moorish way (*moreschisch*) or in the Spanish way (*valencianisch*). Veils are referred to as being made in the Slav (*Schlauisch*) or Calabrese (*Calabresisch*) way. Some more linen cloth is given as a kind of stock for Paula's future needs, and she

83 'Item ein langen gulden weissen rock mit offnen erblen / undterfǔtert mit silbren praẘn tuech und der / bǔst vom rockh mit schilher. / Item ein gulden grǔen rockh mit offn erbln, underzogen mit / gulden roten tǔech und der bǔst mit prawn zendl. / Item ein gulden rotten rock mit engen erblen, gesprengt / mit perlein auf dem prăm und auf den erblen, / unndtertzogen mit grǔnem zendel […] / Item ein rock von lebervarbm atlas mit engen erbln. Ist der / gehefft von perl und rubin. Sein der perlein 450, / der rubin zwǒlff. Ist undterzogen mit vechwammen.' TLA Inventare A 202.8 fol. 2v; Kollreider, 'Paola', 141.

84 *Plûm/phlûm* designates down feathers, see *Mittelhochdeutsches Wörterbuch* von Benecke, Müller, Zarncke, PLÛME *bis* PÔGRÂT (Bd. 2, Sp. 523b *bis* 524a), online: http://woerterbuchnetz.de/ (accessed 27 February 2014).

85 For the whole inventory, see Kollreider, 'Paola', 140–48.

is accompanied by a tailor who supposedly would make clothes for her. As mentioned earlier, Paula would continue to purchase textiles from Italy in her future years while living in the county of Görz (now Eastern Tyrol).

The Semantics of Textiles: Political Communication and Social Interaction via Textiles and Clothes

Clothes as Marker of Social Status

To explore further the questions expressed in the introductory paragraph, this chapter will investigate some of the central meanings conveyed by cloths and clothes and focus on textiles as means for social interaction and political action or communication.[86] As stated in the previous section, textiles fulfilled a basic function of representation, which became most obvious when they were displayed on walls and in rooms. However, textiles were also permanently exhibited on people's bodies and it was in these spheres that they acquired a multitude of meanings. As Evelyn Welch stresses in her essay *Women in Debt*, 'issues of credit were very visible on the female body'.[87] Women's dresses and the jewels they wore expressed not only their social status but their personal financial situation. Welch details the situation of Girolamo Riario's wife, whose jewels had been pawned, which restricted her capacity to move freely since she did not want to be seen in public without her jewels.[88] A similar situation is found with Emperor Maximilian's second wife, Bianca Maria Sforza. Because of his constant lack of money, Maximilian had quickly spent Bianca Maria's enormous dowry and was not able to provide her with the luxurious garments necessary for an empress. In 1505 the emperor even wanted to avoid his wife meeting the French ambassadors since she was not well equipped (*nit wol gestaffirt*).[89] In the same year, the head of her court, Nikolaus Firmian, complained in a long letter that the female court had not received winter clothes in three years and that they were freezing in the cold. Debts had also been taken on in order to pay for clothes. Maximilian prevented his wife from meeting French ambassadors, because of her miserable attire.[90]

86 Following the central theories of speech acts (Austin and Searle) communication is of course also action and actions are forms of communication; in this sense, I use both terms in a closely interrelated way.

87 Welch, 'Women', 53.

88 Quoted in Welch, 'Women', 52–3. Welch quotes Pasolini.

89 Matthäus Lang to the head of court, Serntein, 9th January 1505: 'nachdem sy nit wol gestaffirt ist'; Haus-, Hof- und Staatsarchiv Vienna (HHStA) Maximiliana (Max) 14/9a fol. 14a r; added into this section with corrected date; olim HHStA Max 14/8a/1 fol. 24r; Sabine Weiss, *Die vergessene Kaiserin: Bianca Maria Sforza – Kaiser Maximilians zweite Gemahlin* (Innsbruck-Wien: Tyrolia-Verl., 2010), 122, 291 note 381; Heidemarie Hochrinner, 'Bianca Maria Sforza: Versuch einer Biographie' (PhD diss.: University of Graz, 1966), 83, 85.

90 Hochrinner, 'Bianca Maria', 85.

As a result, Bianca Maria and her ladies were not able to fulfil their official duties and meet guests since they had no proper garments.

The special interest taken in female attire during important feasts is neatly illustrated in a letter by Juan Cristobal Cavete de Estrella where he describes a banquet organised by Ferrante Gonzaga in honour of Philip II's visit to Milan in 1549. In his description he talks about the rich decorations with tapestries (*adereçada de riquísima tapicería*) before going on to describe the ladies present at the banquet.[91] The fact that cloths and jewels literally became part of the female body is beautifully illustrated by the so-called 'dowry portraits' which show the brides wearing all their accessories, clothes, ornaments for the hair as well as jewels. One example can be seen in the 1493 dowry portrait of Bianca Maria Sforza by Giovanni Ambrogio de'Predis.[92] However, the special interest taken in women's clothes and the fact that there are documents reflecting how their financial status was partly expressed by the way they dressed, may be a secondary impression for an audience, given the fact that women depended financially on men. Therefore, money-saving measures affected women before they affected men. These examples do not mean that dresses were particularly important only for women. For example, while Maximilian did not dress his wife properly, he of course continued to represent his status as emperor by being dressed in the proper way. Dresses were therefore equally important for women and men to express their status and be seen in public.[93] The importance clothes played for both men and women as a form of extension of their individual body is further underlined by Valentin Groebner. In his work on forms of identification in pre-modern Europe he noted the way in which garments generally formed parts of people's identity and physical appearance; remarkable garments became a *pars pro toto* for the individual wearing it, and people were often named according to their conspicuous clothes.[94]

The interest in the way men were dressed is evident in a letter concerning the marriage of Paula Gonzaga (*1464 †1496) and count Leonhard of Görz (*1444 †1500) (see colour plates 3 and 4). The couple had experienced serious problems in the first year of marriage, culminating in a miscarriage in August 1479, after which Paula returned to Mantua, officially for some days, a visit which finally extended to a period of more than four months. People thought that Paula would not go back to her husband. When she finally did, great interest was placed on the first meeting of the couple, which was described in a letter that Paula's mother, Barbara of Brandenburg, wrote to her son

91 Quot. in Brown and Lorenzoni, 'Ricordi', 236; n. 24.

92 The National Gallery of Art, Washington, DC, Widener Collection 1942.9.53.

93 On the political importance of dresses in medieval society, see Jan Keupp, *Die Wahl des Gewandes. Mode, Macht und Möglichkeitssinn in Gesellschaft und Politik des Mittelalters* (Mittelalter Forschungen 33) (Ostfildern: Thorbecke, 2010).

94 Valentin Groebner, *Who Are You? Identification, Deception, and Surveillance in Early Modern Europe* (New York: Zone Books, 2007).

Federico Gonzaga, summarising the oral report of one of the *familiari* who had accompanied Paula to her husband.

> [W]hen she came near to Lienz she met with the lord count who came to receive her in a very honourable way. He was entirely dressed in white with embroidery in gold and pearls on his cloths and breeches. Many of his people were dressed in a similar way among them eight young men on eight beautiful coursers with beautifully embroidered blankets three of which were embroidered with pearls and here he received her in an affectionate way and with great celebration.[95]

In this report, it is the count's clothes that command the focus of attention, as well as those of his entourage, who multiplied the visual impression of the count by being dressed in a similar manner. Leonhard was completely dressed in white with golden embroideries and pearls on the dress and on the 'breeches' (*calze*). The horses with their beautiful covers embroidered with pearls made another visible statement for the fact that the count paid the greatest honour to his wife and was celebrating her return to their common home. Clothes were moreover a visible marker of people's affiliation, meant in a broader sense, since the term 'cultural marker' may be too wide. In fact, clothes and ways of dressing were not only dominated by big cultural players such as the Burgundian court, they marked individuals and their social pertinence and spheres on a variety of levels. They displayed people's affinities to houses, families, cities, towns and to cultural backgrounds.[96] One of the occasions that clearly demonstrates the social marking rendered by clothes is again the occasion of the wedding. Christiane Klapisch-Zuber has drawn our attention to the importance of the 'undressing' of the bride, who had to take off the clothes owned by her father to put on those owned by her husband and thus visibly demonstrate her passage into the new house of her husband's family.[97] In the case of Paula Gonzaga, the sources document a conflict that took place when Paula, dressed in black for the recent death of her father, was reluctant to take off her clothes and dress in the new wedding clothes on meeting her husband's welcoming committee. However, such behaviour was not tolerated. The source informs us that people from the committee tore down the veil from her head.[98]

[95] '... quando se approximò a Leonza se incontrò in lo signor conte che venne a receverla molto honorevole tuto vestito de biancho cum recamo de oro e perle al vestito e calce cum molti de suoi a simile livrea tra li altri octo regazi su octo bellissimi corsieri cum coperte belle e rechamate tre de lequale erano rechamate de perle e qui la recolse amorevolmente e cum feste assai'. ASMn AG b. 2104b c. 394; 22 July 1480; edited in Antenhofer, *Briefe*, 111.

[96] See on this issue Keupp, *Wahl des Gewandes*.

[97] Christiane Klapisch-Zuber, *La maison et le nom. Stratégies et rituels dans l'Italie de la Renaissance* (Paris: Editions de l'Ecole des hautes études en sciences sociales, 1990).

[98] ASMn AG b. 544 c. 71; Antenhofer, *Briefe*, 82–3; Christina Antenhofer, 'Il potere delle gentildonne. L'esempio di Barbara di Brandenburgo e Paula Gonzaga', in *Donne di potere nel*

Yet, it would be short-sighted to only record the authority exercised by men over women on the question of what to wear. When the Gonzaga and the count of Görz were planning where to celebrate the wedding, the mother of the bride, Barbara of Brandenburg, had given clear instructions to Leonhard of Görz on what to wear if he wanted to celebrate the wedding in Mantua. Again, the biggest instance was the death of Ludovico II, Paula's father, on 12 June 1478. Two days later, Barbara instructed Leonhard, who planned to come to Mantua to take Paula with him, that only his entourage should arrive dressed festively and adorned with jewels and other decoration. She noted that Leonhard and his 'page' should wear black with no ornaments or sword. However, after having been received wearing mourning clothes, they could take off the black clothes, dress cheerfully and celebrate the wedding.[99]

Moreover, weddings were occasions where different ways of dressing met and sometimes even clashed, in the sense that 'other ways of dressing' evoked laughter and comments. There are many examples of these kinds of jokes about dressing, and also of the pleasure people took from dressing in different ways. A famous comment is the one made by the Mantuan chronicler Andrea Schivenoglia on the German clothes of Margareta of Bayern-München, Federico Gonzaga's wife, and her German cortege: he noted that on her arrival in Mantua 'they all were dressed in red which means in rough clothes of ugly colours'.[100] Whereas the Mantuan chronicler mocked the German clothes of the bride and her entourage as being 'gross and of an ugly colour', her mother-in-law was very pleased by the appearance of the young bride.[101] More than 100 years later, when Vincenzo Gonzaga visited his sister Anna Caterina Gonzaga in her new home in Innsbruck, her German way of dressing made him laugh.[102] Bianca Maria Sforza and her ladies amused themselves in the female apartments by 'cross-dressing' in the German or Italian way and dancing 'cross-cultural' dances.[103]

The attractiveness of clothes – whether it be attached to the cultural prestige of the respective court or with pre-modern ideas of fashion – led to remarkable forms of imitation. Imitation is documented for the Gonzaga court by a unique means of transmission of dressing styles, through the use of the fashion doll. In two letters dating from 1515 and 1524 such dolls are

---

Rinascimento, ed. Letizia Arcangeli and Susanna Peyronel (I libri di viella 85) (Roma: Viella, 2008), 67–87.

99 TLA Sigm. 4a.029.072; Antenhofer, *Briefe*, 73–4.

100 'vene tute vestite de rosso zoe de panij grossi et de bruto cholore'. Andrea Schivenoglia, *Cronaca di Mantova dal MCCCCXLV al MCCCCLXXXIV. Trascritta ed annotata da Carlo D'Arco. Dal secondo volume della raccolta di cronisti e documenti storici lombardi inediti pubblicata da Giuseppe Müller* (Milano: Colombo, 1857), 37.

101 Severidt, *Familie*, 205.

102 Vgl. Elena Taddei, 'Anna Caterina Gonzaga und ihre Zeit. Der italienische Einfluss am Innsbrucker Hof', in *Der Innsbrucker Hof. Residenz und höfische Gesellschaft in Tirol vom 15. bis 19. Jahrhundert,* eds. Heinz Noflatscher and Jan Paul Niederkorn (Archiv für österreichische Geschichte 138) (Wien: Verlag der ÖAW, 2005), 213–40, here 236.

103 Hochrinner, 'Bianca Maria', 43.

requested to display Isabella d'Este's way of dressing.[104] The first is to serve as model for some dresses for court ladies in France, whereas the second letter requests a doll displaying the way of dressing in Mantua for some court ladies in Spain.[105] Above all, these fashion dolls document the interest shown in other ways of dressing at different courts and they can be regarded as a source for the use of cloths as cultural markers. With this example we begin to reach the realm of 'fashion' in a modern sense, since some princesses, such as Isabella d'Este, even gained a special reputation for fabricating and creating their own styles of clothes.[106]

Social Interaction via Textiles

Returning to Cohen and Cohen's observation, objects create social interactions above all by their circulation.[107] Whereas the previous section has focused on the immobile display of clothes, this section will examine textiles in motion, giving several representative examples. The interaction created by the buying and commissioning of textiles has been discussed in the previous sections of this chapter; yet three more social forms of interaction have to be taken into consideration: collecting and competing; loaning; and gift giving.

Whereas the display of textiles can be looked at as form of representation, by taking into consideration the final result of the display, namely the decorated walls and impressive rooms, the purchasing of luxurious textiles and above all collecting them amounted to a social action, a basic form of competition that was possible only at the highest level. In this sense, the Gonzaga's collection of tapestries in the sixteenth century were an explicit form of competition with other leading European courts all purchasing at the same Flemish stores. As Brown demonstrates in his introduction, the Flemish tapestry weavers could even reject their prestigious clients by making reference to other wealthy clients. This was the case when cardinal Ercole Gonzaga asked for a sample of a tapestry series: the Flemish tapestry weaver rejected his request, referring to a Spanish merchant who had already shown interest, because sending a sample to Ercole would have delayed the transaction.[108] Contemporary visitors compared the tapestries they were shown and thus prove the point that this was not an individual pleasure of an art lover, but a form of social competition on a high level.[109] In 1519, Marcantonio Michiel compared the

---

104 The first letter is explicitly analysed and integrated in a survey on the special issue of fashion dolls in Yassana C. Croizat, '"Living Dolls". François Ier Dresses His Women', *Renaissance Quarterly*, 60/1 (2007): 94–130.

105 Ferrari, 'Introduction', 20.

106 Ferrari, 'Introduction', 20–21.

107 Cohen and Cohen, 'Postscript'.

108 Brown, 'Introduction', 30.

109 The analogy to the anthropological ways of competition described, for example, by Maurice Godelier are more than obvious. Maurice Godelier, *L'énigme du don* (Paris: Fayard, 1996).

value of the *arrazzi* of the margrave of Mantua designed by Mantegna with the *arrazzi* of Alfonso (d'Este) and Federico, king of Naples, and with those of the *Capella Sistina,* which had been woven on the design of Raffaello.[110] Delmarcel compares the passion of the three Gonzaga brothers – Federico II, Ferrante and cardinal Ercole – for tapestries with those of the Habsburgs of the Netherlands and Spain (Charles Vth, Maria of Hungary and Philip II) and that of their trusted advisor, cardinal Granvelle.[111] Ahrendt speaks of ' [s]trong rivalries among European rulers [that] led them to gather the best and most beautiful tapestries'.[112] She mentions more than 2,000 tapestries of Henry VIII of England and the rivalries with tapestry collections such as that of the duke of Burgundy.

Tapestries appear often as loans; lending tapestries for special occasions established vital bonds among princely families and the respective family members. Of particular interest is a letter in which Ercole Gonzaga responds to a loan request from cardinal Ippolito II d'Este for tapestries, which he needed to honour some strangers (*forastiere*) coming for a visit. Ippolito explicitly asked for 'big tapestries and covers without coat of arms for decorating the halls and the big rooms'.[113] Here it is obvious that he wanted tapestries that did not display the Gonzaga coat of arms so he could use them for his own purpose. From Ahrendt's analysis of the Gonzaga inventories the impression arises that men were more engaged in collecting tapestries than women – men competed with tapestries, while women cared for other forms of textiles. This observation is sustained by the fact that Margherita Paleologa's collection of tapestries was small compared with those of her husband Federico and her co-regents, cardinal Ercole and Ferrante. Moreover, the tapestries were subsequently inherited by the Gonzaga dukes. Margherita was well aware of the prestige of tapestry collections, and she was responsible for them as well as for most of the Gonzaga textiles, yet her own interest was directed towards other objects.[114] However, looking carefully at the examples given by Brown and Lorenzoni, this impression may be true only for the generation of these three Gonzaga brothers, while in later documents we also notice women possessing and inheriting tapestries, even if they might not have developed a particular interest for collecting tapestries.[115]

However, Ahrendt's observation can be important in helping to introduce the category of 'gendered' clothes. Whereas to some extent tapestries could

---

110 Brown, 'Introduction', 24.

111 Guy Delmarcel, 'Introduzione', in *Gli arazzi dei Gonzaga nel Rinascimento,* ed. Guy Delmarcel (Milano: Skira, 2010), 34–5, here 34.

112 Ahrendt, 'Legacy', 146.

113 'razzerie et coltrinaggi alti et senza arme per apparare salle et stantie grandi'. Brown and Lorenzoni, 'Ricordi', 234, n. 16.

114 Ahrendt, 'Legacy', 145–6.

115 Brown and Lorenzoni, 'Ricordi'.

be looked at as a rather 'male' textile, another sort of textile highly marked from a gender perspective is linen, a traditional 'female' textile. While studying Margherita Paleologa, Federico II's wife, Ahrendt detected that Margherita was particularly responsible for the distribution of the linens at court, noting that,

> The documents show that Margherita was steward of a large proportion of linens for herself and for the court. Such custodianship permitted her oversight of court life, since overnight guests required linens for their rooms, dinner guests used table linens, and court textiles decorating reception areas honored important visitors. Besides knowing who was in court, Margherita also projected an image of the Gonzaga family by having her servants choose appropriately refined and decorated examples from the court's collections for any visitor.[116]

While tapestries were a very public and striking form of visual communication, the communication taking place by choice of bed linens for an important guest was a more intimate though not less impressive one, taking place on a more subtle level.

Gifting linens was typical for women. Such gifts were closely connected to the religious field and women could establish networks donating textile gifts to important representatives of the church. One of the most impressive examples is given by Sarah Bercusson in her study of three Habsburg women married to Italian courts. She mentions a box of linens that Giovanna of Austria, married to Francesco I de Medici, gifted to the Pope in 1570. The Pope stressed in his thanks to the Medici ambassador in Rome that these linens and in particular the rochets would supply him for life and that he would honour this gift and place it in his secret writing room where he kept some of the things most dear to him.[117] Female textile gifts abound in correspondence.[118] While they may not earn the adjective 'luxurious' from their monetary value compared with the tapestries, they gain a highly symbolic meaning by the fact that most often these gifts were handmade by women and thus they display the personal effort and intimacy women put into the gifts. This is also expressed explicitly in letters, such as for example in one, with which Antonia del Balzo, wife of Gianfrancesco Gonzaga, sent a hand-fabricated bonnet to her brother-in-law, count Leonhard of Görz, excusing herself at the same time for having taken such a long time to make it, due to an illness. However, she did not want anyone else to finish the bonnet.[119]

---

116 Ahrendt, 'Legacy', 145.

117 Bercusson, 'Gift Giving', 153.

118 See Antenhofer, *Briefe*; Bercusson, 'Gift-Giving'.

119 TLA Sigm. 4a.029.019; 7 October 1493; Antenhofer, *Briefe*, 251.

Conclusion

After this *tour de force* through several generations of Gonzaga princes and their use of textiles, one last question remains to be addressed from the opening paragraph, leading us back to Ercole's letter. Who was the public for this multiple display of textiles and what was their part? From the sources quoted above it becomes obvious that textiles and cloths were displayed on a variety of levels and thus constructed circles of networks starting from the intimacy of homemade textiles and bed linens for exclusive visitors to the publicly displayed tapestries on the façade of the Mantuan cathedral, in the heart of the town. Everybody was involved in textile display, yet on different scales and for different occasions. It was a privilege to be invited to the semi-public rooms of the prince, such as the *Camera degli sposi*, to be allowed to admire the beautiful frescoes there or the rich textiles displayed on beds. Textiles and objects could be immobile, with people being invited to come and visit rooms and decorations; or they might circulate, when being lent to others or gifted, travelling around the country on the bride's journey, or even being displayed via the special medium of the fashion doll that transported Mantuan ways of fashion and dressing to distant courts. The attention contemporaries devoted to these textiles becomes obvious in the comments they made – be it ambassadors who expressed their admiration or chroniclers describing and mocking the behaviour and looks of their princes in Mantua. What becomes evident is that displaying cloths or collecting luxurious textiles was never only because of personal interest in art and luxury as expression of an individual taste of aesthetics, choice of lifestyle or even sense of the arts. Displaying luxury textiles or producing them oneself was part of a huge process of performance that bound together princes, princesses, artists, the major political players of their times, their mighty neighbours, friends and kin as well as the ordinary people on the streets, who were never only apt to admire but also to criticise and mock.[120]

---

[120] In this sense I refer to the analysis of the ancient historian Egon Flaig, who in his book on how to challenge the Emperor outlines the mutual interdependence between the Roman emperor and the different social groups of the *Imperium Romanum*, such as the aristocracy, the Roman *plebs* and the *milites*. The mutual interdependence becomes above all evident in what Flaig calls 'symbolically regulated gestures', visible in donations and interactions on the occasions of the *ludi*, the big public games. This interaction builds up an affective relationship between the Emperor and the different social groups. Egon Flaig, *Den Kaiser herausfordern. Die Usurpation im Römischen Reich* (Historische Studien 7) (Frankfurt/New York: Campus, 1992).

Bibliography

Manuscript Sources

Archivio di Stato di Mantova (ASMn)
registro (r.) 6514 carte (cc.) 16–17
ASMn Archivio Gonzaga (AG)
AG busta (b.) 219 c. 4, c. 5
AG b. 544 c. 71
AG b. 1909 cc. 256–7
AG b. 2103bis c. 545
AG b. 2104b c. 394
Haus-, Hof- und Staatsarchiv Vienna (HHStA)
Maximiliana (Max) 14/9a
Tiroler Landesarchiv Innsbruck (TLA)
Inventare A 202.8
Sigmundiana (Sigm.) 16.31
Sigm. 4a.029.014
Sigm. 4a.029.019
Sigm. 4a.029.072

Published Primary Sources

Antenhofer, Christina, Axel Behne, Daniela Ferrari, Jürgen Herold, and Peter Rückert, eds. *Barbara Gonzaga: Die Briefe/Le Lettere (1455–1508). Edition und Kommentar deutsch/italienisch*. Stuttgart: Kohlhammer, 2013.

Brown, Clifford M., and Anna M. Lorenzoni. 'Ricordi dell'archivio'. In *Gli arazzi dei Gonzaga nel Rinascimento*, edited by Guy Delmarcel, 223–63. Milano: Skira, 2010.

Ferrari, Daniela, ed. *Le collezioni Gonzaga: L'inventario dei beni del 1540–1542*. Fonti, repertori e studi per la storia di Mantova. Collana del centro internazionale d'arte e di cultura di Palazzo Te 1. Milano: Silvana Editoriale Spa, 2003.

Kollreider, Maria. 'Madonna Paola Gonzaga und ihr Brautschatz'. In *Lienzer Buch: Beiträge zur Heimatkunde von Lienz und Umgebung*. 137–48. Schlern-Schriften 98. Innsbruck: Wagner, 1952.

Leverotti, Franca, ed. *Carteggio degli oratori mantovani alla corte sforzesca (1450–1500). Vols. I–XVI*. Pubblicazioni degli archivi di stato. Roma: Ministero per i beni e le attività culturali, 1999ff.

Morselli, Raffaella. *Le collezioni Gonzaga: L'elenco dei beni del 1626–1627*. Fonti, repertori e studi per la storia di Mantova. Collana del centro internazionale d'arte e di cultura di Palazzo Te 2. Milano: Silvana Editoriale Spa, 2000.

Schivenoglia, Andrea. *Cronaca di Mantova dal MCCCCXLV al MCCCCLXXXIV. Trascritta ed annotata da Carlo D'Arco. Dal secondo volume della raccolta di cronisti e documenti storici lombardi inediti pubblicata da Giuseppe Müller*. Milano: Colombo, 1857.

Published Sources

Ahrendt, Martha S. 'The Cultural Legacy and Patronal Stewardship of Margherita Paleologa (1510–1566), Duchess of Mantua and Marchesa of Montferrat'. PhD thesis, Washington University, December 2002.

Ajmar-Wollheim, Marta, Flora Dennis, and Elizabeth Miller. *At Home in Renaissance Italy: [published to coincide with a major exhibition at the Victoria and Albert Museum]*. London: V&A Publishing, 2006.

Antenhofer, Christina. *Briefe zwischen Süd und Nord: Die Hochzeit und Ehe von Paula de Gonzaga und Leonhard von Görz im Spiegel der fürstlichen Kommunikation (1473–1500)*. Schlern-Schriften 336. Innsbruck: Universitätsverlag Wagner, 2007.

Antenhofer, Christina. 'Il potere delle gentildonne. L'esempio di Barbara di Brandenburgo e Paula Gonzaga'. In *Donne di potere nel Rinascimento*, edited by Letizia Arcangeli, and Susanna Peyronel, 67–87. I libri di viella 85. Roma: Viella, 2008.

Antenhofer, Christina. 'Der Fürst kommuniziert. Die *Camera Picta* des Andrea Mantegna'. In *Bildmagie und Brunnensturz: Visuelle Kommunikation von der klassischen Antike bis zur aktuellen medialen Kriegsberichterstattung*, edited by Elisabeth Walde, Monika Fink, and Thomas Steppan, 217–37. Innsbruck–Wien–Bozen: StudienVerlag, 2009.

Antenhofer, Christina. 'Familien-Körper. Die Organisation der Körper in adeligen Familien'. In *Körper er-fassen: Körpererfahrungen, Körpervorstellungen, Körperkonzepte*, edited by Kordula Schnegg, and Elisabeth Grabner-Niel, 113–33. Innsbruck, Wien [u.a.]: Studien Verl., 2010.

Antenhofer, Christina. 'From Local *Signori* to European High Nobility. The Gonzaga Family Networks in the Fifteenth Century'. In *Transregional and Transnational Families in Europe and Beyond: Experiences Since the Middle Ages*, edited by Christopher H. Johnson, David Warren Sabean, Simon Teuscher, and Francesca Trivellato, 55–74. New York-Oxford: Berghahn Books, 2011.

Antenhofer, Christina. 'Meeting the Prince between the City and the Family: The Resignification of Castello San Giorgio in Mantua (14th–16th Centuries)'. In *The Key to Power? The Culture of Access in Early Modern Courts, 1400–1700*, edited by Sebastiaan Derks, and Dries Raeymaekers. Leiden–Boston: Brill, forthcoming.

Battaglia, Salvatore. *Grande dizionario della lingua italiana*, vols 1–21. Torino: Unione Tipografico–Ed. Torinese, 1961–2002.

Bercusson, Sarah J. 'Gift-Giving, Consumption and the Female Court in Sixteenth-Century Italy'. PhD thesis, Queen Mary College, University of London, 2009.

Bourne, Molly. *Francesco II Gonzaga: The Soldier-Prince as Patron*. Biblioteca del Cinquecento 138. Roma: Bulzoni, 2008.

Brown, Clifford M., and Guy Delmarcel, in collaboration with Anna M. Lorenzoni. *Tapestries for the Courts of Federico II, Ercole, and Ferrante Gonzaga, 1522–63*. Seattle and London: College Art Association in association with University of Washington Press, 1996.

Brown, Clifford M. Introduction to *Gli arazzi dei Gonzaga nel Rinascimento*, edited by Guy Delmarcel, 21–31. Milano: Skira, 2010.

Calzona, Arturo, Francesco P. Fiore, Alberto Tenenti, and Cesare Vasoli, eds. *Il principe architetto: Atti del convegno internazionale, Mantova, 21–23 ottobre 1999*. Centro Studi Leon Battista Alberti Ingenium 4. Firenze: Leo S. Olschki, 2002.

Calzona, Arturo. *La rotonda e il palatium di Matilde*. Parma: Università degli Studi di Parma, Istituto di Storia dell'Arte, Centro di Studi Medievali, 1991.

Chambers, David S., and Jane Martineau, eds. *Splendours of the Gonzaga: Catalogue, exhibition, 4. Nov. 1981 – 31 Jan. 1982*. London: V&A Museum, 1981.

Chambers, David S. *A Renaissance Cardinal and His Worldly Goods. The Will and Inventory of Francesco Gonzaga (1444–83)*. Warburg Institute Survey and Texts 20. London: Warburg Institute, 1992.

Cohen, Thomas V., and Elizabeth S. Cohen. 'Postscript: Charismatic Things and

Social Transaction in Renaissance Italy'. *Urban History* 37 (2010): 474–82.
Coniglio, Giuseppe, *I Gonzaga*. Grandi famiglie 13. Varese: Dall'Oglio, 1967.
Croizat, Yassana C. ' "Living Dolls": François Ier Dresses His Women'. *Renaissance Quarterly* 60, 1 Spring (2007): 94–130.
Delmarcel, Guy, ed. *Gli arazzi dei Gonzaga nel Rinascimento*. Guy Delmarcel and Clifford M. Brown. Milano: Skira, 2010.
Delmarcel, Guy. Introduction to *Gli arazzi dei Gonzaga nel Rinascimento*, edited by Guy Delmarcel, 34–5. Milano: Skira, 2010.
Delmarcel, Guy. 'Prefazione'. In *Gli arazzi dei Gonzaga nel Rinascimento*, edited by Guy Delmarcel, 13–16. Milano: Skira, 2010.
De Mauro. Il dizionario della lingua italiana, Paravia 2000, edition on CD-Rom
'Epilogo'. In *Gli arazzi dei Gonzaga nel Rinascimento*, edited by Guy Delmarcel, 265–6. Milano: Skira, 2010.
Elias, Norbert. *Die höfische Gesellschaft. Untersuchungen zur Soziologie des Königtums und der höfischen Aristokratie*. Suhrkamp Taschenbuch Wissenschaft 423. Frankfurt am Main: Suhrkamp, 1989 [1969].
Ferrari, Daniela. Introduction to *Le collezioni Gonzaga: L'inventario dei beni del 1540–1542*, edited by Daniela Ferrari, 9–27. Fonti, repertori e studi per la storia di Mantova. Collana del centro internazionale d'arte e di cultura di Palazzo Te 1. Milano: Silvana Editoriale Spa, 2003.
Flaig, Egon. *Den Kaiser herausfordern. Die Usurpation im Römischen Reich*. Historische Studien 7. Frankfurt/New York: Campus, 1992.
Godelier, Maurice. *L'énigme du don*. Paris: Fayard, 1996.
González García, Juan L. 'Charles V and the Habsburgs' Inventories: Changing Patrimony as Dynastic Cult in Early Modern Europe'. *RIHA Journal* 0012, 11. November (2010): 1–19.
Grazzini, Nello F. '1. Annunciazione'. In *Gli arazzi dei Gonzaga nel Rinascimento*, edited by Guy Delmarcel, 36–45. Milano: Skira, 2010.
Grieco, Sara F. Matthews. 'The Body, Appearance, and Sexuality'. In *A History of Women in the West. 3. Renaissance and Enlightenment Paradoxes*, edited by Natalie Zemon Davis, and Arlette Farge, 46–84. Cambridge, MA–London: Belknap Press of Harvard University Press, 1994.
Groebner, Valentin. *Who Are You? Identification, Deception, and Surveillance in Early Modern Europe*. New York: Zone Books, 2007.
Guerzoni, Guido. 'La corte gonzaghesca in età moderna. Struttura, ordini e funzioni'. In *I Gonzaga: Moneta, arte, storia*, edited by Silvana Balbi de Caro, 90–6. Milano: Electa, 1995.
Hochrinner, Heidemarie. 'Bianca Maria Sforza'. PhD diss., Graz, 1966.
Huizinga, Johan. *Herbst des Mittelalters: Studien über Lebens– und Geistesformen des 14. und 15. Jahrhunderts in Frankreich und in den Niederlanden*, edited by Kurt Köster. 12th ed. Kröners Taschenausgabe 204. Stuttgart: Kröner, 2006.
Kantorowicz, Ernst H. *The King's Two Bodies: A Study in Mediaeval Political Theology*. Princeton, N.J: Princeton University Press, 1997 [1957].
Keupp, Jan. *Die Wahl des Gewandes. Mode, Macht und Möglichkeitssinn in Gesellschaft und Politik des Mittelalters*. Mittelalter Forschungen 33. Ostfildern: Thorbecke, 2010.
Klapisch-Zuber, Christiane. *La maison et le nom: Stratégies et rituels dans l'Italie de la Renaissance*. Paris: Editions de l'Ecole des hautes études en sciences sociales, 1990.
Kress, Susanne. 'Frauenzimmer der Florentiner Renaissance und ihre Ausstattung: Eine erste "Spurensuche"'. In *Das Frauenzimmer: Die Frau bei Hofe in*

Spätmittelalter und Früher Neuzeit, edited by Jan Hirschbiegel, and Werner Paravicini, 91–113. Residenzenforschung 11. Ostfildern: Thorbecke, 2000.

Lazzarini, Isabella. *Fra un principe e altri stati: Relazioni di potere e forme di servizio a Mantova nell'età di Ludovico Gonzaga*. Istituto storico italiano per il Medioevo/ Nuovi studi storici 32. Roma: Nella sede dell'Istituto, 1996.

Lévi-Strauss, Claude. *Les structures élémentaires de la parenté*. Paris: Presses Universitaires de France, 1949.

Luzio, Alessandro. *L'Archivio Gonzaga di Mantova. La corrispondenza familiare, amministrativa e diplomatica. Vol. II*. Rist. anastatica [Verona: Mondadori 1922]. Pubblicazioni della R. Accademia Virgiliana di Mantova. Serie I = Monumenta II. Mantova: Grassi, 1993.

Mozzarelli, Cesare, Robert Oresko, and Leandro Ventura, eds. *La corte di Mantova nell'età di Andrea Mantegna, 1450–1550 / The Court of the Gonzaga in the Age of Mantegna, 1450–1550: Atti del convegno (Londra, 6–8 marzo 1992; Mantova, 28 marzo 1992)*. Europa delle Corti. Centro studi sulle società di antico regime. Biblioteca del Cinquecento 75. Roma: Bulzoni, 1997.

Romani, Marina. *Una città in forma di palazzo: Potere signorile e forma urbana nella Mantova medievale e moderna*. Quaderni di Cheiron 1. Mantova: Publi Paolini, 1995.

Rückert, Peter, ed. *Von Mantua nach Württemberg: Barbara Gonzaga und ihr Hof*. Stuttgart: Kohlhammer, 2012.

Sandtner, Claudia. 'Zum Brautschatz der Antonia Visconti: Kleidung, Stoffe und Schmuck'. In *Antonia Visconti (+ 1405): Ein Schatz im Hause Württemberg: Begleitbuch und Katalog zur Ausstellung des Landesarchivs Baden-Württemberg – Hauptstaatsarchiv Stuttgart = Antonia Visconti (+ 1405): un tesoro in casa Württemberg: libro e catalogo sulla mostra del Landesarchiv Baden-Württemberg – Hauptstaatsarchiv Stoccarda*, edited by Peter Rückert, 72–7. Stuttgart: Landesarchiv Baden-Württemberg – Hauptstaatsarchiv, 2005.

Severidt, Ebba. *Familie, Verwandtschaft und Karriere bei den Gonzaga: Struktur und Funktion von Familie und Verwandtschaft bei den Gonzaga und ihren deutschen Verwandten (1444–1519)*. Leinfelden-Echterdingen: DRW, 2002.

Signorini, Rodolfo. *La più bella camera del mondo: La Camera Dipinta di Andrea Mantegna detta 'degli sposi'*. Mantova: Ed. MP, 2002 .

Signorini, Rodolfo. *Opus hoc tenue. La camera dipinta di Andrea Mantegna. Lettura storica iconografica iconologia*. Parma: Artegrafica Silva, 1985.

Spagnoletti, Angelantonio. *Le dinastie italiane nella prima età moderna*. Bologna: Il Mulino, 2003.

Sutter Fichtner, Paula. 'Dynastic Marriage in Sixteenth-Century Habsburg Diplomacy and Statecraft. An Interdisciplinary Approach'. *The American Historical Review* 81/2 (1976): 243–65.

Taddei, Elena. 'Anna Caterina Gonzaga und ihre Zeit. Der italienische Einfluss am Innsbrucker Hof'. In *Der Innsbrucker Hof: Residenz und höfische Gesellschaft in Tirol vom 15. bis 19. Jahrhundert*. Edited by Heinz Noflatscher, and Jan P. Niederkorn, 213–40. Archiv für österreichische Geschichte 138. Wien: Verlag der Österreichischen Akademie der Wissenschaften, 2005.

Tamalio, Raffaele. *La memoria dei Gonzaga. Repertorio bibliografico Gonzaghesco 1473–1999*. Biblioteca di bibliografia italiana CLVIII. Firenze: Olschki, 1999.

Trevisani, Filippo, ed. *Andrea Mantegna e i Gonzaga. Rinascimento nel Castello di San Giorgio*. Milano: Electa, 2006.

Weiss, Sabine. *Die vergessene Kaiserin: Bianca Maria Sforza – Kaiser Maximilians zweite Gemahlin*. Innsbruck–Wien: Tyrolia-Verl, 2010.

Welch, Evelyn. 'The Art of Expenditure: The Court of Paola Malatesta Gonzaga in Fifteenth-Century Mantua'. *Renaissance Studies* 16, no. 3 (2002): 306–317.

Welch, Evelyn. 'Women in Debt: Financing Female Authority in Renaissance Italy'. In *Donne di potere nel Rinascimento*, edited by Letizia Arcangeli, and Susanna Peyronel, 45–65. I libri di viella 85. Roma: Viella, 2008.

3

Between Mass and 'Mystère': The *Life of Saint Remigius* and the Ceremonial Function of Choir Tapestries[1]

Laura Weigert

In 1531, Robert Lenoncourt donated to the monastery of Saint-Remi a tapestry depicting the life of its patron saint.[2] The circumstances of this gift are included in the last panel (see colour plate 5), where they are described as follows:

> In the year one thousand five hundred and thirty plus one,
> the reverant Robert de Lenoncourt
> had me made word is still circulating
> to decorate this site on all sides.
> In honor of God and his celestial court,
> Within which is the blessed saint Remigius.[3]

Following the very clear wishes of the donor, Archbishop of Reims from 1508 to 1532 and Abbot of Saint-Remi from 1480 to 1523, the *Life of Saint Remigius* was displayed in the monks' choir of the abbey church "on all sides" during

[1] I would like to thank Katherine Wilson for her editorial suggestions and Mario Longtin for his generous help with the French translations.

[2] General discussions of this tapestry include: Marguerite Sartor, *Les Tapisseries, toiles peintes et broderies de Reims* (Reims: L. Michaud, 1912); Alain Erlande-Brandenburg, *La Tenture de saint Remi, exposée au musée Saint-Remi* (Reims: Centre regional de documentation pédagogique, 1983; Audrey Nassieu-Maupas, 'La tenture de *La Vie de saint Remi* du musée Saint-Remi de Reims,' *Travaux de l'Académie nationale de Reims* 174 (2000): 49–92.

[3] 'L'an mil cinq centz trente et ung adjouste
Le Révérand Robert de Lenoncourt
Pour décorer ce lieu de tous coustez
Me fist parfaire encore le bruyt en court
Honorant Dieu et sa celeste court
En laquelle est le benoist sainct Remy.
Il me donna pour le cas faire court
C'est demonstré de son salut amy'

(Inscription on the final panel of the Life of Saint Remigius (Reims, Musée de Saint-Remi).

major feast days. Like other examples of woven saints' lives, also donated by high-ranking clerics to their churches and displayed above the stalls reserved for the canons or monks, these tapestries were only seen on designated occasions.[4] The specificity with which the spatial and temporal display of such tapestries is documented offers a unique opportunity to explore the role luxury textiles played in particular ceremonial events.

Although textiles were an integral part of many important occasions in the fifteenth and sixteenth centuries, their material specifications and subject matter rarely leave a trace in the historical record. Descriptions of royal and ducal entries, beginning in the fourteenth century, state again and again that a city was "parée" (clothed) or that a procession was "tapissée" (draped with hangings) from its beginning to end point.[5] Yet these documents do not specify the pattern or subject matter of the woven adornment, nor is it clear whether such hangings were produced with a tapestry weave, as opposed to being made of a less expensive material, such as painted linen cloth.[6] In the case of many of the most well-known tapestries, the only evidence for their site of display significantly postdates the time of their production. The first reference to the display of the Angers Apocalypse, for instance, woven in the 1370s, dates to the 1470s when it hung along the walls of the nave in the cathedral of Saint Maurice.[7]

Where we have more specific references to the choice of subject matter and material structure of textiles is in the case of banquet festivities. For instance, historiated tapestries of the Labors of Hercules adorned the main hall during the celebration of the Feast of the Pheasant (1454);[8] those depicting the exploits of Jason were displayed at the banquet held in honor of the wedding

---

4 For a larger study of this type of tapestry, please see my: *Weaving Sacred Stories: French Choir Tapestries and the Performance of Clerical Identity* (Ithaca: Cornell University Press, 2004).

5 Froissart's description of Isabeau of Bavaria's entry into Paris in 1389 is unusually precise and provides one of the few documents that specify that these hangings were historiated tapestries. He writes, ' … toutes les maisons, à deux côtés de la grand rue Saint-Denis jusques en Châtelet, voire jusques au grand pont de Paris, étoient parées et vêtues de drap de haute lice de diverses histoires, dont grand plaisance et oubilance étoit au voir.' Froissart, *Chroniques*, book IV, chapter 1, *Les Chroniques de Sire Jean Froissart*, Ed. J.A.C. Buchon (Paris: Au Bureau du Panthéon Littéraire, 1852), 3:5.

6 Given the fragility of the latter, few examples of painted cloths survive. An exception is the group of paintings on linen/hemp cloth preserved in the Musée des Beaux Arts in Reims. On the possible use of these painted cloths in entry processions, please see: Laura Weigert, 'Visualizing the Movement of Urban Drama in the Late Middle Ages: the 'Mystère' of the Lord's Vengeance in Reims,' in *Meaning in Movement. The Semantics of Movement in Medieval Art*, Eds. Giovanni Freni and Nino Zchomelidse, Princeton: Princeton University Press, 2011, 161–87.

7 Francis Muel et al., *La tenture de l'Apocalypse d'Angers. Cahiers de l'Inventaire* 4. 2d ed. (Nantes: Association pour le développement de l'Inventaire general des monuments et des richesses artistiques en region des Pays de la Loire, 1987).

8 *Chronique de Mathieu d'Escouchy*, ed. G. Du Fresne de Beaucourt (Paris: Renouard, 1864), vol. 2, 131, 144–151.

of Margaret of York and Charles the Bold (1467).[9] Even when we know the subject matter of tapestries, though, it is difficult to gauge to what extent the theme was chosen based on the nature of the occasion. In many cases the fact that tapestries lined the walls seems to be more important for chroniclers to mention than it was to specify their content. Certainly the decision to hang the story of Gideon at meetings of the order of the Golden Fleece was linked to the occasion, since the tapestries depicted what were considered the historical origins of the Order. However, the series was also displayed in conjunction with the story of Alexander at a banquet following the coronation of Louis XI. [10] On this occasion the combination of events featuring the two heroes served to demonstrate the ruler's magnificence, power, and wealth. The connection between the subject matter of a tapestry and the event at which it was displayed seems to have been quite often of this more general nature.[11]

The exceptional detail of documentation on the location and timing of the display of choir tapestries provides an opportunity to describe more specifically the reception and function of individual tapestries within the site and set of circumstances for which they were made. The luxury of these tapestries lay not only in the material value of the fabric, their scale, the expense involved in their production, and the high quality of their design, but also in the fact that they were reserved for specific ceremonial occasions, and conversely, that they were withheld from view at all other times of the year. As a product of Flemish painters and weavers, many choir tapestries and the *Life of Saint Remigius* in particular, provide material evidence of the extensive geographic network these artisans established in the fifteenth and sixteenth centuries.

Reception and Function of Choir Tapestries

The demand for choir tapestries can be circumscribed both geographically and chronologically. The *Life of the Virgin and Christ*, now in Aix cathedral, was made for Christ Church, Canterbury;[12] Anna Rapp Buri and Monica Stucky-Schürer have described the three extant examples, which were made for German churches, as well as the *Life of Vincent*, made for the cathedral

---

9 'Elle [la salle] était tendue par en haut de drap de laine bleu et blanc, et par les côtés tapissée et tendue d'une riche tapisserie représentant l'histoire de Jason, où était narré le mystère de la Toison d'Or.' Olivier de la Marche, *Mémoires*, vol. 3, 114–201.

10 Jeffrey Chipps Smith, 'Portable Propaganda-Tapestry as Princely Metaphors at the Courts of Philip the Good and Charles the Bold,' *Art Journal*, 48 (1989), 123–129.

11 Thomas P. Campbell et al. Tapestry in the Renaissance: Art and Magnificence, Exh. Cat. (New Haven: Yale University Press, 2002), 13-27; Wolfgang Brassat, *Tapisserien und Politik. Funktionen, Kontexte und Rezeption eines repräsentativen Mediums* (Berlin: Mann, 1992).

12 *Saints de Choeur. Tapisseries du Moyen Age et de la Renaissance*, Exhibition catalogue under the direction of Catherine Arminjon (Milan: 5 Continents Editions, 2004), 104–111.

of Bern in 1515.[13] However, the vast majority of choir tapestries were made for churches located within the realms of the French kings and Burgundian dukes. Although individual commissions might have existed in the fourteenth century, the first references to and extant examples of choir tapestries date from the early fifteenth century. The *Lives of Piat and Eleutherius*, a tapestry woven in Arras for the cathedral of Tournai in 1402, is the earliest documented example (see colour plate 6).[14] The *Life of Saint Remigius* was produced at the end of the period during which this type of tapestry was most popular. Choir tapestries continued to be made through the seventeenth and even eighteenth centuries. The *Life of Maurille* was woven in 1616 for the parish church of Saint-Maurille in Angers, for instance, and some wealthy cathedrals replaced their tapestries in the seventeenth century. These isolated examples, however, do not constitute a coherent group or a true revival of what had been the fashion during a defined chronological period.

As is the case for most tapestries, documentation that attests to the designer and weavers of an extant choir tapestry is the exception, rather than the rule. The *Lives of Piat and Eleutherius*, made for the cathedral of Tournai, and the *Life of Saint Anathoile*, given to the church Saint-Anathoile in Salins in 1501 (see colour plate 7), are exceptional in this respect.

In both of these cases, the name of the master weaver and the city in which he worked was incorporated into the last section of the tapestry. These inscriptions are now lost, yet they were both transcribed prior to the disappearance of the panels on which they were woven. Pierot Feré is credited with the former, which, according to the inscription, was woven in Arras.[15] The inscription on the latter read, "Ces quatorze pièces de tapis furent à Bruges faites et construites à l'hostel de Jehan Sauvage."[16] The cities of Arras, and Bruges, along with Tournai and Brussels, constituted the centers of tapestry production during the fashion for choir tapestries.[17] Recent scholarship has located the production of some choir tapestries in Paris where Flemish weavers took up residence and established workshops.[18] Although we cannot specify the place of production for most examples, choir tapestries provide

[13] Anna Rapp Buri and Monika Stucky-Schürer, *Burgundische Tapisserien* (Munich: Hirmer, 2010).

[14] Laura Weigert, 'Performing the Past,' *Gesta* 38 (1999): 154–170.

[15] Weigert, ibid., 167.

[16] Bernard Prost, 'La tapisserie de Saint-Anatoile de Salins,' *Gazette des beaux-arts* 3.8 (1892): 496–507.

[17] On Bruges as a center of tapestry production, please see: Guy Delmarcel and Erik Duverger.

[18] Audrey Nassieu-Maupas, 'La Vie de saint Jean-Baptiste d'Angers et la production de tapisseries à Paris dans la première moitié du XVIe siècle,' *Revue de l'Art* 145 (2004): 41–53.

evidence for the contact Flemish weavers in these cities maintained with French ecclesiastic patrons.

The visual impact and meaning of these tapestries as a group were linked to their display in the choir on certain occasions. The length of the tapestries, which measure between forty and sixty metres, was determined by the dimensions of the stalls, which in turn were constructed according to the size of the choir and the number of clerics who occupied it. Ecclesiastical officials commissioned these tapestries; their display in the choir, which was separated from the nave by a rood screen, restricted their audience to the clergy. The *Life of the Virgin and Christ* still *in situ* in the choir of the abbey of La Chaise-Dieu allows us to imagine what this display of tapestries would have looked like (see colour plate 8). That the series hangs permanently, however, prevents us from appreciating the contribution their display made to the audience's experience of ceremonial occasions, for the temporal limitation of their viewing was an essential component of their donation. Not only were the days on which they were to be seen specified but a donation could also include funds to pay for them to be hung and taken down and to pay for chests in which they would be stored at other times of the year.[19]

The saints selected for these woven *vitae* were the objects of devotion and donations of a community from the founding of each particular church. Events in the lives of the patron saint or saints of the church, of the Virgin, or in rare cases of Christ, as at the Chaise-Dieu, unfold along the length of the tapestries. The cult of these saints focused on their relics, housed most commonly in reliquaries located in the choir of the church. So, in the case of the cathedral of Tournai, the *Lives of Piat and Eleutherius* were displayed around the walls of the choir, within which the relics of the latter saint were housed in a reliquary behind the high altar.

Both in the choice of events and the relationship of these events to a church's relics, choir tapestries call attention to a community's devotion to their patron saints and establish its privileged relationship to their cult. On the one hand, the events chosen in the saints' *vitae* often integrate the posthumous events relating to the devotion to and miracles performed by their relics. In many cases, the tapestries shift attention from the physical life of the saints to the invention and multiple translations of their relics. These woven legends thereby provide both a model for and a mirror of a community's devotion to their patron saint. On the other hand, the tapestries provide a pictorial legend that enhances a viewer's experience of the saints' relics in the choir. Through images of the miraculous power of these relics or the circumstances

[19] Chests were part of the donation of choir tapestries to the cathedrals of Bayeux and Sens (Eucher Deslandes, *Etude sur l'église de Bayeux* (Caen: E. Dominin, 1917), 420; Michel Hérold, 'Aux sources de l' 'invention': Gaultier de Campes, peintre à Paris au début du XVIe siècle,' *Revue de l'Art* 120 (1998): 50.

surrounding their origin and the life of the saint, these woven narratives provide a historical account of the relics they surround. At the same time, these accounts of the saints that, in turn, are physically and visually juxtaposed with the reliquaries situated in the choir serve to authenticate and legitimate the relics they house.

In a similar conjunction of the woven events themselves and their situation in the choir, these tapestries honor the donor and the clerical or monastic community in which he played a role. As in the case of the *Life of Saint Remigius*, a written inscription on the first or last panel of these tapestries documents the individual responsible for and the circumstances surrounding their donation. At each display of the tapestry, the memory of this individual and his gift to the church is evoked through a combination of a portrait and the dedicatory inscription. Moreover, the placement of this commemorative panel over the seat of the donor himself and those who assumed this office after his death, enhanced his status by underscoring his role in the tapestry's making and positioning him within a lineage of generous benefactors to the church. The juxtaposition of living cleric and pictorial representation became even more significant in cases where the donor and the patron saint had occupied the same ecclesiastic or monastic office. In these cases, the individual associated with the donation after his death or seated in a prominent location in the choir was identified as the successor of the saint, whose woven *vita* adorned the walls. The tapestry, in turn, united the larger clerical or monastic community through the continuous scroll of tapestry that spanned above the heads of its members.

Choir tapestries also prompt intriguing questions about the overlap between forms of visual representation made for these restricted religious communities and those associated with a broader civic audience. References to choir tapestries in inventory accounts, for instance, can often be confused with documentation on the performance or script of a mystery play, since the language used for each is so similar.[20] The word "mystère" is used in these records to refer to a text that was used for or commemorated a play with a large and diverse audience as well as to a tapestry whose audience was restricted to individuals with access to the choir. In another telling example, the same author is credited with the composition of both a Passion play and with the instructions to artists for the making of a choir tapestry. A lengthy description of the *Lives of Urban and Cecilia* was composed for the artists involved in the design and weaving of a tapestry for the royal collegiate church of Saint-Urbain in Troyes.[21] Its author has been identified as Pierre

---

20 D. Mater, 'Les Anciennes Tapisseries de la Cathédrale de Bourges. Pierre de Crosses,' *Mémoires de la Société des Antiquaires du Centre*, 27, 1903, 357–58.

21 Philippe Guignard, 'Mémoire fournis aux peintres chargés d'exécuter les cartons d'une tapisserie destinés à la collegiale Saint-Urbain de Troyes, représentant les legends de St. Urbain et Sainte Cécile,' *Mémoires de la Société d'Agriculture, Sciences et Arts de l'Aube*

Desrey, who also wrote part of the Troyes Passion play, performed in the city in 1482.[22] Finally, the appearance of unusual episodes in the play of Saint Martin and in the choir tapestry devoted to his *vita*, made for the collegiate church of Saint-Martin in Montauban, provides just one example of the shared source material that defined both visual representations of a saint's life.[23]

Choir tapestries served the general needs and desires of ecclesiastic and monastic patrons at a time in which luxury textiles were considered essential elements within the orchestration of ceremonial occasions. Their similarities to contemporary saints' plays ask us to broaden our discussion of ceremony in the choir to encompass a larger urban performance culture in the fifteenth and sixteenth centuries. That examples of this type of tapestry share common features and a general set of functions, however, does not deny the specificity of each one. Although the patterns for discrete sections of figures and motifs were reused in different choir tapestries, the overall subject matter, and the order and composition of individual events was unique to each one. Moreover, their format and the choice of events were determined by their display in the choir of a particular church. The way each tapestry intersected with such a ceremonial setting can only be appreciated if we turn to a single example.

The *Life of Saint Remigius*

The *Life of Saint Remigius* attests to the effectiveness with which painters and weavers produced a tapestry that satisfied the requirements of a specific architectural, liturgical, and civic context at the same time that they met the demands of a larger market for choir tapestries. The similarity between individual figures and motifs in the *Life of Saint Remigius* and several other choir tapestries confirms that the same preliminary patterns were reused for different tapestries. Audrey Nassieu-Maupas has argued that the painter known as the Maître de Montmorency produced the cartoons for this larger group of choir tapestries; Guy-Michel Leproux, in turn, identifies this master as a Flemish painter working in Paris named Gauthier de Campes.[24]

Drawing on stylistic evidence, these arguments allow us to circumscribe a group of choir tapestries that derive from a common artistic milieu. The

15 (1849–50): 421–534; now reprinted with translation and introduction by Tina Kane (*The Troyes Mémoire: The Making of A Medieval Tapestry* (Rochester: The Boydell Press, 2010).

22 Théophile Boutiot, *Histoire de la ville de Troyes et de la Champagne Méridionale* (Troyes: Dufey-Robert, 1874), vol. 4, 271; Jean-Claude Bibolet ed. *Le Mystère de la Passion de Troyes: Mistere de la Passion Nostre Seigneur, Troyes XVe siècle* (Geneva: Droz, 1987).

23 Gustave Cohen, 'Rabelais et la légende de Saint-Martin,' in *Etudes d'Histoire du Théâtre en France au Moyen-Age et à la Renaissance* (Paris: Gallimard, 1956), 341.

24 Audrey Nassieu-Maupas, 'Peinture, vitrail et tapisserie au début du XVIe siècle: l'exemple du Maître de Montmorency,' *Les Cahiers de la Rotonde* 22 (2000): 45–60 and 'La tenture'; Guy-Michel Leproux; Michel Hérold, 'Aux sources de l' 'invention': Gaultier de Campes, peintre à Paris au début du XVIe siècle,' *Revue de l'Art* 120.2 (1998): 49–57.

earliest example, the *Life of Stephen*, donated by bishop Jean Baillet to the cathedral of Auxerre, dates to around 1500; the last, the *Life of Saint Remigius*, to 1531. The chronologic span during which the tapestries were woven testifies to the longevity of the popularity of stylistic forms and a shared set of figures and motifs. The argument that a painter trained in Brussels or his workshop was responsible at some point during this time for producing or circulating these patterns is convincing. It is also possible, however, that similarities between tapestries were not the result of this painter or workshop intervening in the making of each choir tapestry. It could be that the weavers themselves preserved and circulated the patterns that they then arranged and supplemented according to the specifications of an individual commission.[25]

In the case of the *Life of Saint Remigius* the compositional format of earlier choir tapestries was significantly modified. The narrow scrolls of fabric that unfolded around the walls of the choir changed to ten individual squares, each one measuring approximately five by five metres. The total length of the ten tapestries corresponded with that of a choir much smaller than the expanse of the stalls reserved for cathedral chapters and their dignitaries, which measured up to forty metres. Rather than beginning and ending at the north and south entrances into this choir, the *Life of Saint Remigius* continued around the walls of the sanctuary, linking this area with that containing the monks' stalls. Unlike other choir tapestries, whose width corresponded with that of the wooden backs of the stalls, the *Life of Saint Remigius* stretched up to the beginning of the vaults of the choir. The change of format would have been all the more striking, since Robert de Lenoncourt's donation replaced a choir tapestry of the earlier format, given to Saint-Remi by its abbot, Jean Canart, in 1419.[26]

As is commonly the case with scholarship on tapestries, literature on the series has focused primarily on questions of artistic style, patronage, and iconography.[27] Scholarship on the *Life of Saint Remigius*, however, is unusual in that the earliest studies devoted to the series called attention to the coexistence of this woven version of the saint's life and a mystery play that takes the same theme. Henri Jadart emphatically stressed the connection between the two in his study of 1894, in which he claims that the *Life of Remigius* in tapestry is "the translation of a mystery play." He does not, however, identify the play and it is not clear whether he actually knew of the existence of a Saint Remigius play.[28] In a more recent study, Jelle Koopmans provides a possible

25 On such questions of authorship, please see: Guy Delmarcel, 'L'auteur ou les auteurs en tapisserie: quelques réflexions critiques,' in *Le Dessin sous-jacent dans la peinture* IV (Louvain-la-Neuve: Université Catholique de Louvain, Institut Supérieur d'Archéologie et d'Histoire de l'Art, 1982), 43–48.

26 Sartor, 'Tapisseries,' 22–23.

27 Erlande-Brandenburg, 'La tenture'; Nassieu-Maupas, 'La tenture de la vie.'

28 Henri Jadart, 'La vie de saint Remi dans la poésie populaire. Anciens hymnes et proses, le mystère de saint Remi, les tapisseries,' *Travaux de l' Académie National de Reims* 97

source for the tapestry in a surviving play script.[29] This script survives in a single copy now in the Bibliothèque de l'Arsenal in Paris.[30] Its first owner is not documented but it came into the hands of a family in Amiens in 1528. Based on this fact and his analysis of the manuscript, Jelle Koopmans dates it to between 1520 and 1528.[31] When scholars take this script into account, however, they still consider it source material for the woven events, which are: "true pictorial summaries of descriptions in the mystery play."[32]

The survival of both a play script and a tapestry of the *Life of Remigius* offers the opportunity to explore with greater nuance the interaction between two roughly contemporaneous representations of the saint's *vita*. The architectural and temporal specificity of the display of the tapestry, in turn, makes this interaction particularly telling for a potential exchange between performance within the choir and in city streets. As this chapter will suggest, the ceremonial occasion to which the tapestry contributed incorporated elements from both liturgical and urban drama; the *Life of Remigius* was seen in relation to the "Mass" and to a "Mystère."

The events included in the woven *vita* recount the saint's birth, his entry into an ecclesiastical career, the miracles performed during his lifetime and through the agency of his relics, after his death. The famous baptism of Clovis takes an important place among these miracles, but others, less well known, also are conveyed in detail. We see the saint resurrect a young girl from Toulouse and cause an empty barrel of wine to overflow. Other panels place us within the fray of battle led by Clovis or lead us through the efforts of the people of Reims to extinguish a fire in their city (see colour plate 9). Under each scene, woven *tituli* summarize the action, taking place within the panel. However, it is the life-size figures depicted in each panel that present the story of the saint's life to viewers.

The scale of these woven figures evoke the human actors, and the new format of this choir tapestry parallels the organization of plays in which multiple place marks and actors appear simultaneously within a viewer's visual field. But the tapestry also presents more specific parallels with the extant Saint Remi play. As Jelle Koopmans points out, the text is organized as a series of independent and discrete episodes. Each one concludes with the word, "explicit," and begins with the signal, "Here begins how … ."[33] Jelle Koopmans accounts for the composite nature of the text by suggesting that it brings together different plays about Saint Remi, which

(1894–95): 115–169.

29 Jelle Koopmans ed., *Mystère de Saint-Remi* (Geneva: Droz, 1997).

30 Paris, Bibliothèque de l'Arsenal Ms. 3364.

31 Koopmans, 'Le Mystère,' 59.

32 ' … véritables résumés picturaux des descriptions du mystère' (Nassieu-Maupas, 'La tenture de la vie,' 71).

33 'Ci commence comment … '

would have been performed on a series of stages erected at different locations in Reims. The tapestry is also organized as a series of discrete episodes. Rather than the continuous pictorial stories that unfold along the length of the scroll-like format of other woven *vitae*, the *Life of Saint Remigius* is divided into individual pictorial units, within which three, four, or sometimes five events in the life of the saint transpire in relation with each other. The designers of the series did not provide visual cues to link the individual panels together; each one exists as a self-contained unit.

The two visual versions, one woven and one performed, are particularly close in their choice of events. Most of the events common to the script of the saint's play and the tapestry can be found in Hincmar's ninth-century life of Remigius;[34] Flodoard's tenth-century account of the history of Reims expands on the fate of his relics.[35] Jacobus de Voragine made other events accessible in his two-part life of Remigius, distributed in the Golden Legend between the feasts of the saint on October 1 and on January 13, which commemorated the translation of his relics.[36] None of these written texts, however, includes all of the events depicted in the tapestry or preserved in the play's script.

In all but its last two panels, the tapestry follows almost step by step the development of the saint's life in the script. We begin with God surrounded by the celestial hierarchy, who announces the birth of Remigius to the hermit Montain; move to his election; and then on to a succession of miracles, which the saint performs, including his baptism of Clovis, the first Christian king of France. In both accounts, the city of Reims and the saint's role in its protection figure prominently, as in the moment Remigius extinguishes the fire raging within its walls (see colour plate 9). Devils and demons make their usual appearance, both in the tapestry (see colour plate 9) and engaging in lengthy debates in the play.

The strongest link between the play and the tapestry is their inclusion of an episode not found in any other known account of the saint's life (see colour plates 10 and 11).[37] Saint Remigius, sleepy in the early morning, forgets the lessons for the reading of the Matins office. He prays to God and, miraculously, Peter and Paul appear and prompt him on his lines. This miracle is observed by a priest, whom Saint Remigius confronts making him promise not to reveal what he has seen. Both the tapestry and the play devote significant attention to this otherwise unrecorded episode.

---

34 Hincmar, *Vita Remigii* (*Acta Sanctorum* (Paris and Rome: Palmé, 1867) vol. XLIX (October 1), 131–67.

35 Flodoard, *Ex Historia ecclesiae Remensis* (*Acta Sanctorum* (Paris and Rome: Palmé, 1867) XLIX (October 1), 172–76.

36 Jacobus de Voragine, *The Golden Legend*, trans. William Granger Ryan (Princeton: Princeton University Press), vol. 1, 85–87 (Jan. 13), vol. 2, 216–218 (Oct. 1).

37 'Le Mystère de saint Remi,' verses 14,020–14,477 (Koopmans, 'Le Mystère,' 733–751).

The play stages this episode in two different locations. The episode begins in Paradise, where God engages and addresses saints Michael and Gabriel in praise and support of Remigius. We then move to the chapel in which Remigius will say Matins. The saint arrives and his prayers to God create a bridge between these two locations as God responds to him from Paradise. A second bridge is created as Peter and Paul descend to the chapel and subsequently return to Paradise. The exchange between the spying priest and Remigius concludes the episode and the play.

Of all the episodes in the saint's play, this is the one that refers most directly and repeatedly to both the spoken words and the adornment that defined ceremony in the choir. The readings spoken by the figures of Remigius, Peter, and Paul are in Latin and begin with the recognizable liturgical refrain: "Jube domine benedicere."[38] The saint's play, in turn, describes in copious detail the adornment of the church interior on festive occasions. Even more relevant for a potential exchange between the tapestry and play of Saint Remigius, the display of a tapestry becomes the topic of a lengthy passage. Prior to Remigius's entrance, a priest named Liénart prepares the chapel where the saint will say Matins, with the words:

In honor of the beautifully born,
who carried the true son of God,
I will now go to adorn the place,
Where my Lord will say Matins ... [39]
I will have a beautiful and finely worked tapestry.
Tapestry? It is *sarrasinois,*
I can see from the craftmanship.
It is made to adorn the front of the altar,
to the ground. Ho! There is nothing like it!
And this one: it is exactly what I need.
It is beautiful, it will be placed on the upper part,
It is woven in gold throughout.
Even Nebuchadnezzar,
Who had countless riches,
Noble treasures and high nobleties,
I think did not have the like of it.
Here is another one, red this time,
I'm not sure what it's called,
But the colour of it is extremely beautiful,
One has given it to him in Spain,

[38] 'Lord, grant me thy blessing;' 'Le Mystère de saint Remi,' verses 14305–14308.
[39] ' ... En l'onneur de la belle nee
Qui porta le vrai filz de Dieu
M'en vueil aler parer le lieu
Ou mon seigneur dira matines ... ' (verses 14116–14119)

And this one other one came from Britain
On my soul, it is beautiful and fine
As if woven by a seraphin,
Joyous and full of life.
And this one is the work of angels,
Hahay! It is the work of a master hand,
From here to heaven on earth,
One will not find one of finer craftsmanship … [40]

With vibrant imagery and extensive detail, Liénart differentiates between the woven ornamentation before and around the altar. The material of the fabric is insistently and distinctly related to tapestry weave through the word "sarazinois," a term that first designated one group of weavers in Parisian guild regulations.[41] The nature of the dyes, their colours, and the presence of gilt silk threads are emphasized in the account of the precious hangings. The skill of the weavers is equated with angelic intervention and the tradition of adorning a sacred and ritual site is linked back to the traditions of kings. The speech thereby vacillates between a historically accurate description of actual display practices and the metaphoric status of textiles to both conceal and enhance the sacred site of the altar.[42]

40 'Aray je tappis bel et bon
Tappis? Il est sarazinois,
A l'ouvraige bien le congnois.
C'est pour parer devant l'autel
A terre. Ho! Y n'y a tel
Et cestui, c'est quanque il me fault,
Il est bel, c'est pour mettre en haut:
Il est tretout tissu a or.
Oncques Nabugodonosor,
Qui sans nombre avoit richesses,
Nobles tresors, belles noblesses,
Ce croy, n'avoit point de pareil.
Vez en ci ung aultre vermeil,
Je ne sçai comment on l'apelle,
Mais la couleur en est moult belle:
On li donna en Espaingne.
Et cestui ci vint de Behaingne,
Pour mon ame, il est bel et fin
Et l'eust tissu ung seraphin
Joieux et fricque.
Et cestui, c'est euvre angelicque,
Hahay! Il est de main de maistre:
De ci en paradis terrestre
Ne trouveroit on mieux ouvré … ' (verses14129–14152).

41 Etienne Boileau René de Lespinasse, de François Bonnardot, eds. *Histoire générale de Paris, les métiers et corporations de la ville de Paris* (*XIIIe siècle, Le Livres des Métiers d'Etienne Boileau*) (Paris: Imprimerie Nationale, 1879).

42 Johann Konrad Eberlein, *Apparatio Regis—revelatio veritatis. Studien zur Darstellung des Vorhangs in der bildenden Kunst von der Spätantike bis zum Ende des Mittelalters* (Wiesbaden: Dr. Ludwig Reichert, 1982).

The tapestry relates this episode in a three-part sequence that appears in the top register of the eighth panel (see colour plate 11). On the left, Peter and Paul appear in the chapel next to Remigius, who celebrates the office at the altar. The central panel represents Remigius also before the altar, above which God appears surrounded with a celestial cloud and angels. On the right, Remigius confronts the priest who has witnessed the miracle of Peter and Paul's intervention. The spatial relationship between the three events solves the problem of incorporating the temporal sequence of the play, which moved back and forth between the chapel and Paradise. The designers established the prominence of the central scene based on its placement and the way that it protrudes slightly into the viewer's space, in contrast to the two flanking events. This arrangement also allows us to read the central event as preceding the one represented on its left. Consequently, it can refer both to the moment of Remigius's prayers to God before he sends Peter and Paul, and to that in which he says another prayer, following their appearance and help. The designers thereby condensed events that are represented separately in the written narrative into a single image and emphasized the significance of God's appearance to Remigius. On the right, the sequence ends with his confrontation with the priest, a more mundane event that is presented as occurring outside of the sacred site of the chapel.[43]

The parallels between the two *vitae* of Remigius go beyond their incorporation of this unusual episode; the tapestry creates a similar visual and experiential environment to that evoked by the play. The display of textile adornment described in the saint's play is included with equal specificity in the representation of the chapel in the tapestry. The central and right-hand event include a silk brocade patterned altar frontal, with an orange ground and burgundy pomegranate motif, bordered by a striped red and blue fringe. The left-hand depiction of the chapel includes blue and yellow striped altar curtains, for which the hanging system is fully visible, and a baldachin with fringe of the same colour sequence. A hint of these colours also appears in the central event, suggesting that the altar was adorned with the same curtains and baldachin. The absence of these textiles in the right-hand event differentiates this architectural setting from the sacred space of the chapel. However, the description of luxury adornment of a sacred site emphasized in the play would have been more visibly demonstrated in the actual display of

---

43 The tituli read:
1) 'Saint Pierre et Pol d'admirable façon
Viennent des cieux soubs terrestre courtines
Et chacun d'eulx entonne une leçon
Puis saint Remy paracheve matines.'
2) 'Voyant qu'ils sont remontez es sainctz cieulx
Demande a Dieu sa benediction
Saint Thierry homme devocieux
Se musse et cache en contemplation.'

the tapestry in the choir of Saint-Remi. The vibrancy and expensive threads of the tapestry equaled the diverse colours and luxury fabrics described by Liénart. As it took its place around the walls of Saint-Remi, the tapestry created a sacred space that corresponded with the one evoked through an actor's words and the accompanying stage props.

A similar correspondence between the visual experience of the play and that of the tapestry is suggested in the latter's incorporation of spoken words. The key exchange between the Archdeacon is included in the right-hand section of the tripartite sequence in the tapestry. In a banderole stretching from his mouth, the figure of Remigius requests that, "Now that you have seen this beautiful mystery, I beg that you keep quiet about it."[44] This woven figure then becomes associated and speaks the words, as if it were an actor playing a role in a performance of the saint's life. The inclusion of *Antiphons* and *Responses* in the written version of the play would have evoked those words spoken in the liturgy, creating an association for its audience between ceremony in the choir and the performance of a mystery play. Conversely, the monks in the choir of Saint-Remi would have associated the woven images of Peter, Paul, and Remigius celebrating Matins with the words they either spoke or heard during liturgical celebrations in their choir. In this process, they would have participated in the telling of the saint's life as it took place in the choir.

The eighth panel departs, however, in significant ways from the written play and this departure is crucial for understanding how the tapestry version of the saint's life relates distinctly to its display in the choir of Saint-Remi. First, the spying priest called the "Archdeacon" in the play, identified merely by his status within the ecclesiastical hierarchy, becomes Theodoric or Thierry in the tapestry. His name appears in the three scenes and in the inscription. Saint Theodoric was a disciple of Saint Remigius, whom he ordained and appointed abbot of the newly founded monastic community of the Mont d'Or.[45] The monastery of Saint Remigius played an important role in the propagation of his cult, protecting his relics in their basilica in the tenth century.[46] The tapestry version of the event thereby emphasizes their patron saint's monastic connections and through him those of Robert de Lenoncourt, the tapestry's donor, who had given up his actual status as Abbot of Saint-Remi but remained the direct successor of Remigius as Archbishop of Reims.

The second significant departure of this episode from its representation in the play of Saint Remigius is what it includes after the three-part sequence relating to the Matins office. Whereas the play ends with Remigius's

---

44 'Puisque vous avez vu ce beau mistaire
Je vous supplie de le taire.'

45 Rombaut van Doren, 'Teodorico,' in *Bibliotheca Sanctorum* vol. 12 (Rome: Istituto Giovanni XXIII, 1969), 230–231.

46 Lacatte-Joltrois, *Histoire et description de l'église de Saint-Remi de Reims* (Reims: P. Dubois, 1868).

confrontation with the priest and the saint's final speech, invoking God to bless France with peace, the tapestry combines this episode with another three-part sequence of events. In the same panel we see the drafting of Remigius's will, the saint's celebration of Mass and Communion, and his final moments, with his soul transported by angels. Jelle Koopmans suggests that the text might be incomplete, which makes it possible that the play of the saint's life included this episode. Even if this were the case, however, the tapestry would still depart from the play in that it links the two episodes by combining them in a single panel.

The parallels the tapestry creates between these two episodes underscore the relationship between these events and ceremony in the choir. Although the content of the story suggests that Saint Remigius celebrates Communion in the cathedral, the ornamentation of the altar resembles that of the chapel, thereby creating a visual link between the sites in which the two events occur. The tripartite division of events is maintained for both of the episodes, as is the prominence accorded the central event. That the saint has celebrated Mass before offering Communion is specified in the titulus that links this central event with that on its right, "He says Mass then gives the Host to his clerics."[47] As in the upper register, the central event is situated in front of the ground plane upon which the events that flank it are placed. This spatial organization encourages the viewer to begin the story with and privilege the central event. The ceremonial finery of the liturgical vestments equals that of those worn by Remigius in his other appearances (see colour plate 9). The expensive materials of the vestments are conveyed in these instances through shades of yellow that create a shimmering effect similar to that created by the use of gilt threads. In these instances, his cope and miter emphasize his status and that of the Episcopal office in general. The choice of pattern on the vestments within the scene of Mass and Communion relates directly to its subject matter. Not only does a wafer hover in mid action, as Remigius delivers it to the open mouth of the cleric kneeling before him, but it is also prominently displayed above a chalice, within the pattern of the saint's embroidered cope. Remigius's vestments reiterate the focus of the event on the sacrament of the Eucharist. Read in conjunction with the event immediately above it, God's appearance in Paradise confirms His presence in the Host below.

The last two panels in the tapestry, depicting Remigius's burial and the miracles performed by his relics (see colour plates 12 and 13), relate the story of the saint to his relics housed in the sanctuary and to the monks of Saint-Remi. A single procession carrying the body of the saint and then his relics winds through a series of distinct events, transpiring in different places and times. At one point, the procession leading the body to its burial merges with a later procession of his relics that saved the city from the plague. This procession

[47] 'La messe il dict puis à ses clercs il donne le corps de Dieu.'

continues into the city gates but a canon on the outer edge of the panel offers an alternate direction, gesturing to the final panel of the series, where the procession of Remigius's relics continues. But rather than reaching its destination at this juncture in the tapestry, the coffin, held by four angels, hovers in an intermediary space, between the imaginary space in which the story takes place, and that of the choir in front of the tapestry. Situated at the easternmost end of the choir, this image established a divine provenance for the relics, protected by the monks of Saint-Remi.

In turn, the tapestry solidified the position of Robert de Lenoncourt within the monastic community of Saint-Remi. The circumstances of the donation of the *Life of Saint Remigius* and its intended display are documented in the final panel, where, as we have seen, the tapestry itself speaks in rhymed verse, saying that: "in the year 1531, the reverent Robert of Lenoncourt, had me made … to decorate this site, on all of sides." Following the expressed wishes of its donor, the *Life of Saint Remigius* was hung in the choir of the abbey church during the celebration of high feast days. The centerpiece of these celebrations was the Mass, performed by the Archbishop of Reims, who acted as celebrant on these occasions. The eighth panel, in particular, served to legitimate the Eucharistic sacrament and the bishop's privileged role in its celebration. Furthermore, as the Archbishop's presence on these occasions brought the monastery and cathedral together, the tapestry at this juncture joined Remigius's celebration of the monastic office above with his celebration of Mass below, in which the status of his Episcopal office is emphasized.

Within the circumscribed arena of liturgical celebration in the church of Saint-Remi, the tapestry fulfilled thereby a variety of political and religious functions. With this donation, the Archbishop of Reims, Robert Lenoncourt, confirmed his devotion to Saint Remigius, the Virgin and God. The privileged position accorded his portrait at the end of the story, and the appearance of his arms throughout the hangings, reflect his role in its production. The donation was meant to serve in his salvation: it represented a righteous deed and provided the monks of Saint-Remi with an incentive to pray for his soul every time the tapestry was displayed. With this gift, Robert de Lenoncourt also highlighted his ties with the monastery, where he had served as abbot, and conveyed a broader alliance between the Archbishop of Reims and the monastery of Saint-Remi. For the monks, the tapestry transformed the choir during the celebration of festivals in the church, as it integrated an account of the patron saint into this space. In addition, the monks, seated under the images of their illustrious predecessor, were associated with him and with the events in the history of France in which he played an important role.

Conclusion

Historians of art and of theatre of the late Middle Ages have long recognized the shared subject matter, motifs, and costumes in civic drama and art of this period.[48] The relationship between the two visual forms is described most commonly in terms of the influence of one medium on the other. This example suggests instead a mutual exchange between pictures and plays, in which producers and designers relied on an audience's familiarity with one medium to enhance their appreciation and understanding of the other. The woven and performed *vitae* of Saint Remigius draw on the same series of events, emphasize the same attributes of the saint, and locate his *vita* firmly within the city of Reims. The script encourages viewers to recall liturgical ceremony in the choir as they watch the performance of the saint's life. Conversely, the scale, format, and display of the tapestry meant that its viewers were both surrounded by and incorporated into the story in a way that resembled the audience's experience of large-scale urban drama.

The display of the *Life of Remigius*, moreover, points to the overlap between liturgical and civic performances of the lives of saints. As the woven saint's life became part of the liturgical furnishings on high feast days, the events the tapestry shared with a saint's play became part of the performance of Mass. Its display suggests, in turn, that tapestries could create an experience that was considered to be homologous to that of a saint's play. The textual description of the *Lives of Cecilia and Urban* implies, for instance, that the woven figures were understood to perform their roles. Similarly, the figures in the *Life of Saint Remigius* speak by means of banderoles that extend from their mouths. And, to return to the final inscription, we learn that the tapestry itself performs, as it proclaims in the first person its own role in honoring God, the celestial choir, and the saint.

Bibliography

Arminjon, Catherine. *Saints de Choeur. Tapisseries du Moyen Age et de la Renaissance.* Milan: 5 Continents Editions, 2004.

Bibolet, Jean-Claude. ed., *Le Mystère de la Passion de Troyes: Mistere de la Passion Nostre Seigneur, Troyes XVe siècle.* Geneva: Droz, 1987.

Boutiot, Théophile. *Histoire de la ville de Troyes et de la Champagne Méridionale.* Troyes: Dufey-Robert, 1874.

Brassat, Wolfgang. *Tapisserien und Politik. Funktionen, Kontexte und Rezeption eines repräsentativen Mediums.* Berlin: Mann, 1992.

Campbell, Thomas P., et al. Tapestry in the Renaissance: Art and Magnificence, Exh.

---

48 Emile Mâle, 'Le renouvellement de l'art par les 'mystères,'' *Gazette des beaux-arts* 3rd series, 31 (1904): 89–106, 215–230, 283–301, 379–394; Gustave Cohen, 'The Influence of the Mysteries on Art in the Middle Ages,' *Gazette des Beaux Arts*, 1943, 328.

Cat. (New Haven: Yale University Press, 2002

Chipps Smith, Jeffrey. 'Portable Propaganda-Tapestry as Princely Metaphors at the Courts of Philip the Good and Charles the Bold.' *Art Journal* 48 (1989): 123–129.

Cohen, Gustave. 'Rabelais et la légende de Saint-Martin.' In *Etudes d'Histoire du Théâtre en France au Moyen-Age et à la Renaissance*. Paris: Gallimard, 1956.

Delmarcel, Guy. 'L'auteur ou les auteurs en tapisserie: quelques réflexions critiques.' In *Le Dessin sous-jacent dans la peinture IV*, 43–48. Louvain-la-Neuve: Université Catholique de Louvain, Institut Supérieur d'Archéologie et d'Histoire de l'Art, 1982.

Deslandes, Eucher. *Etude sur l'église de Bayeux*. Caen: E. Dominin, 1917.

De Voragine, Jacobus. *The Golden Legend*. Translated by William Granger Ryan. Princeton: Princeton University Press, 2012.

Du Fresne de Beaucourt, G. *Chronique de Mathieu d'Escouchy*. Paris: Renouard, 1864.

Eberlein, Johann Konrad. *Apparatio Regis-revelatio veritatis. Studien zur Darstellung des Vorhangs in der bildenden Kunst von der Spätantike bis zum Ende des Mittelalters*. Wiesbaden: Dr. Ludwig Reichert, 1982.

Erlande-Brandenburg, Alain. *La Tenture de saint Remi, exposée au musée Saint-Remi*. Reims: Centre regional de documentation pédagogique, 1983.

Flodoard. *Ex Historia ecclesiae Remensis Acta Sanctorum*. Paris and Rome: Palmé, 1867.

Froissart, Jean. *Les Chroniques de Sire Jean Froissart*. Edited by J.A.C. Buchon Paris: Au Bureau du Panthéon Littéraire, 1852.

Guignard, Philippe. 'Mémoire fournis aux peintres chargés d'exécuter les cartons d'une tapisserie destinés à la collegiale Saint-Urbain de Troyes, représentant les legends de St. Urbain et Sainte Cécile.' *Mémoires de la Société d'Agriculture, Sciences et Arts de l'Aube* 15 (1849–50): 421–534.

Hérold, Michel. 'Aux sources de l' 'invention': Gaultier de Campes, peintre à Paris au début du XVIe siècle.' *Revue de l'Art* 120 (1998): 49–57.

Hincmar. *Vita Remigii Acta Sanctorum*. Paris and Rome: Palmé, 1867.

Jadart, Henri. 'La vie de saint Remi dans la poésie populaire. Anciens hymnes et proses, le mystère de saint Remi, les tapisseries.' *Travaux de l' Académie National de Reims* 97 (1894–95): 115–169.

Kane, Tina. *The Troyes Mémoire: The Making of a Medieval Tapestry*. Rochester: The Boydell Press, 2010.

Koopmans, Jelle. ed., *Mystère de Saint-Remi*. Geneva: Droz, 1997.

Lacatte-Joltrois. *Histoire et description de l'église de Saint-Remi de Reims*. Reims: P. Dubois, 1868.

Lespinasse, René de and François Bonnardot. eds., *Histoire générale de Paris, les métiers et corporations de la ville de Paris* (*XIIIe siècle, Le Livres des Métiers d'Etienne Boileau*). Paris: Imprimerie Nationale, 1879.

Muel, Francis. *La tenture de l'Apocalypse d'Angers. Cahiers de l'Inventaire*. Nantes: Association pour le développement de l'Inventaire general des monuments et des richesses artistiques en region des Pays de la Loire, 1987.

Nassieu-Maupas, Audrey. 'Peinture, vitrail et tapisserie au début du XVIe siècle: l'exemple du Maître de Montmorency.' *Les Cahiers de la Rotonde* 22 (2000): 45–60.

Nassieu-Maupas, Audrey. 'La tenture de *La Vie de saint Remi* du musée Saint-Remi de Reims.' *Travaux de l'Académie nationale de Reims* 174 (2000): 49–92.

Nassieu-Maupas, Audrey. 'La Vie de saint Jean-Baptiste d'Angers et la production de tapisseries à Paris dans la première moitié du XVIe siècle.' *Revue de l'Art* 145 (2004): 41–53.

Prost, Bernard. 'La tapisserie de Saint-Anatoile de Salins.' *Gazette des beaux-arts* 3.8 (1892): 496–507.

Rapp Buri, Anna and Stucky-Schürer, Monika. *Burgundische Tapisserien*. Munich: Hirmer, 2010.

Sartor, Marguerite. *Les Tapisseries, toiles peintes et broderies de Reims*. Reims: L. Michaud, 1912.

Van Doren, Rombaut. 'Teodorico.' *Bibliotheca Sanctorum* vol. 12 Rome: Istituto Giovanni XXIII (1969): 230–231.

Weigert, Laura. 'Performing the Past.' *Gesta* 38.2 (1999): 154–170.

Weigert, Laura. *Weaving Sacred Stories: French Choir Tapestries and the Performance of Clerical Identity*. Ithaca: Cornell University Press, 2004.

Weigert, Laura. 'Visualizing the Movement of Urban Drama in the Late Middle Ages: the 'Mystère' of the Lord's Vengeance in Reims.' In *Meaning in Movement. The Semantics of Movement in Medieval Art*, edited by Giovanni Freni and Nino Zchomelidse, 161–187. Princeton: Princeton University Press, 2011.

PART II
Commercialisation of Luxury Textiles

4

'Se fist riche par draps de soye' The Intertwinement of Italian Financial Interests and Luxury Trade at the Burgundian Court (1384–1481)[1]

Bart Lambert

'For loans which they have furnished in times of need and necessity, as for the sale and delivery of gold and silver work, jewellery and silk cloth', wrote the Burgundian receiver general in his accounts after having reimbursed a group of Italian merchants in January 1403.[2] For the Burgundian state, which had taken a more definitive shape only twenty years before, both the supply of credit and the purchase of luxury items had always been of paramount importance. Since the revenues from the demesne, the complex of lands and rights held by the prince, were often insufficient and the dream of a permanent contribution from their subjects, based on the example of French royal taxation, was slow in becoming reality,[3] the dukes had to rely on loans both to keep their daily administration running and to set up more ambitious projects such as ducal weddings and military campaigns.[4] The use of luxury goods, such as precious textiles, jewels and objects in gold and silver, had to demonstrate Burgundian wealth and splendour and contribute to the creation of a theatre state, in which state ritual, mostly in a civic setting, visualised the

---

1 The author presented an early version of this paper together with Sophie Jolivet at St Andrews University in 2010. He is grateful to Christine Meek, Francesco Guidi-Bruscoli and Geoff Nuttall for help and advice.

2 Andrée Van Nieuwenhuysen, 'Documents relatifs à la gestion des finances de Philippe le Hardi, duc de Bourgogne et comte de Flandre (1384–1404)', *Bulletin de la Commission Royale d'Histoire* 146 (1980): 290.

3 Marc Boone, 'Les ducs, les villes et l'argent des contribuables: le rêve d'un impôt princier permanent en Flandre à l'époque bourguignonne', in *L'impôt au Moyen Age. L'impôt public et le prélèvement seigneurial (fin XIIe – début XVIe siècle). II. Les espaces fiscaux*, ed. Philippe Contamine, Jean Kerhervé and Albert Rigaudière (Paris: Comité pour l'Histoire Economique et Financière de la France, 2002), 323–41.

4 Jelle Haemers and Bart Lambert, 'Pouvoir et argent. La fiscalité d'Etat et la consommation du crédit des ducs de Bourgogne', *Revue du Nord* 91 (2009): 35–59.

ruling dynasty and convinced urban groups to take part in the Burgundian project.[5] On numerous occasions throughout the Burgundian period, the moneylending business and the trade in luxury goods, that of luxury textiles in particular, at the ducal court were closely connected. They involved the same groups of people, who were able to establish personal relationships with the dukes that were advantageous to both buyers and sellers.

Running in the Family: A Perfect Marriage between Financial and Commercial Interests (1384–1430)

After a series of bankruptcies in the second half of the fourteenth century had ousted the Florentine companies from the foreground of international trade and banking,[6] the dukes of Burgundy had to turn to merchants of the nearby city of Lucca to relieve their financial and commercial needs. This enabled a dynasty of Lucchese businessmen, all of them professionally and personally related, to win over ducal favour and to keep hold of it for the next 45 years. The first and by far the most successful of them was Dino Rapondi. Rapondi had worked his way up in international trade in Bruges and had occasionally provided money to Philip the Bold, younger brother of the French king, during the 1360s and 1370s.[7] The merchant's star rose even higher when Philip succeeded Louis of Male as count of Flanders in 1384: Rapondi was appointed ducal counsellor, would advise his employer in all financial matters and would negotiate innumerable loans. Having moved to Paris, he became the duke's banker in everything but in name, supplying hundreds of thousands of pounds from 1392 onwards, from modest daily advances to colossal credits, and transferring the contributions from the Flemish cities to the ducal treasury. At the same time he sold cartloads of satin, silk cloth, and gold and silver thread to the ducal family, who wore his fabrics on every important occasion.[8]

Upon his death in 1415, Dino's place was taken by his brother Filippo and Bartolomeo Bettini. Bettini was a long-time friend and associate of the family, who had started his career as a clerk in Dino's service in 1413. Together or on their own, he and Filippo, having relocated to Bruges after political circumstances had forced John the Fearless to leave Paris in 1413, rendered numerous financial services to the duke, worth more than £800 groat (gr.),

---

5 Wim Blockmans and Walter Prevenier, *De Bourgondiërs. De Nederlanden op. weg naar eenheid, 1384–1530* (Amsterdam/Leuven: Meulenhoff/Kritak, 1997), 32, 67, 127. Elodie Lecuppre-Desjardin, *La ville des cérémonies : essai sur la communication politique dans les anciens Pays-Bas bourguignons* (Turnhout: Brepols, 2004), passim.

6 Edwin Sydney Hunt, *The Medieval Super-Companies : a Study of the Peruzzi Company of Florence* (Cambridge: Cambridge University Press, 1994), 156–246.

7 Jean Rauzier, *Finances et gestion d'une principauté. Le duché de Bourgogne de Philippe le Hardi 1364–1384* (Paris: Ministère de l'Economie et des Finances, 1996), passim.

8 Bart Lambert, *The City, the Duke and their Banker: The Rapondi Company and the Formation of the Burgundian State (1384–1430)* (Turnhout: Brepols, 2006), 79–141.

and continued to provide silks.[9] After Bettini's death in 1420, Filippo would sell luxury textiles and lend another £5,000 gr. to John the Fearless' successor Philip the Good.[10] However, it was another intimate of the Rapondi family who emerged as the leading Lucchese in ducal service during the 1420s: after having served as a moneylender and a silk supplier at the court of John IV of Brabant, Marco Guidiccioni, executor of Dino's will in 1413, associate of Filippo and husband of their niece Giovanna,[11] eclipsed all competitors by obtaining a near monopoly of ducal silk purchases after 1423 and lending no less than £110,000 gr. between 1420 and 1428. His factor Parente Fava contributed another £23,000 gr. during the next three years.[12] According to an *estat abregie*, an embryonic form of budget, drawn up by the Burgundian administration in 1428, £74,343 13 s. 6 d. of 40 groats or 44.65 per cent of all revenues from the Transport Tax, annuity rents, receivers and bailiffs in the county of Flanders during the years 1425 to 1428 were spent on reimbursing Guidiccioni, another £8,773 6 s. 8 d. of 40 groats or 5.27 per cent on Filippo Rapondi.[13] Because of the debts owed to him, Guidiccioni was even mentioned among the members of the ducal household and the many charitable institutions in Philip the Good's first will, drawn up in 1426.[14]

Dino Rapondi, his brother Filippo, their protégé Bartolomeo Bettini, their in-law Marco Guidiccioni and his factor Parente Fava figured on the Burgundian payrolls as financiers and silk merchants. The links between these activities were manifold and diverse. Although they were usually registered in separate chapters of the ducal accounts, merchants were often reimbursed for loans and silk purchases at the same time. When, sometime before 1420, an overview was made by the ducal administration of all the arrears owed to Bartolomeo Bettini, including no less than 58 payment orders to ducal functionaries and cities, the amounts owed for his deliveries of satin and silk cloth were simply added up with the money owed for his advances.[15] Often, the Lucchese supplied credit and sold silks on the same occasion. In 1404, Dino Rapondi furnished 2,024 *écus* to finance Philip the Bold's funeral and made his brother Jacopo deliver several pieces of gold cloth to decorate the churches where the duke's body would be laid to rest.[16] In 1415, Marco Guidiccioni

9 Michel Mollat, ed., *Comptes généraux de l'Etat bourguignon entre 1416 et 1420* (Paris : Imprimerie Nationale, 1965–9), nos. 266, 583, 949, 970, 984, 1200, 1400–1403, 1436, 1467, 2278, 4083, 4086, 6339–40, 6923, 7590, 7643, 7657, 7789, 8209, 8211, 8791, 8902, 8910, 8919, 8930, 9623, 9665, 9667–8, 9670, 9683, 9691, 9693, 9748, 9793, 9796–7, 9849.

10 Lille, Archives Départementales du Nord (hereafter referred to as ADN), B 1925, f. 76 v. ADN, B 1927, f. 134 v. Claude De Smet, 'Les emprunts de Philippe le Bon, d'après les comptes de la recette générale de l'Etat bourguignon' (Diplôme d'études supérieures: Université de Lille III, 1956), 148.

11 Lambert, *The City, the Duke and their Banker*, 145.

12 De Smet, 'Emprunts de Philippe le Bon', 149–50.

13 Dijon, Archives Départementales du Côte-d'Or, B 488, unfoliated.

14 ADN, B 456, no. 15507.

15 ADN, B 17634, no. 145874.

16 Lambert, *The City, the Duke and their Banker*, 123.

supplied 3,000 *écus* to pay for the tailors who had to cut the costumes for John the Fearless' meeting with the duke of Gloucester[17] and passed the counter again when gold, silver and silk thread were bought to embellish the outfits.[18]

Payments for both credit and silk purchases were either assigned to a local receiver, as in the case of Bettini's debt settlement, or were made using the revenues from the *aides*, the subventions granted by the duke's subjects. Dino Rapondi collected £16,000 of 40 groats for a loan on the *aide* of 1410, Bettini £1,000 for a loan and £360 for silk cloth in 1416, Filippo £10,000 for a loan in 1417, and both Guidiccioni and Filippo £27,630 for loans and silks in 1422–1423.[19] Fully exploiting their position at the Burgundian court, they had also negotiated these *aides* and sometimes even advanced or transferred the money to the ducal treasury: between 1388 and 1407, all Bruges' subventions to Philip the Bold and John the Fearless, or roughly £14,038 gr., passed through the eager hands of Dino Rapondi.[20] In 1445, the same city was still paying off the heirs of Marco Guidiccioni, who had provided similar services until his death in 1430.[21] In short, the Lucchese merchants working for the Burgundian dukes supplied the money to set up ducal projects, sold the luxury textiles that added the necessary splendour, negotiated the contributions that enabled the reimbursement of both their loans and sales and in some cases also carried out their payment. By doing so, they guaranteed the continuity of their own success.

An original way in which the Burgundian administration could make liquidities available, and one in which financial and commercial interests almost completely intertwined, were buy-and-sell-back operations. These kinds of transactions involved the purchase of goods on credit and their immediate resale. They often resulted in a considerable loss, given the short term in which the operation was to take place, but they were still more advantageous than high interest loans.[22] The most frequently bought merchandise included spices, metals and precious cloth, the latter provided exclusively by Lucchese traders. In August 1418, Marco Guidiccioni ordered his factor Parente Fava to supply 85 pieces of silk cloth to the court. After the ducal officials had committed to paying £3,060 of 40 groats for the fabrics at a later date, they sold them on the spot to the Castilian Dyago de Morande for £2,550 of 40 groats, or £510 less than what they owed Guidiccioni. The whole operation had been set up to obtain ready cash to pay back a loan from Venetian, Florentine, Lucchese

---

17 ADN, B 1935, f. 61 v. For the duke's meeting with Gloucester, see Richard Vaughan, *John the Fearless: The Growth of Burgundian Power* (Woodbridge: Boydell Press, 2002), 213.

18 ADN, B 1931, f. 81 v.

19 Antoine Zoete, 'De beden in het graafschap Vlaanderen onder de hertogen Jan zonder Vrees en Filips de Goede (1405–1467)', *Verhandelingen van de Koninklijke Academie voor Wetenschappen, Letteren en Schone Kunsten van België* 149 (1995): 144–5.

20 Lambert, *The City, the Duke and their Banker*, 95–127.

21 Bruges, Stadsarchief, City Accounts, 1445–1446, f. 62 v.

22 Georges Bigwood, *Le Régime juridique et économique du commerce de l'argent dans la Belgique du moyen âge* (Brussels: Maurice Lamertin, 1921–2), 92–3.

and Genoese merchants that had been brokered by Guidiccioni himself and for which Bartolomeo Bettini had stood surety.[23]

It should be stressed, however, that buy-and-sell-back operations were originally an urban practice and were used much more frequently by cities, in particular by the authorities in Bruges at the beginning of the fifteenth century. Here too, Lucchese merchants were active as sellers or buyers. In 1422, Marco Guidiccioni got £670 gr. for 300 pieces of velvet, 27 pieces of sendal, 71 dozens of hoods and 130.5 lb. of fine silk, which Bruges sold on with a loss of £72 19 s. 11 d. gr.[24] The true champion of these purchases on credit was another confidant of the Rapondi clan. Giovanni di Arrigo Arnolfini had made his first steps in business as Marco Guidiccioni's factor and was married to Dino's great niece Giovanna Cenami.[25] Between 1420 and 1422, he was involved in six sales to the city and one to the duke, probably laying the first foundations of his later commercial success. It is remarkable that some of the goods sold were bought back at a lower price by fellow Lucchese. In March 1421, Urbano Domaschi delivered 17 pieces of silk cloth to the city which were then obtained by his compatriot Arnolfini with a profit of £8 3 s. 4 d. gr.[26] Given the small size and the strong interconnectedness of the Lucchese community in Bruges,[27] it seems fair to assume that price agreements were made and that the Lucchese were doing business at the expense of the Bruges tax payer.[28]

The advantages of the strong ties between the moneylending business and the trade in luxury textiles at the Burgundian court were numerous both for the dukes and the merchants involved. Philip the Bold, John the Fearless and Philip the Good knew that they could rely on a limited number of devoted financiers with substantial financial reserves who would damage their own commercial interests by keeping their purses shut, something that was particularly valuable at a time when government finance was considered extremely hazardous. For Dino and Filippo Rapondi, Bartolomeo Bettini, Marco Guidiccioni and Parente Fava, what had begun as a profitable way to invest their idle capital quickly turned into both a core business in its own right and a strategy that enabled them to reinforce their own commercial position. On top of this they were rewarded, or compensated, with often honorary but invariably lucrative offices within the Burgundian administration or parts of the ducal demesne. All of them served as ducal counsellors and all but Fava were appointed *maîtres d'hôtel*.[29] Dino was given the usufruct of the ducal

23 ADN, B 1923, f. 61 r.

24 Bigwood, *Régime juridique*, 132–3, 140–41.

25 ADN, B. 1923, f. 148. Cenami was the niece of Giovanni Rapondi, Dino's nephew.

26 Bigwood, *Régime juridique*, 92 bis, 138–141.

27 At the end of the fourteenth century, the Lucchese community only had about twenty members. Raymond De Roover, 'La communauté des marchands Lucquois à Bruges de 1377 à 1404', *Annales de la Société d'Emulation de Bruges* 86 (1949), 88–9.

28 Interest rates varied from 15 to 24 per cent, making these transactions not automatically cheaper than pure credit operations. Bigwood, *Régime juridique*, 133.

29 Lambert, *The City, the Duke and their Banker*, 93, 154.

Figure 4.1: Statue representing Dino Rapondi, erected by Philip the Good in the ducal Sainte Chapelle in Dijon, Bibliothèque nationale de France, Bibliothèque de l'Arsenal, ms. 3901, c. 22.

lands in Knesselare and pocketed the rights paid on the loading of ballast in the harbour of Sluys, passed on to Filippo in 1415.[30] Bettini collected the tax of two groats on every sealed piece of cloth produced in the Flemish town of Wervik and acquired the shrievalty and the exploitation of the prisons in Courtrai.[31] Guidiccioni was made keeper of the Flemish dunes[32] and Fava was invested with the water bailiwick of Sluys in 1436.[33] At the same time, the Lucchese's commercial success at court reflected positively on their business with other wealthy purchasers: during the second half of the 1380s and the first half of the 1390s, the Rapondi company sold many more luxuries to the duke's French royal relatives, his courtiers and urban political elites.[34]

Following years of reliable service, the relationship between the duke and his suppliers became one of a very personal nature: in 1417 Bartolomeo Bettini was given a quantity of silver for his wedding by John the Fearless.[35] Upon the death of the last of the Rapondi brothers, Philip the Good even ordered a statue representing Dino Rapondi to be erected in the *Sainte Chapelle,* the ducal chapel in Dijon which was usually reserved for members of the ducal family (see Figure 4.1), and a memorial service to be held.[36] This very direct bond cemented an exceptional continuity, with only four closely related businessmen dominating Burgundian finance and silk trade in the Low Countries for more than forty-five years.

After 1430: Lucchese Merchants and Florentine Moneylenders

From 1430 onwards, the mechanism that underpinned Lucchese activities in the Burgundian territories started to fall apart. The Lucchese silk trade at the ducal court continued to flourish: the space left by Marco Guidiccioni was filled by his former attorney in London Paolo Meliani, who, having settled in both Bruges and Antwerp, delivered more than 2,737 ells and 81 pieces of silk cloth, damask and gold cloth between 1428 and 1441, worth more than £27,764 of 40 groats, to the Burgundian duke. Meliani's most fierce competitor, Carlo Gigli, had married Guidiccioni's widow Camilla Cagnoli.[37] He made more

30 Tim Soens, *De rentmeesters van de graaf van Vlaanderen. Beheer en beheerders van het grafelijk domein in de late middeleeuwen* (Brussels: Paleis der Academiën, 2002), 283, 317.

31 ADN, B 1601, f. 88 r.–v., 92 r., 93 r., B 4086, f. 22 v. and B 4088, f. 188 v.

32 Brussels, Algemeen Rijksarchief, Fonds Rekenkamers, I002, 13695, f. 21 r., 35 r., 49 r.

33 Bart Lambert, 'The Political Side of the Coin: Italian Bankers and the Fiscal Battle between Princes and Cities in the Late Medieval Low Countries', in *Economies, Public Finances and the Impact of Institutional Changes in Interregional Perspective: The Low Countries and Neighbouring German Territories (14th-17th Centuries),* ed. Remi W.M. van Schaïk (Turnhout: Brepols, 2015), 109–110.

34 Lambert, *The City, the Duke and their Banker,* 97–102.

35 Mollat, *Comptes Généraux,* no. 266.

36 Lambert, *The City, the Duke and their Banker,* 141, 153.

37 Helen Bradley, 'The Italian Merchants in London c1350–c1450' (PhD diss., Royal Holloway, University of London, 1992), 298–300.

than £36,758 of 40 groats with the sale of 2,010 ells and 82 pieces from 1430 to 1443.[38] Meliani and Gigli supplied the silk cloth for the wedding of Philip the Good and Isabella of Portugal in 1430,[39] for which they were reimbursed £18,000 and £13,438 respectively from the 150,000 nobles *aide* in 1431.[40] Once again the personal relationship the merchants maintained with the duke proved crucial for their business interests. According to a genealogy written by a seventeenth-century descendant, Carlo Gigli could even call himself Philip the Good's friend.[41] During the 1440s, however, Gigli fell out with the prince, his supplies to the court stopped and he left the Low Countries for England, where he obtained English denizenship in 1460.[42]

If merchants of Lucca maintained a firm grip on the silk business, the other component of their pre-1430 activities was lacking. This is not to say Lucchese silk merchants did not furnish credit anymore: Paolo Meliani advanced 4,174 *saluts d'or* to duchess Isabella of Portugal in 1436[43] and accepted the reimbursement for his deliveries at the 1430 wedding to be spread over several years.[44] The systematic and large-scale capital supply, which before 1430 had equalled or even surpassed their silk trade in size, and the mutually beneficial combination of both activities, had disappeared though. Meliani even made a physical distinction between his silk business and his financial affairs: his fabrics were sold in Bruges whereas his loans, including the very occasional ones to the ducal household, were issued in Antwerp.

Highly illustrative in this respect is the career of the aforementioned Giovanni Arnolfini. After having entered the Bruges business world in the footsteps of Marco Guidiccioni,[45] Arnolfini made his first dealings with the court, selling six tapestries to Philip the Good in 1423[46] and luxury fabrics in

---

38 Sophie Jolivet, 'Les Italiens et le commerce de luxe à la cour de Philippe le Bon', *Publications du Centre Européen d'Etudes Bourguignonnes (XIVe–XVIe s.)* 49 (2009): 246–7.

39 For the ducal wedding, see Richard Vaughan, *Philip the Good: The Apogee of Burgundy* (Woodbridge: Boydell Press, 2002), 54–7.

40 Zoete, *Beden in het graafschap Vlaanderen*, 145.

41 'Hebbe amicitia di principi grandi come delli ... duci di Borgogna'. Biblioteca Statale di Lucca, Ms. 1008, Martino Gigli, Descrizione della famiglia dei Gigli copiata da una fatta da me Martino di Martino di Niccolò di Martino Gigli il 1618, f. 19–20.

42 *Calendars of the Patent Rolls Preserved in the Public Record Office: Henry VI. Volume 6: 1452–1461* (London: His Majesty's Stationery Office, 1910), 579.

43 Monique Sommé, *Isabelle de Portugal, duchesse de Bourgogne. Une femme au pouvoir au XVe siècle* (Villeneuve d'Ascq: Presses Universitaires du Septentrion, 1998), 209.

44 Bigwood, *Régime juridique*, 189. ADN, B 1991, f. 170 r. Jolivet, 'Italiens et commerce de luxe', 246.

45 From 1428 to 1431, Arnolfini acted as a factor and representative for Guidiccioni in his dealings with the Burgundian court and before the Ghent bench of aldermen. Ghent, Stadsarchief, Series 301, no. 30, 1428–1429, f. 89 r., no. 31, 1430–1431, f. 74r. Jeanine Ruckebusch, 'Les Finances de Philippe le Bon à l'époque de la paix d'Arras' (Université de Lille III, Diplôme d'études supérieures, 1954), 63.

46 Lorne Campbell, *National Gallery Catalogues: The Fifteenth Century Netherlandish Schools* (London: Yale University Press, 1998), 198.

1424.[47] He ran his own silk shop in the 1430s, became a regular court merchant in 1439 and was appointed ducal counsellor one year later. During the next four years, he ousted all of his competitors until, in 1443, he was the only supplier of luxury textiles left at court. Between 1439 and 1455, Arnolfini sold 19,352 ells and 72 pieces of silk for the staggering amount of £131,568 of 40 groats. Only in 1461, when he deserted Philip the Good's son Charles the Bold and sided with Burgundian archenemy Louis XI of France, would his near monopoly on the ducal purchases of luxury textiles come to an end.[48]

During these same twenty years Arnolfini was recorded in the financial chapters of the ducal accounts only twice. In 1455, he acted as a broker for Bruges merchants who lent £12,000 of 40 groats to the duke[49] and in 1461 he provided £1,200 parisis on his own account.[50] The chronicler Georges Chastellain said that Arnolfini, who, just like Dino Rapondi, was one of the most consulted ducal advisors on financial affairs and who, in 1449, was given the lease of the important Burgundian wool toll in Gravelines, arrived as a pauper in Bruges and made his fortune thanks to his activities in the silk trade.[51] About loans and credit, however, Chastellain did not say a word.

The money needed to run the Burgundian state now came from others, who did not have any involvement in the trade in luxury textiles. Several Genoese merchants provided liquidities, but none of them was able to achieve any prominence.[52] The court also dealt with several autochthonous bankers. Among them, the Bruges brokers Louis and Chrétien Le Bakre, who advanced £106,000 p., including more than £27,000 p. on their own account, and the Burgundian officer Pieter Bladelin or de Leestmaker, are most worth mentioning.[53] From the 1440s onwards, the Florentines moved to the foreground again, spearheaded by the firm of Bernardo Cambi and Forese de Rabatta, who lent over £43,000 p. to the duke.[54] They, and everyone else involved in ducal finance, would soon be completely overshadowed by the Medici company.

If the Florentine Medici family, who were well on their way to become 'the biggest firm' that, according to Burgundian chronicler Philippe de

47 Peter Stabel, *A Capital of Fashion: Luxuries, Guilds and Economic Change in Late Medieval Bruges* (Oxford: Oxford University Press, forthcoming).

48 Jolivet, 'Italiens et commerce de luxe', 247. His reimbursements on the aides between 1445 and 1460 add up to £133,394 of 40 groats. Zoete, *Beden in het graafschap Vlaanderen*, 145.

49 ADN, B 2020, f. 46 r.

50 De Smet, 'Emprunts de Philippe le Bon', 149.

51 'Un marchant de Bruges, Lucois, qui vint audit Bruges, povre compagnon chantre, et se fist riche de deux cent mille florins, par livrer draps de soye en la maison du duc et par tenir le tonlieu de Gravelines'. Joseph Kervyn de Lettenhove, ed., *Oeuvres de Georges Chastellain. Tome Quatrième* (Brussels: Heussner, 1866), 33.

52 De Smet, 'Emprunts de Philippe le Bon', 149–50.

53 De Smet, 'Emprunts de Philippe le Bon', 145–6. For Pieter Bladelin, see Wim De Clercq, Jan Dumolyn and Jelle Haemers, 'Vivre Noblement': Material Culture and Elite Identity in Late Medieval Flanders', *Journal of Interdisciplinary History* 38 (2007): 1–31.

54 De Smet, 'Emprunts de Philippe le Bon', 154.

Commynes, 'had ever existed in this world',[55] were quite reluctant to furnish liquidities to the duke at first, representatives Agnolo Tani and, above all, Tommaso Portinari dropped all prudence from 1457 onwards. They would channel more than £126,000 p. to the *recette générale* from 1444 until the end of Philip the Good's reign,[56] an amount that would only increase under the rule of his money-hungry son and successor. Portinari, christened 'Charles the Bold's Dino Rapondi' by historian Richard Vaughan,[57] spent thousands of pounds on Charles' military campaigns,[58] obtaining ducal counsellorship, the wool toll in Gravelines and the monopoly on the sale of alum in the Low Countries in return.[59]

At the same time, Portinari, who, as Marc Boone has shown, was not afraid to consciously use Medici money to further his own interests,[60] deployed his financial services to gain predominance in the silk trade, in the same way as his Lucchese colleagues had done before him. In a letter to his superior Cosimo de Medici, dated 1 July 1464, the manager justified his long stays with the duke by saying that, for the first time in 85 years, he had been able to break the Lucchese silk monopoly at the Burgundian court. To boost his new business, he even asked permission to hire a new factor who was perfectly fluent in French.[61] In 1468, the year that Charles the Bold married Margaret of York, his supplies, produced by the Medici's own silk manufactures in Italy,[62] already accounted for more than 55 per cent of the ducal expenditure in the accounts of the *argentier*.[63]

Here too, the relationship between the silk merchant and his ducal customer soon became more than just an economic one. In the 1471 contract between Portinari and the Medici company, Lorenzo de Medici explicitly allowed Tommaso to continue to do business with Charles the Bold 'given the virtues and the goodness of this illustrious prince and the affection and familiarity the

---

55 ''La plus grand' maison que ie croy qui iamais ait esté au monde', in Johannes Sleidanus, ed., *Les Mémoires de Messire Philippe de Commines, chevalier, seigneur d'Argenton sur les principaux faits et gestes de Louys XI et Charles VIII, son fils, Rois de France* (Rouen: Iean Berthelin, 1625), 607. The Medici holding had branches in Rome, Naples, Geneva, Bruges and London and interests in very diverse domains of economic life. Raymond De Roover, *The Rise and Decline of the Medici Bank, 1397–1494* (Cambridge, MA: Harvard University Press, 1963), passim.

56 De Smet, 'Emprunts de Philippe le Bon', 153–154. Before 1457, the only loans were one by Bernardo Portinari in 1444, one by Tani in 1450 and one by Francesco Sassetti in 1454.

57 Richard Vaughan, *De Bourgondiërs* (Haarlem: Fibula-Van Dishoeck, 1976), 97.

58 Xavier Maeght, 'Les emprunts de Charles le Téméraire d'après les Comptes de la Recette Générale de l'Etat Bourguignon, et quelques comptes urbains' (Université de Lille III, Diplôme d'études supérieures, 1956), 79–84.

59 Marc Boone, 'Apologie d'un banquier médiéval : Tommaso Portinari et l'Etat bourguignon', *Le Moyen Age* 105 (1999): 38–47. Richard J. Walsh, *Charles the Bold and Italy (1467–1477): Politics and Personnel* (Liverpool: Liverpool University Press, 2005), 129–33.

60 Boone, *Apologie d'un banquier médiéval*, 52–4.

61 Florence, Archivio di Stato, Mediceo Avanti il Principato, filza 73, no. 315.

62 De Roover, *Rise and Decline*, 168–71.

63 Stabel, *Capital of Fashion*.

aforementioned Tommaso Portinari enjoys with his illustrious highness and his court'.[64] Portinari genuinely admired the new ruler and was convinced he would lead the Burgundian House to unprecedented heights.[65] In 1475, in a letter to duke Galeazzo Maria Sforza of Milan, he referred to Charles as 'glorious', 'undefeated' and 'magnificent'.[66] In 1471, Portinari felt that much at home at court that he was considered 'Burgundian' by the Milanese ducal servant Francesco Salvatico.[67] The 'Burgundian's' luck would not last though. Unexpected political circumstances made Portinari spend much more than his employers ever allowed him to and in the end he overplayed his hand. In 1481, after having made more than £17,500 of 40 groats of losses, Lorenzo de Medici ended the partnership and the Bruges branch was dissolved.[68]

The French Civil War, Italian Factional Conflict and the Expansion of the Burgundian State: Why 1430?

The question remains why the link between Lucchese moneylending and silk trade at the Burgundian court was broken around 1430. The impact of the events in France during the first decades of the fifteenth century could have been significant. At the end of the fourteenth century, Philip the Bold had imposed himself as the guardian of the mentally unstable king Charles VI, obtaining the actual rule over the kingdom. From the 1390s onwards, his authority was contested by Charles' younger brother Louis of Orléans, who did everything he could to obstruct the Burgundian duke. When Philip died in 1404, this escalated into an open conflict, which only ended when the new duke John the Fearless had his rival murdered in 1407. The result was a civil war between the Bourguignons, the party of the Burgundian duke, and the Armagnacs, the supporters of Louis of Orléans,[69] which was particularly devastating for the Lucchese community in Paris.

The Lucchese merchants in the capital had been the bankers of choice of the French princes and at the beginning of the fifteenth century each of them

64 'Attesa la virtù e bontà di quello illustrissimo principe e la grazia e familiarità del sopradetto Thommaso Portinari con la sua illustrissima signoria e sua chorte'. Heinrich Sieveking, 'Die Handlungsbücher der Medici', Österreichische Akademie der Wissenshaften, Sitzungsberichte: *Philosophisch-historische Klasse* 151 (1906): 52.

65 Armand Grunzweig, ed., *Correspondance de la filiale de Bruges des Medici* (Bruxelles: Lamertin, 1931), 140.

66 'Glorioso', 'invicto' and 'magnifico'. Ernesto Sestan, ed., *Carteggi diplomatici fra Milano sforzesco e la Borgogna. Volume I* (Roma: Istituto Storico per l'Età Moderna e Contemporanea, 1985), no. 271.

67 'Borgonione'. Joseph Calmette and Georges Périnelle, *Louis XI et l'Angleterre* (Paris: Éditions Auguste Picard, 1930), 327.

68 Boone, 'Apologie d'un banquier médiéval', 47. De Roover, *Rise and Decline*, 274–275.

69 Bertrand Schnerb, *Les Armagnacs et les Bourguignons. La maudite guerre* (Paris: Librairie Académique Perrin, 1988), passim.

was either involved with the Burgundians or with Orléans.[70] The Armagnac supporters lost more than £150,000 tournois following the death of their employer in 1407, the losses in the other camp will not have been much less. The warfare between the two parties, combined with the renewed hostilities with the English from 1415 onwards, halted all commercial activities in Paris. When John the Fearless re-entered the capital in 1418, the businesses of numerous Lucchese Orléans supporters were plundered; some of whom were even killed. By the beginning of the 1420s, the once thriving Lucchese community in Paris had virtually ceased to exist. Several Lucchese families, including the Rapondi, moved to Bruges, which regained its position as the centre of banking and luxury trade.[71] Following the losses incurred in France, however, more than one Lucchese might have been either incapable or unwilling to lend to princes ever again, a handicap their Genoese and Florentine counterparts did not encounter.

More clatter of war, but then in Italy, might have inspired the Lucchese to stop lending to the Burgundian dukes. From the 1370s onwards, internal tensions in Lucca between the supporters of the Guinigi family and the partisans of the Rapondi family had been running high. In 1392, this erupted into a direct confrontation, won by the Guinigi. The victors imposed a dictatorship in the *commune* and banished their rivals from the city.[72] In 1430, around the time when financial activities at the Burgundian court started to slow down, the rule of Paolo Guinigi came to an end and the exiles were allowed to return home. Several of them, including Filippo Rapondi, seem to have done so straight away.[73] It is possible that this renewed interest in their hometown could no longer be combined with both the silk trade – which, after decades of emigration of Lucchese silk workers to other parts of Italy seems to have known a revival in Lucca in the post-Guinigi era[74] – and moneylending in the Low Countries. Is it a coincidence that the Rapondi, who had already been selling large quantities of silks to the Burgundian prince for years, only started supplying credit on a massive scale in 1392, the year they were banished from Lucca?

---

70 Although some, such as Guglielmo Cenami, were able to skilfully manoeuvre between both sides, depending on their economic interests. Florence Berland, 'Les marchands italiens et le duc de Bourgogne à Paris: engagement politique ou intérêts économique? Le cas de Guillaume Cename (v. 1372–v. 1454)', *Publications du Centre Européen d'Etudes Bourguignonnes (XIVe–XVIe s.)* 49 (2009): 227–42.

71 Léon Mirot, 'La colonie lucquoise à Paris du xiiie au xve siècle', *Bibliothèque de l'Ecole des Chartes* 88 (1927): 83–5.

72 Christine E. Meek, *Lucca 1369–1400: Politics and Society in an Early Renaissance City-State* (Oxford: Oxford University Press, 1978), 194–299.

73 Michael E. Bratchel, *Lucca 1430 – 1494: The Reconstruction of an Italian City-Republic* (Oxford: Clarendon Press, 1995), 118.

74 Michael E. Bratchel, 'The silk industry of Lucca in the fifteenth century', in *Tecnica e Società nell'Italia dei Secoli XII–XVI* (Pistoia: Centro Italiano di Studi di Storia e d'Arte, 1987), 189–90.

The end of the massive Lucchese loans could have had a more structural cause as well. It was not only the nature of Lucchese activities in the Low Countries that was changing around 1430. This was also the period in which the Burgundian state underwent an enormous territorial expansion, with the addition of Namur in 1429, Brabant and Limburg in 1430, Hainaut, Holland and Zeeland in 1433 and Luxemburg in 1443. Government institutions were centralised and civil service was professionalised.[75] All this resulted in an explosion of the Burgundian budget,[76] which might have exceeded the capacities of the Lucchese merchant community. The amounts of money needed by the booming Burgundian state had just become too big for men whose first and most important job still was and always had been the trade in silks.

Conclusions

Far more than a mere function of market variables, the trade in luxury textiles at the Burgundian court was part of a wider web of interests. Economic historians such as Raymond De Roover and Yves Renouard could not help being struck by the Lucchese predominance on the Burgundian silk market between 1384 and 1461.[77] In sharp contrast with cities like London or Paris, outside competitors in Bruges had to wait more than 75 years before they were able to breach the Lucchese monopoly in the trade in luxury textiles. Key to this success was a remarkably high level of mutual confidence and personal appreciation between these suppliers and the main consumers of luxuries in the Low Countries, the Burgundian dukes, buttressed by an often kin-based professional continuity and, for 36 of those 75 years, a combination of luxury trade with financial services. It took Tommaso Portinari all these ingredients and the opportunism of Giovanni Arnolfini, who before had competed his fellow Lucchese out of the luxury market, to land the first Florentine silk contract with the Burgundian dukes in 1464. He was able to integrate financial and commercial interests in the way his Lucchese predecessors had done, until his rashness and the political circumstances decided otherwise.

---

75 Vaughan, *Philip the Good*, 29–53.

76 Maurice Arnould, 'Une estimation des revenus et des dépenses de Philippe le Bon en 1445', *Acta Historica Bruxellensia* 3 (1974): 131–219. Michel Mollat, 'Recherches sur les finances des ducs Valois de Bourgogne', *Revue Historique* 219 (1958): 310.

77 De Roover, *Rise and Decline*, 190–1. Yves Renouard, *Les hommes d'affaires italiens du Moyen Age* (Paris: Colin, 1968), 169, 220.

Bibliography

Manuscript Sources

Bruges, Stadsarchief
City Accounts: 1445-1446.
Brussels, Algemeen Rijksarchief
Fonds Rekenkamers, I 002: 13695.
Dijon, Archives Départementales du Côte-d'Or (ACO)
Série B (Chambre des Comptes): 488
Florence, Archivio di Stato
Mediceo Avanti il Principato: filza 73, no. 315.
Ghent, Stadsarchief
Series 301: 30, 31.
Lille, Archives Départementales du Nord (ADN)
Série B (Chambre des Comptes): 456, 1601, 1923, 1925, 1927, 1931, 1935, 1991, 2020, 4086, 4088, 17634
Lucca, Biblioteca Statale
Ms. 1008, Martino Gigli, Descrizione della famiglia dei Gigli copiata da una fatta da me Martino di Martino di Niccolò di Martino Gigli il 1618.

Published Sources

Arnould, Maurice. 'Une estimation des revenus et des dépenses de Philippe le Bon en 1445'. *Acta Historica Bruxellensia* 3 (1974): 131–219.

Berland, Florence. 'Les marchands italiens et le duc de Bourgogne à Paris: engagement politique ou intérêts économique? Le cas de Guillaume Cename (v. 1372–v. 1454)'. *Publications du Centre Européen d'Etudes Bourguignonnes (XIVe–XVIe s.)* 49 (2009), 227–242.

Bigwood, Georges. *Le régime juridique et économique du commerce de l'argent dans la Belgique du moyen âge*. Brussels: Maurice Lamertin, 1921–1922.

Blockmans, Wim and Prevenier, Walter. *De Bourgondiërs. De Nederlanden op. weg naar eenheid, 1384–1530*. Amsterdam/Leuven: Meulenhoff/Kritak, 1997.

Boone, Marc. 'Apologie d'un banquier médiéval: Tommaso Portinari et l'Etat bourguignon'. *Le Moyen Age* 105 (1999): 31–54.

Boone, Marc. 'Les ducs, les villes et l'argent des contribuables: le rêve d'un impôt princier permanent en Flandre à l'époque bourguignonne'. In Philippe Contamine, Jean Kerhervé and Albert Rigaudière, eds., *L'impôt au Moyen Age. L'impôt public et le prélèvement seigneurial (fin XIIe – début XVIe siècle). II. Les espaces fiscaux*. Paris: Comité pour l'Histoire Economique et Financière de la France, 2002, 323–341.

Bradley, Helen. 'The Italian Merchants in London c1350–c1450'. PhD diss., Royal Holloway, University of London, 1992.

Bratchel, Michael E. *Lucca 1430–1494: The Reconstruction of an Italian City-Republic*. Oxford: Clarendon Press, 1995.

Bratchel, Michael E. 'The silk industry of Lucca in the fifteenth century'. In *Tecnica e Società nell'Italia dei secoli XII–XVI*. Pistoia, Centro Italiano di Studi di Storia e d'Arte, 1987.

Calmette, Joseph and Périnelle, Georges. *Louis XI et l'Angleterre*. Paris: Éditions Auguste Picard, 1930.

Campbell, Lorne. *National Gallery Catalogues: The Fifteenth Century Netherlandish Schools*. London: Yale University Press, 1998.

Clough, Cecil H. 'Three Gigli of Lucca in England during the Fifteenth and Early Sixteenth Centuries: Diversification in a Family of Mercery Merchants', *The Ricardian. Journal of the Richard III Society* 13 (2003): 121–147.

De Clercq, Wim, Dumolyn, Jan and Haemers, Jelle. ' "Vivre Noblement": Material Culture and Elite Identity in Late Medieval Flanders'. *Journal of Interdisciplinary History* 38 (2007): 1–31.

De Roover, Raymond. *The Rise and Decline of the Medici Bank, 1397–1494*. Cambridge, MA: Harvard University Press, 1963.

De Roover, Raymond. 'La communauté des marchands Lucquois à Bruges de 1377 à 1404'. *Annales de la Société d'Emulation de Bruges* 86 (1949): 23–89.

De Smet, Claude. 'Les emprunts de Philippe le Bon, d'après les comptes de la recette générale de l'Etat bourguignon'. Université de Lille III, Diplôme d'études supérieures, 1956.

Grunzweig, Armand, ed. *Correspondance de la filiale de Bruges des Medici*. Brussels: Lamertin, 1931.

Haemers, Jelle and Lambert, Bart. 'Pouvoir et argent. La fiscalité d'Etat et la consommation du crédit des ducs de Bourgogne (1384–1506)'. *Revue du Nord* 379 (2009): 35–60.

Hunt, Edwin Sydney. *The Medieval Super-Companies: A Study of the Peruzzi Company of Florence*. Cambridge: Cambridge University Press, 1994.

Jolivet, Sophie. 'Les Italiens et le commerce de luxe à la cour de Philippe le Bon'. *Publications du Centre Européen d'Etudes Bourguignonnes (XIVe–XVIe s.)* 49 (2009): 242–258.

Jolivet, Sophie. 'Pour soi vêtir honnêtement à la cour de monseigneur le duc: costume et dispositif vestimentaire à la cour de Philippe le Bon, de 1430 à 1455'. PhD diss., Université de Bourgogne, 2003.

Lambert, Bart. *The City, the Duke and their Banker: The Rapondi Company and the Formation of the Burgundian State (1384–1430)*. Turnhout: Brepols, 2006.

Lambert, Bart. 'The Political Side of the Coin: Italian Bankers and the Fiscal Battle between Princes and Cities in the Late Medieval Low Countries'. In *Economies, Public Finances and the Impact of Institutional Changes in Interregional Perspective: The Low Countries and Neighbouring German Territories*, edited by Remi W.M. van Schaïk. Turnhout: Brepols, 2015, 103–112.

Maeght, Xavier. 'Les emprunts de Charles le Téméraire d'après les Comptes de la Recette Générale de l'Etat Bourguignon, et quelques comptes urbains'. Université de Lille III, Diplôme d'études supérieures, 1956.

Meek, Christine E. *Lucca 1369–1400: Politics and Society in an Early Renaissance City-State*. Oxford: Oxford University Press, 1978.

Mirot, Léon. 'La colonie lucquoise à Paris du xiiie au xve siècle'. *Bibliothèque de l'Ecole des Chartes* 88 (1927): 50–86.

Mirot, Léon. 'La société des Raponde. Dine Raponde'. *Bibliothèque de l'Ecole des Chartes* 89 (1928): 299–389.

Mollat, Michel, ed. *Comptes généraux de l'Etat bourguignon entre 1416 et 1420*. Paris: Imprimerie Nationale, 1965–9.

Mollat, Michel. 'Recherches sur les finances des ducs Valois de Bourgogne'. *Revue Historique* 219 (1958): 285–321.

Rauzier, Jean. *Finances et gestion d'une principauté. Le duché de Bourgogne de Philippe le Hardi 1364–1384*. Paris: Ministère de l'Economie et des Finances, 1996.

Renouard, Yves. *Les hommes d'affaires italiens du Moyen Age*. Paris: Colin, 1968.

Ruckebusch, Jeanine. 'Les finances de Philippe le Bon à l'époque de la paix d'Arras'. Université de Lille III, Diplôme d'études supérieures, 1954.

Schnerb, Bertrand. *Les Armagnacs et les Bourguignons. La maudite guerre*. Paris: Librairie Académique Perrin, 1988.
Sestan, Ernesto, ed. *Carteggi diplomatici fra Milano sforzesco e la Borgogna*. Roma: Istituto Storico per l'Età Moderna e Contemporanea, 1985–7.
Sleidanus, Johannes, ed. *Les mémoires de Messire Philippe de Commines, chevalier, seigneur d'Argenton sur les principaux faits et gestes de Louys XI et Charles VIII, son fils, Rois de France*. Rouen: Iean Berthelin, 1625.
Soens, Tim. *De rentmeesters van de graaf van Vlaanderen. Beheer en beheerders van het grafelijk domein in de late middeleeuwen*. Brussels: Paleis der Academiën, 2002.
Sommé, Monique. *Isabelle de Portugal, duchesse de Bourgogne. Une femme au pouvoir au XVe siècle*. Villeneuve d'Ascq: Presses Universitaires du Septentrion, 1998.
Spufford, Peter. 'Coinage, Taxation, and the Estates General of the Burgundian Netherlands'. *Anciens pays et Assemblées d'Etats (Standen en Landen)* 40 (1966): 63–88.
Spufford, Peter. *Monetary Problems and Policies in the Burgundian Netherlands, 1433–1496*. Leyden: Brill, 1970.
Stabel, Peter. *Capitals of Fashion: Luxuries, Art and the City*. Cambridge: Cambridge University Press, forthcoming.
Van Nieuwenhuysen, Andrée. *Les finances du duc de Bourgogne Philippe le Hardi (1384–1404). Economie et Politique*. Brussels: ULB, 1984.
Vaughan, Richard. *De Bourgondiërs*. Bussum: Fibula-Van Dishoeck, 1976.
Vaughan, Richard. *John the Fearless: The Growth of Burgundian Power*. Woodbridge: Boydell Press, 2002.
Vaughan, Richard. *Philip the Good: The apogee of Burgundy*. Woodbridge: Boydell Press, 2002.
Walsh, Richard J. *Charles the Bold and Italy (1467–1477): Politics and Personnel*. Liverpool: Liverpool University Press, 2005.
Zoete, Antoine. 'De beden in het graafschap Vlaanderen onder de hertogen Jan zonder Vrees en Filips de Goede (1405–1467)'. *Verhandelingen van de Koninklijke Academie voor Wetenschappen, Letteren en Schone Kunsten van België* 149 (1995), 1–275.

5

Florence, Nuremberg and Beyond: Italian Silks in Central Europe during the Renaissance

Francesco Guidi-Bruscoli

This chapter will mainly focus on the export of Florentine luxury textiles to Central Europe in the first half of the sixteenth century. The German area was not the main market for silks woven in Florence, which found rich buyers in many areas, from Western Europe to the Levant. But from the fourteenth century Nuremberg had begun to gain importance as a local and international market, partly because of its position at the crossroads of major European land routes. Towards the end of the fifteenth century the town reached the peak of its success, and at that point Florentine merchants (among others) increased their presence in that market, while at the same time starting to look towards Poland.

Only limited evidence concerning the activities of Florentines in Central European towns can be found in German archives, in the form of notarial acts, minutes from trials and lists of expenses written during the fairs. The latter, however, only establish the presence of a merchant at a fair, and nothing more, although it is not always easy to identify the people, whose names have been 'Germanised'. However, the Stadtarchiv of Nuremberg, especially the *Libri Conservatorii* collection, contains some scattered mentions of Italian merchants active in town during the first half of the sixteenth century.[1]

On the Florentine side sources are richer and more detailed, especially in two archives: the State Archive of Florence and the Bartolini family private archive, which hold letters, sent and received, and accounts or receipts, though no ledger kept directly in Nuremberg has survived. The material in

---

1 See, for example, Kurt Weissen, 'I mercanti italiani alle fiere tedesche nel tardo medioevo', in Simonetta Cavaciocchi (ed.), *Fiere e mercati nella integrazione delle economie europee, secc. XIII-XVIII*, Proceedings of the 'Trentaduesima Settimana di Studi dell'Istituto Internazionale di Storia economica F. Datini', Prato, 8–12 May 2000, ed. Simonetta Cavaciocchi (Florence: Le Monnier, 2001), 900–901.

the Florentine State Archive allows research in particular on two companies (the Olivieri and Saliti), and on their long-term partners in the silk trade: the Torrigiani, Acciaioli, Bartolini, Bonsi, Carletti and Talani. Sources concerning the Olivieri are found in the *Galli Tassi* collection.[2] The *Compagnie religiose soppresse da Pietro Leopoldo* collection contains a series of documents produced in Germany such as balance sheets, statements, lists of merchandise and letters. These missives (about 120 for the period 1534–56) were either sent to Florence, or to/from representatives of the Bartolini-Saliti company within Germany (e.g. Frankfurt to Nuremberg or vice versa).[3] A mass of information on the latter company can also be found in the Bartolini archive, which contains several sources belonging to the commercial firms of the family in the sixteenth century: in particular, there are 46 letters written from Florence to Nuremberg or Vienna (1529–43), in addition to a series of accounts of Gherardo Bartolini & Partners *battilori* (manufacturers of gold thread), who also dealt with Germany.[4] In total the letters from the last two groups amount to about 160, sent between Florence and Nuremberg (especially), Frankfurt, Leipzig or Vienna in the period 1529–56. The letters of the *Compagnie religiose soppresse* collection are the originals sent to Florence and then bound into folders; the letters kept in the Bartolini archive are the copies of those sent to Germany. Interestingly they concern the same company and people, though only occasionally do they overlap chronologically.

It is beyond the scope of this article to write a history of Florentine activity in Central Europe during the late Middle Ages, for which we refer to the existing bibliography.[5] One problem is the lack of quantitative data: several studies carried out by Italian and German scholars assess the presence in Nuremberg of merchants from the peninsula through time, but they tell us very little about their commercial activities, apart from general comment. The best of these studies are by Kurt Weissen who drew on both German and Italian sources and covered both the fourteenth and fifteenth centuries.[6] Another field of research, for a slightly later period, deals with the social and

---

2 Florence, Archivio di Stato (ASF), *Galli Tassi*, 1824, 1926, 1959–1962, 2294.

3 ASF, *Compagnie Religiose Soppresse da Pietro Leopoldo (CRSPL)*, 2037.

4 Archivio Bartolini, vols 243, 246 and 255. Already from the first half of the fifteenth century *setaioli* (silk manufacturers) began to invest in companies of *battilori*; by the end of the century 'many battiloro companies were indistinguishable from manufacturers of silk cloth, some identifying themselves as companies of both or alternatively as battilori and setaioli': Richard A. Goldthwaite, *The Economy of Renaissance Florence* (Baltimore: The Johns Hopkins University Press, 2009), 312.

5 The most complete work on Florentines in Germany is the – unfortunately – yet unpublished thesis by Kurt Weissen, 'Florentiner Bankiers und Deutschland (1275 bis 1475). Kontinuität und Diskontinuität wirtschaftlicher Strukturen' (Habilitationsschrift, University of Basel, 2001). Accessed June 21, 2011. http://kweissen.ch/docs/weissen%20-%20 2000%20-%20Habil%20-%20ganz.pdf. The only discussion on the trade between Florence and Germany and its significance within the economic history of Late Medieval and Early Modern Florence can be found in Goldthwaite, *Economy of Renaissance Florence*, 194–202.

6 Weissen, 'I mercanti italiani', 887–908; Kurt Weissen, 'I mercanti italiani e le fiere in Europa centrale alla fine del Medioevo e agli inizi dell'età moderna', in Paola Lanaro (ed.),

religious integration during the time of the Reformation.[7] But very few works have looked closely at the economic activity of these merchants and most of these articles have drawn solely on Florentine sources, where presumably even more material could be found.[8] Apart from a few names (Agli, Macci) in the fourteenth century, and one or two particularly active agents in the first half of the following century (e.g. Gherardo Bueri), it is not possible to see an established presence of Florentines in Germany until the 1470s, when merchants such as Benvenuto di Daddo Aldobrandi and Lorenzo di Giovanni Villani moved to Nuremberg. In the early sixteenth century the list of names becomes richer, with the addition of more or less illustrious Florentine families: from the better known Antinori and Torrigiani, to the less familiar Acciaioli, Bonsi, Carletti, Lapi, Nobili, Olivieri, Saliti, Talani and Villani. Some of them worked for one company only, others for several companies belonging either to their family or to compatriots before establishing their own firms. For some of these merchants we can only ascertain a presence in Nuremberg or at the fairs of Frankfurt and Leipzig; for others we have more abundant sources, allowing us to study their commercial activities.

In 1512 Zanobi Saliti and Bernardo Acciaioli created an *accomandita* (limited partnership) with the agreement that the latter should move to Germany. Clearly business was profitable, because by 1515 the two decided to develop a closer business relationship, founding a commercial company styled Bernardo Acciaioli and Bernardo (di Zanobi) Saliti & Partners. The company was renewed in 1518 with a capital of 6,500 florins. In 1527 there is evidence of the existence of two companies, one in Florence (Piero and Giovan Battista Saliti & Partners) and one in Nuremberg (the heirs of Zanobi Saliti & Partners). It is interesting that the capital of the Florentine company (9,000 florins) was to be

---

La pratica dello scambio, Sistemi di fiere, mercanti e città in Europa (1400–1700) (Venice: Marsilio, 2003), 161–176.

7 See, for example, Rita Mazzei, 'Convivenza religiosa e mercatura nell'Europa del Cinquecento. Il caso degli italiani a Norimberga', in *La formazione storica della alterità. Studi di storia della tolleranza nell'età moderna offerti a Antonio Rotondò, promossi da H. Méchoulan, R. H. Popkin, G. Ricuperati, L. Simonutti* (3 vols, Florence: Olschki, 2001), vol. 1, 395–428; and also her wider analysis, Rita Mazzei, *La trama nascosta. Storie di mercanti e altro (secoli XVI-XVII)* (Viterbo: Sette Città, 2006).

8 Francesco Guidi-Bruscoli, 'Der Handel mit Seidenstoffen und Leinengeweben zwischen Florenz und Nürnberg in der ersten Hälfte des 16. Jahrhunderts', *Mitteilungen des Vereins für Geschichte der Stadt Nürnberg*, 86 (1999), 81–113; Francesco Guidi-Bruscoli, 'Drappi di seta e tele di lino tra Firenze e Norimberga nella prima metà del Cinquecento', *Archivio Storico Italiano*, CLIX (2001): 359–394; Marco Spallanzani, 'Le compagnie Saliti a Norimberga nella prima metà del Cinquecento (un primo contributo dagli archivi fiorentini)', in Jürgen Schneider (ed.), *Wirtschaftskräfte und Wirtschaftswege. Festschrift für Hermann Kellenbenz* (5 vols, Nuremberg: Klett-Cotta, 1978–81), vol. 1, *Mittelmeer und Kontinent*, 603–620; Marco Spallanzani, 'Tessuti di seta fiorentini per il mercato di Norimberga intorno al 1520', in *Studi in memoria di Giovanni Cassandro* (3 vols, Rome: Ministero per i beni culturali e ambientali, Ufficio centrale per i beni archivistici, 1991), vol. 3, 995–1016. See also Bruno Dini, 'L'economia fiorentina e l'Europa centro-orientale nelle fonti toscane', *Archivio Storico Italiano*, CLIII (1995): 633–655, reprinted in Bruno Dini, *Saggi su una economia-mondo. Firenze e l'Italia fra Mediterraneo ed Europa (secc. XIII-XVI)* (Pisa: Pacini, 1995), 271–288.

sent from Germany and that the capital of the Nuremberg company (10,000 florins) consisted entirely of goods (i.e. silks). Both companies were soon closed, however, because Piero Saliti was not sending money from Germany. Nevertheless, a few years later Saliti was still active in Nuremberg, this time in association with Gherardo Bartolini, a *battiloro*, and with Francesco Carletti, a *setaiolo* (silk manufacturer), both active in Florence.[9]

Raffaello Torrigiani was in Frankfurt as early as 1515. Soon after, he created a company in Nuremberg with Iacopo Bettoni and Alessandro Antinori, and a company in Florence with Ridolfo Torrigiani, which had the export of Florentine silks to Germany as one of its main aims. In 1521 the Nuremberg company was also styled Raffaello and Ridolfo Torrigiani & Partners; it was renewed in 1526 and Giovanni Olivieri, who had previously acted as an employee, was now promoted to partner and manager. In the same way as the Saliti, the Torrigiani also had as their capital silks worth 4,200 florins. In 1531 Olivieri again appeared in the firm's trading name, but this was just the prelude to disagreements between the Torrigiani and their partners, which came to a head in 1536. The Torrigiani, however, continued business in Nuremberg until 1612, providing an impressive example of continuity (one century of uninterrupted activity), even after the Reformation, when Nuremberg became a Lutheran city and attempts were made, also by the Papacy, to force them out of the town.[10]

Giovanni di Piero Olivieri began his business career in Florence in the 1510s, as an employee of Paolo and Amadio Del Giocondo. He then moved to Nuremberg, where as we have seen he collaborated with the Torrigiani. Towards the end of the 1530s he became a partner of his cousin, Michele di Paolo Olivieri, in a company based in Florence. At the same time, Michele also opened a business in Naples together with his brother Alessandro, who had been active in the South of Italy for some years. The Neapolitan company had branches in Cosenza (Donato di Michele Olivieri and Francesco Vecchietti & Partners) and in L'Aquila (Paolo di Michele Olivieri and Giandonato Barbadori & Partners). Eventually, in 1542, the Florentine and Neapolitan companies joined forces in order to create a partnership in Nuremberg. This organisation, revolving around the Naples–Florence–Nuremberg axis, was the key to Olivieri's success because it provided the perfect network for a business concentrated on the coordinated trade in raw materials and finished products.[11]

---

9 Spallanzani, 'Le compagnie Saliti a Norimberga', 603–620.

10 Guidi-Bruscoli, 'Drappi di seta e tele di lino', 361–368; Mazzei, 'Convivenza religiosa e mercatura', 403–420.

11 Guidi-Bruscoli, 'Drappi di seta e tele di lino', 368–372.

Trade

The companies in Florence were the intermediaries and coordinators of the North-South trade. They had representatives (if not sister companies) in Nuremberg and, through their network, they could obtain the raw silk from the South of the Italian peninsula. In some cases, such as the Olivieri's, the companies of Florence and Naples provided the capital for the Nuremberg company; in other cases, such as the Torrigiani or the Saliti, there were firms of *setaioli* or *battilori* directly connected to the company in Germany.

Raw Silk from the Kingdom of Naples

The greatest share of the raw silk used by the Florentine manufacturers throughout the sixteenth century came from outside Tuscany, despite the attempts, made first by the Republican government and then by the Medici Grand Dukes, to make the region as self-sufficient as possible. Our data, mainly concerning the 1540s, show a dominance of silk from Calabria: this confirms the data of Roberta Morelli, who studied the registers of various Florentine silk manufacturers in the sixteenth century and noticed a preponderance of silk from Messina up to the 1540s, then the emergence of silk from Calabria around mid-century, and eventually the progressive increase in the import of North-Eastern ('vicentina') silk from the 1570s.[12]

It was therefore not by chance that in the South of Italy, as we have seen, the Olivieri had branches in L'Aquila and Cosenza, staffed and financed by the Neapolitan company.[13] The raw silk from those areas was shipped to Florence on the initiative of the local company, sometimes on behalf of the Olivieri company of Nuremberg (see Table 5.1). It was then delivered to Florentine *setaioli,* who wove it into finished silks or cloths of gold/silver; in the latter case, the precious metal could have come from Germany itself as part-payment for the silks sent northwards. For example, in the period September–November 1545, the Olivieri of Florence sold to Florentine *setaioli,* on behalf of the Olivieri of Nuremberg, 2,350 lbs (760–800 kg.) of raw silk, to the value of

12 Roberta Morelli, *La seta fiorentina nel Cinquecento* (Milan: Giuffrè, 1976), 34–39. Calabria was by far the most important land of origin of raw silk for the Martelli-Del Giocondo company still in 1584–91, accounting for one third of the total, the second being Tuscany with 18%. Richard A. Goldthwaite, 'Le aziende seriche e il mondo degli affari a Firenze alla fine del '500', *Archivio Storico Italiano,* CLXIX (2011): 291–292.

13 Incidentally, Nuremberg merchants had direct connections with L'Aquila (and Bari), where they bought saffron for the German market: Rainer Gömmel, 'Die Vermittlerrolle Nürnbergs zwischen Italien und Deutschland vom Spätmittelalter bis zum 18. Jahrhundert aus wirtschaftshistorischer Sicht', in *Nürnberg und Italien. Begegnungen, Einflüsse und Ideen,* ed. Volker Kapp et al. (Tübingen: Stauffenburg Verlag, 1991), 41. For a more detailed account on the export of saffron to Germany see Kurt Weissen, 'Safran für Deutschland. Kontinuität und Diskontinuität mittelalterlicher und früneuzeitlicher Warenbeschaffungsstrukturen', in *Beschaffungs- und Absatzmärkte oberdeutscher Firmen im Zeitalter der Welser und Fugger,* ed. Angelika Westermann et al. (Husum: Matthiesen Verlag, 2011), 61–78.

4,920 ducats; the *setaioli* paid this sum (plus 141 ducats of expenses) partly in cash and partly in silks, as we shall see.[14]

Table 5.1 Raw silk sent from Calabria to Florence, on behalf of the Olivieri of Nuremberg (Sept–Nov 1545)
1 ducat = 7 *lire di piccioli*

date	**place of origin**	**weight in lbs**	**unit price in *lire di piccioli***	**buyers**	**total price in ducats**
07-09-45	Torre e Squillace	236.50	14.65	P. Gondi and P. Velluti & co.	495.66
07-09-45	Montalto	215.35	14.20	Giovanni Mormorai & co.	437.32
07-09-45	Montalto	217.00	14.25	Paolo Tolomei & co.	441.75
23-09-45	Montalto	240.35	14.20	Rinaldo Corsini & co.	488.04
24-09-45	Montalto	240.30	14.25	Gherardo Barbadori & co.	489.59
26-09-45	Montalto	239.55	14.20	Cristofano Bucetti & co.	486.69
24-10-45	Montalto	241.35	14.25	Paolo Tolomei & co.	491.79
24-10-45	Montalto	241.05	14.20	Jacopo Sangalletti & co.	489.05
24-10-45	Licatura	242.40	16.00	Bastiano Antinori & co.	554.67
23-11-45	Licatura	235.25	16.20	Paolo Tolomei & co.	544.82
total	**10 bales**	**2,349.10**			**4,919.38**

Source: ASF, *Galli Tassi*, 2294, fol. 230*d*.

Occasionally the raw silk owned by partnerships between companies from Florence, Nuremberg and the Kingdom of Naples was sent directly to Nuremberg, where it was presumably used to embellish locally produced tapestries and wall hangings.

[14] The silk from Calabria, which was mainly used for the velvet's weft, was the least expensive on the Florentine market: this was true a century earlier (the price being florins 1 5s per lb. if paid in cash and florins 1 12s if given in exchange for other merchandises) and forty years later, when the average price was 18.22 *lire* per lb. (Florence Edler de Roover, 'Andrea Banchi, Florentine Silk Manufacturer and Merchant in the Fifteenth Century', *Studies in Medieval and Renaissance History*, 3 (1966): 239; Goldthwaite, 'Le aziende seriche', 292).

Plate 1 Andrea Mantegna, *The Encounter*, Camera degli Sposi, West Wall, Palazzo Ducale, Castello San Giorgio, Mantua. Used with permission of the Archivio di Stato di Mantova and the Ministero dei Beni e delle

Plate 2 Andrea Mantegna, *The Court*, Camera degli Sposi, North Wall, Palazzo Ducale, Castello San Giorgio, Mantua. Used with permission of the Archivio di Stato di Mantova and the Ministero dei Beni e delle Attività Culturali e del Turismo.

Plate 3 Simon von Taisten, *Mary's Death and the Donors Leonhard von Görz and Paula Gonzaga*, Chapel Schloss Bruck, Lienz. Used with permission of the Museum Schloss Bruck.

Plate 4 Simon von Taisten, *The Miracle of the Cross of St. Elisabeth of Thüringen* (detail), Museum der Stadt Lienz, Schloss Bruck, Lienz. Inv. Used with permission of the Museum Schloss Bruck.

Plate 5 Portrait of Robert de Lenoncourt, Panel 10 of the *Life of Saint Remigius*, Reims, Musée de Saint Remi (detail). Copyright Camara StudioDVL, Reims, France.

Plate 6 *Lives of Piat and Eleutherius* (detail), Tournai, Notre-Dame Cathedral. Copyright KIK-IRPA, Brussels.

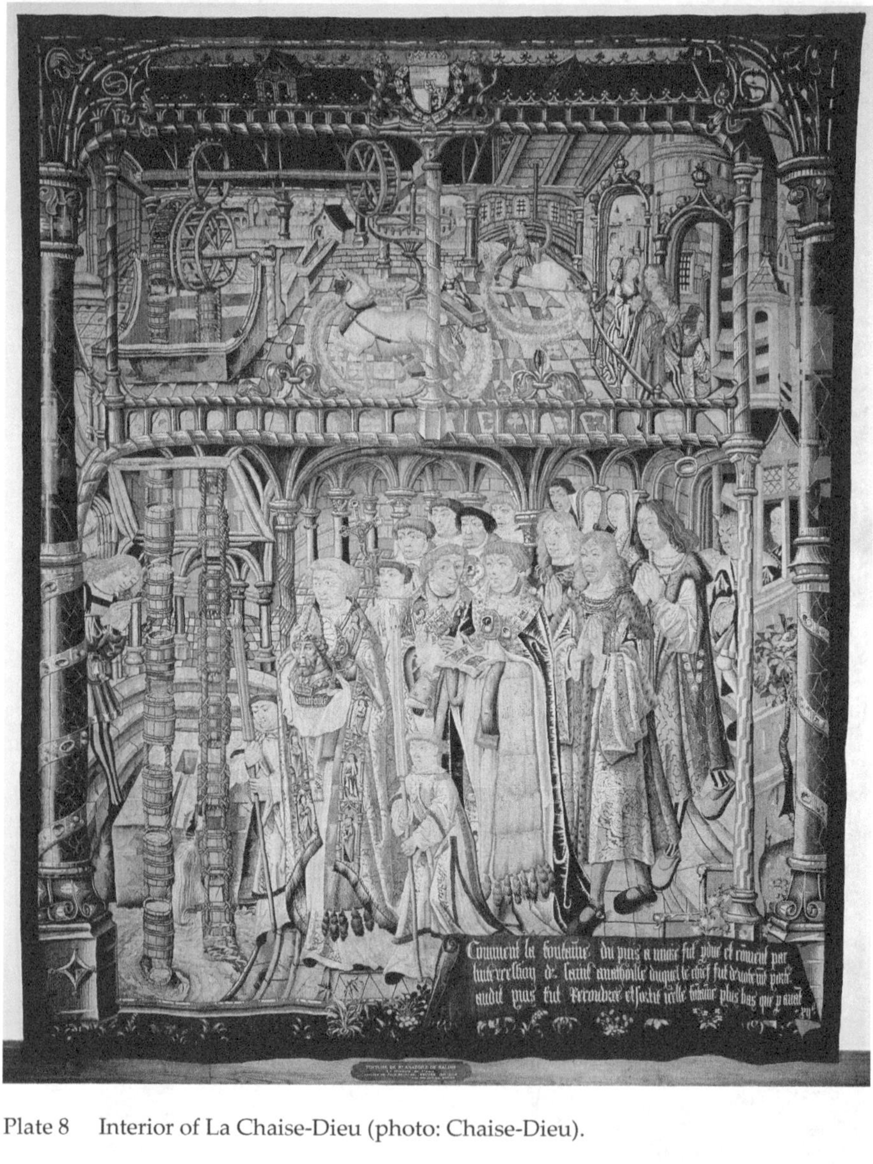

Plate 8 Interior of La Chaise-Dieu (photo: Chaise-Dieu).

Plate 9 Panel 3 of the *Life of Saint Remigius*, Reims, Musée de Saint Remi. Copyright Camara StudioDVL, Reims, France.

Plate 10 Panel 8 of the *Life of Saint Remigius*, Reims, Musée de Saint Remi. Copyright Camara StudioDVL, Reims, France.

Plate 11 Detail of panel 8 of the *Life of Saint Remigius*, Reims, Musée de Saint Remi. Copyright Camara StudioDVL, Reims, France.

Plte 12 Panel 9 of the *Life of Saint Remigius*, Reims, Musée de Saint Remi. Copyright Camara StudioDVL, Reims, France.

Plate 13 Panel 10 of the *Life of Saint Remigius*, Reims, Musée de Saint Remi. Copyright Camara StudioDVL, Reims, France.

Plate 14 Chasuble with embroidered scene of the Passion, Genoese velvet embroidered with dyed silk and gold thread, c.1530, Maagdenhuis, Antwerp. Copyright KIK-IRPA, Brussels

Plate 15 Large leaf verdure with Hercules killing the Stymphalian birds, Wool & silk, 1541–1560, Provinciebestuur Oost–Vlaanderen, Ghent. Copyright KIK-IRPA, Brussels.

Plate 16 The Mechelen cloth hall in the first half of the 19th century Jan-Baptist De Noter, *Mechelen Cloth Hall*, Collection Schoeffer, City Archives Mechelen. Copyright City Archives Mechelen-www.beeldbankmechelen.be.

Plate 17 Sandro Botticelli, *Portrait of a Young Man*, 1485, Private Collection.

Plate 18 Domenico Ghirlandaio, *Stories of Saint Francis (detail)*, 1485, Santa Trinita, Sassetti Chapel, Florence. Used with permission of the Ministero dei Beni e delle Attività Culturali e del Turismo.

Plate 19 School of Agnolo Gaddi, *Stories of Saint Nicholas (detail)*, circa 1385, Santa Croce, Castellani Chapel, Florence. Used with permission of the Fondo Edifici di Culto, Ministero dell' Interno.

Florentine Silks

Florentine silks were sold on many markets but their quality differed according to their destination: for example, cloths going to London and Antwerp were only rarely of the highest quality, whereas Hungary and the Levant mainly attracted heavy cloths or cloths of gold. Lyon, Central Europe and Spain stood somewhat in the middle, with variety in quality as the major feature.[15]

The silk cloths were sent to Germany following detailed requests made by the representatives of the Florentine companies in Nuremberg. They were then sold there, at the company's warehouse, or at the fairs of Frankfurt and Leipzig.[16] The quantities kept in stock are impressive: according to a 1519 inventory, the Acciaioli-Saliti warehouse contained 9,559.18 Florentine *braccia* (more than 5,000 metres) of silk cloth worth as much as 17,000 Rheinish florins or 12,500 Florentine florins, which was about eight times the annual production of Iacopo di Tedesco, presumably the most important silk-weaver of Florence during those years.[17] One can assume a seasonality in the stocks: this inventory was drawn just after Leipzig's Easter fair and it is therefore likely that the stock in the warehouse was at a below-average level. In 1527 Piero Saliti transferred 2,380.5 *braccia* (=1,389.26 metres, of which 859 were damasks) plus 128 pieces of camelot, to the value of 6,820 Rheinish florins to the 'new' company.[18] In order to meet the tastes of its clients, each company had cloths of a large variety in stock, with a wide range of

---

15 Morelli, *La seta fiorentina*, 88–90. In mid-fifteenth century the Geneva fairs would be the place where Florentine silks were sold to rich South-German merchants, who seemed to prefer them to the Venetian silks: Florence Edler de Roover, *L'Arte della seta a Firenze nei secoli XIV e XV* (Firenze: Olschki, 1999), 109. For a synthesis of the trends of the Florentine silk production and export in the sixteenth century see Sergio Tognetti, *Un'industria di lusso al servizio del grande commercio internazionale. Il mercato dei drappi serici e della seta nella Firenze del Quattrocento* (Florence: Olschki, 2002), 39–42, and Jordan Goodman, 'Tuscan Commercial Relations with Europe, 1550–1620: Florence and the European Textile Market', in *Firenze e la Toscana dei Medici nell'Europa del '500* (3 vols, Florence: Olschki, 1983), vol. 1, *Strumenti e veicoli della cultura. Relazioni politiche ed economiche*, 337–338.

16 On these fairs and on their importance, see for example: Nils Brübach, *Die Reichsmessen von Frankfurt am Mein, Leipzig und Braunschweig (14.-18. Jahrhundert)* (Stuttgart: Franz Steiner Verlag, 1994) (there are few mentions of Florentine merchants at 191–93, 432); Michael Rothmann, *Die Frankfurter Messen in Mittelalter* (Stuttgart: Franz Steiner Verlag, 1997); Herbert Eiden, 'The Fairs of Leipzig and the Eastern European Economies (15th-18th centuries)', in Cavaciocchi (ed.), *Fiere e mercati*, 723–739. Some useful information also in the already cited works by Kurt Weissen (see footnote 6). The Frankfurt fairs were the main reference point for trade with the West and the South, whereas the Leipzig fairs attracted trade towards Eastern Europe.

17 Spallanzani, 'Tessuti di seta fiorentini', 997–998, 1006; on Jacopo di Tedesco's production see Richard A. Goldthwaite, 'An Entrepreneurial Silk Weaver in Renaissance Florence', *I Tatti Studies*, 10 (2005): 82. The Florentine *braccio* was equivalent to 0.5836 mt. In 1553 the inventory of the Milanese Giovanni Antonio Orombelli shows that his warehouses contained 13,175 Milanese *braccia* of silks and 4,827 *braccia* of cloths of gold (the Milanese *braccio* being equivalent to 0.5949 mt); but he was presumably the most important silk merchant-entrepreneur of Milan (Aldo De Maddalena, '"Excolere vitam per artes". Giovanni Antonio Orombelli mercante auroserico milanese del Cinquecento', in Aldo De Maddalena, *Dalla città al borgo. Avvio di una metamorfosi economica e sociale nella Lombardia spagnola* (Milan: Franco Angeli, 1982), 36, 41.

18 Spallanzani, 'Le compagnie Saliti a Norimberga', 615.

prices, from the *arricciati,* woven with gold thread and valued at as much as 16 florins per *braccio,* to the far less expensive *ermisini* or *taffetà,* which rarely reached one florin per *braccio.* It is not the aim of this article to go into too much detail, but it is important to point out the variety of products. The list includes *altobassi, arricciati,* baldachins, brocades and *broccatelli,* camelots, damasks, *ermisini,* satins, *telette, taffettà,* velvets and *zetani;* they were dyed with a single colour or a combination of colours (sometimes one for the warp the other for the weft). Moreover, the cloths could be in one or two *camini, alla piana, a poste,* with old or new *opera,* have more or less water, or could be identified with a specific regional type (*alla fiorentina, alla genovese, alla lucchese* or *alla veneziana*), even if they were produced elsewhere. After mid-sixteenth century the Florentine output would tend to concentrate on the lower scale of the production, with light silks like *taffetà, ermisini* and *rasi* accounting for the lion's share of the production.[19]

More rarely the letters describe the decoration: flowers, pomegranates,[20] pine cones, small leaves and nests are sometimes mentioned. In one case a light blue *altobasso* had to be embellished 'on each side' with 'two gilded letters, decorated by some golden images, B D, according to the sample we sent to you'.[21] But another motif recurs and was clearly successful for decades: in 1537 Piero Saliti wrote to Carletti to ask him among other things for 'big flowers […] with the big capers, in the style of the Lucchese […] and they are much appreciated'.[22] About twenty years later, in 1555, another letter was sent to Florence with an even more precise description, which is accompanied by a drawing: as Villani wrote in this letter, 'it is a decoration that people here appreciate'.[23] The proof of the long-standing appreciation of this motif can be seen in a series of German paintings, where different types of cloths, but with the same motif, recur from the 1510s.[24]

---

19 Tognetti, *Un'industria di lusso,* 40–41.

20 Silks with a pomegranate decoration were exported to Germany since at least the mid-fifteenth century: see for example Hans Pleydenwurff's portrait of Georg, Count von Löwenstein: *Gothic and Renaissance Art in Nuremberg, 1300–1550* (New York and Munich: Metropolitan Museum of Art and Germanischen Nationalmuseums, 1986), 170–171 no. 41. They were also imitated in the local production of tapestries and wall-hangings, Ibid., pp. 200, 208–209 nos 58, 68, 69. On the pomegrate motif see for example: Rosalia Bonito Fanelli, 'The Pomegranate Motif in Italian Renaissance Silks: a Semiological Interpretation of Pattern and Color', in Simonetta Cavaciocchi (ed.), *La seta in Europa, secc. XIII-XX,* Proceedings of the 'Ventiquattresima Settimana di Studi dell'Istituto Internazionale di Storia economica F. Datini', Prato, 4–9 May 1992 (Florence: Le Monnier, 1993), 507–30.

21 ASF, *CRSPL,* 2037, fols 182*r*, 191*v*, 195*r*, 213*r*: Piero Saliti, in Nuremberg and Leipzig, to Francesco Carletti, in Florence, 2 February, 16 April, 21 July 1537 and 5 June 1538.

22 ASF, *CRSPL,* 2037, fol. 183*v*: Piero Saliti, in Leipzig, to Francesco Carletti, in Florence, January 1537.

23 Spallanzani, 'Le compagnie Saliti a Norimberga,' 610 (drawing), 616 (description).

24 See, for example, Lucas von Cranach's portrait of Weißenfels' mayor of 1515 (*Gemäldegalerie Berlin: Gesamtverzeichnis der Gemälde. Complete Catalogue of the Paintings* (London: Weidenfeld & Nicolson, 1986), 25, 107 no. 61), Conrad Faber von Creuznach's portrait of Johann Reiss of 1529 (Wolfgang Brücker, *Conrad Faber von Creuznach* (Frankfurt am Main: Kramer, 1963), 164 no. 10) and Bartholomaeus Bruyn's portrait of a gentleman of 1534 (*Gemäldegalerie Berlin,* 19, 97 no. 31).

The orders were very precise, but were not always followed as desired: more than once Saliti complained about the quality of the products he received from Italy. Sometimes he was concerned about the thickness of the gold thread: 'we do not like any of the silks of the last chest you have sent […] moreover, the *telette a uno oro* have such a thick weft and such a thin gold thread that we can barely see it. Make them more beautiful, with better silk and with thicker gold thread!' On other occasions the complaints concerned the quality of the colours: 'it seems to me that your production is getting worse; […] make sure you do not use bad colours'. But reproaches could in general point out the fact that the producer in Florence had not followed the detailed instructions: 'I cannot avoid telling you that, among the damasks you produce, there are always some where the colours are reversed: if you looked at the note we sent, this would not have happened, because you know […] that the first colour to be mentioned must be the warp and the second the weft. […] We write black and grey and you make it grey and black; and the same with the other colours. Moreover, even among the silks of only one colour some are badly coloured'. Sometimes dissatisfaction was shown with bitter irony: 'you are not able to make the *tané* [brown-red] colour, neither for them [the *ermisini*] nor for the damasks; many times I sent you the samples of the colours but you must have lost them'.[25]

Silks on display were supposed to look expensive: 'they should appear [of good quality] even if they are not. And make sure the gold of the gold *telette* is rich, because sometimes they appear white and we feel ashamed with the customers';[26] because after all 'the eye is the judge of everything'.[27] In fact, in 1526, when they renewed their partnership in Nuremberg, the Torrigiani had written into the contract a clause agreeing that they would buy the silks from the sister company in Florence, but with a reduction of ½ ducat per *braccio*. However, the agreement also stated that they should 'make them of lower quality, but make them appear like the previous ones'.[28]

Table 5.2 shows a sample of silks manufactured by Florentine *setaioli* and sent to Germany by the Olivieri of Florence on behalf of the Olivieri of Nuremberg: in 10 ½ months the value of the cloths amounted to c. 3,650 ducats (other sources show that until 15 April 1544 – but starting at an unknown date – the value of silks sent to Germany amounted to 6,270 ducats).[29]

25 ASF, *CRSPL*, 2037, fols 175*r*, 195*r-v*, 203*v*, 206*v*: Piero Saliti, in Nuremberg, to Francesco Carletti, in Florence, letters of 6 November 1536, 21 July 1537, 4 March 1538, 22 April 1538. Similar complaints were issued also from correspondents based in other parts of Europe: see for example Bini's letters from Lyon (Morelli, *La seta fiorentina*, 85–86).

26 ASF, *CRSPL*, 2037, fol. 190*v*: Piero Saliti, in Nuremberg, to Francesco Carletti, in Florence, 16 April 1537.

27 ASF, *CRSPL*, 2037, fol. 183*v*: Piero Saliti, in Leipzig, to Francesco Carletti, in Florence, January 1537.

28 ASF, *Galli Tassi*, 1824, folder 10, fol. 1*r*.

29 ASF, *Galli Tassi*, 2294, fol. 183.

Table 5.2 Florentine silks sent to Nuremberg (21 July 1544–6 June 1545)

date	producer[1]	cloth description	unit price	total price (ducats)
21-07-44	Heirs of N. Machiavelli & co.	*più domaschi in 1 e in 2 camini di sete stiette*		240.7
10-11-44	B. Antinori & co.	*2 drappi d'oro*		246.7
13-11-44	B. Antinori & co.	*1 pezza di teletta d'oro*		86.0
13-11-44	P. Tolomei & co.	*1 pezza di teletta gialla d'oro tirato a 2 ori (braccia 45.3)*	duc. 3 / br.	135.8
03-12-44	L. and N. Bardi & co.	*1 broccatello rosso in 1 camino (braccia 59.5)*	*lire* 6.3 / br.	53.8
03-12-44	L. and N. Bardi & co.	*telette gialle piane d'oro tirato a 2 ori (braccia 60.25)*	duc. 2.7 / br.	165.7
05-12-44	P. Tolomei & co.	*1 pezza di ermisino nero (braccia 35, libbre 6.2)*	*lire* 24 / lb., [duc. 0.6 / br.]	21.7
09-12-44	B. and R. Machiavelli & co.	*2 pezze di velluti rossi di chermisi di Spagna (braccia 84.25)*	[duc. 1.6 / br.]	134.6
11-12-44	Heirs of N. Machiavelli & co.	*più drappi di seta stietti*		499.8
11-12-44	L. and heirs of B. Steccuti & co.	*più drappi di seta stietti*		352.9
11-12-44	R. Corsini & co.	*ermisini neri (libbre 44.35)*	*lire* 24 / lb.	152.9
11-12-44	F. Antinori & co.	*broccatelli (braccia 82.5)*	*lire* 5.2 / br.	61.3
11-12-44	P. Corsini & co.	*più drappi d'oro e stietti*		207.3
16-12-44	N. and B. Del Nente & co.	*7 pezze 'leggiere' di taffettà (libbre 76.3)*	[*lire* 18.1 / lb.]	196.9
16-12-44	Heirs of N. Machiavelli & co.	*2 pezze di ermisini neri (libbre 22.2)*	*lire* 25.5 / lb.	81.9
14-02-45	B. Antinori & co.	*più drappi d'oro e di seta stietti*		455.0
14-02-45	B. Antinori & co.	*1 pezza di raso rosso d'argento in 1 camino a 2 ori*		114.8
14-02-45	C. Dini, A. Michelozzi & co.	*2 pezze di domaschi in 2 camini*		101.0
13-05-45	D. Angiolieri & co.	*più drappi d'oro, d'argento e stietti*		231.4
06-06-45	P. Gondi, P. Velluti & co.	*1 broccatello rosso e 1 domasco pagonazzo*		113.0

Source: ASF, *Galli Tassi*, 2294, fols 81, 131, 142.

Note [1] Richard Goldthwaite has recently published an inventory of account-books relating to the Florentine silk industry from mid-fourteenth to the beginning of the seventeenth century; unfortunately no surviving account-book exists for any of the manufacturers mentioned in the table: Goldthwaite, 'Le aziende seriche', 281–341 (inventory at 329–337).

Silks were an important part of this Florentine export trade, but not to the exclusion of all other products. The merchants had to be ready to meet the requests of their rich clientele. For example, in 1534, sixteen carpets ('tappeti alla morescha') were sent to Piero Saliti, in Nuremberg, to be sold in Hungary (most likely to the Hungarian court): the estimated value of these goods was c. 103 Florentine ducats, equivalent to 90 Hungarian ducats.[30]

Products from the North

As widely known, the balance of the North–South trade was highly unfavourable for the North and could only be balanced through the use of cash or precious metals, as we shall shortly see. Nuremberg was a major hub for goods coming from Central and Eastern Europe, but there were not many products that the Florentines wanted in exchange for the luxury goods they exported. Among them were cloths of lesser quality (cotton, linen, hemp), leather, furs (wolf, marten, sables, etc.), metal wares and sometimes horses.[31] In 1545 the Antinori of Nuremberg wanted to sell some sables to Rome and managed to do so, thanks to the services of the Olivieri. It was not easy to sell them, however, because the prospective clients (coming from the higher echelons of the Papal bureaucracy) had seen the sables bought by Cardinal Farnese, which were much more beautiful than those sold by the Antinori; eventually a buyer, Cardinal Santa Fiora, was found who paid 650 golden *scudi* for them.[32]

In its position at the centre of the Central-Eastern European trading area, Nuremberg attracted inexpensive linen cloth from the surrounding regions (Bohemia, Saxony and Silesia) and dyed and refined it before shipping it towards the Mediterranean countries.[33] The surviving letters show a relevant amount of low quality cloth sent towards the Italian peninsula. Table 5.3, for example, shows that c. 3,800 pieces of these unspecified cloths were sent to Florence, to a relatively small number of *setaioli*, in about a year.

[30] Archivio Bartolini, 246, fol. 237.

[31] Metalwork constituted about half of the craft production of Nuremberg in the fifteenth and sixteenth century (Alfred Wendehorst, 'Nuremberg, the Imperial City: From Its Beginnings to the End of Its Glory', in *Gothic and Renaissance Art in Nuremberg, 1300–1550* (New York: The Metropolitan Museum of Art, 1986), 22).

[32] ASF, *Galli Tassi*, 1959, letters of 26 July, 16 October, 11 December and 16 December 1545.

[33] Wendehorst, 'Nuremberg, the Imperial City', 24–25.

Table 5.3 German cloths sold to Florentine *setaioli* on behalf of the Olivieri of Nuremberg (Feb 1545–Mar 1546)

date	buyers	description of cloth	no. of pieces	total value in ducats
21-02-45 / 02-03-46	P. Tolomei & co.	*tele (bottane) tinte alte e basse*	1,315	1,177.6
21-02-45 / 09-09-46	B. Antinori & co.	*tele (bottane) tinte basse*	926	793.8
15-05-45	D. Angiolieri & co.	*tele bottane tinte basse*	424	363.4
07-09-45 / 02-03-46	P. Gondi, P. Velluti & co.	*tele (bottane) tinte basse*	380	325.7
21-02-45 / 07-09-45	L. Steccuti & co.	*tele (bottane) tinte basse*	344	294.9
16-01-46	G. Barbadori & co.	*tele tinte basse*	184	157.7
21-02-45 / 31-07-45	R. Mormorai & co.	*tele (bottane) tinte basse*	124	106.2
16-01-46 / 02-03-46	P.F. Gucci & co.	*tele (bottane) tinte basse*	93	79.7
02-03-46	L. Berardi & co.	*tele tinte basse*	6	5.3
			3,796	3,304.3

Source: ASF, *Galli Tassi*, 2294, fols 163, 228.

However, as already pointed out, an important part of the trade consisted of metals (copper) or precious metals (gold and, mainly, silver), both in coins and in ingots. Between July 1544 and March 1546 the Olivieri company of Nuremberg sent to Piero Tolomei & Partners, *setaioli*, 21.5 *centi* (hundredweights) of Cologne gold for a value of 191.7 ducats: it is possible that this would then be used by some *battiloro* to produce the gold thread the Tolomei would then weave into their precious cloths of gold.[34] The Saliti company even attempted an investment in a silver mine, but the venture did not provide the profits they had hoped for.[35]

Shipping cash or precious metals was risky, however, and not always desirable. Sometimes transfers had to be made by way of exchange operations, but it was not always easy to finalise them, in a town that was at the margins of the main financial axis. For example, in May 1555, Villani wrote that he was 'unable to find someone who sells bills of exchange'; he was only able to solve the problem when he found a merchant from Padua who had bought products in Germany (and therefore he had debts there) and who transferred the money after his return to Italy, through a bill of exchange from Venice to Florence.[36]

34 ASF, *Galli Tassi*, 2294, fols 84, 232.

35 Saliti complained: 'our mines performed badly, we do not work there anymore and we are tired of not finding silver' (ASF, *CRSPL*, 2037, fol. 174*v*: Piero Saliti, in Nuremberg, to Francesco Carletti, in Florence, 6 November 1536).

36 ASF, *CRSPL*, 2037, fols 340*r*, 342, 346: Lorenzo Villani, in Frankfurt, to Francesco Carletti, in Florence, 7 May, 27 May and 27 June 1555.

The Importance of Counter-Exchange

The international trading network we have just been describing was centred on Florence. The Tuscan town was the fulcrum where activity was coordinated. Requests from Nuremberg were received and production was then organised, in collaboration with the local *setaioli*. Florentine companies with a branch in Nuremberg were at times also manufacturers, as in the case of the Torrigiani, *setaioli*, the Bartolini, *battilori*, and Carletti, another *setaiolo*. The same companies organised and managed the provision of raw silk coming from Southern Italy, where they had sister companies or at least compatriots acting as agents.

What it is noticeable is that a major part of this trade was carried out without the use of cash: the parties adopted counter-exchange.[37] Despite being commonly considered a primitive trading technique, in reality it was frequently used even by the international merchants who were surely able to adopt alternative and 'more refined' business practices, if they wished. When the Torrigiani were about to establish their company in Nuremberg, in 1526, they provided cloths of gold and silver to two German merchants ('Chrapffen' and 'Oberlinden') and, in exchange, they received 22,850 backs (leather), which formed part of the starting capital of the Torrigiani company.[38] Despite the apparent simplicity of operations of this kind, the difficulties in striking a balance between goods from Germany, Florence and the South of Italy being exchanged should not be underestimated. In a long letter of January 1537, Alessandro Talani discussed the possibility of selling berets in exchange for other goods: at the moment they were in Palermo, but they could be shipped to Marseille or to Leghorn. Even though – he continued – 'la morte loro', the most profitable destination, would be France or Germany, where they could easily be sent through Genoa: the moment was convenient, because 'the pirates are in the ports'.[39]

Counter-exchange did not only characterise trade with Germany, but was a common feature also between other commercial centres. It is well known that in the first half of the sixteenth century Lyon was still a centre of attraction for Florentine mercantile and banking companies. Many Florentine *setaioli* associated with these companies (e.g. the Strozzi with the Bini or the Capponi) for the export of their products to the French town and – from there – to the rest of France but also to the Low Countries, England and even Spain. And again, counter-exchange was one of the means of trade: in 1522, for example, Lorenzo and Filippo di Filippo Strozzi & Partners of Florence, *battilori*,

---

37 We are using here the term 'counter-exchange', instead of barter, even when the sources use the term 'baratto', because it is more precise way to define these operations: counter-exchange – unlike barter – is in fact based on the common denominator of money.

38 ASF, *Galli Tassi*, 1824, folder 10, fol. 4*r*.

39 ASF, *CRSPL*, 2037, fol. 356*r-v*: Alessandro Talani, in Nuremberg, to Francesco Carletti, in Florence, 9 January 1537.

used the services of Stefano Del Benino of Lyon to dispatch some of their cloths of gold to Paris, in exchange for 108 pieces of cloth of Southampton.[40] Woollen and silks were exchanged for raw silk also in fifteenth-century Pera (Constantinople).[41]

Counter-exchange, as we have already seen, can be found at any level of this network. On one side, silks were sold in Nuremberg using this method. Sometimes Florentine merchants tried to use lower quality silks with this aim, and at times this was the only way to get rid of certain cloths: in 1537, for example, Piero Saliti instructed his company in Florence to 'send better cloths in the future, so that we don't need to resort to counter-exchange'. In other occasions, however, the quality of these cloths was so low and unsatisfactory for local costumers that the Florentines had to add 'five or six pieces of reasonable damasks, in order to attract them'.[42]

Counter-exchange could also be a quicker way to close a commercial deal. In the early 1540s Gherardo Bartolini's company of *battiloro* incurred huge losses in Lyon and Florence. Hoping to repay his debts, he wrote many letters to his employees in Nuremberg with instructions to sell things quickly, 'even overlooking the price, because I need to sell everything in order […] to pay my creditors'; 'it is necessary not to look for profit in order to sell them'.[43] In July 1542 he sent his trusted collaborator Francesco Carletti to Nuremberg and insisted that if he could not sell 'the remainder of the silks' for cash, he had to sell through counter-exchange (if that was easier) because this could be a faster way.[44]

Occasionally even imported products were obtained in Nuremberg, in exchange for Florentine silks: for example, in 1531, light damasks (*domaschi leggieri*) were given away in order to obtain kermes; and 2–3 barrels of the same – or other – kermes were then shipped to Bologna, another centre of production of silks.[45]

Most of the time, however, silks were exchanged with local goods, such as leather, furs or low quality German clothes that, in turn, could be used to pay the Florentine *setaioli*. In this case, the company in Germany would send them to its parent company in Florence, which would use them to pay for at least part of the silks. The sources clearly specify the nature of the exchange, as they

---

40 ASF, *Carte Strozziane*, V series, 100, *Libro giornale e Ricordanze segnato F di Lorenzo e Filippo di Filippo Strozzi e compagni battilori di Firenze*, 1519–30, fol. 281*r*. For Antwerp see, in this volume, Jeroen Puttevils, *Trading Silks and Tapestries in sixteenth-century Antwerp*, 135–55.

41 Edler de Roover, 'Andrea Banchi', 272.

42 ASF, *CRSPL*, 2037, fol. 183*r*: Piero Saliti, in Leipzig, to Francesco Carletti, in Florence, January 1537.

43 Archivio Bartolini, 255, fols 89*r*, 103*r*: Gherardo Bartolini, in Florence, to Alessandro Talani, in Nuremberg, 4 and 25 February 1542.

44 Archivio Bartolini, 255, fol. 185*v*: Gherardo Bartolini, in Florence, to Francesco Carletti, in Nuremberg, 11 July 1542. Prices of goods in fact differed, depending on the means of payment: obviously they were cheaper when bought in cash.

45 Archivio Bartolini, 243, fols 88*v*, 95*v*: Gherardo Bartolini, in Florence, to Piero Saliti, in Nuremberg, 10 January and 4 February 1532.

underline that these cloths reached their final destination (i.e. the Florentine *setaioli*) 'for the trade made with them in exchange for silks'.[46] Unfortunately the descriptions of the cloths are far from detailed, as they are often indicated as 'coloured cloths' (*tele tinte*), made presumably of cotton, hemp and linen. What use the *setaioli* made of these huge quantities of cloth needs further investigation: presumably some of the cloths were used as packaging (i.e. wrapping the much more precious silks), others for accessories, but most of them must have been sold on the local market.

On the other hand, the Florentine *setaioli* could also receive raw silk in exchange for the finished silks they were producing. The Olivieri company of Nuremberg, for example, used the services of its sister companies in Florence and Naples (and the latter's branches in L'Aquila and Cosenza) to send this product, which came from the South of Italy, to the *setaioli*. Looking at the matter from the other point of view, we could say that the *setaioli* paid for the raw silk not only in cash, but also by giving finished silks in return. The 1543 balance sheet of the Olivieri company of Florence clearly shows that, as a payment for the consignment of raw silk, 'we have received [from Florentine *setaioli*] silks for ours of Nuremberg', in addition to a certain amount of cash.[47]

In January and in February 1538, Michele and Alessandro Olivieri & Partners of Naples were given crimson red velvet, both times in exchange for a bale of Montalto silk (valued respectively at 415 and 417 ducats); the velvet only covered part of the value of the silk, the rest had to be settled (presumably in cash) after a year.[48] The following May, two pieces of crimson velvet and one piece of 'di lacca' velvet were used to cover the cost of Montalto silk worth about 220 ducats.[49] Alternatively, raw silk could also be exchanged against the gold thread manufactured by some *battilori*, as in the same May 1538, when the cost of c. 415 ducats was covered by lb. 39.2.19 of gold thread.[50]

Table 5.4 shows the situation from the point of view of the *setaioli*, who – as has been said – offered silks and received both raw silk and German cloths. Unfortunately the data is scattered and, even when the same people are involved, dates do not always coincide and, certainly, some cash payments, often delayed, were also being made. But the Table can nonetheless illustrate the point being made.

46 ASF, *Galli Tassi*, 2294, fols 158, 163.
47 ASF, *Galli Tassi*, 1926, fols 3*r*, 4*r*.
48 Archivio Bartolini, 246, fol. 360.
49 Archivio Bartolini, 246, fol. 372.
50 Archivio Bartolini, 246, fol. 372.

Table 5.4 Sales of silks and purchases of raw silk and German cloths by Florentine *setaioli* (1544–46)

SETAIOLO	date	**value of silks (in ducats)**	date	**value of raw silk (in ducats)**	date	**value of german cloths (in ducats)**
D. Angiolieri & co.	13.05.45	**231.4**			15.05.45	**363.4**
B. Antinori & co.	10.11.44 / 14.02.45	**902.5**	24.10.45	**554.7**	21.02.45 / 09.09.46	**793.8**
F. Antinori & co.	11.12.44	**61.3**				
G. Barbadori & co.			24.09.45	**489.6**	16.01.46	**157.7**
L. and N. Bardi & co.	03.12.44	**219.5**				
L. Berardi & co.					02.03.46	**5.3**
C. Bucetti & co.			26.09.45	**486.7**		
P. Corsini & co.	11.12.44	**207.3**				
R. Corsini & co.	11.12.44	**152.9**	23.09.45	**488.0**		
N. and B. Del Nente & co.	16.12.44	**196.9**				
C. Dini, A. Michelozzi & co.	14.02.45	**101.0**				
P. Gondi, P. Velluti & co.	06.06.45	**113.0**	07.09.45	**495.7**	07.09.45 / 02.03.46	**325.7**
P.F. Gucci & co.					16.01.46 / 02.03.46	**79.7**
B. and R. Machiavelli & co.	09.12.44	**134.6**				
Heirs of N. Machiavelli & co.	21.07.44 / 16.12.44	**822.4**				
G. Mormorai & co.			07.09.45	**437.3**		
R. Mormorai & co.					21.02.45 / 31.07.45	**106.2**
J. Sangalletti & co.			24.10.45	**489.1**		
L. and heirs of B. Steccuti & co.	11.12.44	**352.9**			21.02.45 / 07.09.45	**294.9**
P. Tolomei & co.	13.11.44 / 05.12.44	**157.5**	07.09.45 / 23.11.45	**1478.4**	21.02.45 / 02.03.46	**1177.6**

Source: elaboration of Tables 5.1, 5. 2 and 5.3.

Commercial Strategy

Obviously, external factors affected the commercial strategy. One of them was war, because of its disruptive consequences for transport: in fact, it could make the traditional routes insecure, thus forcing the merchants to look for alternative – and often more expensive – routes. But on other occasions a whole area was considered commercially unviable, as a consequence of a turbulent situation: in 1537, for example, Cosimo Bonsi wrote that the Hungarian area 'is a country where there is always confusion or war, or there is expectation that it could erupt'.[51] Conversely, other events could enhance the possibilities of trade: positive news was therefore sought after and transmitted, as in 1542 when Bartolini wrote to the Olivieri of Nuremberg that 'we hear that this year the Turks should not cause troubles in those areas'.[52] As we shall see, high-ranking marriages would also trigger the enthusiasm of the merchants who envisaged a source of enormous profits.

It was important that the warehouse was always provided with all kinds of silks at any time, as one or a few types were not sufficient to cover demand: 'And you need to know that whoever wants to take part in this trade cannot deal exclusively with cloths of gold: we need to acquire the reputation of dealing with everything. In conclusion we need to have everything [in stock]'.[53] One passage of a 1537 letter by Saliti to Carletti is very clear: 'If we stayed six months or a year with little supply, we would lose our customers; and if they get used to dealing with others it is impossible to get them back, unless you sell to them without making profits. But once you lower the price things can go wrong'. In the same year, the Saliti-Bartolini company remained without camelots for 6 months: Saliti estimated the missed profit for not having been able to sell them at 100 florins, and at another 100 florins the missed profit from the loss of customers, who turned to other sellers.[54]

Generally speaking, there was a mixture of competition and collaboration between Florentine companies active in Nuremberg, as in the many places where they settled. All companies obviously sought profits, but it is debatable how far they were prepared to go in preventing the others from doing so and therefore excluding them from the market; moreover, price policies could be dangerous, as shown above. Also, it must be said that they all knew each other very well and often worked – especially in the early stages of the career – in compatriots' companies, developing a sense of trust and mutual respect.

---

51 ASF, *CRSPL*, 2037, fol. 269*r*: Cosimo Bonsi, in Leipzig, to Francesco Carletti, in Florence, 8 January 1537.

52 Archivio Bartolini, 255, fol. 89*r*: Gherardo Bartolini, in Florence, to the Olivieri company, in Nuremberg, 4 February 1542.

53 ASF, *CRSPL*, 2037, fol. 269*v*: Cosimo Bonsi, in Leipzig, to Francesco Carletti, in Florence, 8 January 1537.

54 ASF, *CRSPL*, 2037, fol. 200*r*: Piero Saliti, in Nuremberg, to Francesco Carletti, in Florence, 28 August 1537.

Olivieri, as we have seen, started working with the Torrigiani; Bonsi was with the Saliti-Bartolini first, then moved to work with the Olivieri and eventually established his own company. Florentine merchants were all selling and buying similar products on the same markets and therefore constantly monitored each other's activities: those based in Nuremberg sent detailed information to their Florentine partners on the dealings of their compatriots in Germany and the sale price of certain products. In 1537, for example, a rumour spread that Piero Antonio de' Nobili had in his warehouse three pieces of *arricciati* he was about to sell 'to the Turks'. They must have been really beautiful, because Piero Saliti went to visit Nobili in order to see them; however, he could only see 'some cloths of gold and a few damasks' as Nobili did not want to show the '*arriccati richissimi*' for fear of imitation.[55] Sometimes unpleasant incidents happened: in 1554, during the Lent fair at Leipzig, some German merchants contacted Lorenzo Villani in order to buy silks, because their usual supplier, the Antinori company, was providing a more limited stock than agreed. Villani therefore sold them some of his cloths of gold, but was severely reproached by a factor and a partner of the Antinori.[56] But overall, despite personal incompatibility and disagreements, which were always possible (many letters, for example, underline Villani's difficult personality), everyone benefited from the avoidance of harsh competition: disputes and litigations were likely to damage the reputation of the national community as a whole and therefore weaken the position of every single merchant belonging to it.

The Clientele

Unfortunately if most of the letters sent from Germany are very precise in describing the requested type, colour and quantity of cloths, they much more rarely give evidence about the clientele. It is obvious that silks were at the top end of the market and were therefore destined for only a small percentage of the population. In a growing urban economy, however, rising fashion awareness and the increasing wealth in the hands of the mercantile class and the richest artisans certainly widened the potential clientele and stimulated the demand for variety.[57]

The 1527 balance sheet of Piero Saliti & Partners of Nuremberg and the 1551 balance sheet of Michele, Alessandro and Giovanni Olivieri & Partners of Nuremberg show a long list of German clients from Nuremberg, Cologne,

55 ASF, *CRSPL*, 2037, fol. 198*v*: Piero Saliti, in Nuremberg, to Francesco Carletti, in Florence, 26 August 1537.

56 ASF, *CRSPL*, 2037, fol. 327*v*: Lorenzo Villani, in Nuremberg, to Francesco Carletti, in Florence, 18 May 1554.

57 See, for example, the chapter dedicated to Matthäus Schwarz, the accountant of the Fugger firm, in Ulinka Rublack, *Dressing Up: Cultural Identity in Renaissance Europe* (Oxford: Oxford University Press, 2010), 33–80.

Erfurt, Frankfurt, Halle, Leipzig, Lübeck, Straubing but also from areas east of Germany such as Bratislava, Bohemia (Prague) or Hungary.[58] Most of the time, however, silks were not sold directly to the final customer, but to German merchants: this happened at the fairs of Leipzig and Frankfurt (which the Nuremberg-based Florentines never missed), but also at Nuremberg itself. Additionally, some silks were sold to fellow Florentine merchants, especially when they had not received the consignments they expected and were therefore in need of products to sell in the forthcoming fairs.

The documents clearly highlight the ups and downs of the market. Obviously, demand for luxury goods would be stimulated by important events such as the marriage of a local lord. The rumour of these events was very much sought after by the merchants, who were ready to write home and to press for an increase in production: as Piero Saliti wrote from Leipzig, 'they say that a certain marriage could be agreed, but I don't want to give you too much hope, to avoid your disappointment if it eventually does not take place'; 'and they foresee the marriage of a lord, which could imply the sale of many silks'.[59]

However, at times these local elites proved to be less than reliable in making payments (or repayments). In 1541 Gherardo Bartolini wrote to Vienna, to Agnolo Acciaioli, concerning the 'marchese Bonndeburgh', who still had to repay a loan: on one side, 'he is so noble […] that I reckon he will not miss the payment'; on the other, however, 'as I know that he does not have much money and has many debts, I cannot stop worrying until I see the payment'. The general conclusion was that 'when we give huge amounts [of money] to such people, we need to be extremely cautious'.[60]

A few years earlier, in 1537, Alessandro Talani, through an intermediary, was trying to make contacts 'with two or three merchants who follow the [Imperial] court', at the time in Bohemia: the merchants were reliable, whereas 'it is difficult to rely on the king or the queen, because they always have debts and are not good payers'.[61]

---

58 Spallanzani, 'Le compagnie Saliti a Norimberga', 611–613. Guidi-Bruscoli, 'Drappi di seta e tele di lino', 392–394.

59 ASF, *CRSPL*, 2037, fols 173*r*, 183*v*: Piero Saliti, in Nuremberg, to Francesco Carletti, in Florence, 31 October 1534 and January 1537.

60 Archivio Bartolini, 255, fol. 34*r*: Gherardo Bartolini, in Florence, to Agnolo Acciaioli, in Vienna, 25 June 1541.

61 ASF, *CRSPL*, 2037, fol. 363*r-v*: Alessandro Talani, in Nuremberg, to Francesco Carletti, in Florence, 28 August 1537.

Conclusion

This chapter deals with a slightly peripheral area compared to the main trading partners for Italian luxury products. In the early sixteenth century the trade with Germany was more recent and less developed than the trade with the Low Countries, for example; most of the time Florentine companies exporting silks to Central and Eastern Europe were also selling the same products to Antwerp, Lyon, London or the Levant. For the period 1450–1530, of 461 *accomandita* (limited partnership) contracts drawn up in Florence, only three concerned trade with Central and Eastern Europe. Obviously there were other possible forms of association, but this figure still gives an idea about the relative importance of the region for the Florentine trade. One of the contracts concerns Hungary (Francesco Bini, Giannozzo Pucci and Cardinale Rucellai with Filippo Cavalcanti), and two concern trade in the German area ('nelle parti della Magnia'): Niccolò di Tommaso Antinori provided Raffaello di Iacopo Vecchietti and Iacopo Bettoni with 400 florins in 1499 and Zanobi Saliti – as we have seen – conferred 4,000 florins to Bernardo Acciaioli in 1512. Another sign of the importance attributed to the region by Florentines is given by the status of the people implicated in these ventures: we generally do not find the most important mercantile families, but mainly newcomers to Florentine business circles (e.g. Saliti or Olivieri), even though some of the most established families (e.g. the Antinori or the Torrigiani) appear as well.[62]

Nuremberg – as we said – reached the peak of its success towards the end of the fifteenth century and maintained it for some decades. After the mid-sixteenth century, however, the Lisbon–Antwerp axis gradually replaced the traditional Mediterranean cities with which Nuremberg had dealt (Venice, Milan and Genoa). Initially, merchants from Nuremberg were able to adapt and to assert their presence in the new leading towns, where they had branches or agents. But when Antwerp was eventually overtaken by Amsterdam, the South German town saw all its connections disappear.[63]

Sources kept in the Florentine archives allow us to take a snapshot of the period when the Florence–Nuremberg trade was at its peak. Traditionally Florence was not Nuremberg's main market in the Italian peninsula. Merchants from the German town preferred to go to Venice first and then to Milan or Genoa, from the late fifteenth century.[64] But these sources also show that substantial quantities of luxury Italian cloths were sold at Nuremberg

---

62 Dini, 'L'economia fiorentina e l'Europa centro-orientale', 275–276.

63 Gerald Strauss, *Nuremberg in the Sixteenth Century. City Politics and Life between Middle Ages and Modern Times* (Bloomington & London: Indiana University Press, 1976), 147–149.

64 In the late sixteenth century, however, German merchants would buy silks directly in Florence: for example, in the 1580s the *setaioli* Martelli-Del Giocondo sold 18% of their silks to Germans, some of whom were based in other Italian cities (Goldthwaite, 'Le aziende seriche', 322).

and at the German fairs by Florentine merchants. Profits for them could be very good: in 1543, writing to Francesco Carletti who was in Florence, Lorenzo Villani encouraged him to invest more money in trade with Germany, an activity – he said – whose profits were higher than 20% per year.[65]

The strategies of different companies – as we have seen – could vary slightly from one another, but the common feature was the organisation of a network revolving around Florence. The Tuscan town was the place where the silks came from; it was also the place to which products from the North were sent, before being sold to the local market or re-exported. On the other hand, the Florentine silk industry could only meet the demand coming from Northern Europe and elsewhere because its looms were continuously fed by the raw materials arriving from the South of the Italian peninsula. The system worked because the mercantile companies shipped products in all directions and – remarkably – did so without having to move excessive amounts of cash.

Bibliography

Manuscript Sources

Florence, Archivio di Stato
Carte Strozziane, V series, 100.
Compagnie Religiose Soppresse da Pietro Leopoldo, 2037.
Galli Tassi, 1824, 1926, 1959–1962, 2294.
Vicchio di Mugello, Archivio Bartolini
vol. 243.
vol. 246.
vol. 255.

Published Sources

Bonito Fanelli, Rosalia. 'The Pomegranate Motif in Italian Renaissance Silks: a Semiological Interpretation of Pattern and Color', in *La seta in Europa, secc. XIII-XX*, Proceedings of the 'Ventiquattresima Settimana di Studi dell'Istituto Internazionale di Storia economica F. Datini', Prato, 4–9 May 1992, edited by Simonetta Cavaciocchi, 507-30. Florence: Le Monnier, 1993.

Brübach, Nils. *Die Reichsmessen von Frankfurt am Mein, Leipzig und Braunschweig (14.-18. Jahrhundert)*. Stuttgart: Franz Steiner Verlag, 1994.

Brücker, Wolfgang. *Conrad Faber von Creuznach*. Frankfurt am Main: Kramer, 1963.

De Maddalena, Aldo. '"Excolere vitam per artes". Giovanni Antonio Orombelli mercante auroserico milanese del Cinquecento'. In Aldo De Maddalena, *Dalla città al borgo. Avvio di una metamorfosi economica e sociale nella Lombardia spagnola*. Milan: Franco Angeli, 1982.

Dini, Bruno. 'L'economia fiorentina e l'Europa centro-orientale nelle fonti toscane'. *Archivio Storico Italiano* CLIII (1995): 633–55. Reprinted in Bruno Dini. *Saggi su una*

[65] ASF, *CRSPL*, 2037, fol. 306: Lorenzo Villani, in Frankfurt, to Francesco Carletti, in Florence, November 1543.

economia-mondo. Firenze e l'Italia fra Mediterraneo ed Europa (secc. XIII-XVI), 271–88. Pisa: Pacini, 1995.

Edler de Roover, Florence. 'Andrea Banchi, Florentine Silk Manufacturer and Merchant in the Fifteenth Century'. *Studies in Medieval and Renaissance History* 3 (1966): 221–85.

Edler de Roover, Florence. *L'Arte della seta a Firenze nei secoli XIV e XV*. Firenze: Olschki, 1999.

Eiden, Herbert. 'The Fairs of Leipzig and the Eastern European Economies (15th-18th centuries)'. In *Fiere e mercati nella integrazione delle economie europee, secc. XIII-XVIII*, Proceedings of the 'Trentaduesima Settimana di Studi dell'Istituto Internazionale di Storia economica F. Datini', Prato, 8–12 May 2000, edited by Simonetta Cavaciocchi, 723–39. Florence: Le Monnier, 2001.

Gemäldegalerie Berlin: Gesamtverzeichnis der Gemälde. Complete Catalogue of the Paintings. London: Weidenfeld & Nicolson, 1986.

Goldthwaite, Richard A. 'Le aziende seriche e il mondo degli affari a Firenze alla fine del '500'. *Archivio Storico Italiano* CLXIX (2011): 281–341.

Goldthwaite, Richard A. 'An Entrepreneurial Silk Weaver in Renaissance Florence'. *I Tatti Studies* 10 (2005): 69–126.

Goldthwaite, Richard A. *The Economy of Renaissance Florence*. Baltimore: The Johns Hopkins University Press, 2009.

Gömmel, Rainer. *Die Vermittlerrolle Nürnbergs zwischen Italien und Deutschland vom Spätmittelalter bis zum 18. Jahrhundert aus wirtschaftshistorischer Sicht*. In *Nürnberg und Italien. Begegnungen, Einflüsse und Ideen*, edited by Volker Kapp and Frank-Rutger Hausmann: 39–48. Tübingen: Stauffenburg Verlag, 1991.

Goodman, Jordan. 'Tuscan Commercial Relations with Europe, 1550–1620: Florence and the European Textile Market'. In *Firenze e la Toscana dei Medici nell'Europa del '500*. 3 vols, vol. 1, *Strumenti e veicoli della cultura. Relazioni politiche ed economiche*, 327–41. Florence: Olschki, 1983.

Gothic and Renaissance Art in Nuremberg, 1300–1550. New York and Munich: Metropolitan Museum of Art and Germanischen Nationalmuseums, 1986.

Guidi-Bruscoli, Francesco. 'Der Handel mit Seidenstoffen und Leinengeweben zwischen Florenz und Nürnberg in der ersten Hälfte des 16. Jahrhunderts'. *Mitteilungen des Vereins für Geschichte der Stadt Nürnberg* 86 (1999): 81–113.

Guidi-Bruscoli, Francesco. 'Drappi di seta e tele di lino tra Firenze e Norimberga nella prima metà del Cinquecento'. *Archivio Storico Italiano* CLIX (2001): 359–394.

Mazzei, Rita. 'Convivenza religiosa e mercatura nell'Europa del Cinquecento. Il caso degli italiani a Norimberga'. In *La formazione storica della alterità. Studi di storia della tolleranza nell'età moderna offerti a Antonio Rotondò, promossi da H. Méchoulan, R. H. Popkin, G. Ricuperati, L. Simonutti*. 3 vols, vol. 1, 395–428. Florence: Olschki, 2001.

Mazzei, Rita. *La trama nascosta. Storie di mercanti e altro (secoli XVI-XVII)*. Viterbo: Sette Città, 2006.

Morelli, Roberta. *La seta fiorentina nel Cinquecento*. Milan: Giuffrè, 1976.

Puttevils, Jeroen. 'Trading Silks and Tapestries in Sixteenth-Century Antwerp'. In *Europe's Rich Fabric: The Consumption, Commercialisation and Production of Luxury Textiles in Italy, the Low Countries and Neighbouring Regions (Fourteenth–Sixteenth Centuries)* edited by Bart Lambert and Katherine Anne Wilson, 131–55. Aldershot: Ashgate, 2016.

Rothmann, Michael. *Die Frankfurter Messen in Mittelalter*. Stuttgart: Franz Steiner Verlag, 1997.

Rublack, Ulinka. *Dressing Up: Cultural Identity in Renaissance Europe*. Oxford: Oxford University Press, 2010.

Spallanzani, Marco. 'Le compagnie Saliti a Norimberga nella prima metà del Cinquecento (un primo contributo dagli archivi fiorentini)'. In *Wirtschaftskräfte und Wirtschaftswege. Festschrift für Hermann Kellenbenz*. 5 vols, edited by Jürgen Schneider, vol. 1, *Mittelmeer und Kontinent*, 603–620. Nuremberg: Klett-Cotta, 1978–81.

Spallanzani, Marco. 'Tessuti di seta fiorentini per il mercato di Norimberga intorno al 1520'. In *Studi in memoria di Giovanni Cassandro*. 3 vols, vol. 3, 995–1016. Rome: Ministero per i beni culturali e ambientali, Ufficio centrale per i beni archivistici, 1991.

Strauss, Gerald. *Nuremberg in the Sixteenth Century. City Politics and Life between Middle Ages and Modern Times*. Bloomington & London: Indiana University Press, 1976.

Tognetti, Sergio. *Un'industria di lusso al servizio del grande commercio internazionale. Il mercato dei drappi serici e della seta nella Firenze del Quattrocento*. Florence: Olschki, 2002.

Weissen, Kurt. 'I mercanti italiani alle fiere tedesche nel tardo medioevo'. In *Fiere e mercati nella integrazione delle economie europee, secc. XIII-XVIII*, Proceedings of the 'Trentaduesima Settimana di Studi dell'Istituto Internazionale di Storia economica F. Datini', Prato, 8–12 May 2000, edited by Simonetta Cavaciocchi, 887–908. Florence: Le Monnier, 2001.

Weissen, Kurt. 'I mercanti italiani e le fiere in Europa centrale alla fine del Medioevo e agli inizi dell'età moderna'. In *La pratica dello scambio, Sistemi di fiere, mercanti e città in Europa (1400–1700)*, edited by Paola Lanaro, 161–176. Venice: Marsilio, 2003.

Weissen, Kurt. 'Safran für Deutschland. Kontinuität und Diskontinuität mittelalterlicher und früneuzeitlicher Warenbeschaffungsstrukturen'. In *Beschaffungs und Absatzmärkte oberdeutscher Firmen im Zeitalter der Welser und Fugger*, edited by Angelika Westermann and Stefanie von Welser, 61–78. Husum: Matthiesen Verlag, 2011.

Weissen, Kurt. 'Florentiner Bankiers und Deutschland (1275 bis 1475). Kontinuität und Diskontinuität wirtschaftlicher Strukturen'. Habilitationsschrift, University of Basel, 2001. Accessed June 21, 2011. http://kweissen.ch/docs/weissen%20-%20 2000%20-%20Habil%20-%20ganz.pdf.

Wendehorst, Alfred. 'Nuremberg, the Imperial City: From Its Beginnings to the End of Its Glory', in *Gothic and Renaissance Art in Nuremberg, 1300–1550*, 11–26. New York: The Metropolitan Museum of Art, 1986.

6

Trading Silks and Tapestries in Sixteenth-Century Antwerp

Jeroen Puttevils

On 14 November 1540, Pieter Van der Molen, the manager of the Antwerp Van der Molen merchant company, wrote to Jeronimo Azeretto di Vivaldis, one of their clients in the Italian city of Genoa: 'there are rumours that the Emperor [Charles V] will announce a new law on velvet and silk cloth, but nothing has happened so far'.[1] The Van der Molen referred to the previous sumptuary law of 1531 issued by the Low Countries central government. This substantive law limited the wearing of gold and silver cloth to the high nobility and the highest officials. Only they could wear crimson silks. The ordinance explicitly tied the permission to wear certain silk varieties to the number of horses one could deliver to the governess in case of war.[2] A year later, on the 8 February 1542, Pieter wrote to Jeronimo again, this time to announce that: 'velvets and silk cloths are at their usual price level. The court [Charles V and governess Mary of Hungary] has promulgated a new law: nobles or those who act like nobles who wear garments made of velvet, satin or damask, have to keep two horses of fifteen hands high to serve the court when necessary. So that it will be too difficult for most to pay for silk garments and keeping two horses'. Pieter suggestively added that probably this law would fade into obscurity as other laws often did.[3]

In May 1550 the Hapsburg central government issued another sumptuary law in which it castigated its subjects for wearing clothes that were too costly and excessive, especially when this sartorial display of silk cloth, gold and silver thread, embroidery, fringes and ribbons did not befit their rank and status. The

1 City Archive, Antwerp, Insolvente Boedelkamer, IB 2898, Copy-letterbook of Pieter Van der Molen 1538–1544, fol. 186r. Hereafter CAA. Unless otherwise noted, all translations are the author's.

2 Charles Laurent, Jules-Pierre-Auguste Lameere, and Henri Simont, *Recueil des ordonnances des Pays-Bas: 2e série, 1506–1700*, 6 vols. (Brussels: Goemaere, 1893–1922). III, October 7 1531, 265–273.

3 CAA, IB 2898, Copy-letterbook of Pieter Van der Molen 1538–1544, fol. 225v.

law text meticulously lists who could wear what and explicitly forbade mercers and merchants to sell textiles to people whose rank did not match the textiles they were to acquire, and stipulated that crimson silk cloths could be worn only by the nobility. The penalty for this offence would be the forfeiture of the fabric and a fine.[4] In that same year an interpretation of this law was pronounced which partially overturned the original ordinance by stating that small pieces of silk such as velvet and satin, even in crimson, were allowed. Camlets and ostades that were not made from silk could be worn by everybody.[5] Earlier, in 1527, Margaret of Austria, in a letter to the Antwerp magistracy, linked this display of silk cloth to the large amounts of bullion leaving the Low Countries to pay for silk.[6] These references to sumptuary legislation point out the government's efforts to control display. Between 1300 and 1600, European dress was targeted by sumptuary laws. However, in the densely commercialised Low Countries such sumptuary legislation was very sparse.[7]

The growth of commerce throughout Europe gave new people access to luxuries that had once been the sole preserve of the nobility. This eroded the ability of dress to do what it had traditionally been thought able to do: reliably express identity. Therefore, commerce caused social disorder and moral rot in the eyes of princes, urban magistrates, church officials and scholars.[8] This chapter focuses on two types of frequently traded luxury goods subject to sumptuary legislation, silks and tapestries, which were traded *en masse* in sixteenth-century Antwerp, Europe's pivotal market. Silk was imported mostly from Italy but gradually the Low Countries developed a native silk industry. Tapestries were a commercial hit of the Low Countries' industrial apparatus and formed a substantial part of the export market. Supply and demand will be reconstructed for these products by using gross supply estimates derived from toll accounts and merchants' documents. Information on the marketing of these products can be found in several ledgers of merchants trading silks and tapestries.[9] A selection of probate inventories and merchant's ledgers will provide more information on the more elusive actual demand for these goods. One of the central questions of this volume is how supply and demand interacted and how local production reacted on the extensive importation of Italian silk. Did this lead to import substitution and the production of imitative products?

4 Laurent, Lameere and Simont, *Recueil des ordonnances des Pays-Bas*, VI, May 27 1550, 80–83.

5 Laurent, Lameere and Simont, *Recueil des ordonnances des Pays-Bas*, VI, December 2 1550, 128–129.

6 CAA, Privilegiekamer, received letters, Pk#271, 1527.

7 Martha Howell, *Commerce before Capitalism in Europe, 1300–1600* (Cambridge: Cambridge University Press, 2010), 236.

8 Howell, *Commerce before Capitalism in Europe*, 208.

9 Roger De Peuter, 'Mooie kleren voor hoge heren. Beschouwingen over de textielhandel te Brussel in het midden van de zestiende eeuw', *Textielhistorische bijdragen* 34 (1994); Jan Denucé, *Antwerpsche tapijtkunst en handel* (Antwerpen: Sikkel, 1936).

In the first two sections of the chapter, the volume of tapestries and silks – both as imported semi-finished and finished products and native goods produced in the Low Countries, sometimes as a part of an import substitution strategy – traded through the city of Antwerp are put together. The subsequent sections of the chapter examine the role of merchants and commercial middlemen, their contacts with foreign suppliers and buyers, and with local producers and consumers. The final section tackles the issue of demand: were silks and tapestries still the preserve of a noble and ecclesiastical elite or were they accessible to broader groups in society?

Antwerp's Sixteenth-Century Tapestry Trade

Antwerp's initial success and growth in the late fifteenth and early sixteenth century was largely supported by the annual Brabant fairs held in the city itself and in the nearby town of Bergen op Zoom and by the relative decline of the Bruges market caused by the political struggles in the county of Flanders. In this period, Antwerp's trade was characterised by what Herman Van der Wee called the 'tripod of English textiles, South German metals, and Portuguese spices'.[10]

The Southern Netherlands were the most important producer of tapestries in Europe from the fifteenth to the seventeenth century. Antwerp acted as the major distribution centre for this product, despite being only a minor production centre. Most tapestries were produced in Brussels, Sint-Truiden, Oudenaarde and Tournai.[11] Between 1488 and 1514, roughly the first growth phase of the Antwerp market, tapestries and silks can be found in the transactions registered in the aldermen's registers and certification books,

---

10 Herman Van der Wee, *The Growth of the Antwerp Market and the European Economy (Fourteenth-Sixteenth Centuries)*, 3 vols, vol. 2 (Den Haag: Nijhoff, 1963); Herman Van der Wee, 'Handel in de Zuidelijke Nederlanden', in *Nieuwe Algemene Geschiedenis der Nederlanden* (Haarlem: Fibula-Van Dishoeck, 1978). For the presence of Italians in this first growth phase of the Antwerp market, see: Peter Stabel, 'Italian merchants and the fairs in the Low Countries (12th–16th centuries)', in *La pratica dello scambio. Sistemi di fiere, mercanti e città in Europa (1400–1700)*, ed. Paola Lanaro (Venetië: Marsilio, 2003); Peter Stabel, 'Venice and the Low Countries: commercial contacts and intellectual inspirations', in *Renaissance Venice and the North. Crosscurrents in the Time of Bellini, Dürer and Titian*, ed. B. Aikema and B.L. Brown (Milan: Bompiani, 1999); Jim L. Bolton and Francesco Guidi Bruscoli, 'When did Antwerp replace Bruges as the commercial and financial centre of north-western Europe? The evidence of the Borromei ledger for 1438', *The Economic History Review* 61 (2008): 360–379.

11 Filip Vermeylen, *Painting for the Market: Commercialization of Art in Antwerp's Golden Age* (Turnhout: Brepols, 2003), 87–91. Fine introductions: Guy Delmarcel, *Het Vlaamse wandtapijt van de 15de tot de 18de eeuw* (Tielt: Lannoo, 1999); Thomas P. Campbell, ed. *Tapestry in the Renaissance: Art and Magnificence* (New York: Metropolitan Museum of Art, 2006); van G. T. Ysselsteyn, *Tapestry, the Most Expensive Industry of the 15th and 16th Centuries: A Renewed Research into Technic, Origin and Iconography* (The Hague: Van Goor, 1969); Roger A. d'Hulst, *Vlaamse wandtapijten van de 14de tot de 18de eeuw* (Brussel: Arcade, 1960).

which merchants often used to obtain written proof of their transactions.[12] Tapestries, usually without further details, are listed in these documents from 1490 on a frequent basis. One document provides the details of the Brussels tapestry merchant Gabriel de Leenere who sent 138 ells of gold tapestry to the Duke of Buckingham.[13]

After a period of stagnation in the 1520s caused by the Valois–Habsburg conflict and the resultant economic destabilisation, the Antwerp market experienced a second growth spurt from the middle of the 1530s onwards. The renewed trade with the Mediterranean was essential for the commercial growth of the city. The 1529 Peace of Cambrai reinforced Habsburg power in Italy and allowed for the recovery and intensification of commercial relations between the Low Countries and Italy.[14] The political instability in Italy and the resulting wars during the first half of the sixteenth century hit Italian industry and trade hard. This crisis in the Italian supply enabled a powerful growth in sales of Netherlandish products on the European market.[15] Foreign trade was crucial for Antwerp and for the Low Countries' economy in general. In the middle of the sixteenth century, at the height of Antwerp's second growth phase imports to the Low Countries amounted to 7 guilders per capita, while England and France had only an import of 1.5 guilders per capita, a staggering difference. Moreover, a quarter of the industrial production of the Low Countries was destined for export.[16] By then, Antwerp had seized a dominant position as the main gateway for trade over land and by sea in the Low Countries and connected Europe's economic regions to each other.[17] For the 1540s and 1550s toll statistics and other witness accounts such as ambassador reports allow the quantification of trade flows for specific products between Italy, Germany, the Iberian peninsula and the Low Countries and in particular, Antwerp.[18]

---

12 Renée Doehaerd, ed. *Etudes anversoises: documents sur le commerce international à Anvers, 1488–1514*, 3 vols. (Paris: SEVPEN, 1962–1963).

13 Doehaerd, *Etudes anversoises*, III, 223.

14 Van der Wee, *The Growth of the Antwerp Market*, 2, 180–82, 431.

15 Van der Wee, 'Handel in de Zuidelijke Nederlanden', 87–89.

16 Wilfrid Brulez, 'The balance of trade of the Netherlands in the middle of the 16th century', *Acta historiae Neerlandica* 4 (1970): 48.

17 For the most recent interpretation, see: Clé Lesger, *The Rise of the Amsterdam Market and Information Exchange: Merchants, Commercial Expansion and Change in the Spatial Economy of the Low Countries, c. 1550–1630* (Aldershot: Ashgate, 2006), 15–100; Michael Limberger, 'No town in the world provides more advantages: economies of agglomeration and the golden age of Antwerp', in *Urban Achievement in Early Modern Europe: Golden Ages in Antwerp, Amsterdam and London* ed. Patrick O'Brien et al. (Cambridge: Cambridge University Press, 2001).

18 For export from the Low Countries to Italy and the Iberian Peninsula: Algemeen Rijksarchief Brussels, Rekenkamer (from now on ARB), 23357–23364, Accounts of Gaspar Ducci, collector of the 100th Penny on foreign exports, 1543–1545. For import and export between the Netherlands and the Iberian Peninsula: ARB, Rekenkamer, 23469–23474, Accounts of the 2 % tax on export and import, 1552–1553. Jeroen Puttevils, 'Klein gewin brengt rijkdom in: de Zuid-Nederlandse handelaars in de export naar Italië in de jaren 1540', *Tijdschrift voor sociale en economische geschiedenis* 6 (2009).

Table 6.1 Tapestry exports based on toll records, mid sixteenth century[19]

Destination	Year	Value in £ Fl. gr.	Percentage of total export
Italy	1544	4,982	0.03%
Germany	1544	246	0.07%
Iberian Peninsula	1552/1553	66,250	11.5%

Table 6.1 demonstrates that little tapestry was exported to Italy and Germany in 1544. English and Netherlandish cloth were the most important products to be exported to Germany and Italy. For Germany, spices were dominant as well. Yet, ten years later in the trade with Portugal and Spain, tapestries had become a popular export product. It is not clear why there is such a large difference between these numbers. Possibly, the Iberian demand was heightened by the inflow of bullion and goods from the Americas and the East, explaining the large imports of high-value luxury products such as Flemish tapestries.[20] Overall, England, France and the Iberian peninsula were the most important importers of Flemish tapestry.[21]

Table 6.2 Share of Netherlandish tapestry production centres in the export to Iberia in 1553 (January 1–June 30 1533)[22]

Production centre	# ells	Share in total tapestry exports in %	Average value per ell in £ Fl. gr. (in 1553)
Oudenaarde	16,715	48.5	1
Sint-Truiden	12,429	36	0.04
Brussels	1,194	3.5	1–5
Doornik	600	1.7	1
Diest	578	1.7	0.2
Herentals	300	0.9	0.5
Edingen	245	0.7	1
Unknown	34,431	7	

19 Martine Vanwelden, *Productie van wandtapijten in de regio Oudenaarde: een symbiose tussen stad en platteland (15de tot 17de eeuw)* (Leuven: Universitaire Pers, 2006), 208–09. Values are given in pounds Flemish groat. £ 1 Fl. gr. = £ 2/3 Brabant groat = 6 guilders. For comparison: a mason in Antwerp in 1550 had an annual real wage of around £ 20 Brabant groat or £ 13.33 Fl. gr. or 180 guilders.

20 Jeroen Puttevils, 'A servitio de vostri sempre siamo. De effecten van de handel tussen Antwerpen en Italië op. de koopmansfamilie Van der Molen' (MA, University of Antwerp, 2007); Jeroen Puttevils, 'Klein gewin; Brulez', The balance of trade; Herman Van der Wee, 'Industrial dynamics and the process of urbanization and de-urbanization in the Low Countries from the late Middle Ages to the eighteenth century. A synthesis', in *The Rise and Decline of Urban Industries in Italy and in the Low Countries (Late Middle Ages – Early Modern Times)*, ed. Herman Van der Wee (Leuven: Leuven University Press, 1988), 336–38.

21 Filip Vermeylen, 'De export vanuit de Zuidelijke Nederlanden naar Duitsland omstreeks het midden van de 16de eeuw' (MA, Catholic University of Louvain, 1989), 88–91.

22 Vanwelden, *Productie van wandtapijten*, 212.212. She based her numbers on Louis Bril: Louis Bril, 'De handel tussen de Nederlanden en het Iberisch schiereiland (midden XVIe eeuw)' (Universiteit Gent, 1962), 166.

The above table of the provenances of these tapestries and their production centres in the Low Countries shows that Oudenaarde tapestries constituted the bulk of tapestry exports to Spain and Portugal, together with Sint-Truiden tapestry work, which was inexpensive and had an average value below that of Oudenaarde work. Diest and Herentals also exported cheap tapestries. The relatively low share of Brussels tapestries and their significantly higher value are remarkable. It has been claimed that Brussels tapestries were mostly made on order by well-known tapestry entrepreneurs such as Willem de Pannemakere, Pieter Coecke van Aalst or Bernaert van Orley.[23] But that argument can be countered by the fact that when Brussels tapestries would be exported after finishing, they would still be listed in the same toll lists as the other types. So quantitatively, the more expensive and more renowned Brussels tapestries were less important than the cheaper Oudenaarde ones, which were exported on a grand scale.[24] Estimates suggest that Brussels tapestry production nonetheless provided work for between 12,000 and 15,000 Brussels labourers, or almost one third of the city's inhabitants.[25]

Antwerp's Sixteenth-Century Silk Trade

The Low Countries' trade in silk fabrics is much harder to quantify.[26] No data for imports from Italy are available and it is hard to distinguish between fabrics produced in the Low Countries and silk fabrics coming from abroad. Silks such as satin, taffetas, damask, silk cloth and silk ribbons start to pop up from 1491 and regularly appear from 1507 in the registers and certificates of the Antwerp aldermen.[27] Antwerp increasingly became Europe's commercial gateway and transit centre: according to the Antwerp magistracy in 1552, silk fabrics were re-exported from Antwerp to London for a value of 372,000 guilders.[28] Silks were also exported from Antwerp to France and the Baltic. Small quantities of *camelotti* (silk cloths) and satins (a mix of silk and wool or linen) were exported from the Low Countries to the Iberian peninsula in 1552–1553.[29] In the middle of the sixteenth century, silk textiles estimated at a value of 500,000 guilders were exported annually out of the Low Countries.[30] An anonymous silk merchant registered all his purchases and sales in a well-preserved ledger. Between 1548 and 1557 he bought 1,439 pieces of mainly

23 Campbell, *Tapestry in the Renaissance*, 131–44.

24 Vanwelden, *Productie van wandtapijten*, 207–13.

25 Campbell, *Tapestry in the Renaissance*, 279; Vanwelden, *Productie van wandtapijten*, 101.

26 A thorough introduction to the silk industry and trade is: Luca Molà, *The Silk Industry of Renaissance Venice* (Baltimore: The Johns Hopkins University Press, 2000).

27 Doehaerd, *Etudes anversoises*.

28 Brulez, 'The balance of trade', 42. Or £ 62 000 Fl. gr.

29 Bril, 'De handel', 52.

30 Brulez, 'The balance of trade', 42. Or £ 83 333 Fl. gr.

silk fabric, which was cut up to be sold in retail.[31] The merchant traded velvet, satin, taffetas, caffa and damask linen in more than twenty-five colour combinations.

Eyewitnesses such as the Venetian ambassador in the Low Countries, Marino Cavalli, set the total import value of Italian cloth-of-gold, camlets, fustian and silk at more than one million Venetian ducats or £308,333 Fl. gr. (on a total import of £ 3.35 million) in 1551, while his countryman the Florentine Lodovico Guicciardini in his *Descrittione Di Tutti I Paesi Bassi* arrives at a number of six million guilders (or one million £ Fl. gr.) for silk imports from Italy in 1567.[32] From these numbers it is evident that the Low Countries had a deficit on their balance of trade with Italy, but this deficit was compensated by a surplus on the Low Countries balance of trade with Spain, Portugal, England, France, and possibly Germany.[33] A price list for the organisation of a tax on trade in 1575 offers an intriguing insight into the range of silk fabrics that were available on the Antwerp market.[34] The list mentions gold and silver silk cloth, crimson velvet, damask, satin, taffetas, camlets, gold and silver thread, sewing silk, silk ribbons in all colours, and silk stockings. The origins are not clear for every type of textile but most of these luxury textiles were produced in Italy, the Middle East and the Netherlands. The most expensive types were gold and silver silk cloth from Italy, silk stockings both from Italy and the Netherlands, and silk cloth with gold and silver thread from the Low Countries. In the lower end of the Antwerp silk market satins from Bruges and Tournai and dyed sewing silk from Bruges and Antwerp are listed. Of course, native woollen cloth was also extensively available on the Antwerp market and can be found in both the high and low end of the market.[35] There are only a few observations on price data of linen which have been excluded from Figure 6.1. The linen price ranged from 16 d. Fl. gr. to 720 per ell. Much of this linen was produced in the Low Countries' countryside; cities such as Antwerp, Cambrai, Courtrai, Lille, Mechelen, Tournai and Valenciennes specialised in the production of luxury linen such as damask, napkins and figurative linen.[36]

---

31 ARB, 1548–1557, Handschriften, 2784, anonymous ledger. De Peuter, 'Mooie kleren voor hoge heren'.

32 Brulez, 'The balance of trade', 22 & 36. 1 Venetian ducat = 74 d. Fl. groat. Raymond De Roover, 'Anvers comme marché monétaire aux XVIe siècle', *Revue belge de philologie et d'histoire* 31 (1953): 1003–1047.

33 Brulez, 'The balance of trade', 46.

34 CAA, Tresorij 737. Published as: Alfons K.L. Thijs, 'Les textiles au marché anversois au XVIe siècle', in *Textiles of the Low Countries in European Economic History, Proceedings of the Tenth International Economic History Congress*, ed. Eric Aerts and John H. Munro (Leuven: Leuven University Press, 1990).

35 Herman Van der Wee, 'The western European woollen industries, 1500–1750', in *The Cambridge History of Western Textiles*, ed. David Jenkins (Cambridge: Cambridge University Press, 2003); Van der Wee, 'Industrial dynamics and the process of urbanization'.

36 The seminal work on Low Countries linen, with many errors however, is: Etienne Sabbe, *De Belgische vlasnijverheid. Deel 1: De Zuid-Nederlandse vlasnijverheid tot het verdrag van*

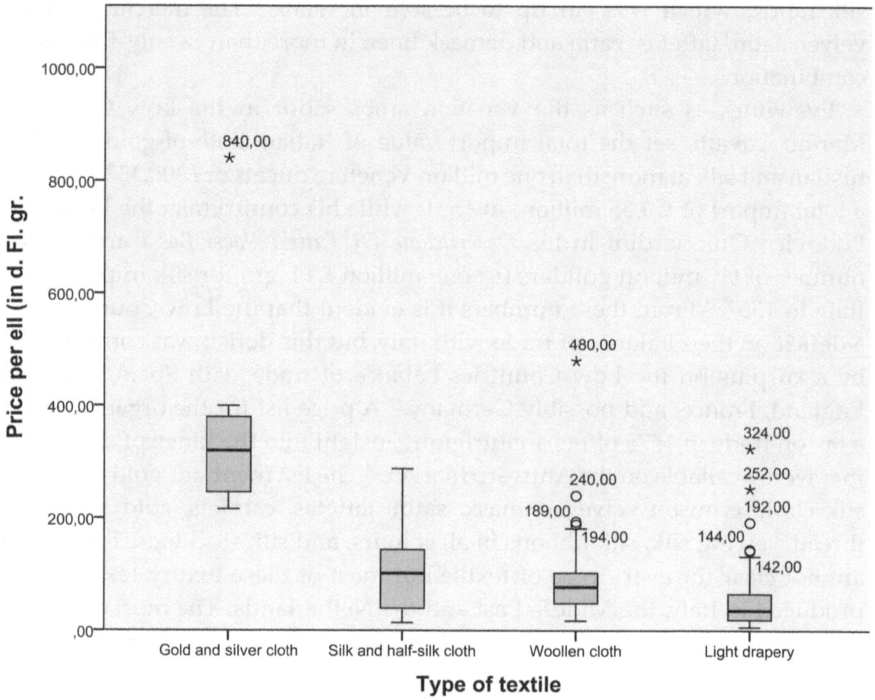

Figure 6.1: Prices of textiles available on the Antwerp market in 1575.

Source: Based on Thijs, 'Les textiles'.

Gold and silver cloth were unsurprisingly the most precious textiles available on the Antwerp market c.1575. Silk and half-silk products were only slightly more expensive than the most expensive woollen cloth, English Coggeshall cloth. Light drapery offered cheaper textile alternatives. The presence of Netherlandish satins and dyed silk for sewing, embroidering and ribbon-making in the tax list of 1575 demonstrates the existence of a native silk industry. Economic historians such as Herman Van der Wee and Alfons Thijs have argued that the development of the silk industry in the Netherlands was part of the restructuring of the economy in the fifteenth and sixteenth century: traditional cloth production declined and was partially replaced by the growing fashion, luxuries, arts and services sector.[37] Concentration of industry and the growing trade volumes that passed through cities as Antwerp enabled all kinds of product innovations, of which the silk industry is a fine example.

Utrecht (1713) (Kortrijk: Nationaal Vlasmuseum, 1975).

37 Van der Wee, 'Industrial dynamics and the process of urbanization', Herman Van der Wee, 'Structural Changes and Specialization in the Industry of the Southern Netherlands, 1100–1600', *The Economic History Review* 28 (1975): 203–221.

Because Antwerp enjoyed good connections with Italy, it became an important market and distribution centre for raw silk and silk thread. Both silk processing (twining and dyeing) and silk weaving enterprises became established in sixteenth-century Antwerp. Satin weaving (a mix of silk and linen or wool) appears for the first time in the Scheldt city in 1500, thus only after Bruges, Antwerp's commercial predecessor, where satin production began in the late fifteenth century. Commercially, satin weaving was an excellent choice: the cheaper half-silk product could not compete with the extensive imports of expensive Italian or Eastern silk cloths, but precisely this price difference allowed it to open up a different and larger group of potential buyers.[38] The 1530s and 1540s reveal a search for product differentiation and the beginning of the production of the more expensive damask and velvet. Jan Nuyts, an immigrant from Brabant, set up a firm specialising in crimson and violet silk cloth weaving and dyeing and other typically Italian silk products, for which he was granted a subsidy by the city government, a policy often pursued by the government to selectively attract economically useful migrants. His output was mainly sold in the Low Countries.[39] Immigration of silk weavers from other centres in the Low Countries to Antwerp exploded from 1566 onwards, the year of the Iconoclasm in the Low Countries, and contributed to the growth in production of not only satin but also grosgrains, *bourats* (mixed silk and wool) and velvets and led to a more international commercial orientation. In 1584 more than 4,000 workers were active in Antwerp silk weaving in a city of around 80,000 inhabitants, although it needs to be said that this growth came at the cost of other production centres in the Low Countries that were temporarily forced out of business because of the Dutch Revolt.[40] Moreover, the last third of the sixteenth century witnessed the breakthrough of silk trimmings and silk ribbons production and of silk twining and dyeing. This was possibly facilitated by a knowledge transmitted through the presence of Italian producers in Antwerp such as the Genoese dyer Stefano de la Torre and the Venetian silk twiner Ambrosius Spiritellus.[41] What began as a strategy of import substitution through the production of more inexpensive silk products and the gradual move towards more expensive silk fabrics imitating Italian and Eastern products, became an export sector at the end of the sixteenth century.[42] Tellingly, this process closely resembles

---

38 Alfons K.L. Thijs, *Van 'werkwinkel' tot 'fabriek': de textielnijverheid te Antwerpen, einde 15de – begin 19de eeuw* (Brussel: Gemeentekrediet, 1987), 123–24. For silk in Antwerp, see especially: *De zijdenijverheid te Antwerpen in de zeventiende eeuw* (Brussel: Pro Civitate, 1969).

39 Alfons K.L. Thijs, 'Een ondernemer uit de Antwerpse textielindustrie, Jan Nuyts (ca. 1512–1582)', *Bijdragen tot de geschiedenis* 51(1968).

40 Thijs, *Van werkwinkel tot fabriek*, 124–27.

41 Thijs, *Van werkwinkel tot fabriek*, 140.

42 Alfons K.L. Thijs, 'Structural changes in the Antwerp industry from the fifteenth to the eighteenth century', in *The Rise and Decline of Urban Industries in Italy and in the Low Countries (Late Middle Ages – Early Modern Times)*, ed. Herman Van der Wee (Leuven: Leuven University Press, 1988), 207–08.

the development of Italy's own silk industry in the thirteenth and fourteenth centuries; Italian silk production too started out as an import substitution industry for Eastern silks to became an export industry later on.[43]

It is no coincidence that centres such as Lille and Tournai and others in French Flanders specialised in the production of corduroys, camelots and satins that imitated silk products. *Changeants* looked like taffetas and *mockados* and *tripes de velours* were meant to resemble velvet. Ostades and rasses (arras) had long-stapled, highly-twisted yarns. The prices of these Netherlandish silk imitations ranged between seven and forty-four d. Fl. gr. and were thus much cheaper than real silks.[44] This so-called nouvelle draperie légère of smooth, light and thin fabrics was highly expansive throughout the entire sixteenth century and large volumes were exported to England, Spain, Portugal, Italy and Germany.[45] But it was also a feverish and unstable development vulnerable to fast changing tastes: the decline of one type of production could be partially set off by the rise of another, often in another town.[46] Much of this production was also performed by rural labourers in the surrounding countryside.[47] A true silk industry was also set up besides half-silk and silk imitation production in Tournai and Lille: because the same terminology is used its products are very hard to distinguish from the imitations. Courtrai vainly tried to set up an imitation silk industry by subsidising immigrant Lille satin and velvet weavers in 1528 and again in 1538.[48]

This native silk and silk imitation industry could only partially compensate for the decline of the traditional woollen drapery in the sixteenth century.[49] In 1497 Archduke Philip the Fair announced a new sumptuary law that specifically targeted the wearing of velvet and silk because it was harming the native cloth industry, preserving silk dress for the happy few. Only the high

---

[43] Rosamond E. Mack, *Bazaar to Piazza: Islamic Trade and Italian Art, 1300–1600* (Berkeley: University of California Press, 2002); Lisa Monnas, *Merchants, Princes and Painters: Silk Fabrics in Italian and Northern Paintings, 1300–1550* (New Haven: Yale University Press, 2008); Anna Muthesius, 'Silk in the medieval world', in *The Cambridge History of Western Textiles*, ed. David Jenkins (Cambridge: Cambridge University Press, 2003).

[44] Thijs, 'Les textiles', 84.

[45] Van der Wee, 'The western European woollen industries', 434–36; Patrick Chorley, 'The "draperies légères" of Lille, Arras, Tournai, Valenciennes: new materials for new markets?', in *La draperie ancienne des Pays-Bas: débouchés et stratégies de survie (14e-16e siècles) / Drapery Production in the Late Medieval Low Countries: Markets and Strategies for Survival (14th-16th Centuries)*, ed. Marc Boone et al. (Leuven: Garant, 1993), 159–61.

[46] Robert S. Duplessis, *Lille and the Dutch Revolt: Urban Stability in an Era of Revolution, 1500–1582* (Cambridge: Cambridge University Press, 1991), 96.

[47] Hugo Soly and Alfons K.L. Thijs, 'Nijverheid in de Zuidelijke Nederlanden 1490–1580', in *Algemene geschiedenis der Nederlanden*, ed. Dirk Peter Blok (Haarlem: Fibula-Van Dishoeck, 1979), 43.

[48] Peter Stabel, *De kleine stad in Vlaanderen: bevolkingsdynamiek en economische functies van de kleine en secundaire stedelijke centra in het Gentse kwartier (14de-16de eeuw)* (Brussel: Paleis der Academiën, 1995), 197–98.

[49] For the decline of and changes in traditional woollen industry, see: Van der Wee, 'Structural changes'; Van der Wee, 'Industrial dynamics and the process of urbanization'; Van der Wee, 'The western European woollen industries'.

nobility and high-ranking ducal officials and their wives and children could wear silk; all others had to wear clothes made from native cloth.[50] However, it was not so much the rise of silk dress as the success of the draperie légère producing lighter fabrics from cheaper wool varieties, mixed fabrics as fustians and the large volumes of Low Countries linen that spelled the doom of the traditional drapery.[51]

The Van der Molen's Trade in Luxury Textiles

The next section will focus on the micro-level, on the experience of individual traders and producers marketing luxury goods. One of them was Frederick Van der Molen, originally from Haarlem in Holland, who established himself as a merchant in Antwerp in the first years of the sixteenth century, after being trained by Cornelis Van Bombergen, a Flemish merchant active in Venice.[52] The first traces of his transactions as a merchant demonstrate an active trade with Italy and an involvement in the tapestry trade, as well as various other products. In one of his first documented transactions he bought 250 ells of tapestry from Henricks van Inecke, a tapestry master from the village of Sint-Geertruiden, on the Bergen op Zoom fair.[53] In the first quarter of the sixteenth century Frederick formed a partnership with Bernardo di Zanchi, an Italian merchant from Verona active in Venice. This partnership lasted until the winter of 1537 when both Frederick and Bernardo died. The sons of Frederick decided not to renew the partnership with the Zanchi family, as was stipulated in Frederick's testament.[54] Like most merchants at that time, the Van der Molen combined trading on their own account with commission trading for correspondents. Three brothers Pieter, Ghijsbrecht and Cornelis

---

50 Raymond Van Uytven, 'Showing off one's rank in the Middle Ages', in *Showing Status: Representation of Social Positions in the Late Middle Ages*, ed. Wim Blockmans and Antheun Janse (Turnhout: Brepols, 1999), 29–30.

51 Peter Stabel, ''Dmeeste, oirboirlixste ende proffitelixste let ende neringhe': een kwantitatieve benadering van de lakenproductie in het laatmiddeleeuwse en vroegmoderne Vlaanderen', *Handelingen van de Maatschappij voor Geschiedenis en Oudheidkunde te Gent* 51(1997); Soly and Thijs, 'Nijverheid in de Zuidelijke Nederlanden', 40–41.

52 On the Van der Molen: Florence Edler, 'The Van der Molen, Commission Merchants of Antwerp: Trade with Italy, 1538–44', in *Medieval and Historiographical Essays in Honour of James Westfall Thompson*, ed. James Lea Cate and Eugene N. Anderson (Chicago: The University of Chicago Press, 1938); Puttevils, 'A servitio de vostri'. On the Van Bombergen: Wilfrid Brulez, 'Lettres commerciales de Daniel et Antoine de Bombergen à Antonio Grimani (1532–43)', *Bulletin de l' Institute Historique Belge de Rome* 31(1958).

53 CAA, Certificatieboek, 3, 1510, f° 70v. 'Frederic vander Moelen, coopman alhier in der stadt frequenterende, jur[avit] van alsulcken twee hondert ende vijftich ellen tapicherie oft daer omtrent als hy nu in de leste merct van Berghen opten Zoom gecocht heeft jegens Henricks van Inecke, tapichier van Sinte Gheertruyden ende cortelings aldaer gepact selen worden in een pac gemerct metten mercke, in de margie van desen geteyckent, omme die alhier in der stad gebracht te wordene quod pertinent sibi et nemo altri'.

54 Zeeuws Archief Middelburg, Familie De Jonge van Ellemeet 40, Testament of Frederick van der Molen and Allijt Ballincx, 1534.

were working in Antwerp, while Daniel, Frederick's youngest son, worked in the Venice branch of the firm. The Van der Molen had a network of agents in the production centres of various textiles in the Low Countries: Bruges, Hondschoote and Holland, and shipping agents in Arnemuiden and London. They appear frequently in the records of the tax on trade with Italy during the years 1543–5 and they mainly shipped English and Flemish cloth, Flemish sayes (a saye is a lightly twilled woollen textile) and English kerseys to Venice, Ancona and Ferrara.[55] Besides some fragments in a range of diverse sources, only the ledger containing copies of letters sent to commission correspondents for the years 1538–1544 remains. The Van der Molen documentation is unique for it is the only extensive one remaining for the first half of Antwerp's golden sixteenth century and thus offers an exclusive insight in the marketing of luxury textiles from the city of Antwerp. The company acted as both purchasing and selling agents for principals in Rome, Ferrara, Mantua, Brescia, Genoa, Bologna, Ancona and Venice. Broadly, the Van der Molen sent English and Netherlandish textiles to Italy and imported Italian and Levantine textiles, spices, precious stones, and semi-finished products such as gold and silver thread. For their services as commission agents, the Van der Molen received a commission of three per cent on the value of the transaction, the usual fee at that time. This percentage could be lowered as a client favour.

Marketing Silk on the Antwerp Market in the Middle of the Sixteenth Century

Several of their clients sold silks through the Van der Molen on the Antwerp market. The company of Geronimo Azeretto, based in Genoa and with branches in Ferrara, Venice, Messina, Palermo and the Greek island of Chios, sent the Van der Molen Genoese velvets (see colour plate 14), Venetian tapestry silk and camlets. The Bolognese Davizani brothers sold sewing silk and two merchants from Ancona, Bernardo Morando and Giovanni Senati, sold Levantine camlets and mohair (a mixed silk fabric, using goat's hair or wool). The Venetian merchants Martino Bragadini and Martino Zerchiari exported camlets, Venetian satins and mohair to Antwerp. Mercers from Antwerp, the rest of the Netherlands and England bought the velvets, camlets and silk thread from the Van der Molen: the Bruges mercer Pieter De Rais bought twenty-six camlets on credit because of his outstanding credit record or *fama*.[56] Tapestry weavers obtained raw materials such as silk thread from

[55] ARB, Rekenkamer, 23357–23364, Accounts of Gaspar Ducci, collector of the 100th Penny on foreign exports, 1543–1545.

[56] 'Pietro le Rais merzer di Brugia qual e de principali merzeri de bona fama e credito'. CAA, Insolvente Boedelkamer, IB 2898, Copy-letterbook of Pieter Van der Molen 1538–1544, fol. 153r.

the Van der Molen.[57] The aforementioned anonymous silk merchant bought his silks from Italian, often Lucchese, merchants operating in Antwerp such as Bartolomeo Cenami and Paulo Burlamacchi, from the Antwerp merchant Gillis van Breuseghem and from retail merchants.[58]

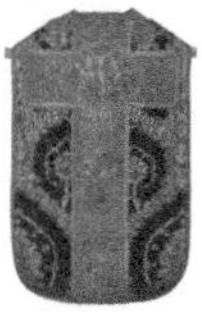

Most of these products were sold on credit with the bi-annual fairs of Bergen op Zoom and those of Antwerp as clearing terms of three months to two years. Two fairs, about six months, was the most frequent credit term. Barter, a primitive selling technique at first sight, took place as well. The values of the products were expressed in money value and each merchant slightly augmented the real value to get a bonus from the barter transaction. Part of the transaction could be settled in cash to enhance trust. For example, the Van der Molen bartered some Genoese velvets for Geronimo Azeretto in return for English kerseys.[59] *Baratto* was mainly used for commodities that were hard to sell and offered a handy strategy for cashless transactions.[60] However, barter was not always an option: the Van der Molen wrote to their Genoese client Jeronimo Azeretto di Vivaldis that they could not barter Hondschoote sayes for cloth-of-gold since the Hondschoote weavers were too poor for such a luxury product.[61] Some products such as the much-demanded high-quality English kerseys could easily be sold for cash or short-term credits and therefore did not require barter transactions. The monetary revaluations and regulations of 1539 and 1542 obliged cash payment of two thirds of the value of bills of exchange.[62] An anonymous request was sent to the Antwerp government to pressure the central government to abandon this rule. The request argued that many merchants had turned to barter to avoid this cash payment. But not all merchants could barter, it was not easy to find the right merchant who wanted to sell the commodity another merchant required. Merchants who sent their goods to agents in Antwerp for sale and did not make any purchases could not barter either.[63]

---

57 See infra, footnote 76.

58 ARB, 1548–1557, Handschriften, 2784, anonymous ledger. De Peuter, 'Mooie kleren voor hoge heren', 35–36.

59 CAA, Insolvente Boedelkamer, IB 2898, Copy-letterbook of Pieter Van der Molen 1538–1544, fol. 105v.

60 Wilfrid Brulez, *De firma Della Faille en de internationale handel van Vlaamse firma's in de 16de eeuw* (Brussel: Paleis der Academiën, 1959), 379–85.

61 CAA, Antwerp, Insolvente Boedelkamer, IB 2898, Copy-letterbook of Pieter Van der Molen 1538–1544, fol. 6r.

62 Florence Edler, 'The effects of the financial measures of Charles V on the commerce of Antwerp, 1539–1542', *Belgisch tijdschrift voor filologie en geschiedenis* 16 (1937).

63 'Item quil nargue de riens ce quon pourra dire que les marchans peuvent baratter une marchandise a laultre et ainsy eviter la constraincte de lordonnance/ pour ce nestre faisable/ ne a tous marchans convenable a cause que plussieus marchans nont besoing daultres marchan-dises/ et plussieurs diceulx envoyont icy leur marchandises faire sur leurs respondantz/ quant a quant/ tractz de changes a payer iceulx changes des mesmes deniers de leurs marchandises' CAA, Privilegiekamer, Pk 1018, undated, anonymous piece, fol. 2r.

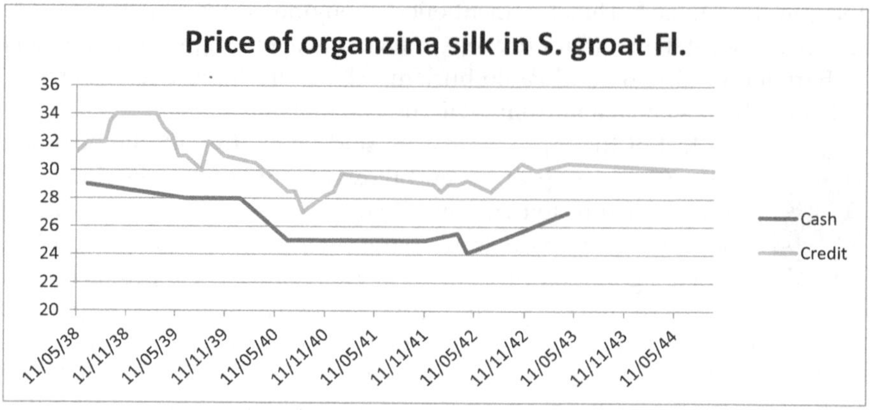

Figure 6.2: Price quotations of organzina silk in the Van der Molen letters, 1538–1544, s. Flemish groat

Note: 1 shilling Flemish groat = 0,05 £ Fl. groat

Samples of fabrics were used by the clients of the Van der Molen to obtain the right colours and quality, as did another Antwerp firm the Della Faille. Descriptions of colours and types of textiles could be tricky and ambiguous. A sample piece of textile sent together with a letter eliminated that risk.[64] Using the price quotations in the Van der Molen letters for organzina silk, raw silk that was used as the warp thread for silk cloth, the ups and downs of the market for silk products can be determined (see Figure 6.2).[65]

In October 1538 silk prices went up coinciding with the pending visit of Mary of Hungary, governor of the Low Countries, to her sister Eleanor, queen of France.[66] Prices went down in the spring of 1539 because of the death of empress Isabella of Portugal, wife of Charles V, in May. During the subsequent mourning period, the courtiers wore black woollen cloth instead of silk and velvet, causing demand to shrink.[67] This shows that the demand

[64] Edler, 'The Van der Molen', 99–100; Brulez, *De firma Della Faille*, 388–89.

[65] I use organzina silk because it is standardised product. Other silk products are less uniform, since these differed in both quality and their place of origin, which is not always clear. The data from Herman Van der Wee, 'Economic activity and international trade in the Southern Netherlands, 1538–1544', in *The Low Countries in the Early Modern World*, ed. Herman Van der Wee (Aldershot: Ashgate, 1993) have been used, adapted and combined with my own, more extensive data from the copy-book.

[66] 'La regina e partita con tuta la corte per Franza e li velutj per questi trionfi sono un pocho montati da d4 per braccio' CAA, Insolvente Boedelkamer, IB 2898, Copy-letterbook of Pieter Van der Molen 1538–1544, fol. 39r.

[67] 'La corte sono statto qui xv giorni ma non hano megliorato le facende de drapi de seta per che limperatore et tutta la corte vano anchor vestiti de panno nero' CAA, Insolvente Boedelkamer, IB 2898, Copy-letterbook of Pieter Van der Molen 1538–1544, fol. 155v. Later, in 1611, when Queen Margaret of Austria, spouse to Philip III, king of Spain, died, Marcq van Zeverdoncq supplied all the courtiers and state officials with black cloth for the mourning

exerted by the court had a large influence on price levels which stresses the size limitations of the silk market. The Habsburg war against Francis I and his allies, William, duke of Cleves, Julich and Guelders, and Christian III of Denmark, temporarily caused the closure of the Rhine route to Italy and prices went up again, after which they declined again when the route reopened and stocks could be replenished. The presence of the prince and his court procured higher profits and larger turnovers for textile merchants. Political and military crises had the opposite effect. The ledger of the anonymous silk merchant supplying the court show that the merchant bought and sold large amounts of silks in the years 1548–1549, when the Emperor Charles V and his son, the future King Philip II were in the Low Countries, and in 1555–1556 when Philip was installed as prince. Sales stalled in 1552–1553, a period of political disaster with Charles V's defeat against the French and the victories of the Lutheran princes in the Holy Roman Empire.[68] War and peace with the Ottoman empire had an effect on the price of Levantine silks as well. Note that buying silk in cash was always cheaper than buying on credit. Herman Van der Wee argues that in the years after 1544 organzina prices rose because silk clothing, traditionally limited to the court, the aristocracy and the Church, became popular among the well-to-do urban middle classes, although this is not quantitatively proven.[69] Trading luxury textiles was definitely profitable. The purchase and sales ledger of an anonymous silk merchant who bought his products, which included damask, velvet, satin, and taffeta, from Italian merchants in Antwerp and Antwerp traders and then sold them to various consumers, shows that he had a then substantial profit rate of around ten to fifteen per cent per year (or 1440 guilders per year, twenty-nine times a mason's journeyman's annual wage). The merchant only sold five pieces of silk at a loss.[70]

Marketing Flemish Tapestries

Antwerp had become the commercial gateway for tapestries at the end of the fifteenth century. Antwerp merchants and financiers such as Joris Vezeleer, Peter van der Walle and Erasmus Schets became actively involved in tapestry production and trade because of the capital demands in this sector and the

period, for the impressive amount of £ 40 265 Fl. gr. Courtesy of dr. Dries Raeymaekers (University of Antwerp). ARB, Raad van State, 157, Declaration des parties de draps et toilles d'or et d'argent, de soie et laine, 1611.

68 ARB, 1548–1557, Handschriften, 2784, anonymous ledger. De Peuter, 'Mooie kleren voor hoge heren', 39.

69 Van der Wee, 'Economic activity and international trade', 122.

70 ARB, 1548–1557, Handschriften, 2784, anonymous ledger. De Peuter, 'Mooie kleren voor hoge heren', 43–44.

access of such high-flying financiers to European courts.[71] Low Countries merchants were not the only ones active in the export of these Netherlandish products: large Italian merchant houses such as the Affaitadi shipped large quantities to Italy.[72] Between 1498 and 1502 Pieter Coecke van Aalst had a partnership with two important Florentine merchants Ludovico della Fava and Lorenzo Barducci.[73] Flemish tapestries were another luxury article often traded by the Van der Molen.[74] Tapestries with foliage or *verdure* (see colour plate 15) often appear in the correspondence; less frequent are the tapestries with figures or *tapezerie a figure*. The tapestries came in different forms and shapes: not only as wall hangings, but also as door hangings and table covers. The provenance of these products is hard to verify: sometimes there is mention of 'tapezerie a verdure dudenarde'[75] and in the correspondence the writers often refer to contacts with Brussels *tapezeri*. Subjects of the figurative tapestries such as the Story of Venus and Aeneas,[76] the Destruction of Troy and the History of Jupiter[77] are sometimes given in the correspondence.

These tapestries were sent to specialised customers in Rome, Ferrara, Mantua and Venice. Some of those can be tied directly to Italian courts. Two bankers from Como, Francesco Formento and Baldassare Olgiato, extended large loans to the Apostolic Chamber and thus enjoyed connections with the papal court in Rome.[78] Geronimo Piperario often travelled to Antwerp to purchase tapestries on behalf of cardinal Ercole Gonzaga of Mantua.[79] A typical order for tapestries went as follows: in a letter of August 1538 the Van der Molen wrote that they had ordered a tapestry with a surface of thirty-one hand palms, depicting St Martin, for the Venetian merchant Martino di Zerchiari. The Van der Molen had it designed and woven in Brussels. The design cost £ 1 6s. Fl. gr., the weaving 4s. 6d. Fl. gr.per ell (a total of £ 6 19s. Fl. gr.). With the commission fee and transport costs added, the St Martin tapestry came at a price of £ 8 18s. 2d. Fl. gr., to be paid

71 Campbell, *Tapestry in the Renaissance*, 280–82.

72 Jan Denucé, *Inventaire des Affaitadi, banquiers italiens à Anvers de l'année 1568* (Antwerpen: De Sikkel, 1934).

73 Campbell, *Tapestry in the Renaissance*, 132.

74 Some references on the tapestry trade of the Van der Molen can be found in: Denucé, *Antwerpsche tapijtkunst en handel*, 2–18.

75 CAA, Insolvente Boedelkamer, IB 2898, Copy-letterbook of Pieter Van der Molen 1538–1544, fol. 43v.

76 CAA, Insolvente Boedelkamer, IB 2898, Copy-letterbook of Pieter Van der Molen 1538–1544, fol. 73.

77 CAA, Insolvente Boedelkamer, IB 2898, Copy-letterbook of Pieter Van der Molen 1538–1544, fol. 161.

78 Francesco Guidi Bruscoli, *Papal Banking in Renaissance Rome: Benvenuto Olivieri and Paul III, 1534–1549* (Aldershot: Ashgate, 2007), 19, 89, 91–92, 107–08.

79 Clifford M. Brown, Guy Delmarcel, and Anna Maria Lorenzoni, *Tapestries for the Courts of Federico II, Ercole, and Ferrante Gonzaga, 1522–63* (Seattle, WA: College Art Association, 1996), 109–10.

to Joan Battista di Zanchi in Venice, the partner of the Van der Molen.[80] The tapestry must have pleased Zerchiari because a year later he ordered another one. The tapestry, however, was not made on order, but bought readymade on the market.[81] Hence, tapestries could be both produced on order and could be purchased when they were already finished. Precise measurements were needed and so the Van der Molen repeatedly had to write back to their Italian customers to know the missing width or length, which might suggest that the Italian customers were unfamiliar with the product and might have expected the same standardisation as in Netherlandish cloth. Orders could experience significant delays because of bad weather. For example, in January 1542 delivery was delayed because of work overload, disease or serious road traffic disruption caused by the winter weather, and terms of delivery often had to be renegotiated with the tapestry masters.

Almost no names of tapestry producers can be found in the letters. Moreover, the term *tapizero* is ambiguous: it can denote middlemen, tapestry masters and humble tapestry weavers at the same time. The Van der Molen were writing about the tapezeri of Brussels and ordering tapestries from 'el meglior maestro' of Oudenaarde.[82] Merchants and dealers such as the Van der Molen must have been in a powerful position to bargain with the tapestry makers: tapestries could be paid on delivery or cash advances could be made before the tapestries were finished. By granting the weavers cash advances, merchants and entrepreneurs could bind weavers to them.[83] The Van der Molen not only bought from tapestry masters, they also sold them raw materials. Tapestry silk from Venice was sold to (Brussels?) *tapezieri* such as Henrick Pipe and Hans Van Brecht who bought 36 pounds for £ 7 4s. Fl. gr. and 56 pounds for £ 16 9 s. Fl. gr. respectively.[84] It was these entrepreneurs travelling back and forth to Antwerp or who had agents in the Scheldt city, who were crucial for the success of both the Brussels and Oudenaarde tapestry industries: they had access to an international market for the sale of their produce and purchases of raw materials, patterns and other necessary goods.[85]

80 CAA, Insolvente Boedelkamer, IB 2898, Copy-letterbook of Pieter Van der Molen 1538–1544, fol. 45r.

81 CAA, Insolvente Boedelkamer, IB 2898, Copy-letterbook of Pieter Van der Molen 1538–1544, fol. 61r, 68v, 92r.

82 CAA, Insolvente Boedelkamer, IB 2898, Copy-letterbook of Pieter Van der Molen 1538–1544, fol. 3v, 190r.

83 Edler, 'The Van der Molen', 100; Paul Huys Janssen, *Werken aan kunst: economische en bedrijfskundige aspecten van de kunstproduktie, 1400–1800* (Hilversum: Verloren, 1995), 76; Erik Duverger, *Jan, Jacques en Frans de Moor, tapijtwevers en tapijthandelaars te Oudenaarde, Antwerpen en Gent (1560 tot ca. 1680)* (Gent: Interuniversitair Centrum voor de geschiedenis van de Vlaamse tapijtkunst, 1960), 50.

84 CAA, Insolvente Boedelkamer, IB 2898, Copy-letterbook of Pieter Van der Molen 1538–1544, fol. 63v.

85 Vanwelden, *Productie van wandtapijten*, 204–07; Erik Duverger, 'De Steurbouts, een Oudenaards-Antwerps tapissiersgeslacht', *Artes Textiles* 6 (1965); *Jan, Jacques en Frans de Moor*.

Venetian ambassador Michele Suriano was impressed by the perfection of Low Countries tapestry production: 'like mosaic makers with their small coloured stones, Low Countries tapestry weavers, with very thin wool and silk thread, can not only imitate the most diverse of colours but can also simulate shadow and light to put figures in relief, with all the nuances produced by the most skilled painter'.[86] Indeed, quality was a primary concern in the tapestry trade: in 1539 the Van der Molen corresponded on a case of litigation between the Brussels court and the Brussels tapestry makers. A member of the court bought tapestries that afterwards appeared to be more than usually retouched by dyeing over small flaws in the weave.[87] After that, not only fine Brussels but also Oudenaarde tapestries were confiscated in Antwerp. Oudenaarde was hit hard by the confiscations and the resulting problems: on 16 March 1539 the Oudenaarde bailiff Philippe de Lalaing wrote to Mary of Hungary, governor of the Low Countries, to end the sales prohibition because some 12,000 inhabitants of Oudenaarde and its surroundings, who lived off tapestry production, were then unemployed.[88] This litigation finally ended in the *Generale Ordonnantie* on tapestry trade and production in the Low Countries, arranging quality control by craft guilds, enforcing the insertion of city and weaver marks on the tapestries, and organising a legal frame for specialised tapestry brokers: they had to stand surety for insolvent buyers or delayed payments and received a fixed commission of 4 d. per £ Fl. gr. worth of tapestries.[89]

Given the fact that tapezeri are always mentioned during the Antwerp fairs in the Van der Molen correspondence, it is not unreasonable to think that meetings between merchants and producers were held and tapestries were acquired in the usual vending location for this product, the Dominicans' Pand.[90] In 1551 a new specialised Tapestry Pand was erected and sales on a permanent base were to take place there. Tapestry makers and dealers had to sell their products there or in shops without windows.[91] In the Tapestry Pand, not only tapestries of all sorts and provenances could be acquired, but also wool, tapestry silk, colourants, gold and silver thread, cartoons, and even looms, as is attested in the inventories of the shops of Hendrik van Beeringhen (1581) and Frans de Neve (1583) in the Pand.[92] It was merchants such as the

---

86 Louis-Prosper Gachard, *Relations des ambassadeurs vénitiens sur Charles-Quint et Philippe II* (Bruxelles: Hayez, 1856), 103.

87 CAA, Insolvente Boedelkamer, IB 2898, Copy-letterbook of Pieter Van der Molen 1538–1544, fol. 60, 63, 64v, 67v, 70v, 71v, 76v.

88 Martine Vanwelden, *Het tapijtweversambacht te Oudenaarde, 1441–1772* (Oudenaarde: Stadsarchief, 1979), 13; Vanwelden, *Productie van wandtapijten*, 98–101.

89 Vanwelden, *Productie van wandtapijten*, 95–98.

90 Denucé, *Antwerpsche tapijtkunst en handel*, xi-xii.

91 Hugo Soly, *Urbanisme en kapitalisme te Antwerpen in de 16de eeuw: de stedebouwkundige en industriële ondernemingen van Gilbert van Schoonbeke* (Brussel: Gemeentekrediet, 1977), 221–23 & 34–38; Vermeylen, *Painting for the Market*, 47–48.

92 Denucé, *Antwerpsche tapijtkunst en handel*, 30–42.

Van der Molen, brokers and specialised vending locations that could solve information asymmetries and who could connect buyers and sellers who were separated in time and place.[93]

Demand for Luxury Textiles

If the supply and marketing side of luxury textiles allows a sketchy but revealing insight, the demand side is even more problematic. Three types of demand for luxury textiles can be distinguished: foreign demand and local demand, which can be split up in terms of elite status – nobility and the Church – and general demand. Herman Van der Wee has claimed that besides the large international demand for these products, the growing ranks of the urban middle classes exerted a powerful demand for products such as silks and tapestry of which the possession used to be a prerogative of the nobility and the Church.[94] Two different perspectives might gauge Van der Wee's assertions.

A representative sample of 112 Antwerp probate inventories from the Antwerp orphan chamber, notary deeds, testaments from the Church of Our Lady, and confiscations by the Antwerp sheriff in civil cases, for the period 1530–1550, precisely a period of substantial growth of the silk and tapestry industries, shows a staggering variety of fabrics and textile types. Of the 2077 references to pieces of clothing, 383 or 18.4% were silk. Wool and linen clothing were dominant.[95] Entire pieces of clothing made of silk were presumably still rare possessions reserved for the higher and richer ranks of society. Yet, small pieces of silk such as silk accessories, embroidery, trimmings and ribbons are present in quite a few probate inventories, indicating that these could be bought by larger groups of society. This could explain the quick growth of the native silk industry in Antwerp, which specialised precisely in these products, first satisfying home demand and only later on becoming an export industry.[96] Moreover, we have already seen that silk imitations were produced in the Low Countries and were available at relatively low prices, thus open for a broader clientele.

---

93 Denucé, *Antwerpsche tapijtkunst en handel*, xiv-xv, xxxiv; Huys Janssen, *Werken aan kunst: economische en bedrijfskundige aspecten van de kunstproduktie, 1400–1800*, 95–98, 204–07; Ysselsteyn, *Tapestry, the Most Expensive Industry of the 15th and 16th Centuries: A Renewed Research into Technic, Origin and Iconography*, 75–78; Delmarcel, *Het Vlaamse wandtapijt van de 15de tot de 18de eeuw*, 189.

94 For example: Van der Wee, 'Economic activity and international trade', 122. Also: Soly and Thijs, 'Nijverheid in de Zuidelijke Nederlanden'.

95 Véronique Vandenbossche, '"Item eenen dronckemansstoel" Een historisch onderzoek naar de materiële cultuur: boedelinventarisonderzoek in de stad Antwerpen (1530–1550)' (MA, KU Leuven, 2000), 143–45.

96 Monnas, *Merchants, Princes and Painters: Silk Fabrics in Italian and Northern Paintings, 1300–1550*, 28–29; Muthesius, 'Silk in the medieval world'.

The ledgers of merchants provide an insight into the social distribution of luxury textiles as well. The Van der Molen mostly sold to local producers, retailers and foreign merchants. The aforementioned anonymous silk merchant and court supplier meticulously listed the pieces of silk sold to his clients, writing down their name and the amounts of fabric they had bought between 1548 and 1557. The majority of this merchant's identifiable clients were members of the nobility and government, such as Mary of Austria, governor of the Low Countries, Lamoral, count of Egmont, and even Emperor Charles V himself, besides many other aristocrats. The anonymous merchant also sold to other merchants and retailers.[97] The fact that the merchant sold large pieces of silk underlines that his clientele automatically consisted of the more well-to-do. An approximate proxy for the popularity of silk products is the number of silk merchants and retailers migrating to Antwerp and registering as new citizens. Between 1534 and 1597 fifty-six new silk merchants and retailers were registered in Antwerp, forty-six of them between 1540 and 1579.[98]

Conclusion

Substantial volumes of tapestries and silks worth thousands of pounds Fl. gr. changed hands on Antwerp's sixteenth-century market. Local demand in the Low Countries combined with a large demand abroad for tapestries and silks fuelled commerce in the city and allowed scores of merchants to earn their livelihood. Traders such as the Van der Molen family brought consumers and producers of luxury products in contact through the truly international Antwerp market. Through their local contacts with producers and their foreign correspondents they were able to match supply and demand, extended credit to both producers and consumers, and made use of an impressive market infrastructure such as the Tapestry Pand and the more invisible web of information linking various European cities. They supplied silks and gold and silver thread to tapestry weavers and sold the tapestries on Europe's markets. Given the high price of most of the luxury textiles, these were intended for a rich clientele and the nobility. The demand exerted by the rich and powerful is clearly visible in the price level of silk, which was highly sensitive to events at court. It was through the conspicuous consumption of luxury textiles that the rich and powerful wished to distinguish themselves from the rest of society. Sumptuary laws were installed to enforce dress as a reliable indication of social position. Yet, the concentration of commerce in luxury textiles in the city of Antwerp and its accessibility rendered

97 De Peuter, 'Mooie kleren voor hoge heren', 37–38.

98 Jan Van Roey, *Antwerpse poortersboeken*, 6 vols. (Antwerpen: Stadsarchief, 1978). Dr. Jan De Meester has made a database of these Poortersboeken, which we used to calculate this number.

such rigorous boundaries of social position increasingly obscure. Also, the development of a native silk industry, specialising in silk ribbons, fringes and mixed silk fabrics, and the production of silk imitations made these little luxuries come into the reach of larger groups in society. It is no coincidence that exactly these products were mentioned in the sumptuary laws as well, indicating that lower groups in society could acquire and wear a piece of silk as well, which the central government tried to forbid. Moreover, with the production of cheaper silk look-a-likes 'luxury' textiles were accessible to large groups of society, not to mention the second-hand market for silk fabrics which multiplied the group of silk wearers. By then, the relationship between dress and status had become totally obscure, no matter how hard legislators tried to set up social hierarchies (for example, one based on the number of horses one could deliver in case of war).[99] Production of silk and tapestries not only affected the consumers, it also created jobs, albeit very specialised jobs and very locally. Oudenaarde's economy and its countryside was largely dominated by the production of lower end verdure tapestries, providing work for a large mass of people rendering it very dependent on a commercial product that found capricious demand throughout Europe. Antwerp's own silk industry employed thousands of workers. All this shows that it matters to consider the production, commerce and consumption of luxury products: such an analysis allows for the discovery of the basic structure of the early modern commercial economy and the profound social changes it generated.

Bibliography

Manuscript Sources

Algemeen Rijksarchief Brussels

Handschriften, 2784, anonymous ledger.

Raad van State, 157, Declaration des parties de draps et toilles d'or et d'argent, de soie et laine, 1611.

Rekenkamer, 23357–23364, Accounts of Gaspar Ducci, collector of the 100th Penny on foreign exports, 1543–1545.

Rekenkamer, 23469–23474, Accounts of the 2% tax on export and import, 1552–1553.

Felixarchief Antwerp

Certificatieboeken, 3, 1510.

Insolvente Boedelkamer, IB 2898, Copy-letterbook of Pieter Van der Molen 1538–1544.

Privilegiekamer, letters received by the city magistracy, Pk 271, 1527.

Privilegiekamer, anonymous piece, Pk 1018, undated.

Zeeuws Archief Middelburg

Familie De Jonge van Ellemeet 40, Testament of Frederick van der Molen and Allijt

99 Howell, *Commerce before Capitalism*, 256.

Ballincx, 1534.

Published Sources

Bolton, Jim L., and Francesco Guidi Bruscoli. 'When did Antwerp replace Bruges as the commercial and financial centre of north-western Europe? The evidence of the Borromei ledger for 1438'. *The Economic History Review* 61 (2008): 360–79.

Bril, Louis. 'De handel tussen de Nederlanden en het Iberisch schiereiland (midden XVIe eeuw)'. Universiteit Gent, 1962.

Brown, Clifford M., Guy Delmarcel, and Anna Maria Lorenzoni. *Tapestries for the Courts of Federico II, Ercole, and Ferrante Gonzaga, 1522–63*. Seattle, WA: College Art Association, 1996.

Brulez, Wilfrid. 'The balance of trade of the Netherlands in the middle of the 16th century'. *Acta historiae Neerlandica* 4 (1970): 20–48.

Brulez, Wilfrid. *De firma Della Faille en de internationale handel van Vlaamse firma's in de 16de eeuw*. Brussel: Paleis der Academiën, 1959.

Brulez, Wilfrid. 'Lettres commerciales de Daniel et Antoine de Bombergen à Antonio Grimani (1532–43)'. *Bulletin de l' Institute Historique Belge de Rome* 31 (1958): 169–205.

Campbell, Thomas P, ed. *Tapestry in the Renaissance: Art and Magnificence*. New York: Metropolitan Museum of Art, 2006.

Chorley, Patrick. 'The "draperies légères" of Lille, Arras, Tournai, Valenciennes: new materials for new markets?' In *La Draperie ancienne des Pays-Bas: débouchés et stratégies de survie (14e-16e Siècles) = Drapery Production in the Late Medieval Low Countries: Markets and Strategies for Survival (14th–16th Centuries)*, edited by Marc Boone and Walter Prevenier. 151–66. Leuven: Garant, 1993.

d'Hulst, Roger- A. *Vlaamse wandtapijten van de 14de tot de 18de eeuw*. Brussel: Arcade, 1960.

De Peuter, Roger. 'Mooie kleren voor hoge heren. Beschouwingen over de textielhandel te Brussel in het midden van de zestiende eeuw'. *Textielhistorische bijdragen* 34 (1994): 30–49.

De Roover, Raymond. 'Anvers comme marché monétaire au XVIe siècle'. *Revue belge de philologie et d'histoire* 31 (1953): 1003–47.

Delmarcel, Guy. *Het Vlaamse wandtapijt van de 15de tot de 18de eeuw*. Tielt: Lannoo, 1999.

Denucé, Jan. *Antwerpsche tapijtkunst en handel*. Antwerpen: Sikkel, 1936.

Denucé, Jan. *Inventaire des Affaitadi, banquiers italiens à Anvers de l'année 1568*. Antwerpen: De Sikkel, 1934.

Doehaerd, Renée, ed. *Etudes anversoises: documents sur le commerce international à Anvers, 1488–1514*. 3 vols. Paris: SEVPEN, 1962–1963.

Duplessis, Robert S. *Lille and the Dutch Revolt: Urban Stability in an Era of Revolution, 1500–1582*. Cambridge: Cambridge University Press, 1991.

Duverger, Erik. 'De Steurbouts, een Oudenaards-Antwerps tapissiersgeslacht'. *Artes Textiles* 6 (1965): 31–74.

Duverger, Erik. *Jan, Jacques en Frans De Moor, tapijtwevers en tapijthandelaars te Oudenaarde, Antwerpen en Gent (1560 tot ca. 1680)*. Gent: Interuniversitair Centrum voor de geschiedenis van de Vlaamse tapijtkunst, 1960.

Edler, Florence. 'The effects of the financial measures of Charles V on the commerce of Antwerp, 1539–1542'. *Belgisch tijdschrift voor filologie en geschiedenis* 16, no. 3–4 (1937): 665–73.

Edler, Florence. 'The Van Der Molen, commission merchants of Antwerp: trade with

Italy, 1538–44'. In *Medieval and Historiographical Essays in Honour of James Westfall Thompson*, edited by James Lea Cate and Eugene N. Anderson. 78–145. Chicago: The University of Chicago Press, 1938.

Gachard, Louis-Prosper. *Relations des ambassadeurs vénitiens sur Charles-Quint et Philippe II*. Bruxelles: Hayez, 1856.

Guidi Bruscoli, Francesco. *Papal Banking in Renaissance Rome: Benvenuto Olivieri and Paul III, 1534–1549*. Aldershot: Ashgate, 2007.

Howell, Martha. *Commerce before Capitalism in Europe, 1300–1600*. Cambridge: Cambridge University Press, 2010.

Huys Janssen, Paul. *Werken aan kunst: economische en bedrijfskundige aspecten van de kunstproduktie, 1400–1800*. Hilversum: Verloren, 1995.

Laurent, Ch., J. Lameere, and H. Simont. *Recueil des ordonnances des Pays-Bas: 2e série, 1506–1700*. 6 vols. Brussels: Goemaere, 1893–1922.

Lesger, Clé. *The Rise of the Amsterdam Market and Information Exchange: Merchants, Commercial Expansion and Change in the Spatial Economy of the Low Countries, C. 1550–1630*. Aldershot: Ashgate, 2006.

Limberger, Michael. 'No town in the world provides more advantages: economies of agglomeration and the golden age of Antwerp'. In *Urban Achievement in Early Modern Europe: Golden Ages in Antwerp, Amsterdam and London* edited by Patrick O'Brien, Derek Keene and Marjolein 't Hart. 39–62. Cambridge: Cambridge University Press, 2001.

Mack, Rosamond E. *Bazaar to Piazza: Islamic Trade and Italian Art, 1300–1600*. Berkeley, CA: University of California Press, 2002.

Molà, Luca. *The Silk Industry of Renaissance Venice*. Baltimore: The Johns Hopkins University Press, 2000.

Monnas, Lisa. *Merchants, Princes and Painters: Silk Fabrics in Italian and Northern Paintings, 1300–1550*. New Haven, CT: Yale University Press, 2008.

Muthesius, Anna. 'Silk in the medieval world'. In *The Cambridge History of Western Textiles*, edited by David Jenkins. 325–54. Cambridge: Cambridge University Press, 2003.

Puttevils, Jeroen. 'Klein gewin brengt rijkdom in: de Zuid-Nederlandse handelaars in de export naar Italië in de jaren 1540'. *Tijdschrift voor sociale en economische geschiedenis* 6, no. 1 (2009): 26–52.

Puttevils, Jeroen. 'A servitio de vostri sempre siamo: de effecten van de handel tussen Antwerpen en Italië op de koopmansfamilie Van Der Molen'. MA, University of Antwerp, 2007.

Sabbe, Etienne. *De Belgische vlasnijverheid. Deel 1: de Zuid-Nederlandse vlasnijverheid tot het verdrag van Utrecht (1713)*. Kortrijk: Nationaal Vlasmuseum, 1975.

Soly, Hugo. *Urbanisme en kapitalisme te Antwerpen in de 16de eeuw: de stedebouwkundige en industriële ondernemingen van Gilbert van Schoonbeke*. Brussel: Gemeentekrediet, 1977.

Soly, Hugo, and Alfons K.L. Thijs. 'Nijverheid in de Zuidelijke Nederlanden 1490–1580'. In *Algemene geschiedenis der Nederlanden*, edited by Dirk Peter Blok. 27–57. Haarlem: Fibula-Van Dishoeck, 1979.

Stabel, Peter. *De kleine stad in Vlaanderen: bevolkingsdynamiek en economische functies van de kleine en secundaire stedelijke centra in het Gentse kwartier (14de-16de eeuw)*. Brussel: Paleis der Academiën, 1995.

Stabel, Peter. '"Dmeeste, oirboirlixste ende proffitelixste let ende neringhe": een kwantitatieve benadering van de lakenproductie in het laatmiddeleeuwse en vroegmoderne Vlaanderen'. *Handelingen van de Maatschappij voor Geschiedenis en Oudheidkunde te Gent* 51 (1997): 113–53.

Stabel, Peter. 'Italian merchants and the fairs in the Low Countries (12th–16th centuries)'. In *La pratica dello scambio. Sistemi di fiere, mercanti e città in Europa (1400–1700)*, edited by Paola Lanaro. 131–60. Venetië: Marsilio, 2003.

Stabel, Peter. 'Venice and the Low Countries: commercial contacts and intellectual inspirations'. In *Renaissance Venice and the North. Crosscurrents in the Time of Bellini, Dürer and Titian*, edited by B. Aikema and B.L. Brown. 30–42. Milaan: Bompiani, 1999.

Thijs, Alfons K. L. A. *De zijdenijverheid te Antwerpen in de zeventiende eeuw*. Brussel: Pro Civitate, 1969.

Thijs, Alfons K.L. 'Een ondernemer uit de Antwerpse textielindustrie, Jan Nuyts (ca. 1512–1582)'. *Bijdragen tot de geschiedenis* 51 (1968): 53–68.

Thijs, Alfons K.L. 'Les textiles au marché anversois au XVie siècle'. In *Textiles of the Low Countries in European Economic History, Proceedings of the Tenth International Economic History Congress*, edited by Eric Aerts and John H. Munro. 76–86. Leuven: Leuven University Press, 1990.

Thijs, Alfons K.L. 'Structural changes in the Antwerp industry from the fifteenth to the eighteenth century'. In *The Rise and Decline of Urban Industries in Italy and in the Low Countries (Late Middle Ages – Early Modern Times)*, edited by Herman Van der Wee. 105–13. Leuven: Leuven University Press, 1988.

Thijs, Alfons K.L. *Van 'werkwinkel' tot 'fabriek': de textielnijverheid te Antwerpen, einde 15de – begin 19de eeuw*. Brussel: Gemeentekrediet, 1987.

Van der Wee, Herman. 'Economic activity and international trade in the Southern Netherlands, 1538–1544'. Translated by Lizabeth Fackelman. Chap. 6 In *The Low Countries in the Early Modern World*, edited by Herman Van der Wee. 115–25. Aldershot: Ashgate, 1993.

Van der Wee, Herman. *The Growth of the Antwerp Market and the European Economy (Fourteenth-Sixteenth Centuries)*. 3 vols Den Haag: Nijhoff, 1963.

Van der Wee, Herman. 'Handel in de Zuidelijke Nederlanden'. In *Nieuwe Algemene Geschiedenis Der Nederlanden*. 75–95. Haarlem: Fibula-Van Dishoeck, 1987.

Van der Wee, Herman. 'Industrial dynamics and the process of urbanization and de-urbanization in the Low Countries from the late middle ages to the eighteenth century. A synthesis'. In *The Rise and Decline of Urban Industries in Italy and in the Low Countries (Late Middle Ages – Early Modern Times)*, edited by Herman Van der Wee. 307–88. Leuven: Leuven University Press, 1988.

Van der Wee, Herman. 'Structural changes and specialization in the industry of the Southern Netherlands, 1100–1600'. *The Economic History Review* 28, no. 2 (1975): 203–21.

Van der Wee, Herman. 'The western European woollen industries, 1500–1750'. In *The Cambridge History of Western Textiles*, edited by David Jenkins. 397–472. Cambridge: Cambridge University Press, 2003.

Van Roey, Jan. *Antwerpse poortersboeken*. 6 vols. Antwerpen: Stadsarchief, 1978.

Van Uytven, Raymond. 'Showing off one's rank in the Middle Ages'. In *Showing Status: Representation of Social Positions in the Late Middle Ages*, edited by Wim Blockmans and Antheun Janse. 19–34. Turnhout: Brepols, 1999.

Vandenbossche, Véronique. '"Item eenen dronckemansstoel". Een historisch onderzoek naar de materiële cultuur: boedelinventarisonderzoek in de stad Antwerpen (1530–1550)'. MA, KU Leuven, 2000.

Vanwelden, Martine. *Het tapijtweversambacht te Oudenaarde, 1441–1772*. Oudenaarde: Stadsarchief, 1979.

Vanwelden, Martine. *Productie van wandtapijten in de regio Oudenaarde: een symbiose tussen stad en platteland (15de tot 17de eeuw)*. Leuven: Universitaire Pers, 2006.

Vermeylen, Filip. 'De export vanuit de Zuidelijke Nederlanden naar Duitsland omstreeks het midden van de 16de eeuw'. MA, Catholic University of Louvain, 1989.
Vermeylen, Filip. *Painting for the Market: Commercialization of Art in Antwerp's Golden Age*. Turnhout: Brepols, 2003.
Ysselsteyn, van G. T. *Tapestry, the Most Expensive Industry of the 15th and 16th Centuries: A Renewed Research into Technic, Origin and Iconography*. The Hague: Van Goor, 1969.

PART III
Production of Luxury Textiles

7

The Move to Quality Cloth. Luxury Textiles, Labour Markets and Middle Class Identity in a Medieval Textile City. Mechelen in the Late Thirteenth and Early Fourteenth Centuries

Peter Stabel

The period around 1300 witnessed a fundamental breakthrough in the social history of the pre-modern cities of the Low Countries. The period not only meant the end of the long period of urban growth, in which the urban element in the core principalities of the southern Low Countries, Flanders and Brabant, accounted for over a third of the total population, a percentage unequalled anywhere else in Northern Europe, but these changes also included structural shifts in the social balance within most cities, as guild-organised middle groups of manufacturers and retailers were able to gain access to political and economic power.[1] Moreover, their impact on urban society as a whole became much greater and most social historians would agree with naming the middle groups of guild craftsmen and retailers as constituting the backbone of late medieval and early modern urban society in this region.[2] As Catharina Lis and Hugo Soly have argued very convincingly in their recent study on attitudes to work and workers in pre-industrial Europe, these societal middle groups, however diverse and heterogeneous they were, developed their own ideological tools to value the place of work in urban society.

In a breathtaking process of rapid social change shortly before and after 1300, they were also able to gain access to power and set new standards for

---

1 On the urban system Peter Stabel, 'Composition et recompositions des réseaux urbains des Pays-Bas au bas moyen âge', in *Villes de Flandre et d'Italie : relectures d'une comparaison traditionnelle*, ed. Elisabet Crouzet-Pavan et al. (Turnhout: Brepols, 2007), 29–64.

2 See the recent synthesis by Bruno Blondé, Frederik Buylaert, Jan Dumolyn, Jord Hanus and Peter Stabel, 'Samenleven in de stad: sociale relaties tussen ideaal en realiteit', in *Een stadsgeschiedenis van de Nederlanden 1100–1600*, ed. Bruno Blondé et al., forthcoming.

organising the urban economy.[3] Their struggle to compete with the leading social groups of traditional land-owning and mercantile urban elites would, however, never yield complete hegemony and in most cities a political compromise between the two groups led to systems of sharing power, in often very complicated institutional arrangements whereby guilds achieved access to city councils or benches of aldermen. From the 1300s the craft guilds became a force to be reckoned with, even in cities where access to political power would prove only temporary.[4] The rising importance of guild-organised urban middle classes in the larger cities of Flanders and Brabant is also strangely linked to important industrial changes, whereby the dominant textile industries shifted from being a mass producer of all kinds of (woollen) fabrics to exclusive manufacturing centres aiming at the highest niches of luxury textiles. One might say that social change was triggered as well by entrepreneurial responses to economic difficulty, which resulted in directing efforts towards luxury segments of the market.

There is little doubt that the revolutionary period before and after 1300 had been crucial in achieving this shift. But most authors remain vague as to the particularities of this development. Even Lis and Soly are unclear about this issue.[5] Therefore, what constituted a worker's identity in this period remains to a large extent elusive. It is clear from recent scholarship that there was no such thing as a common worker's ethic.[6] Not even the powerful late medieval and early modern craft guilds of the southern Low Countries were able to structure their ideological tools and their attitudes to work into one single

3 Catharina Lis and Hugo Soly, *Worthy Efforts: Attitudes to Work and Workers in Pre-Industrial Europe* (Leiden: Brill, 2012) and Hugo Soly, 'The Political Economy of Guild-Based Textile Industries: Power Relations and Economic Strategies of Merchants and Master Artisans in Medieval and Early Modern Europe', in *The Return of the Guilds*, ed. Jan Lucassen et al. (Cambridge: Cambridge University Press, 2008); *International Review of Social History, Supplement* 53 (2008): 45–71.

4 Most prominently in the cities of Flanders: Jan Dumolyn, 'Guild Politics and Political Guilds in Fourteenth-Century Flanders', forthcoming; Wim Blockmans, 'Regionale Vielfalt im Zunftwesen in den Niederlanden vom 13. bis zum 16. Jahrhundert', in *Handwerk in Europa vom Spätmittelalter bis zur Frühen Neuzeit*, ed. Knut Schulz, (Munich: Oldenbourg, 1999), 51–63. In Brabant the final result was much more mixed; see Raymond Van Uytven, 'Plutokratie in de 'oude demokratieën der Nederlanden' Cijfers en beschouwingen omtrent de korporatieve organisatie en de sociale struktuur der gemeenten in de late middeleeuwen', *Handelingen van de Koninklijke Zuidnederlandse Maatschappij voor Taal- en Letterkunde en Geschiedenis*, 17 (1962): 373–409. More recently, see also: Maarten Prak, 'Corporate politics in the Low Countries: Guilds as Institutions, 14th to 18th Centuries', in *Craft Guilds in the Early Modern Low Countries: Work, Power, and Representation*, ed. Maarten Prak et al. (Aldershot: Ashgate, 2006), 74–106

5 Lis and Soly, *Worthy Efforts*, 323ff.

6 On medieval labour identities, see also Heather Swanson, *Medieval Artisans: An Urban Class in Late Medieval England* (Oxford and New York: Blackwell, 1989). Robert S. DuPlessis and Martha C. Howell have provided the analytical framework of the small-commodity producer in, 'Reconsidering the Early Modern Urban Economy: the Cases of Leiden and Lille', *Past and Present* 94 (1982): 49–84.

set of values.[7] Social, economic and even political hierarchies among guild masters; sectorial differences between manufacturing and retailing guilds and between local and regional supply and export industries; hierarchies of access to economic opportunity between masters, skilled journeymen, apprentices and unskilled workers; subcontracting among masters; varying access to capital and credit: all of these elements presented too great an obstacle to allow the dominance of one single and homogenous guild identity.[8]

There was, of course, still some common class identity of workers. From the late Middle Ages onwards, guilds spent a great deal of effort (and money) on the fashioning of guild ideology (often with different access of the various constituencies within the guild: guild administrators, masters, journeymen and apprentices). Common meals, common rituals (burials), a common chapel with collective liturgical celebrations, common pageants where often the order of the participating guilds proved a major element of political competition, common membership of the city militia, sometimes even common dress, needed to accentuate the brotherhood of all guild members.[9] Most guilds used the rhetoric of equal opportunity and brotherhood to smooth relations within the group or to ease the burden of economic competition. There is no doubt whatsoever that ideas of brotherhood and solidarity penetrated into the psyche of guildsmen and guildswomen. Recently, I have shown with Anke De Meyer that even in very different juridical settings (such as the urban civil court that settled conflicts in urban society and princely pardon for criminal offenders), guildsmen in the fifteenth century constructed their guild identities to present themselves as hardworking, modest subjects where guild

---

7 On retailing, see Peter Stabel, 'Markets in the cities of the late medieval Low Countries: retail, commercial exchange and socio-cultural display', in *Fiere e mercati nella integrazione delle economie europee, secoli 13–18*, ed. S. Cavaciocchi, (Firenze: Istituto di storia economica F. Datini, 2001), 797–817.

8 Jean-Pierre Sosson, 'Les métiers: norme et réalité. L'exemple des anciens Pays-Bas méridionaux aux XIVe et XVe siècles', in *Le travail au Moyen Âge: une approche interdisciplinaire*, ed. J. Hamesse et al. (Louvain-la-Neuve: Publications de l'Institut d'Etudes Médiévales, 1990), 339–348; Stephan R. Epstein, 'Craft Guilds, Apprenticeship and Technological Change in Pre-Industrial Europe', *Journal of Economic History* 58 (1998): 684–713. Various contributions in *Craft Guilds in the Early Modern Low Countries*, ed. Prak et al. (Aldershot: Ashgate, 2006) and *Guilds, Innovation, and the European Economy, 1400–1800*, ed. Stephan R. Epstein et al. (Cambridge: Cambridge University Press, 2008).

9 Gervase Rosser, 'Crafts, Guilds and the Negotiation of Work in the Medieval Town', *Past and Present*, 154 (1997): 3–31, Peter Stabel, 'Guilds in Late Medieval Flanders: Myths and Realities of Guild Life in an Export-Oriented Environment', *Journal of Medieval History*, 30 (2004): 187–212. Similar developments can be found for other guilds, organising military, religious and cultural activities in the urban social fabric of the Low Countries. Peter Arnade, *Realms of ritual. Burgundian ceremony and civic life in late medieval Ghent* (Ithaca/London: Cornell University Press, 1996) and Laura Crombie, 'Honour, Community and Hierarchy in the Feasts of the Archery and Crossbow Guilds of Bruges, 1445–81', *Journal of Medieval History*, 37 (2011): 102–113 discuss the shooting guilds; Paul Trio, *De Gentse broederschappen (1182–1580): ontstaan, naamgeving, materiële uitrusting, structuur, opheffing en bronnen* (Ghent, 1990) talks about religious fraternities; and Anne-Laure Van Bruaene, *Om beters wille. Rederijkerskamers en de stedelijke cultuur in de Zuidelijke Nederlanden(1400–1650)* (Amsterdam: Amsterdam University Press, 2008) discusses the Chambers of Rhetoricians.

values such as solidarity and mutual assistance were no empty words.[10] In contemporary literature, urban writers and playwrights constantly referred to markers of guild identity.[11] When in the course of the seventeenth and eighteenth centuries a wave of more formal behaviour entered guild life, this is considered by many scholars to be a sign that the old communal ideas of solidarity and brotherhood gradually lost their pre-eminence.[12]

If there is little doubt about the craft guild's agency as a set of values with which manufacturers and retailers alike could identify, the relation with something like a worker's identity is much less clear. Many of the recent syntheses on guilds fail to a certain extent to discuss the chronological development of guild and worker identities. It is as if, when guilds started to appear (in the southern Low Countries this is a gradual process that can be situated in the thirteenth century), they straightaway embodied these identities. Their political agency even brought their attitudes to work on a higher (i.e. urban) level. But guilds were slow to grow. They often started as informal (or even illegal) religious fraternities and solidarities. Their early name of charities ('charités' or 'cariteyt') in the Artesian and Flemish cities also points at mutual assistance as one of the core activities of these associations, even when formal systems of assisting poor or sick guild members with a 'bourse' or 'bus' appeared only much later in the fifteenth century.[13] Even when, in the second half of the thirteenth century, craft guilds became influential economic institutions and gradually started regulating economic manufacture and exchange, this was always a gradual process contested by other stakeholders in the urban economy, of course firstly by the merchant and landowning elites.

Moreover, even in cities where guilds could rise to municipal power, effects of social polarisation within the guild favoured wealthier and better connected entrepreneurs (guild masters), who often conspired with the merchants to control access to political power and power within the guild.[14] The process of increasing control of the craft guilds on economic life could also be reversed.

---

10 Anke De Meyer and Peter Stabel, 'Fashioning the self in courts of law. Performance of guild identities in the late medieval Low Countries', *Cultural and Social History*, forthcoming.

11 Jan Dumolyn and Jelle Haemers, 'Patterns of Urban Rebellion in Medieval Flanders', *Journal of Medieval History*, 31 (2005): 369–393; Dumolyn and Haemers, '"A Bad Chicken was Brooding": Subversive Speech in Late Medieval Flanders', *Past and Present*, 214 (2012): 45–68.

12 Bert De Munck, 'From brotherhood community to civil society? Apprentices between guild, household and the freedom of contract in early modern Antwerp', *Social History*, 35 (2010): 1–20.

13 Carlos Wyffels, *De oorsprong der ambachten in Vlaanderen en Brabant* (Brussels: Koninklijke Vlaamse academie voor wetenschappen, letteren en schone kunsten van België, 1951) and Jean-Pierre Sosson, 'Die Körperschaften in den Niederlanden und Nordfrankreich: neue Forschungsperspektiven', in *Gilden und Korporationen in den nordeuropäischen Städten des späten Mittelalters*, ed. Klaus Friedland (Cologne: Böhlau, 1984), 79–90.

14 Processes of growing polarisation in political guild ideology are discussed in Jan Dumolyn and Jelle Haemers, 'Let each man carry on with his trade and remain silent'. Middle class ideology in the urban literature of the late medieval Low Countries', *Cultural and Social History*, 10 (2013): 169–189.

When in 1438 Bruges suffered a defeat against their prince, Duke Philip the Good of Burgundy, the reins of political power were placed within the hands of the bench of aldermen, again controlled by the urban elites rather than by the middle groups of associated craftsmen, and the craft guilds had to suffer again the sanctioning of the city's aldermen for all their actions.[15] A similar fate befell the Ghent guilds after their failed revolt in 1540 against Charles V.[16]

In order to assess how workers' identities shifted in the process, we need to look more closely at how they were expressed in these changing environments. We will look at the first stage of this development, when workers' identities were slowly integrated into a guild framework across the thirteenth and fourteenth centuries. Although Mechelen hosted a number of industrial activities, the manufacture of woollen cloth, by far the most important until the early sixteenth century, was taken as a test case. In the major cloth-producing cities of the Southern Low Countries, textile manufacture employed more than half of the working population, which included many women.[17] Moreover, as the industry transformed itself from mass production of a wide range of fabrics into a luxury industry aiming for the highest niches in the market and producing only the finest and most expensive woollens for export in exactly the period we are studying, a major shift of workers' identities can be anticipated.[18] From proletarianised craftsmen, without much control of the manufacturing process, many textile workers became quasi-independent small-commodity producers, some of them even succeeding in controlling the manufacturing process instead of the merchant-entrepreneur.[19] Sadly, except for the regulatory environment of cloth manufacture (statutes), precious little

15 Stabel, 'Guilds in late medieval Flanders', and Jan Dumolyn, *De Brugse opstand van 1436–1438* (Kortrijk: UGA, 1997).

16 Johan Dambruyne, *Corporatieve middengroepen. Aspiraties, relaties en transformaties in de 16de-eeuwse Gentse ambachtswereld* (Gent: Academia Press, 2002).

17 Walter Prevenier, 'Bevolkingscijfers en professionele strukturen der bevolking van Gent en Brugge in de 14de eeuw', in *Album Charles Verlinden* (Wetteren: Universa, 1975); Peter Stabel, *Dwarfs among giants: the Flemish urban network in the late Middle Ages* (Studies in urban social, economic and political history of the medieval and modern Low Countries 8, Leuven/Apeldoorn, 1997).

18 On this shift, see Herman Van der Wee, 'Industrial dynamics and the process of urbanization and de-urbanization in the Low Countries from the late middle ages to the eighteenth century. A synthesis', in *The rise and decline of urban industries in Italy and in the Low Countries (late middle ages - early modern times)*, ed. Herman Van der Wee, (Leuven: Leuven University Press, 1988); John H. Munro, 'Industrial Transformations in the North-West European Textile Trades, c. 1290-c. 1340: Economic Progress or Economic Crisis?', in *Before the Black Death. Studies in the 'Crisis' of the Early Fourteenth Century*, ed. Bruce M.S. Campbell (Manchester: Manchester University Press, 1991), 110–148, Patrick Chorley, 'The Cloth Exports of Flanders and Northern France during the Thirteenth-Century: a Luxury Trade?', *Economic History Review* 40 (1987): 349–379 and Peter Stabel, 'Dmeeste, oirboirlixste ende proffitelixste let ende neringhe': een kwantitatieve benadering van de lakenproductie in het laatmiddeleeuwse en vroegmoderne Vlaanderen', *Handelingen van de Maatschappij voor Geschiedenis en Oudheidkunde te Gent*, new series 51 (1997): 113–153.

19 Hans Van Werveke, 'De Koopman-ondernemer en de ondernemer in de Vlaamsche lakennijverheid van de Middeleeuwen', *Mededeelingen van de Koninklijke Vlaamsche Academie voor Wetenschappen, Letteren en schoone Kunsten van België. Klasse der Letteren* 8 (1946).

documentation has survived that can comment on workers' identities. But recent research amply demonstrates how the regulatory environment was also an economic instrument allowing change and conversion, and catering therefore for social change within the industries or retailing activities. These frequently adapted statutes can therefore also be revealing of changing attitudes to work.[20]

Cloth Production in Medieval Mechelen

Mechelen is, together with its Flemish counterparts Ypres and Douai, one of the few medieval cloth cities from the Low Countries for which extensive source materials have survived from the thirteenth and early fourteenth centuries that can document these processes.[21] But in order to interpret these materials, a closer look at how the textile industry was organised in this period is necessary. As such the development of cloth manufacture follows, be it with a certain chronological distance, the trajectory of most major Flemish and Artesian textile cities.[22] Mechelen's textile industry must have been closely associated with the city's urban growth in the twelfth and early thirteenth centuries. Already in 1213 a cloth hall (greatly expanded in the fourteenth century, see colour plate 16) was mentioned and even before 1235 Mechelen cloth was exported to England. However, Jean Paul Peeters, the leading historian of the Mechelen and Brabantine textile manufacture, considers that the main flowering of the industry took place only from the 1270s.[23] If

20 Peter Stabel, 'Working women and guildsmen in the Flemish textile industries (13th and 14th century). Gender, labor and the European marriage pattern in an era of economic change', forthcoming on the role of women on the textile labour markets in medieval Flanders and Artesia.

21 These data have been published in Henri Joosen, 'Recueil de documents relatifs à l'histoire de l'industrie drapière à Malines (des origines à 1384)', *Bulletin de la Commission royale d'histoire* 99 (1935): 365–572. Mechelen is one of the major towns in today's province of Antwerp, Belgium, and is roughly halfway between Antwerp and Brussels. The town is often called by its French name of 'Malines' in historical literature.

22 The most recent works of synthesis about the economic and social history of medieval Mechelen remain Raymond Van Uytven and Marc De Laet, 'Een bloeiende laken- en stapelstad van het midden van de dertiende eeuw tot 1473. Het sociaal-economische leven', in *De geschiedenis van Mechelen. Van heerlijkheid tot stadsgewest*, ed. Raymond Van Uytven (Tielt: Lannoo, 1991), 41–57, and Wenceslaus Mertens, 'Een prinselijke stad 1473–1530. Toenemende economische welvaart' in *De geschiedenis van Mechelen*, 83–93. Useful data about population development and industrial expansion in this period can also be found in Jos Verbeemen, 'De demografische evolutie van Mechelen 1370–1800', *Handelingen van de Koninklijke Kring voor Oudheidskunde, Letteren en Kunst van Mechelen* 57 (1953): 63–97.

23 Jean Paul Peeters, 'De produktiestructuur der Mechelse lakennijverheid en de ambachten van wevers en volders van 1270 tot 1430', *Handelingen van de Koninklijke Kring voor Oudheidskunde, Letteren en Kunst van Mechelen* 88 (1984): 93–158, and Peeters, 'Aspecten van de structurele mutatie der Mechelse lakennijverheid in het midden van de 15de eeuw (1430–1470)', *Handelingen van de Koninklijke Kring voor Oudheidskunde, Letteren en Kunst van Mechelen* 82 (1978): 65–131, Roger Trouvé, 'Belangrijke keerpunten voor wevers, weefnijverheid en economie te Mechelen in 1436 en 1458', *Studia Mechliniensia. Bijdragen aangeboden aan dr.*

this was the case – but data is scarce to make very bold statements about textile output before that period – Mechelen's textile manufacturers must have profited from the troublesome period of Flemish textile manufacture that started around this period. More difficult European outlets because of trade insecurity, higher taxes on English wool exports and social revolt in the major Flemish textile cities led to changing manufacturing strategies and huge unemployment.[24] Mechelen seems to have escaped miraculously from this predicament and Mechelen textiles appeared in full force on the European market from the Mediterranean to Central Europe.[25] Only shortly before 1350, Mechelen entrepreneurs started to experience the problems their Flemish colleagues had known half a century before, and their reaction was, unsurprisingly, very similar. They changed, or were forced to change, more and more to the manufacture of luxury textiles, made from the finest (and most expensive) English wool and using increasingly expensive dyes. Furthermore, they capitalised on skilled labour and luxury, rather than on lower wages for semi-skilled craftsmen and mass production.

The gradual change to a niche market for luxury textiles must have, as in the Flemish and Artesian cities, affected the labour relations in early fourteenth-century Mechelen to no small extent. As textile output dropped from 30,000 at the peak of the industry in the 1330s to 10,000 in the 1350s and even to about 5,000 in the early fifteenth century, many craftsmen saw opportunities to work in textile manufacture dwindle away, while others could claim a new position as small-scale entrepreneurs in what had effectively now become a luxury industry.[26] Mechelen luxury textiles even survived the hecatomb of Low Countries cloth industries in the latter part of the fifteenth century. Even on the Antwerp market in the 1570s expensive Mechelen cloth was still among staple textiles, in the same range of quality as the cloth from its Flemish counterpart Ypres and the most expensive English broadcloth finished in

H. *Joosen*, Mechelen (1976): 31–68, and a couple of studies by Raymond Van Uytven, '(De omvang van de Mechelse lakenproductie vanaf de 14de eeuw tot de 16de eeuw', *Noordgouw* 5 (1965): 1–22 and 'La draperie brabançonne et malinoise du XIIe au XVIIIe siècle: grandeur éphémère et décadence', in *Produzione, commercio e consumo dei panni di lana*, ed. Marco Spallanzani (Florence, 1976), 85–97.

24 John H. Munro, 'Medieval Woollens: Textiles, Textile Technology, and Industrial Organisation, c. 800–1500', in *The Cambridge History of Western Textiles*, ed. David Jenkins (Cambridge: Cambridge University Press, 2003) 181–227, and Munro, 'Medieval Woollens: The Western European Woollen Industries and their Struggles for International Markets, c.1000–1500', *The Cambridge History*, 228–324.

25 The importance of Mechelen's textiles in the general cloth exports of the Low Countries is discussed in Robert-Henri Bautier, 'La place de la draperie brabançonne et plus particulièrement bruxelloise dans l'industrie textile du moyen âge', *Annales de la Société Royale d'Archéologie de Bruxelles* 51 (1966): 31–63, and, of course, Hektor Ammann, 'Deutschland und die Tuchindustrie nordwesteuropas im mittelalter', *Hansische Geschichtsblätter* 72 (1954): 1–65.

26 Van Uytven and De Laet, Een bloeiende laken- en stapelstad, 41–57, and Mertens, Een prinselijke stad, 83–93.

Antwerp itself.[27] Production in Mechelen, however, had dropped by this time to a mere 2,500 pieces and employment in woollen textile manufacture had become only marginal to the total urban economy.

From Merchant Control to Guild Agency: The Late Thirteenth Century

Like in Flanders, the change also implied a shifting political balance in the city, as the new craftsmen wanted a tighter grip on the urban administration. In the symbolic year of 1302 the bench of aldermen, the playground of a few elite families, was opened to the influence of the craft guilds.[28] Twelve councillors or *iurati*, chosen from the city's merchant guilds by the city's craft guilds complemented the elitist bench of aldermen, but this gesture of the city's elite was not enough to stop the ambition of the stronger urban middle groups. A revolt was suppressed by the city's lord, Jan Berthout, and the Duke of Brabant in 1303, but even by 1305 a new charter was granted whereby the guilds could now appoint their own representatives in the council. As a result, the bench of aldermen also became less exclusive and from 1338 onwards, the craft guilds (and above all textile weavers) were even able to have their representatives among the aldermen and from the 1380s they would also be represented in the financial administration of the city.

This political development also reflects the changing balance of power within the city's main industry. From the late thirteenth century onwards the guilds started to appear as a new force in the regulatory environment of the textile industry. However, this means that most of the cloth regulation before that date emanates from the commercial elites of the city, the members of Mechelen's merchant guild, and that once the craft guild came into play, regulation was becoming more and more of a compromise between the merchants on the one hand and the craft guild's leaders on the other.[29]

---

27 Alfons K.L. Thijs, 'Les textiles au marché anversois au XVI Siècle', in *Textiles of the Low Countries in European Economic History, Proceedings of the Tenth International Economic History Congress*, ed. Eric Aerts et al. (Leuven: Leuven University Press, 1990). For a survey of the fifteenth and sixteenth-century developments of Mechelen's cloth industry, see: Jean Paul Peeters, 'Sterkte en zwakte van de Mechelse draperie in de overgan van middeleeuwen naar nieuwe tijd (1470–1520)', *Handelingen van de Koninklijke Kring voor Oudheidskunde, Letteren en Kunst van Mechelen* 90 (1986): 129–176 and Peeters, 'Het verval van de lakenijverheid te Mechelen in de 16de eeuw en het experiment met de volmolen 1520–1580', *Handelingen van de Koninklijke Kring voor Oudheidskunde, Letteren en Kunst van Mechelen* 89 (1985): 143–195.

28 Van Uytven and De Laet, 'Een bloeiende laken- en stapelstad', 60–62.

29 Only in Bruges, the most important trading hub in the Low Countries, the merchant guild yielded as much political power, Hans Van Werveke, 'Hansa in Vlaanderen en aangrenzende gebieden', *Handelingen van het Genootschap voor Geschiedenis te Brugge* 90 (1953): 60–87, Van Werveke, 'Das Wesen der flandrischen Hansen', *Hansische Geschichtsblätter* 76 (1958): 88–103; Carlos Wyffels, 'De Vlaamse Hanzen opnieuw belicht', *Academiae Analecta* 53 (1991): 8–13.

Interpreting the status of workers from the industry's regulation must take into account this changing perspective.

The earliest regulation of the textile industry demonstrates unequivocally a merchant's perspective. Merchants dealing in cloth and wool were members of a merchant guild, first mentioned in 1268,[30] and their monopoly on trade in Mechelen was sanctioned by the city lord Wouter Berthout in August 1276, when the merchants were able to institute their own system of officials[31] to control cloth output at the city's cloth press. Henceforth members of the (merchant) guild[32] were to act for the common interest of the community; special measures were taken for auto regulating access to and exclusion from the guild, and guild members received a quasi-monopoly on trade.[33] The presence of Mechelen cloth on the European textile markets became important exactly in this period, from the late thirteenth century onwards.[34] Needless to say, the merchants' grip on textile workers must have been almost unconstrained. Already by the 1240s the Mechelen authorities agreed with Ghent and Antwerp not to employ fugitive textile workers from these other cities.[35] Although little is known about the real impact of the Mechelen merchants on manufacture itself, there is little doubt that they also conformed more or less to the ideal type defined by the Douaisien merchant-entrepreneur Jehan Boinebroke.[36] They formed a closed community, closely associated with political power in the city, the select clique of aldermen stemming from only a couple of elite families and the city lords of the noble Berthout dynasty. Traitors of their interests were banned from the guild and intruders were not welcome, certainly not if they belonged to the 'deceitful trades' (the *fallacis officii* of those living from manual labour). Weavers and fullers, the two most crucial stages of textile manufacture had even to pay a double taxation when they wanted to participate in the city's commerce. Craftsmen were kept away from the lucrative trade that constituted the foundation for the city's ruling elite.[37]

In the meantime, however, the textile workers had succeeded in organising themselves into craft guilds. The first surviving statutes of the Mechelen

30 On 24 May 1268, the guild ('Gulde Machliniensis') received from the city's lord Wouter Berthout the right on the city's ditch and all the fisheries that were organised there (Joosen, *Recueil de documents*, 399 and Peeters, 'Mechelse lakennijverheid', 94).

31 *Custodes*, or in the Dutch texts *warders/wardeerers.*

32 In contrast to the craft guilds, the merchant guild is called the *gulda Machliniensis.* Craft guilds are usually described as craft *(neringe).*

33 Joosen, *Recueil de documents*, 401–404, and Peeters, *Mechelse lakennijverheid*, 94. The statutes were confirmed in 1302 by the Duke of Brabant in a slightly changed version: Joosen, *Recueil de documents*, 415–417.

34 See, for example, the correspondence with the 'gardes des foires' of Champagne and Brie, published in Joosen, *Recueil de documents*, 407–409.

35 Joosen, *Recueil de documents*, 394–396.

36 Georges Espinas, *La draperie dans la Flandre française au moyen âge*, (Paris, 1923); Espinas, *Les origines du capitalisme, 1. Sire Jehan Boinebroke patricien et drapier douaisien (1286 environ)*, (Lille, 1933).

37 Joosen, *Recueil de documents*, 402, and Peeters, Mechelse lakennijverheid, 96.

textile industry, those for textile weavers dating from September 1270, are still a clear testimony of the dominance of the merchants and their guild, but also of a rising labour consciousness among the artisans themselves.[38] The statutes were decreed by the representative of the city lord, Gillis Berthout acting on behalf of his grandfather, by the aldermen of the city and the merchant guild, and witnessed by representatives of the craft guild of the cloth weavers.[39] The formula leaves little doubt as to who was in charge; although it also reveals that the weavers even at this early stage of craft guild development were clearly represented by their own craft guild. The merchant-guildsmen expected any craftsman who noticed a breach of the statutes to come before their dean and denounce the fact, which the officials of the craft guild itself were to corroborate. The latter were appointed in close association with the merchant guild. But respect was not only expected for the officials of the merchant guild. Cloth weavers who insulted their own craft guild officers were also forbidden to execute their trade until amends were made.[40] The statutes of 1270 were to a certain extent already a compromise between the merchant elites and the craftsmen in this most essential of Mechelen's industries.

It was, however, still the needs of the merchant-entrepreneur that were at the heart of most regulation. Hence weavers could not abandon their work or go on strike (*uutganc*), in order not to jeopardise the output for the merchants, nor were they allowed to put themselves in debt for their trade, so limiting in this way possibilities of expanding their workshop and become competitors for the merchants.[41] On regular weekdays, even on blue Mondays, when absenteeism from work was considered a problem, weavers had to be available for the entrepreneur to be hired. Once a labour contract was negotiated, they were not allowed to abandon this contract to get a better deal elsewhere, and, if they did, they risked an extremely high fine and payment of all the damages caused.[42] Weavers could not exercise their trade in Mechelen if they had been condemned (banned from their hometown) for theft or another felony and had not sat out their punishment. In addition, solidarity among the weavers was severely restricted. Journeymen craftsmen, struck by illness, were allowed to only once undertake a tour[43] or collection of alms among their colleagues for support, and in order to be allowed to do this they had to ask permission from the officials of the craft guild, but also from those of the merchant guild. In the same way weavers were not allowed

38 Joosen, *Recueil de documents*, 462–468.

39 The merchants are called *guldebruedere van Mechelen*, the representatives of the craft guild who witnessed the event *den gemeinen getuge sambochts van den weveren van Mechelen* (Joosen, *Recueil de documents*, 463).

40 Joosen, *Recueil de documents*, 467–468.

41 Joosen, *Recueil de documents*, 465.

42 Joosen, *Recueil de documents*, 463–464.

43 The word used, '*ommeganc*', has the connotation of a very public event.

to make a round of the 'looms' (workshops) to ask for a gratuity from their colleagues (*drincpenninge*).[44] Restrictions for all craftsmen were important. These were surely not yet independent master weavers, and indications for clear hierarchies between master employers and journeymen employees are almost absent. They were in all but name mere workers for the merchant's entrepreneurial activities.

But not all was bleak for the textile workers. Already in 1270 the statutes had been to some extent a compromise between merchants and craftsmen. Not only was the craft guild's existence formally recognised by the merchants united in the guild and by the urban ruling elites, but its authority in controlling industrial manufacture and its institutional development into a board of officials were also acknowledged, albeit reluctantly. But things went further. Economic relations were changing and the move towards luxury textiles that took place around this period necessitated a different relationship between craftsmen and merchants. Some of the rulings in the 1270 statutes were already pointing in the direction of the regulatory environment that fully fledged craft guild organisation would achieve in the course of the fourteenth century. Training of apprentices was restricted to a limited circle of relatives or people of *good fame and conduct*, which must have limited to no small extent competition among skilled artisans and must have reinforced at the same time their bargaining power with the commercial elites. The increasing quality of Mechelen textiles was not only a matter of technical skill, expensive raw materials and commercial strategy. It was also something that needed to be constructed in social relations, in institutional arrangements and, last but not least, in entrepreneurial and labour identity. The tide was turning in favour of the middle-class craftsmen, as small-commodity producers, at the expense of the merchant's control of industrial relations. The shift to luxury textiles and the guild control it required proved a real catalyst in this.

Hence the strange 'moralistic' notions already present in the 1270 regulations must not necessarily be interpreted, as Mechelen cloth specialist Jean Paul Peeters did, as a way for the ruling elites to force a bunch of craftsmen into adopting 'civilised behaviour'.[45] In the course of the fourteenth and fifteenth centuries these rulings would be as much part of the construction of a master craftsman's identity. Reputation was to be one of the cornerstones of guild ideology. It was the instrument used to pursue social, economic and political aspirations, from setting standard qualities to maintaining relations of trust and credit. Hence fines for not wearing decent (of course woollen) dress during work for both employers and employees (masters and journeymen) and bans on living with a prostitute or on not paying your drinking debt in due time, can be seen as tools of identity and as instruments in building a workman's

44 Joosen, *Recueil de documents*, 465.
45 Peeters, *Mechelse lakennijverheid*, 94ff.

reputation in a period when it was reputation that decided the success of the industry as a whole. As such these 'moralistic' aspects of medieval industrial regulation complement more obvious rulings against cheating and theft.[46]

Employers and Employees: Hierarchies and Luxuries in a Guild Economy c.1300

The weavers' statutes of 1270 are not only indicative of the still overwhelming dominance of the merchant class and of an embryonic development of what would become the guildsman's identity, it also demonstrates how the Mechelen textile industry at the brink of an industrial change towards ever more expensive luxury woollens already constituted a very complex labour market, where relations, not only between workers and merchants, but also between masters and their employees, the journeymen and apprentices had become crucial for the success of the industry as a whole. Hence most attention was paid to the way the labour market had to be organised. The time of work, the place where entrepreneurs could recruit their work force, and so on, all received ample attention.[47] Market transparency had to limit transaction costs for what still were very vulnerable small-commodity producers.

Although weavers were still cut off from the market for finished commodities (fabrics) or raw materials (wool), they were already moulding the labour market for their own purposes. A standard weaver's workshop usually had more than one large loom, and a fully employed workshop therefore needed, besides the labour input of the master himself, at least three skilled journeymen and a couple of unskilled servants or apprentices. Being able to hire these journeymen according to the work that was available was therefore necessary to guarantee the economic success and even the survival of the workshop. Moreover, working for time rate wages (*dagelijcse hure*) was a normal part of the labour market for everyone, and not only for journeymen but also for the masters themselves. Gradually masters developed hierarchical networks of subcontracting, whereby masters sold the industrial output of their own workshop to other masters who had the necessary capital or access

46 For the fifteenth century, see Myriam Carlier and Peter Stabel, 'Questions de moralité dans les villes de la Flandre au bas moyen âge: sexualité et activité urbaine (bans échevinaux et statuts de métiers)', *'Faire Banz, edictz et statuts'* légiférer dans la ville médiévale, ed. Jean-Marie Cauchies, (Brussels, 2002), 241–262. Recent literature on the use of morality in the construction of the craftsman's identity and the construction of value of his products can be found in Lis and Soly, *Worthy Efforts,* and Bert De Munck, 'The agency of branding and the location of value : hallmarks and monograms in early modern tableware industries', *Business history* 54 (2012): 1055–1076.

47 Stabel, 'Labour time, guild time? Working hours in the cloth industry of medieval Flanders and Artois (thirteenth-fourteenth centuries)', *The Low Countries Journal of Social and Economic History,* forthcoming.

to larger orders from the merchants.[48] Flexible and transparent markets for labour were crucial in this respect. Weavers, masters and journeymen (the text of 1270 is not that explicit) were to stand each week at the graveyard of the central parish church of Saint Rumbold if they wanted work, and artisans who already had a job for the week were not allowed to be present, in order not to confuse the actors on the market, probably so that these masters and journeymen could profit from labour shortages to raise their price and have employers compete with each other for labour. Workers were also not allowed to do anything more than just wait for a job, as taking the initiative to talk to an employer was discouraged and in particular skilled master weavers working at the premises of other masters were regarded with great suspicion. At the same time, work was forbidden after nightfall (the working bells had to be respected) and working outside the city's jurisdiction was also not allowed for urban craftsmen. The only exceptions where craftsmen were allowed to work were Nieuwland and Nekkerspoel, two of the city's densely populated suburbs, which were counted as being part of the urban environment.

All of these measures were continuously expanded in the course of the following decades. Mechelen became a real guild economy where the construction of quality was achieved in the guild curriculum and through guild-related activities. From the 1290s training became one of the focal points in Mechelen's textile regulation.[49] Guild-organised training in the master's workshop provided one of the prime tools for regulating entrance into the guild and for turning the guild into a community of insiders and outsiders. Formalisation of relations between master and apprentices was paramount in the weavers' statutes of 1295, even more so because the link with training within the close family still present in 1270 was abandoned. The thresholds for admittance depended henceforth on monetised entrance fees and the approval of the guild officials. A fixed training period of at least four years in the same workshop turned the apprentices into a dependable part of the workshop's labour force. Contract enforcement was crucial in this relationship, and guilds catered mostly for the needs of the master employers when they took action against apprentices who left their workshop, in claiming paternal-like power of the master over the apprentice.

But apprenticeship was not the only way of organising the community. Guilds did not aim for equality despite the fact that equal opportunity was paramount in their ideological discourse. The master weavers, the so-called *drapers*, would become the main recruiting ground for the textile entrepreneurs in the late medieval city of the southern Low Countries. Relations between masters and their skilled employees as such became paramount in

48 General observations in Catharina Lis and Hugo Soly, 'Subcontracting in Guild-Based Export Trades, 13th–18th Centuries' in *Guilds, Innovation, and the European Economy*, ed. Maarten Prak et al. (Cambridge: Cambridge University Press, 2008).

49 Joosen, *Recueil de documents*, 394–396.

constructing quality and guaranteeing the long-term survival in the city of the textile business as a whole. This was particularly true for the main stages of production. Medieval textile manufacture in the cities of the Low Countries as such had always been an extremely fragmented labour market, even before the craft guilds arrived. When guilds came of age around 1300, the process was certainly not reversed. In fact many of the older networks of dependence between various occupations in the treatment of wool and yarn, in the manufacture of the fabric and in the finishing of the woollens, that had existed in the early stages of cloth manufacture in the twelfth and thirteenth century, were maintained. However, the pivotal figure in organising the chain of manufacture changed from the merchants to the drapers, who were usually an elite of the wealthier weavers.

Hence almost everywhere the drapers' interests became the real focus for regulation. As both their economic and non-economic hold on labour relations must have been weaker than that of their predecessor the merchant-entrepreneur, craft guilds came in to reinforce the master's position in the ubiquitous bargaining processes that constituted a medieval labour market. Regulations governing hiring journeymen were very detailed and the conduct of journeymen was strictly defined, including their working hours and lunch breaks and the fact that they could not remain idle once hired. Registers were kept every Monday where all journeymen in the weavers' guild had to matriculate before entering the job market at Saint Rumbold.

Subcontracting proved a much harder issue to integrate into guild regulation. If subcontracting happened through linking the manufacturing capacity of several workshops, there was no real problem. Hierarchical networks of workshops were at the heart of the guild system. Differential access to capital, raw materials and outlets advantaged some masters, and reduced others to working for their more successful colleagues. It became much more awkward if the boundaries between employers and employees became less well defined. Masters working on other men's premises provided such a case. The tools of the trade, which for master weavers were their loom and raw materials, were the essence of a guildsman's identity and they were the foundation for quality control by the guild authorities. Masters in a luxury trade working with tools and materials that were not their own therefore complied less with the required standards. As they were no journeymen either, who fell under the responsibility of the employing master, their economic activity was ill-defined and obscured from the regular systems of control. Mechelen textile entrepreneurs, increasingly aiming at the top end of the market, were particularly hesitant in allowing these kinds of economic relations, although they never completely disallowed them. The textile market was too fluid and unpredictable and a sudden rise or decline in demand was an integral part of the business. The demand needed to be met by flexible labour markets. But mistrust remained and the fear of mixing qualities and blurring notions of standard quality inspired guild regulation to forbid masters from working or even selling their future labour on the labour market elsewhere if they had enough work of their own in their own workshop. And weavers were certainly not allowed to stay the night on the premises of their employer. For the same reasons masters should not accept too much work, for example more than the capacity of their own workshop. This measure, usually seen as a tool of equalisation, was, however, certainly not aimed at limiting the output of the drapers' business, but it required them to make more use of subcontracting, which was easier to control and did not require that much ill-defined labour. The cliché image of the small workshop was certainly not a reality yet in late thirteenth and early fourteenth-century Mechelen. Instead the weavers' guild tried to limit the damage that could potentially result from low levels of control in larger economic entities by developing best practices for drapers, who used journeymen to run their workshop when they were not present, adding extra hierarchy by appointing a master journeyman or *meester cnape*.

However, the guilds did not limit themselves to only regulating the labour market. The economic position of both masters and journeymen, of employers and employees, was continuously linked to moral standing. Construction of quality was achieved through a guildsman's identity. From the 1300s ever more refined systems of fines were levied on excessive drinking, on promiscuity and illicit sexuality, on gambling, not to mention far worse behaviour such as theft, fighting and cheating. Breaching a set code of behaviour was considered unacceptable for a guildsman's proper behaviour. The casuistic nature of fines and other penalties may look like a kind of para-fiscal system to subsidise the guild itself, but there was nothing random about them. They were all intended to promote moral decency that was expected of every guildsman, master and journeyman alike. Reputation was at the heart of construction of quality on which the guild system was built. If guild masters and their employees were to offer a guarantee and a beacon of trustworthiness in a market characterised by ideas of a just price and asymmetrical access to information about the market itself and the products that were manufactured and traded, their behaviour should be beyond reproach.[50] In pre-industrial society, middle-class values of modesty, reliability, truthfulness and hard work entered the realm of the economy.

50 Bo Gustafsson, 'The Rise and Economic Behavior of Medieval Craft Guilds: An Economic-Theoretical Interpretation', *Scandinavian Journal of Economics* 35 (1987): 1–40, and the literature cited in footnote 8.

Consolidation of a Luxury Industry: Labour Relations in the Fourteenth Century

In the early 1300s the pace of regulation increased even further. The weavers' statutes of 1295 would remain the basis for further legislation in the guild and the general pattern would remain more or less the same. If anything, the focus on quality would become more important in this period, as gradually the total volume of cloth output diminished and Mechelen drapers started to focus on fewer but more expensive woollens. This implied that guild statutes increasingly had to focus on the raw materials (wool) and on the technical aspects of production. In particular the statutes of the 1330s provide great detail about the technical requirements of expensive Mechelen plain and striped cloth.[51] But the status of the workers themselves, masters or journeymen, developed further as well. The segmentation of the labour market into masters and journeymen was accentuated even further, but above all the master weaver, or more correctly the successful master weaver, had by now become synonymous for *draper*.[52] Drapers replaced completely the pivotal role of the merchant and master weavers in organising manufacture and they seem to have acted vis-à-vis other occupational groups in the industry much in the same way as the merchants had done in the previous century vis-à-vis the weavers. The fullers were the first to experience this shift in the statutes of the 1330.[53] As in Ghent, the fourteenth century witnessed sharp conflicts between weavers and fullers in Mechelen with an outright revolt in the 1360s.[54] In contrast to the Flemish and Artesian cities, women were strangely absent from the legislative framework of textile manufacture in Mechelen, even as drapers.[55]

In 1303, masters working on the premises of other entrepreneurs were completely banned. Every master had to work his own looms and the workforce henceforth consisted of the hierarchically inferior guildsmen, the skilled journeymen.[56] A few years later, the weavers' statutes of 1308 were established in close collaboration with the city aldermen and the craft guild. The direct dominance of the Mechelen merchant guild over the industry had now formally ended. This development took place despite the fact that merchants still very much controlled the bench of aldermen, although, there as well, their hold on political power in the city was more and more contested. In the statutes of 1339 the merchant guild was formally forbidden to intervene in the affairs of the craft guilds of weavers and fullers. Yet, their intervention

51 Joosen, *Recueil de documents*, 504–513.
52 Peeters, *Mechelse lakennijverheid*, 116–117.
53 Joosen, *Recueil de documents*, 506–507.
54 Peeters, *De Mechelse lakennijverheid*, 121, and Van Uytven and De Laet, 'Een bloeiende laken en stapelstad', 61–62.
55 Compare with Stabel, 'Women', forthcoming.
56 Joosen, *Recueil de documents*, 475–476, and Peeters, *Mechelse lakennijverheid*,108–109.

was still possible in other production stages.[57] But as the higher entrance and membership fees for craftsmen in the merchant guild had earlier been abandoned, in fact, many of the textile dealers in Mechelen surely must have been by now the master weavers themselves.

Subsequently, the statutes focused on the group of urban master weavers. Leaving the city without consent from the guild authorities was not allowed without endangering your future prospects in the industry and any manufacturing activity in the countryside was looked upon with great suspicion.[58] Subcontracting was limited to the direct contract between the draper (master weaver) and his dependent master weavers: the latter could not transfer their contract to other masters. In short, the heart of the industry became the workshop of the small-commodity middle-class producer. His economic agency was the driving force, while that of other groups from journeymen to subcontracting masters was severely limited. The authority of the guild officials was reinforced as these continued to control also the non-economic life of guild members. Insulting or contradicting guild officers became a serious and expensive offence.

Conclusions

The period around 1300 witnessed a drastic shift of labour identities in textile manufacture in many textile cities of the Low Countries. As the industry changed under market pressure from a massive producer of all kinds of woollens to a more selective producer of ever more refined and more expensive woollens, the balance of power within urban communities shifted in favour of the middle classes of skilled craftsmen and retailers. As a result the traditional mercantile and landowning elites had to agree to compromise and share access to power. Mechelen, one of the most successful cloth cities in the southern Low Countries, typically follows this trajectory in the late thirteenth and early fourteenth centuries. As master craftsmen – in first instance a select group of wealthier entrepreneurs – could achieve this pivotal role in urban society, they gradually adapted the existing systems of organising labour markets. Great emphasis was placed on the actual labour relations inside the workshop. But they also seem to have adopted a set of values that placed more attention on moral behaviour and strict hierarchies among guild members. Labour identities, therefore, must have shifted considerably. The opposition between manual labour, the deceitful trades, and merchants, which still dominated class struggle in the second half of the thirteenth century, made room for a hierarchical labour market where under

57 Joosen, *Recueil de documents*, 534.
58 Joosen, *Recueil de documents*, 508.

pressure from small-commodity producers, the successful drapers, labour relations were increasingly formalised and focused on quality. This process fundamentally changed the social equilibrium in the manufacturing cities of the Low Countries. The rise of the middle classes, considered by many as one of the fundamental developments in the social history of late medieval and early modern cities, is, therefore, intrinsically linked to the rise of new labour mentalities.

Bibliography

Ammann, Hektor. 'Deutschland und die Tuchindustrie nordwesteuropas im mittelalter'. *Hansische Geschichtsblätter* 72 (1954): 1–65.

Arnade, Peter. *Realms of ritual. Burgundian ceremony and civic life in late medieval Ghent.* Ithaca/London: Cornell University Press, 1996.

Bautier, Robert-Henri. 'La place de la draperie brabançonne et plus particulièrement bruxelloise dans l'industrie textile du moyen âge'. *Annales de la Société Royale d'Archéologie de Bruxelles* 51 (1966): 31–63.

Blockmans, Wim. 'Regionale Vielfalt im Zunftwesen in den Niederlanden vom 13. bis zum 16. Jahrhundert'. In *Handwerk in Europa vom Spätmittelalter bis zur Frühen Neuzeit*, edited by Knut Schulz, 51–63. Munich: Oldenbourg, 1999.

Blondé, Bruno; Buylaert, Frederik; Dumolyn, Jan; Hanus, Jord and Stabel, Peter. 'Samenleven in de stad: sociale relaties tussen ideaal en realiteit'. In *Een stadsgeschiedenis van de Nederlanden 1100–1600*, edited by Bruno Blondé, forthcoming.

Carlier, Myriam and Stabel, Peter. 'Questions de moralité dans les villes de la Flandre au bas moyen âge: sexualité et activité urbaine (bans échevinaux et statuts de métiers)'. In *'Faire Banz, edictz et statuts' légiférer dans la ville médiévale*, edited by Jean-Marie Cauchies, 241–262. Brussels, 2002.

Chorley, Patrick. 'The Cloth Exports of Flanders and Northern France during the Thirteenth Century: A Luxury Trade?'. *Economic History Review* 40 (1987): 349–379.

Crombie, Laura. 'Honour, Community and Hierarchy in the Feasts of the Archery and Crossbow Guilds of Bruges, 1445–81'. *Journal of Medieval History* 37 (2011): 102–113.

Dambruyne, Johan. *Corporatieve middengroepen. Aspiraties, relaties en transformaties in de 16de-eeuwse Gentse ambachtswereld*. Gent: Academia Press, 2002.

De Meyer, Anke and Stabel, Peter. 'Fashioning the self in courts of law. Performance of guild identities in the late medieval Low Countries'. *Cultural and Social History*, forthcoming.

De Munck, Bert. 'From brotherhood community to civil society? Apprentices between guild, household and the freedom of contract in early modern Antwerp'. *Social History* 35 (2010): 1–20.

De Munck, Bert. 'The agency of branding and the location of value: hallmarks and monograms in early modern tableware industries'. *Business History* 54 (2012): 1055–1076.

Dumolyn, Jan and Haemers, Jelle. ' "A Bad Chicken was Brooding": Subversive Speech in Late Medieval Flanders'. *Past and Present* 214 (2012): 45–68.

Dumolyn, Jan and Haemers, Jelle. 'Patterns of Urban Rebellion in Medieval Flanders'. *Journal of Medieval History* 31 (2005): 369–393.

Dumolyn, Jan. 'Guild Politics and Political Guilds in Fourteenth-Century Flanders'.

Forthcoming.
Dumolyn, Jan. *De Brugse opstand van 1436–1438*. Kortrijk: UGA, 1997.
Dumolyn, Jan. 'Let each man carry on with his trade and remain silent'. Middle class ideology in the urban literature of the late medieval Low Countries'. *Cultural and Social History* 10 (2013): 169–189.
DuPlessis, Robert S. and Howell, Martha C. 'Reconsidering the Early Modern Urban Economy: the Cases of Leiden and Lille'. *Past and Present* 94 (1982): 49–84.
Epstein, Stephan R. 'Craft Guilds, Apprenticeship and Technological Change in Pre-Industrial Europe'. *Journal of Economic History* 58 (1998): 684–713.
Georges Espinas. *La draperie dans la Flandre française au moyen âge,* (Paris, 1923), *Les origines du capitalisme, 1. Sire Jehan Boinebroke patricien et drapier douaisien (1286 environ),* (Lille, 1933).
Epstein, Stephan R. and Prak, Maarten. *Guilds, Innovation, and the European Economy, 1400–1800*. Cambridge: Cambridge University Press, 2008.
Gustafsson, Bo. 'The Rise and Economic Behavior of Medieval Craft Guilds: An Economic-Theoretical Interpretation'. *Scandinavian Journal of Economics* 35 (1987): 1–40.
Joosen, Henr. 'Recueil de documents relatifs à l'histoire de l'industrie drapière à Malines (des origines à 1384)'. *Bulletin de la Commission royale d'histoire* 99 (1935): 365–572.
Lis, Catharina and Soly, Hugo. 'Subcontracting in Guild-Based Export Trades, 13th–18th Centuries'. In *Guilds, Innovation, and the European Economy*, edited by Stephan R. Epstein and Maarten R. Prak, 81–113. Cambridge: Cambridge University Press, 2008.
Lis, Catharina and Soly, Hugo. *Worthy Efforts: Attitudes to Work and Workers in Pre-Industrial Europe*. Leiden: Brill, 2012.
Munro, John H. 'Industrial Transformations in the North-West European Textile Trades, c. 1290-c. 1340: Economic Progress or Economic Crisis?'. In *Before the Black Death. Studies in the 'Crisis' of the Early Fourteenth Century*, edited by Bruce M.S. Campbell, 110–148. Manchester: Manchester University Press, 1991.
Munro, John H. 'Medieval Woollens: The Western European Woollen Industries and their Struggles for International Markets, c.1000–1500'. In *The Cambridge History of Western Textiles*, edited by David Jenkins, 228–324. Cambridge: Cambridge University Press, 2003.
Peeters, Jean Paul. 'Aspecten van de structurele mutatie der Mechelse lakennijverheid in het midden van de 15de eeuw (1430–1470)'. *Handelingen van de Koninklijke Kring voor Oudheidskunde, Letteren en Kunst van Mechelen* 82 (1978): 65–131.
Peeters, Jean Paul. 'De produktiestructuur der Mechelse lakennijverheid en de ambachten van wevers en volders van 1270 tot 1430'. *Handelingen van de Koninklijke Kring voor Oudheidskunde, Letteren en Kunst van Mechelen* 88 (1984): 93–158.
Peeters, Jean Paul. 'Het verval van de lakenijverheid te Mechelen in de 16de eeuw en het experiment met de volmolen 1520–1580'. *Handelingen van de Koninklijke Kring voor Oudheidskunde, Letteren en Kunst van Mechelen* 89 (1985): 143–195.
Peeters, Jean Paul. 'Sterkte en zwakte van de Mechelse draperie in de overgan van middeleeuwen naar nieuwe tijd (1470–1520)'. *Handelingen van de Koninklijke Kring voor Oudheidskunde, Letteren en Kunst van Mechelen* 90 (1986): 129–176.
Prak, Maarten, ed. *Craft Guilds in the Early Modern Low Countries*. Aldershot: Ashgate, 2006.
Prak, Maarten. 'Corporate politics in the Low Countries: Guilds as Institutions, 14th to 18th Centuries'. In *Craft Guilds in the Early Modern Low Countries: Work, Power, and Representation*, edited by Maarten Prak, 74–106. Aldershot: Ashgate, 2006.

Prevenier, Walter. 'Bevolkingscijfers en professionele strukturen der bevolking van Gent en Brugge in de 14de eeuw'. In *Album Charles Verlinden*, 269–303. Wetteren: Universa, 1975.

Rosser, Gervase. 'Crafts, Guilds and the Negotiation of Work in the Medieval Town'. *Past and Present* 154 (1997): 3–31.

Soly, Hugo. 'The Political Economy of Guild-Based Textile Industries: Power Relations and Economic Strategies of Merchants and Master Artisans in Medieval and Early Modern Europe'. In *The Return of the Guilds*, edited by Jan Lucassen et al., 45–72. Cambridge: Cambridge University Press, 2008.

Sosson, Jean-Pierre. 'Die Körperschaften in den Niederlanden und Nordfrankreich: neue Forschungsperspektiven'. In *Gilden und Korporationen in den nordeuropäischen Städten des späten Mittelalters*, edited by Klaus Friedland, 79–90. Cologne: Böhlau, 1984.

Sosson, Jean-Pierre. 'Les métiers: norme et réalité. L'exemple des anciens Pays-Bas méridionaux aux XIVe et XVe siècles'. In *Le travail au Moyen Âge: une approche interdisciplinaire*, edited by J. Hamesse, 339–348. Louvain-la-Neuve: Publications de l'Institut d'Etudes Médiévales, 1990.

Stabel, Peter. 'Dmeeste, oirboirlixste ende proffitelixste let ende neringhe': een kwantitatieve benadering van de lakenproductie in het laatmiddeleeuwse en vroegmoderne Vlaanderen'. *Handelingen van de Maatschappij voor Geschiedenis en Oudheidkunde te Gent*, new series 51 (1997): 113–153.

Stabel, Peter. 'Composition et recompositions des réseaux urbains des Pays-Bas au bas moyen âge'. In *Villes de Flandre et d'Italie: relectures d'une comparaison traditionnelle*, edited by Elisabet Crouzet-Pavan, Elodie Lecuppre-Desjardin, Marc Boone, 29–64. Turnhout: Brepols, 2007.

Stabel, Peter. 'Guilds in Late Medieval Flanders: Myths and Realities of Guild Life in an Export-Oriented Environment'. *Journal of Medieval History* 30 (2004): 187–212.

Stabel, Peter. 'Labour time, guild time? Working hours in the cloth industry of medieval Flanders and Artois (thirteenth-fourteenth centuries)'. *The Low Countries Journal of Social and Economic History*, forthcoming.

Stabel, Peter. 'Markets in the cities of the late medieval Low Countries: retail, commercial exchange and socio-cultural display'. in *Fiere e mercati nella integrazione delle economie europee, secoli 13–18*, edited by Simonetta Cavaciocchi, 797–817. Firenze: Istituto di storia economica F. Datini, 2001.

Stabel, Peter. 'Working women and guildsmen in the Flemish textile industries (13th and 14th century). Gender, labor and the European marriage pattern in an era of economic change'. Forthcoming.

Stabel, Peter. *Dwarfs among giants: the Flemish urban network in the late Middle Ages.* Studies in urban social, economic and political history of the medieval and modern Low Countries 8, Leuven/Apeldoorn, 1997.

Swanson, Heather. *Medieval Artisans: An Urban Class in Late Medieval England.* Oxford and New York: Blackwell, 1989.

Thijs, Alfons K.L. 'Les textiles au marché anversois au XVI Siècle'. In *Textiles of the Low Countries in European Economic History, Proceedings of the Tenth International Economic History Congress*, edited by Eric Aerts and John Munro, Leuven: Leuven University Press, 1990.

Trio, Paul. *De Gentse broederschappen (1182–1580): ontstaan, naamgeving, materiële uitrusting, structuur, opheffing en bronnen.* Ghent, 1990.

Trouvé, Roger. 'Belangrijke keerpunten voor wevers, weefnijverheid en economie te Mechelen in 1436 en 1458'. *Studia Mechliniensia. Bijdragen aangeboden aan dr. H. Joosen*, Mechelen (1976): 31–68.

Van Bruaene, Anne-Laure. *Om beters wille. Rederijkerskamers en de stedelijke cultuur in de Zuidelijke Nederlanden (1400–1650)*. Amsterdam: Amsterdam University Press, 2008.

Van der Wee, Herman. 'Industrial dynamics and the process of urbanization and de-urbanization in the Low Countries from the late middle ages to the eighteenth century. A synthesis'. In *The rise and decline of urban industries in Italy and in the Low Countries (late middle ages - early modern times)*, edited by Herman Van der Wee, 307–381. Leuven: Leuven University Press, 1988.

Van Uytven, Raymond and De Laet, Marc. 'Een bloeiende laken- en stapelstad van het midden van de dertiende eeuw tot 1473. Het sociaal-economische leven'. In *De geschiedenis van Mechelen. Van heerlijkheid tot stadsgewest*, edited by Raymond Van Uytven, 41–57. Tielt: Lannoo, 1991.

Van Uytven, Raymond. '(De omvang van de Mechelse lakenproductie vanaf de 14de eeuw tot de 16de eeuw'. *Noordgouw* 5 (1965): 1–22

Van Uytven, Raymond. 'La draperie brabançonne et malinoise du XIIe au XVIIIe siècle: grandeur éphémère et décadence'. In *Produzione, commercio e consumo dei panni di lana*, edited by Marco Spallanzani, 85–97. Florence, 1976.

Van Uytven, Raymond. 'Plutokratie in de 'oude demokratieën der Nederlanden', Cijfers en beschouwingen omtrent de korporatieve organisatie en de sociale struktuur der gemeenten in de late middeleeuwen'. *Handelingen van de Koninklijke Zuidnederlandse Maatschappij voor Taal- en Letterkunde en Geschiedenis* 17 (1962): 373–409

Van Werveke, Hans. 'Das Wesen der flandrischen Hansen'. *Hansische Geschichtsblätter* 76 (1958): 88–103.

Van Werveke, Hans. 'De Koopman-ondernemer en de ondernemer in de Vlaamsche lakennijverheid van de Middeleeuwen'. *Mededeelingen van de Koninklijke Vlaamsche Academie voor Wetenschappen, Letteren en schoone Kunsten van België. Klasse der Letteren* 8 (1946).

Van Werveke, Hans. 'Hansa in Vlaanderen en aangrenzende gebieden'. *Handelingen van het Genootschap voor Geschiedenis te Brugge* 90 (1953): 60–87.

Verbeemen, Jos. 'De demografische evolutie van Mechelen 1370–1800'. *Handelingen van de Koninklijke Kring voor Oudheidskunde, Letteren en Kunst van Mechelen* 57 (1953): 63–97.

Wyffels, Carlos. 'De Vlaamse Hanzen opnieuw belicht'. *Academiae Analecta* 53 (1991): 8–13.

Wyffels, Carlos. *De oorsprong der ambachten in Vlaanderen en Brabant*. Brussels: Koninklijke Vlaamse academie voor wetenschappen, letteren en schone kunsten van België, 1951.

[illegible] Laura. [illegible] Amsterdam: Amsterdam University Press, 2013.

Van der Wee, Herman. "Industrial dynamics and the process of urbanization and de-urbanization in the Low Countries, from the late middle ages to the eighteenth century. A synthesis." [illegible] Leuven: Leuven University Press, [illegible]

[illegible] Raymond. [illegible]

[illegible] de 15[illegible]

Van Uytven, Raymond. [illegible] edited by [illegible] Florence, [illegible]

Van [illegible]

[illegible]

Van [illegible]

Woollen Luxury Cloth in Late Medieval Italy[1]

Franco Franceschi

Within the wide range of activities developed in the cities of late medieval Italy, those related to the production of textiles occupied a crucial position. The processing of wool, cotton and silk drained large proportions of 'industrial' investments and provided a livelihood for thousands of families, all of whose members, the youngest included, were often engaged in the production of its finished products. Driven by diverse demand that ranged from cloth destined for mass consumption to precious textiles requested by a select clientele, the manufacture of wool was by far the most important sector of textile production.[2] Unlike cotton and silk production, which from the outset made use of imported raw materials, its growth drew on local resources and techniques that were traditionally used in rural domestic production. Each city thus witnessed the emergence of its own woollen industry, set on satisfying primarily the demand of the internal market with low value products.[3]

However, in the course of the twelfth century some urban centres in Northern Italy, Lombardy in particular, started to develop industries that produced for export markets. Traces of these activities become more abundant in the documentation from the following century. During the first half of the thirteenth century, the leading centre of wool manufacture on the peninsula,

1 I want to thank Bart Lambert and Katherine Wilson. Without their patience, support, and willingness I would not have been able to accomplish this work.

2 The bibliography on the Italian wool manufacture is very long. See, in first instance, Bruno Dini, 'Gli orizzonti economici', in *Storia della società italiana*, edited by Giovanni Cherubini et al., vol. VII, *La crisi del sistema comunale* (Milan: Teti, 1982), 39–98; Dini, 'L'industria tessile italiana nel tardo Medioevo', (1990), republished in Dini, *Saggi su Firenze e l'Italia fra Mediterraneo ed Europa (secc. XIII–XVI)* (Pisa: Pacini, 1995), 13–49; Giovanni L. Fontana, 'La lana', in *Storia d'Italia. Annali*, vol. 19, *La moda*, edited by Carlo M. Belfanti and Fabio Giusberti (Turin: Einaudi, 2003), 319–361; John H. Munro, 'I panni di lana', in *Il Rinascimento italiano e l'Europa*, vol. IV, *Commercio e cultura mercantile*, edited by Franco Franceschi et al. (Treviso-Costabissara: Fondazione Cassamarca-Angelo Colla editore, 2007), 105–141.

3 Dini, 'Gli orizzonti economici', 58.

both in terms of the quality of the cloth produced and of the number of markets where they were distributed, was Milan. Using wool from the Maghreb, regions across the Alps and, to a lesser extent, from England, as well as dyestuffs from Northern Africa, the Milanese workshops produced different types of textiles, among which the so-called *pecie albe Mediolani* were the most noteworthy. These cloths were taken by Milanese merchants to Genoa (which was also the principal point of entry for the supply of raw materials), from where they were distributed throughout the Mediterranean. By overland transport using the services of Tuscan businessmen, they reached Bologna, Florence, Siena and the markets of central and southern Italy (see colour plate 17). The products of Milan were joined by those of Brescia, Bergamo, Cremona, Monza but most of all those of Como, found in Milan and Venice already by 1216.[4] In the East the most important centre was Verona, where the manufacture made use of local, Tunisian, Algerian, Flemish and German wool. Verona's best known type of cloth, which was exported from Veneto and the Padanian plain very early, was the so-called *santellaro* or *mezzalana,* a peculiar creation of local cloth entrepreneurs combining a wool weft and a warp which used a standard type of linen yarn produced in Lombardy and intended initially for the cotton sector.[5]

From the second half of the thirteenth century onwards the network of wool centres became denser, which may simply have been the result of more abundant documentation for the period. Though in the North, the oldest centres continued to play an important part, they were joined by Mantua, Pavia, Vicenza, Parma, Piacenza, Reggio Emilia and Bologna. In Tuscany sources mention more frequently the cloth of Pisa, Lucca, Pistoia, Prato, Siena and Florence; in Umbria those of Perugia and Orvieto appear, and in Abruzzo we find the fabrics of L'Aquila. During the first decades of the fourteenth century it was the textiles of Como, Verona, Milan and Florence that stood out, at least as far as we can conclude from the customs revenues taken from a number of cities in Central and Northern Italy. Milan and Florence, in particular, distinguished themselves from others because of their production levels and their commercial distribution, but the superior quality of their fabrics

[4] Patrizia Mainoni, *Economia e politica nella Lombardia medievale. Da Bergamo a Milano fra XIII e XV secolo* (Cavallermaggiore: Gribaudo, 1994), 17; Mainoni, 'La fisionomia economica delle città lombarde dalla fine del Duecento alla prima metà del Trecento. Materiali per un confronto', in *Le città del Mediterraneo all'apogeo dello sviluppo medievale. Aspetti economici e sociali, Atti del XVIII Convegno internazionale di Studi. Pistoia, 18–21 maggio 2001)* (Pistoia: Centro italiano di studi di storia e d'arte, 2003), 182; Paolo Grillo, *Milano in età comunale (1183–1276). Istituzioni, società, economia* (Spoleto: Cisam, 2001), 216–217.

[5] Hidetoshi Hoshino, *L'arte della lana in Firenze nel basso Medioevo. Il commercio della lana e il mercato dei panni fiorentini nei secoli XIII-XV* (Florence: Olschki, 1980), 71; Silvana A. Bianchi, 'Il lanificio veronese fra XIII e XIV secolo: strutture organizzative, tecniche, prodotti', in *Tessuti nel Veneto. Venezia e la Terraferma,* edited by Giuliana Ericani and Paola Frattaroli (Verona: Banca popolare di Verona, 1993), 72.

– which were usually made from wool of low or middle value coming from several Italian regions, Northern Africa and other territories in the Western Mediterranean – remains largely undocumented.[6]

Even though the quality of the wool was not the only indicator of the quality of cloth, it remained a factor of the utmost importance. This was exactly the reason why the overwhelming majority of textiles produced in Italian cities in the late thirteenth and early fourteenth centuries, including those of the more important centres, cannot be qualified as luxury cloth. The *stametti*, the *trafilati*, the *tritane*, the *taccolini*, the *saie*, the *biadetti*, the *stamforti* and the *mezzalana* cloths which we find in sources of these decades had market prices that were much lower than those of the fine products obtained in Flanders and Brabant, which met demand for precious fabrics all over Europe.[7] In 1299, for example, Florentine textiles were sold on the market of Orvieto for an average price of 23.2 *soldi* per Florentine *canna*,[8] whereas the cloths labelled as coming 'from France' (*de Francia*) for 43.2 *soldi*. In 1308–1309 in Grasse in Provence, fabrics from Ypres were worth 40–41 *soldi* per local *canna*, those from Châlons 29–38 *soldi*, those from Paris 10–32, from Provins 22–28, from Florence 13–15 and those from Genoa 8. In 1306 the prominent Florentine company of the Alberti had several types of cloth from Brussels in stock whose prices ranged from 58 to 133 *soldi* per *canna*, cloth from Douai at 60–178 *soldi* per *canna*, from Ghent at 53–142 and from Ypres at 55–166, whereas during the same years the market value of Florentine pieces varied between 10 and 53 *soldi* per *canna*.[9]

It must be emphasised that some cloth of higher value left the workshops of the Italian cities whose businessmen maintained close relations with the fairs of Champagne. These were textiles produced with English wool in the Southern Low Countries and Northern France which Italian merchants bought semi-finished, had dyed and finished in their cities of origin and re-exported to various markets in the Mediterranean. Well known in this context are the activities of the members of the Florentine *Arte di Calimala*, the guild founded in the second half of the twelfth century and including the major players in international trade,[10] but surviving documents record the same dynamics taking place in Lucca. Here, from the last twenty years of the twelfth century, there are mentions of *scarlatti* and *vermiglioni*, cloths imported from Northern Europe, meant to be dyed (or dyed again) with grain (*grana*), – a dyestuff extracted from the insect *Kermes vermilio* which produced tones

6 Dini, 'Gli orizzonti economici', 58; Hoshino, *L'arte della lana in Firenze*, 40–41.

7 Munro, 'I panni di lana', 111.

8 The *canna*, consisting of three to four *braccia*, was the most used measurement for full-length cloth in Italy: Carole Collier Frick, *Dressing Renaissance Florence: Families, Fortunes and Fine Clothing* (Baltimore: Johns Hopkins University Press, 2002), 226.

9 Hoshino, *L'arte della lana in Firenze*, 66–71 and 98–100.

10 Armando Sapori, *Una compagnia di Calimala ai primi del Trecento* (Florence: Olschki, 1932), in particular 156–158.

between orange and violet and also the precious scarlet-red –[11] and largely commercialised through the port of Genoa.[12] A similar activity of refinishing Flemish cloth was to be found taking place in Pistoia[13] and has been similarly assumed for Verona.[14] However, even though the processing of these fabrics in the hands of the merchant-entrepreneurs of the peninsula augmented their value, they were still products created elsewhere that did not reflect the technical features and typologies of Italian wool manufacture in this period. It is no coincidence that in the statute of the *Calimala* guild of 1301 these textiles were defined, very precisely, as 'cloths from Ypres dyed in Florence'.[15]

The Conversion to a Luxury Production: Geography and Typology

From the second quarter of the fourteenth century an improvement in the quality of textiles coupled with an added determined orientation of producers towards luxury cloth becomes apparent. The phenomenon, common to other European regions, has been rightly connected by scholars with the changes of international markets, and in particular with the remarkable increase in the transaction and transport costs between the thirteenth and fourteenth centuries. These costs had a smaller impact on the retail price of precious cloth than they had on cheaper fabrics, making it worthwhile to concentrate on the former. Moreover, in attempting to meet a growing discerning demand, the production of precious fabrics resulted in a greater differentiation in types of textiles. Differentiation put producers in a stronger position, certainly when it came to fixing prices for sale.[16] In Italy, the development of the manufacture of luxury cloth is inextricably linked to the introduction of better English wool, especially wool of the Welsh Marches (Herefordshire, Shropshire), the Cotswolds (Gloucestershire, Worcestershire, Oxfordshire, Berkshire) and the surroundings of Lindsey (Lincolnshire); until the sixteenth century

---

[11] Dominique Cardon, *La draperie au Moyen Âge. Essor d'une grande industrie européenne* (Paris: CNRS Editions, 1999), 472 and 476–483.

[12] Patrizia Mainoni, 'La seta in Italia fra XII e XIII secolo. Migrazioni artigiane e tipologie seriche', in *La seta in Italia dal Medioevo al Seicento. Dal baco al drappo*, edited by Luca Molà et al. (Venice: Marsilio, 2000), 377; Alma Poloni, *Lucca nel Duecento. Uno studio sul cambiamento sociale* (Pisa: Plus-Pisa University Press, 2009), 41.

[13] See Federigo Melis, 'Pistoia nei secoli d'oro della sua economia', (1962), republished in Melis, *Industria e commercio nella Toscana medievale*, edited by Bruno Dini (Florence: Le Monnier, 1989), 163.

[14] Bianchi, 'Il lanificio veronese fra XIII e XIV secolo', 60.

[15] 'Panni de Ypro tinti in Florentia': Giovanni Filippi, *L'arte dei mercanti di Calimala in Firenze ed il suo più antico statuto* (Turin: Fratelli Bocca, 1889), book V, chap. XV, 162.

[16] John H. Munro, 'The West European Woollen Industries and their Struggles for International Markets, c.1000–1500', in *The Cambridge History of Western Textiles*, edited by David Jenkins, 2 vols. (Cambridge and New York: Cambridge University Press, 2003), vol. I, 235–239; Munro, 'I panni di lana', 112–115.

these varieties were unrivalled for fineness.[17] Italian producers knew of these wools in previous centuries,[18] but it was only from the middle decades of the fourteenth century that they made widespread use of them. However, the consumption of fleeces from other regions would never halt completely.

How and when producers switched to English wool, considered to be the only raw material that allowed the production of fine cloths modelled after the Flemish ones, has been studied in detail for Florence, where the phenomenon was described by merchant-writer Giovanni Villani in his *Nuova Cronica*.[19] In the city on the Arno, change seems to have taken place in the 1320s, together with the decline of the refinishing of French and Flemish textiles by the *Calimala* merchants (tied to the decline of the Champagne fairs and the commercial networks related to them) and with the increased import of wool by big Florentine companies in England. These new products met with quick success, also benefiting from constant technical and qualitative improvement. Taking advantage of the increasing difficulties of the textile industry of Flanders and Brabant, the wool manufacturers (*lanaioli*) of Florence specialised in the production of luxury cloth and obtained a leading position in this profitable segment of the market particularly in Italy and the Mediterranean from the second half of the fourteenth century onwards. During the first years of the 1370s, some 30,000 bolts of cloth left their workshops a year, a substantial part of which were more precious types of textiles.[20]

During the following decades, however, a reversal of the trend took place. The problems in the supplies of better wool and the competition of new textile centres in England, Catalonia, Flanders and the Languedoc forced the Florentine manufacturers to reduce the volume of their production and to gradually reconvert to the production of cheaper fabrics made of Iberian and Italian (partly *Abruzzese*) wool, which found an outlet in the Ottoman Empire,

17 Peter J. Bowden, 'Wool supply and the Woollen Industry', *The Economic History Review* 9 (1956), 44–58; Giovanni Rebora, 'Materia prima e costi di trasformazione nel promemoria di una lanaiolo veneto della fine del Quattrocento', *Rivista storica italiana* LXXXIII (1971), 149–150; Hidetoshi Hoshino, 'The Rise of the Florentine Woollen Industry in the Fourteenth Century', in *Cloth and Clothing in Medieval Europe. Essays in Memory of Professor E. M. Carus-Wilson*, edited by Negley B. Harte and Kenneth G. Ponting (London: Heinemann, 1983), 191–194; Munro, 'I panni di lana', 107.

18 Egidio Rossini and Maureen F. Mazzaoui, 'Società e tecnica nel Medioevo (La produzione dei panni di lana a Verona nei secoli XIII-XIV-XV)', *Atti e Memorie dell'Accademia d'agricoltura scienze e lettere di Verona* cl. VI, XXI (1969–1970), 592; Federigo Melis, 'La lana della Spagna mediterranea e della Barberia occidentale nei secoli XIV-XV', (1972), republished in Melis, *I mercanti italiani nell'Europa medievale e rinascimentale*, edited by Luciana Frangioni (Florence: Le Monnier, 1990), 234–235; Mainoni, *Economia e politica nella Lombardia medievale*, 23–24; Grillo, *Milano in età comunale*, 216–217; Hoshino, *L'arte della lana in Firenze*, 116.

19 Giovanni Villani, *Nuova Cronica*, edited by Giuseppe Porta, 3 vols. (Parma: Guanda, 1990–1991), vol. I, book XII, chap. XCIV, 199.

20 Hidetoshi Hoshino, 'La tintura di grana nel basso Medioevo', in *Industria tessile e commercio internazionale nella Firenze del tardo Medioevo*, edited by Franco Franceschi and Sergio Tognetti (Florence: Olschki, 2001), 23–39; Hoshino, *L'arte della lana in Firenze*, 115–145 and 199–200; Franco Franceschi, *Oltre il «Tumulto». I lavoratori fiorentini dell'Arte della Lana fra Tre e Quattrocento* (Florence: Olschki, 1993), 3–12.

especially in Turkey. According to Hidetoshi Hoshino, Florence still produced luxury cloth at the end of the fifteenth century, but the ratio between English and Mediterranean wool had now changed dramatically: of an estimated annual production of 17,000 bolts of cloth in 1488, probably no more than 4,000, or less than a quarter of the total amount, were made of wool coming from England.[21] Patrick Chorley, however, pointed out that – according to figures of the Venetian ambassador Marco Foscari – 'c. 1520 the superfine San Martino branch of the Florentine industry still contributed 44-50 per cent of the total value of production', remaining 'a very important component' of the wool manufacture at this time.[22]

The presence of several types of wool in the same city and even in the same firm, used for different products, created problems that were worsened by difficulties Florentine manufacture faced. Seeing that some producers made textiles mixing English wool and other fleeces, which compromised the quality of better cloth, the *Lana* guild took a drastic decision in 1409. It ordered the *lanaioli* of the *convento* of San Martino – the biggest of the four areas of the city where the wool industry was concentrated – to work only with English wool, whereas the remaining districts (San Pancrazio, San Piero Scheraggio and Oltrarno) could still use raw material from other regions, albeit not within the same production process.[23] Thus, a significant distinction among Florentine producers was made; there were those who worked in the better district, the elites of textile entrepreneurs, and those in the remaining three areas, where the use of Mediterranean wool prevailed and which were increasingly known as the *conventi di Garbo*. This distinction was also reflected in the descriptions of the fabrics, which in the fifteenth century were habitually grouped as *San Martino* cloth and *Garbo* cloth.[24]

There are no testimonies on the chronology of the development of a luxury textile production with English wool available for other Italian cities that are as explicit as for Florence. We do know, however, that certainly during the second half of the fourteenth and the first decades of the fifteenth centuries, the phenomenon also occurred in other textile centres. In Tuscany, wool from England was processed in Prato, where it represented about ten per cent of all the raw material used by the well-known firm of Francesco Datini and Agnolo di Niccolò between 1396 and 1399,[25] in Arezzo, where it was recorded in the registers of the *Gabella della Porte*,[26] and in Pistoia, where merchant-entrepreneurs

---

21 Hoshino, *L'arte della lana in Firenze*, 231–244.

22 Patrick Chorley, 'The Volume of Cloth Production in Florence, 1500–1600: An Assessment of the Evidence', in *Wool: Products and Markets (13th-20th Century)*, edited by Giovanni L. Fontana and Gérard Gayot (Padua: Cleup, 2004), 555.

23 Franco Franceschi, 'Lane permesse e lane proibite nella Toscana fiorentina dei secoli XIV-XV: logiche economiche e scelte "politiche"', in *La pastorizia mediterranea. Storia e diritto (secoli XI-XX), Atti del Convegno Internazionale (Alghero, 8–11 novembre 2006)*, edited by Antonello Mattone and Pinuccia F. Simbula (Rome: Carocci, 2011), 884.

24 Hoshino, *L'arte della lana in Firenze*, 144.

25 Federigo Melis, *Aspetti della vita economica medievale. Studi nell'Archivio Datini di Prato* (Siena: Monte dei Paschi di Siena, 1962), 536.

26 Bruno Dini, *Arezzo intorno 1400. Produzioni e mercato* (Arezzo: Grafiche Badiali, 1984), 74.

such as the Guazzalotti, the Visconti and the Mannelli occasionally produced scarlet (*scarlatti*) and pink (*rosati*) cloth of the highest quality.[27] Yet, in none of these cities was the use of English wool as important as it was in Florence and it disappeared from all of them during the fifteenth century. One of the reasons for this was the difficulty that *lanaioli* of smaller centres had in competing with the fiercer Florentine colleagues on the international textile markets. However, we should not neglect the impact of the economic policy of the Florentine republic either. Having become the heart of a regional state that included all of Tuscany's principal cities apart from Lucca and Siena, during the first decades of the fifteenth century Florence used its privileged position to reorganise the whole cloth industry of its dominions through specific legislation. According to these laws, Florentine producers could use both Mediterranean wool, including the best types from Abruzzo, and English raw material, of which they held the monopoly, but it was forbidden for them to use local wool. There were other centres, such as Prato, where they could work with all sorts of wool except English wool. Finally, in rural areas, among which, as a means of punishment, Pisa was included as well, manufacturers were only allowed to produce cloth with exclusively local raw materials.[28] This strategy helped to perpetuate the privileged situation of the Florentine industry but at the same time contributed to the reduction of textile activities in subject centres of the dominion and halted the development of a proto-industry in the Tuscan countryside, in contrast with the development during the same period in regions like Lombardy and Sicily.[29] Outside the Florentine state the picture was slightly different. In Lucca, where in the course of the fifteenth century a strong recovery of cloth manufacture took place, English wool was used, as well as Spanish, African and Provencal varieties.[30] In Siena, where the English wool varieties (*lane francesche e gentili*) already supplied urban workshops before the Black Death, their use was imposed upon the producers by decree. In 1408, in an attempt to revive the textile sector, which was considered to be in a crisis, the Sienese government instructed the *lanaioli* to produce 300 fine cloths made of English wool each year.[31] Even in the second half of the fifteenth century the supply of *francesca* wool did not stop completely.[32]

27 Melis, 'Pistoia nei secoli d'oro della sua economia', 166.

28 Franceschi, 'Lane permesse e lane proibite', 885; Franco Franceschi and Luca Molà, 'Regional States and Economic Development', in *The Italian Renaissance State*, edited by Andrea Gamberini and Isabella Lazzarini (Cambridge: Cambridge University Press, 2012), 453–454.

29 Stephen R. Epstein, *Freedom and Growth, Markets and States in Europe, 1300–1750* (London: Routledge, 2000), 137–138.

30 Michael E. Bratchel, *Lucca 1430–1494. The Reconstruction of an Italian City-Republic* (Oxford: Clarendon, 1995), 151–155.

31 Sandra Tortoli, 'Per la storia della produzione laniera a Siena nel Trecento e nei primi anni del Quattrocento', *Bullettino senese di storia patria* LXXXII-LXXXIII (1975–1976), 229 and 231.

32 See the documents published by Maria Ceppari and Patrizia Turrini, 'Documenti: il commercio delle stoffe; l'abbigliamento e le provvisioni sul lusso; arredi sacri e profani', in *Drappi, velluti, taffettà. Antichi tessuti a Siena e nel suo territorio, Catalogo della Mostra (Siena, 31 maggio-31 luglio 1994)*, edited by Marco Ciatti (Siena: Nuova Immagine, 1994), 252–253.

Outside Tuscany the manufacture of luxury cloths developed in Perugia, Bologna and most of all in the cities and some of the smaller centres of Lombardy and Veneto. Drawing on a lengthy tradition, Milan continued as an important centre of cloth production during the fourteenth and the early fifteenth centuries, but after this period the sector showed signs of a crisis. Yet, the production of precious textiles did not halt, as is clear from the continued presence of wool from England and North Europe on the urban market.[33] The communal statutes of 1396 also specified that so-called cloth of Milan (*panni di Milano*) could only be made of fine and 'ultramontane' wool and this was repeated in 1474, when a ducal decree forbade the use of any wool that did not come from England for these products.[34] That these fabrics were of the highest quality is demonstrated by the prices of 'narrow scarlet cloth in grain' (*scarlatae in grana strictae*) recorded in a list of Milanese merchandise in the second half of the fifteenth century,[35] and those textiles sold in Rome or Pisa during the same decades. Between 1447 and 1486, for example, the Apostolic Chamber bought Milanese *saie lucchesine* at twelve cameral florins per *canna* and *saie rosate* at ten, fourteen and sixteen florins, whereas the price of more expensive Florentine cloths (*lucchesini, lucchesini alla londresca* and *rosati*) did not go above eight to ten florins per *canna*.[36] Good cloth of English wool was also produced in Como, where, as in Milan, regulations were issued at the end of the fourteenth century that prevented processing of 'ultramontane' wool outside the urban centre.[37] Among the smaller centres in Lombardy the case of Torno stands out. It was a borough near Como, where during the fifteenth century German wool of good quality and limited amounts of English wool were supplied.[38]

In the Veneto region a renewal of the production of textiles occurred before the middle of the fourteenth century. Silvana Collodo demonstrated that this renewal probably took place using Florentine specialists as intermediaries.[39] According to an act of the city of Udine of 1348, weavers such as Tizio Nerazzi from Carmignano, close to Florence, were active and were able to make fabrics 'in the way and according to the custom of France [that is of

33 Luciana Frangioni, 'I tessuti di lana e di cotone', in *Artigianato lombardo*, 5 vols. (Milan: Cassa di risparmio delle provincie lombarde, 1977–1981), vol. III, *L'opera tessile*, 14; Patrizia Mainoni, 'Il mercato della lana a Milano dal XIV al XV secolo. Prime indagini', *Archivio storico lombardo* CX (1984), 20–43.

34 Mainoni, 'Il mercato della lana a Milano', 22 and 42.

35 *Liber datii mercantie Communis Mediolani. Registro del secolo XV*, edited by Antonio Noto (Milan: Università L. Bocconi, 1950), 18.

36 Hoshino, *L'arte della lana in Firenze*, 290–291, tables XLVII and XLVIII.

37 Mainoni, 'Il mercato della lana a Milano', 22–23.

38 Paolo Grillo, '«*Vicus Lanificio Insignis*». Industria laniera e strutture sociali del borgo lariano di Torno nel XV secolo', *Studi di Storia Medioevale e di Diplomatica* 14 (1993), 97.

39 Silvana Collodo, 'La produzione tessile nel Veneto medievale', (1993) republished in Collodo, *Società e istituzioni in area veneta: itinerari di ricerca (secoli XII-XV)* (Florence: Nardini, 1999), 85.

Flanders], Florence, Milan, Verona and Como'.[40] Thus, at the end of the 1340s, Verona had joined the bigger Italian wool centres which were renowned for the production of textiles of the highest quality. During the following decades a similar trend occurred in Padua, Vicenza and Venice, as demonstrated by many indicators: the continual increase in width of cloths, the increment of number of threads that the warp was composed of (*portate*) and the introduction of a method of classification of high quality cloths (*panni alti*) based on the number of units that determined the distance between the warp threads (heddles).[41] We should not forget that larger cloth was composed of a higher number of threads and that a higher density of the textiles indicated a qualitative improvement.[42] The number of heddles used also impacted the quality of the product. In Verona, the loom where three heddles were used 'allowed to weave soft yarns crosswise', but weaving with four heddles, also called *alla piana*, 'produced patterned surfaces with sophisticated geometries, such as squares, chequers and twills'. It is no coincidence that this second technique was reserved for cloth made of better raw materials and particularly with *francesca* wool, the distribution of which dates back to the middle of the fourteenth century in the cities of Veneto.[43] Not long afterwards, the existence of luxury production in the region is confirmed. In 1367, a document of the *Lana* guild of Padua mentioned for the first time 'grain and scarlet cloths' (*panni granati e scarlatti*), textiles that had different weaving rates from those of other cloth and that between 1436 and 1440 were sold for very high prices on the market of Constantinople.[44]

The link between fabrics composed of a high number of warp threads, high quality wool and costly dyestuffs is underlined in Venetian legislation. In the Lagune City, where the cloth industry underwent a remarkable development from the end of the fourteenth century onwards, a decree issued by the Senate in 1450 imposed that only cloth made of more than sixty *portate* had to be woven with *francesca* wool and dyed with grain.[45] Legislation in Verona and Vicenza decreed that high quality cloths had to be produced with English wool as well, but introduced a new factor of great importance: the possibility, for the most precious products, to also use local wool (*lane nostrali*), that is obtained in the territories of both cities and – in the case of Vicenza – coming

40 'Ad modum et consuetudinem pannorum de Francia, de Florentia, de Mediolano, de Verona et de Cumis': document cited in Battista Zanazzo, *L'arte della lana in Vicenza (secoli XIII-XV)* (Venice: R. Deputazione veneta di storia patria, 1914), 4.

41 Collodo, 'La produzione tessile nel Veneto medievale', 86–87; Edoardo Demo, *L'«anima della città». L'industria tessile a Verona e Vicenza (1400–1550)* (Milan: Unicopli, 2001), 193–196; Andrea Mozzato, 'Il mercato dei panni di lana a Venezia all'inizio del XV secolo', in *Wool: Products and Markets*, 1045.

42 Cardon, *La draperie au Moyen Âge*, 184.

43 Collodo, 'La produzione tessile nel Veneto medievale', 87–88, citation on page 87.

44 Silvana Collodo, 'Signore e mercanti: storia di un'alleanza', (1987), republished in Collodo, *Una società in trasformazione. Padova tra XI e XV secolo* (Padua: Antenore, 1990), 358 and 365.

45 Mozzato, 'Il mercato dei panni di lana a Venezia', 1045.

from the countryside around Padua (*lana de Scorcia*) and Mantua.[46] The reason for this new direction was no doubt the increasing difficulty in procuring English wool, which has already been discussed for Florence and Tuscany, but also an awareness by manufacturers that wool was available close to their workplaces, the quality of which was very similar to that of the best imported fleeces. This is confirmed by the prices of Mantuan wool on the market of Vicenza at the end of the 1450s,[47] by the descriptions in the guild documents of the same period which talk about cloth made of 'the finest wool and yarn' from the countryside of Padua, Mantua and Verona',[48] and by the judgement of the producers themselves, who – as stated by the anonymous author of a memorandum about cloth production at the end of the century – even considered it to be finer than the *francesca* wool, although noting it was less resistant to general wear and tear.[49]

What is remarkable is that, whether with English or local wool, the production of luxury cloth in the cities of Veneto remained substantial during the whole of the fifteenth century. In Venice, during the last decades of that century, on average 9,500 bolts of cloth a year were made with *francesca* wool alone.[50] In Verona, between 1474 and 1483, urban production ranged between 7,000 and 10,000 pieces. Only five to nine per cent of this were lower quality products while the rest were cloths of the highest level (*panni alti*); moreover, a survey carried out during the period between March and August 1482 showed that over 95 per cent of the precious cloth whose quality could be identified had been made of English or the best varieties of local wool.[51]

A Fundamental Stage in the Improvement of Quality: The Imitation of Foreign Models

One of the most dynamic factors in the development of textile manufacture was the imitation of foreign models, because it often depended on the ability of local entrepreneurs and cloth workers to modify in an original way characteristics of the reproduced goods and to create new products, which could then be imitated in turn. The phenomenon has been acknowledged for all the principal sectors in late medieval Italy. Fabrics models for cotton mainly

46 Demo, *L'«anima della città»*, 39, 196; Edoardo Demo, 'Lane, lanaioli e mercanti nella manifattura vicentina (secc. XIV–XVI)', in *Wool: Products and Markets*, 385–386.

47 Demo, *L'«anima della città»*, 43.

48 'Ex lanis finissimis et fillatis subtilissimis […] de lana scorcia et de lanis mantuanis et veronensibus': cited in Zanazzo, 'L'arte della lana a Vicenza', 300–301.

49 Rebora, 'Materia prima e costi di trasformazione', 149–151.

50 Andrea Mozzato, 'The Production of Woollens in Fifteenth and Sixteenth-Century Venice', in *At the Centre of the Old World. Trade and Manufacturing in Venice and the Venetian Mainland, 1400–1800*, edited by Paola Lanaro (Toronto: Centre for Reformation and Renaissance Studies, 2006), 83.

51 Demo, *L'«anima della città»*, 182, 196–197.

came from the Levant or from the Muslim regions of Africa; for silks they came from the Greek-Byzantine world, which had imitated the techniques and designs of Persian manufacturers in turn;[52] for woollen cloth the major inspiration were the textiles from North-Western Europe, particularly Flanders and Brabant.

Returning to the Florentine case, it allows us to closely observe some of the mechanisms of this important process. In Florence the first clear testimony of the imitation of Flemish and Brabantine fabrics comes from the ledgers of the Rinucci company: from May 1323, this firm started to sell cloths called *mescolati alla francesca* or *mischiati alla francesca*, characterised by a significantly higher price than the fine products that it had been selling up until this point, the *saie* and the *tritane*.[53] The description returns in the statute of the *Lana* guild promulgated in 1331 (but actually drawn up in 1326–27), which speaks of a *tintillano* cloth made *alla francesca*, by adding 'or with cards' (*sive cum scardassis*).[54] Cards were – to use the language of the fifteenth-century Florentine *Trattato dell'Arte della Lana* – tools with 'small and crooked teeth of thin iron wire'.[55] They were used to prepare the short wool (*palmella*) for spinning, whereas the longer fibres (*stame*) were combed. Therefore, the passage in the statute seems to suggest the development of a type of product where at least the weft was made of carded wool, next to a production of textiles made of combed wool, both for the weft and the warp. To be fit for carding, this wool had to meet the standards of elasticity and resistance that was typical of good English varieties.[56]

This 'carding revolution', which from the thirteenth century took place in many European wool centres,[57] had a direct impact on another fundamental stage in the long cloth-making cycle, that of dyeing. Carding, which compacted each tuft of wool and divided the fibres in all directions by mixing them without any loss or damage, was in fact the best way to produce *mélanges* of colour with wool that was already dyed. Using these methods, flecked yarns and marble effects were produced. Colour tones like *monachino* and *bigio*, which required a strict and perfectly homogenous dosage of wool of different grades of blue and red, to which eventually white fibres were added, could also be achieved.[58] It was therefore no coincidence that the first cloths imitating Flemish and Brabantine products in Florence were called *mescolati*, *mischiati* and *tintillani*.

---

52 Mainoni, 'La seta in Italia fra XII e XIII secolo', 367.

53 For the details and archival references, see Hoshino, *L'arte della lana in Firenze*, 133.

54 Hoshino, *L'arte della lana in Firenze*, 129.

55 *Trattato dell'Arte della Lana*, in A. Doren, *Studien aus der Florentiner Wirtschaftsgeschichte*, vol. I, *Die Florentiner Wollentuchindustrie vom 14. bis zum 16. Jahrhundert. Ein Beitrag zur geschichte des modernen Kapitalismus* (Stuttgart: Cotta, 1901), 488.

56 Hoshino, *L'arte della lana in Firenze*, 129–130.

57 Cardon, *La draperie au Moyen Âge*, 184.

58 Cardon, *La draperie au Moyen Âge*, 196–197.

At first there were only a few innovators but these manufacturers became increasingly specialised. By 1340 the firm of Cione Pitti and his brother Neri (father of the more famous Bonaccorso, author of the *Ricordi*)[59] produced cloth that was modelled after the best textiles of Brussels, Douai and Malines, even though their market value was far lower than the originals.[60] After the middle of the fourteenth century, the imitation process became more important. Cloth 'in the way of Brussels' (*a modo di Borsella*) or 'in the way of Douai' (*a modo di Doagio*) appears more often among the goods recorded in the surviving account books of textile firms or in the inventories of goods made in cloth shops.[61] Their quality must have already been fairly high, as in 1360 the Venetian merchants who bought *tintillani* in Florence for re-export to the Levant, obtained that they were subject to the same shipping regulations as the *franceschi* cloth.[62]

During the last quarter of the century the quality and the prices of Florentine fabrics increased further due to the diffusion of dyeing with grain. This kind of dye was characteristic for the most costly types of Franco-Flemish textiles[63] and in Florence it was used for the refinishing of *franceschi* cloth. Curiously, however, these activities passed only slowly from the dyers who worked under the orders of the *Calimala* merchants to those who worked for the *Arte della Lana*. The first mention in the documentation of the *Lana* guild relating to the precious colourant – a provision on the terms of payment for the sale of grain – dates back to 1344. Only in 1372, however, would the *Lana* guild develop specific regulations for the marking of 'grain cloth' (*panni di grana*), whereas another five years would pass before scarlets and *pagonazzi di grana* would appear in the rate table concerning the work done by dyers for wool manufacturers. Right at the end of the 1370s we can detect a wider circulation of the colourant. Thus, it is no coincidence that the wool shop of Jacopo del Bene, active between 1355 and 1370, did not use grain, but it was used by the firm of Francesco Datini in Florence in 1392–1393. In any case, even during the following years, cloth dyed with grain would frequently be produced on commission and the customer would pay the additional cost for the dyestuff and the work.[64]

---

59 Bonaccorso Pitti, *Ricordi*, in *Mercanti scrittori. Ricordi nella Firenze tra Medioevo e Rinascimento*, edited by Vittore Branca (Milan: Mondadori, 1986).

60 Hoshino, *L'arte della lana in Firenze*, 90–94; on page 94 the Japanese scholar gives the example of a 'scarlatto di colpo a modo di doagio', sold by the Pitti for 178 *soldi* per *canna* in 1341 when already in 1325 the original was valued at 240 *soldi*.

61 Hoshino, *L'arte della lana in Firenze*, 144 and 179.

62 Nella Fano, 'Ricerche sull'arte della lana a Venezia nel XIII e XIV secolo', *Archivio veneto* ser. V, XVIII (1936), 135–137.

63 John H. Munro, 'The Medieval Scarlet and Economics of Sartorial Splendour', in *Cloth and Clothing*, 13–70.

64 Hoshino, *L'arte della lana in Firenze*, 183–186; Hoshino, 'La tintura di grana nel basso Medioevo', 27–32.

In turn, Florentine fabrics were imitated by other wool centres. We have already seen that during the middle of the fourteenth century the Commune of Udine had chosen a Tuscan weaver to introduce the production of cloth modelled after the Florentine textiles in the city. In 1369 the statute of the *Lana* guild in Fabriano, in the Marche, mentioned 'mixed and large cloth in the way of Florentine cloth' (*pannos mischiatos et larghos ad modum pannorum florentinorum*),[65] whereas around the middle of the fifteenth century a Venetian document described copying the textiles of the Tuscan city, complaining that the imitations made in the Lagune were, in turn, counterfeited across the Alps: 'In this city the cloth manufacture has just developed and each type of cloth, in particular *garbi* cloth, is produced with the greatest enthusiasm. But there are some merchants here who try to destroy these activities by making sure that in Flanders, in England and in other places *garbi* cloth and other fine cloth in the Florentine way is made. For this purpose they have sent the measurements of the width, the length, the selvedges and the colours abroad'.[66]

The above text confirms that all the main characteristics of the textile were copied. Curiously, however, the imitation also included less essential features, such as the way of folding: in fact some Milanese producers used to fold cloths *alla francesca* 'to counterfeit them'.[67] The Venetian document also makes clear that the transfer of technical knowledge and the production of new types of textile was not always linked to a shift of highly skilled workers. In order to imitate a product it could be enough to have knowledge of its basic characteristics, possibly combined with an accurate investigation of the original. This was probably the case with the imitation of cloth *alla francesca* in Florence, where the will and the choice of the local entrepreneurs prevailed much more than the contribution of foreign specialists. Workers did arrive from Flanders and Brabant, but they did so some decades after the improvement of the fabrics, possibly using the job opportunities that the production of new cloth types gave them. It was mainly from the 1370s and 1380s that groups of weavers and other textile artisans from Flanders and Brabant migrated to Florence, probably attracted by an expanding manufacture, characterised by technical and product affinities with the industry they had left behind.[68]

---

65 *Statuta artis lanae terrae Fabriani* (Rome: Dario Giuseppe Rossi, 1880), chap. LXVII, 30.

66 'El se ha principiado adesso el mestier de la lana in questa cità et lavorasse a grandissima furia de ogni sorta panni, e principalmente panni garbi. Et el si à alguni nostri marchadanti che sotto diversi modi zercha de romper el dicto mestier, havendo ordenado che in Fiandra et Ingeltera et altri luogi se fazi panni garbi e fini lavoradi a la fiorentina, et ha mandado le messure de largeze, longeze, zimose e colori […]' (*La Mariegola dell'arte della lana di Venezia (1244–1595)*, edited by Andrea Mozzato, 2 vols. (Venice: Il Comitato editore, 2002), vol. I, doc. 511, 294.

67 L. Frangioni, *Milano fine Trecento. Il carteggio milanese dell'Archivio Datini*, 2 vols. (Florence: Opus Libri, 1994), vol. I, 236; vol. II, lett. 50, 46.

68 As already noted by H. Laurent, *Un grand commerce d'exportation au Moyen Age: la draperie des Pays-Bas en France et dans les pays méditerranéens (XIIe-XVe siècle)* (Paris: Droz, 1935), 197.

The last theme that needs to be addressed here is the imitation of the most successful precious textiles using materials less costly than the originals. During the 1420s, for example, some wool manufacturers in Arezzo produced *panni alla borsella*, copying the corresponding Florentine fabrics. Unlike the *lanaioli* from Florence, which could use English wool, the producers from Arezzo had to satisfy themselves with Spanish raw materials (wool from San Matteo). Their products took on the name, the colours and the other formal characteristics of the Florentine models, but cost 65 to 70 per cent less.[69] It may have been that this was a way of circumventing the prohibition on wool from England imposed by Florence or possibly an intelligent answer to the desire of the middle and lower middle classes to emulate the consumption of the higher ranks of society.[70] Which one it was is hard to answer, but the fact remains that the activities of the Aretine manufacturers were perfectly legal (if they had not been they would not have been declared for taxation). Real and proper fraud was discovered by the Venetian authorities, according to whom between 1456 and 1458 about 6,000 foreign cloths were imported, subsequently processed by the local producers and refinishers 'in the Venetian way' (*alla veneziana*) and finally re-exported as original products from the City of San Marco.[71] In this case there was only one motive; to make more money by saving on production costs while maintaining the price for sale.

The Labour Process and Production Costs

As is well known, in Italian cities where woollen luxury cloth for an international market was produced, the labour process consisted of a high number of stages (up to 25–30) and was largely decentralised. Manufacturing activities were carried out in a series of centres spread all over the city and even outside the walls, managed with more or less autonomy but connected by the initiative and activity of the wool manufacturer, who often was a merchant.[72]

---

69 Ilaria Becattini, *L'economia aretina nei primi decenni del Quattrocento. Manifattura, industria e commercio attraverso lo spoglio del Catasto fiorentino del 1427* (PhD Dissertation: University of Siena, 2013), 187–188.

70 On the relationship between product imitation and social emulation, see the comments by Guido Guerzoni, 'Novità, innovazione e imitazione: i sintomi della modernità', in *Il Rinascimento italiano e l'Europa*, vol. III, *Produzione e tecniche*, edited by Philippe Braunstein and Luca Molà (Treviso-Costabissara: Fondazione Cassamarca-Angelo Colla, 2007), 77–85.

71 Mozzato, 'The Production of Woollens', 81.

72 On the characteristics of this form of labour organisation, see Melis, *Aspetti della vita economica medievale*, part V; Bruno Dini, *Le origini del capitalismo* (Florence: Le Monnier, 1979), 1–22; Dini, 'L'industria tessile italiana nel tardo Medioevo'. For a critical reflexion, see Franco Franceschi, 'L'impresa mercantile-industriale nella Toscana dei secoli XIV-XVI', in *La storia dell'impresa nella lunga durata: continuità e discontinuità, Atti del Seminario di studi (Venezia, 22–23 Novembre 2002), Annali di Storia dell'impresa* XIV (2003), 229–249.

The heart of the cloth firm was the *bottega di lana*, a large workshop that served as the organising centre, the warehouse for the stocking of the semi-finished products, sales point and production space. Even though individual management was well represented ('if you can do it without a partner, do it', advised the Florentine Giovanni Morelli)[73], wool manufacturers tended to form partnerships. Directly dependent on them were two groups of workers with different roles and characteristics. The first was that of the salaried workers (in Florence called *ciompi*) who took the wool through the preparative stages before the spinning. This was hard and less specialised work using rudimentary and cheap equipment. The second group was composed of apprentices, shop boys and clerks (*discepoli, garzoni, fattori*) who had to assist and control the work force employed in the *bottega di lana* or liaise with external production units. In fact, each wool shop was strictly connected to workplaces for the employees doing the remaining phases of the production cycle, which can be grouped once again into two categories. The first comprised people working at home, with a high female proportion, who using their own equipment took care of the spinning (often in rural environments), the warping and the weaving. The second consisted of artisans who, with the help of dependent workers and at times using expensive equipment such as the dyeing establishments, the tenter sheds (*tiratoi, chiodere*) and the fulling mills, executed the colouring and the refinishing of the textiles.[74] Mutually and internally diverse because of economic composition and social status, members of both groups had the fact in common that they could work on their own, so that the relationship they had with the cloth producers was not, technically, that of a salaried worker but that of an individual who was remunerated for a specific service.[75]

This particular organisation of the wool industry, which avoided the concentration of the production phases in one place and made intensive use of a putting-out system, was a response to two very serious problems textile manufacturers had to face. On the one hand, there was the difficulty in providing capital to directly manage the entire technological cycle. On the other, there was the risk of investing substantial resources for an activity that was heavily dependent on foreign markets for the supplies of raw materials and the sale of textiles, and that was therefore sensitive to sudden fluctuations.

---

73 Giovanni di Pagolo Morelli, *Ricordi*, in *Mercanti scrittori*,177.

74 The bibliography for these aspects is long. For some specific examples, see Melis, *Aspetti della vita economica medievale*, 459–480; Collodo, 'Signore e mercanti', 53–58; Franceschi, *Oltre il «Tumulto»*, 33–77; Pierluigi Castagneto, *L'arte della lana a Pisa nel Duecento e nei primi decenni del Trecento. Commercio, industria, istituzioni* (Pisa: GISEM-Edizioni ETS, 1996), 166–178; Demo, *L'«anima della città»*, 90–110.

75 The technical-economic perspective does not suffice to define the social position of the different categories of workers operating outside the cloth shop. In fact in Italy, unlike other European regions, wool entrepreneurs, supported by their guilds, imposed on external employees particularly severe forms of dependency, which seriously reduced their productive autonomy; see Franco Franceschi, *« … E seremo tutti ricchi». Lavoro, mobilità sociale e conflitti nelle città dell'Italia medievale* (Pisa: Pacini, 2012), 31–52.

In this way, instead, the amount of capital needed to manage a wool shop (at least when compared to investments made in the purely mercantile sector), was not that high. For example, between 1417 and 1456, 63 per cent of the 344 Vicentine firms for which Edoardo Demo had retrieved the partnership contracts worked with amounts between 100 and 300 ducats, whereas only three per cent had access to more than 1,000 ducats. In Verona, during the second half of the fifteenth century, the average capital invested by the *lanaioli* ranged between 500 and 1,500 ducats, even though some rare examples of workshops with lower and much higher amounts are also recorded (as the 7,000 ducats at the disposal of the partnership between Domenico di Uberto and the Stoppa brothers).[76] Venetian firms must have been of similar dimensions to the Veronese, although the data is more impressionistic here.[77] In Florence at the start of the fifteenth century, the sums usually invested in wool firms were significantly higher: according to the figures extracted from the 1427 *Catasto*, 55 per cent of the companies active in the *convent* of San Martino – the only one where al textiles were produced with English wool – had a capital between 1,000 and 4,000 florins, 27.5 per cent had more than 4,000 florins and only 17.5 per cent 1,000 florins or less.[78] In the districts manufacturers principally used Italian or Mediterranean wool the picture was different: there companies working with a capital of 1,000, 600 and even 300 florins were not that exceptional.[79]

Considering that the buildings of the central shop were often rented and that equipment for the production phases was usually cheap, the investment in fixed capital goods was very low. As Richard Goldthwaite has rightly observed, 'what these manufacturers needed was almost exclusively start-up capital so that they could buy raw materials and pay workers to get operations going to the point where income from sales was sufficient to meet ongoing costs'.[80] The impact of the purchase of the wool on the global costs was indeed high: as can be seen in Table 8.1, the minimal percentage recorded was 39 per cent (cloth with wool from Menorca), whereas the highest amounted to 53 per cent (cloth with wool from the countryside around Verona). As for the production process, even taking into account the heterogeneous origins of the data and the differences between the cases, the remarkable weight of the labour costs stands out clearly. The preparation of wool and spinning alone, where the expenses for the equipment were minimal compared to the remunerations, were responsible for 40 to 67 per cent of the manufacturing

76 Demo, *L'«anima della città»*, 110–112.

77 Andrea Mozzato, *L'arte della lana a Venezia nel basso Medioevo. Materia prima, produzione e produttori* (PhD Dissertation, University of Milan, 2003), 421.

78 Hoshino, *L'arte della lana in Firenze*, 232; Raymond De Roover, *The Rise and Decline of the Medici Bank: 1397–1494* (New York: Norton, 1966), 174.

79 Franceschi, *Oltre il «Tumulto»*, 40.

80 Richard A. Goldthwaite, *The Economy of Renaissance Florence* (Baltimore: The Johns Hopkins University Press, 2009), 302.

costs (between 40 and 50 per cent in the Florentine industry). If we look at the absolute numbers, rather than percentages, and we focus on luxury textiles, the factors that had the strongest impact on the production costs of the cloth were the quality of the wool, the type of warp and the kind of dyeing.

To have an idea of the differences in price between the various types of wool it serves to focus on documentation left by the firms of Francesco Datini. In Milan, in the years around 1400, the price of 100 pounds of the best wool from England ranged between 34 and 43 imperial *lire,* that of Flemish wool between 32 and 36 *lire,* and that of German wool between 20 and 24 *lire.* For raw material from Majorca and Menorca one would have paid between 13 and 18 *lire,* for wool from San Matteo between 11 and 14 *lire* and for Provencal fleeces between 8 and 14 *lire.*[81] During the same years (1396–1399) the average prices paid by the Datini company of Prato for 100 pounds of raw material were 32.79 florins for English wool, 19.77 for wool from Menorca, 14.5 from Majorca, 12.41 from Provence and 12.02 from San Matteo.[82] English wool was thus three times more expensive than San Matteo wool. However, with 1,000 pounds of *francesca* wool (or the best from Veneto) one could produce on average 13 cloths, whereas with the same amount of wool from San Matteo only 11.5 could be woven.[83] An indirect consequence of the use of better wools was also that more olive oil was needed to protect the fibres against damage during the various stages of the production process: twice as much oil was necessary to grease English wool, as well as raw material from Verona, Mantua and Vicenza, than for the preparation of wool from San Matteo, Menorca and Abruzzo.[84]

81 Frangioni, *Milano fine Trecento,* vol. I, 230.

82 Melis, *Aspetti della vita economica medievale,* 'prospetto' XXVII.

83 At least according to the calculations by the wool producer active in Veneto at the end of the fifteenth century recorded earlier: Rebora, 'Materia prima e costi di trasformazione', 156.

84 Rebora, 'Materia prima e costi di trasformazione', 146.

Table 8.1 : Composition of the costs of some fine and medium quality cloth (1396–end fifteenth century)

Firm	Datini (Prato, 1396–1400)				Guanti (Florence, 1484–1488)	Anonymous (Verona, 1470s)	Anonymous (Veneto, end XVth century)
Wool	*English*	*Menorca*	*Majorca*	*San Matteo*	*Abruzzo*	*'nostrana'*	*'francesca'*
Preparatory stages	23	27	32	27	21	34	24
Spinning	17	18	18	16	22	33	24
Warping/ weaving	14	14	13	13	13	16	32
Dyeing/ refinishing	45	40	37	44	44	17*	20*
	99	99	100	100	100	100	100
Manufacture	56	-	61	-	56	47	-
Raw material	44	-	39	-	44	53	-

Note * Dyeing excluded

Sources: Melis, *Aspetti della vita economica medievale*, table XXVII (figures elaborated by Richard A. Goldthwaite, 'The Florentine Wool Industry in the Late Sixteenth Century: A Case Study', *The Journal of European Economic History* 32/3 (2003), 537, Table 2); Hidetoshi Hoshino, 'Il commercio fiorentino nell'Impero ottomano: costi e profitti negli anni 1484–1488' (1985), republished in Hoshino, *Industria tessile e commercio internazionale*, 120, Table 1; Demo, *L'«anima della città»*, 204; Rebora, 'Materia prima e costi di trasformazione', 163.

As far as the density of the warp, expressed in the measurement of *portate*, is concerned, it is clear – as we have already discussed – that a piece of cloth made of a higher number of threads required a higher amount of wool, augmenting the costs of its purchase and processing. According to the testimony of an anonymous wool manufacturer from Verona in the 1470s, cloth of local wool made of 60 *portate* cost 16 gold ducats, 55 *soldi* and 6 *denari*, cloth of 70 *portate alla piana* would cost half a ducat more (+ 3 per cent), of 70 *portate a tre licci* a ducat and a half more (+ 9.03 per cent) and of 80 *portate* six and a half ducats more (+ 39.2 per cent) or over 23 ducats altogether.[85] Thanks to a similar document drawn up not much later we can also reconstruct the costs – that of the wool excluded – of producing textiles with the same number of threads but from different raw material: in the Veneto area it would cost 17 ducats to make a cloth of English wool of 70 *portate*, against 8 ducats to produce a piece with the same density but using wool from San Matteo.[86]

85 These figures are compiled on the basis of data provided by Demo, *L'«anima della città»*, 205.

86 Rebora, 'Materia prima e costi di trasformazione', 145.

Dyeing, which could be done on the wool, the thread or the cloth that had left the loom (and could be repeated to widen the range of chromatic possibilities), could have a strong impact on the quality of the fabric. The first factor was the type of colourant. The array of dyestuffs used in the cloth manufacture was large and consisted of products with varying origins and costs: grain, madder, woad, fustic, weld, the bark of alder and walnut trees, brazil wood, orchil, saffron, lotus, dyer's broom, curcuma and others. If grain cost 90 florins per 100 pounds, brazil wood would not be more than 25 florins, madder about 3 and weld 1 florin.[87] A second factor that influenced the cost of dyeing was, again, the quality of the processed wool: according to the Datini documents, it cost little just over 10 florins for a producer to dye English wool *cilestrino* (a shade of dark blue),[88] whereas he would pay 7.5 florins to do this with wool from Majorca and 6 to 6.5 with wool from San Matteo.[89] Yet the dyeing process would also result in significant differences in quality for pieces produced with the same wool. Even though they relate to prices of sold cloth and not the production costs, the data on the commercialisation of Florentine fabrics made of English wool by the company of Pazzino di Luca and Piero di Paolo between 1376 and 1381 confirms this: the prices of the 'grain cloth' ranged between 160 and 205 *soldi* per *canna*, whereas the textiles ready to be treated with this colourant (the 'cloth without grain') ranged between 130 and 158 *soldi*. On average, the first ones cost 30 per cent more than the second.[90] The last factor that might determine the price of dyeing, and thus of the fabric, was the concentration of the colourant used, and consequently the shades obtained. For example, in some Tuscan price lists relating to the dyeing of wool with woad, the most used colourant for blue colours, the costs increased gradually from the lighter shades (*turchino, sbiadato*) to the more intense (*cilestrino, azurrino*) (see colour plate 18).[91] Six dyeing operations done by the Datini of Florence between 1388 and 1399 illustrate even more clearly the relationship between the quantity of the colourant used (in this case grain) and the final cost of the cloth. When textiles whose basic colour was rather dark were treated, the quantity of grain used was lower and the extra cost because of the dyeing was about 22 per cent, whereas in the cases where,

87 Florence Edler De Roover, 'Andrea Banchi, Florentine Silk Manufacturer and Merchant in the Fifteenth Century', *Studies in Medieval and Renaissance history* 3 (1966).

88 As demonstrated by Dominique Cardon, 'Echantillons de draps de laine des Archives Datini (fin XIVe siècle, début XVe siècle). Analyses techniques, importance historique', *Mélanges de l'Ecole Française de Rome. Moyen Age* 103/1 (1991), 368. See also Lisa Monnas, 'Some Medieval Colour Terms for Textiles', *Medieval Clothing and Textiles* 10 (2014), 29.

89 Melis, *Aspetti della vita economica medievale*, 572 and note 1.

90 Hoshino, *L'arte della lana in Firenze*, 221–222, Table XXXI.

91 Doren, *Studien aus der Florentiner Wirtschaftsgeschichte*, vol. I, *Die Florentiner Wollentuchindustrie*, 512; Piero Guarducci, *Un tintore senese del Trecento. Landoccio di Cecco d'Orso* (Siena: Protagon, 1988), 97.

starting from white or clear blue cloths, scarlets were made with the highest quality, the additional costs ranged between 37 and 43 per cent.[92]

During the second half of the fifteenth century, the *lucchesino* stood out among the textiles made in Florence with the best English wool and dyed with higher quantities of colourants than would otherwise be used (see colour plate 19). Represented in the inventories of goods of members of the most important urban families from the Medici to the Strozzi[93] and among the goods purchased by the papal curia, this cloth was the masterpiece of the Florentine luxury production. According to Hidetoshi Hoshino its name should be explained by the fact that the fabric imitated the look of a certain silk cloth from Lucca;[94] at the moment I am not able to confirm his hypothesis, but if it were correct it would be very intriguing. The fact that, during the era of the boom of Florentine and Italian silks,[95] the manufacture of woollen luxury cloth would follow models of the 'sister' industry would confirm that the latter better succeeded in expressing the trends among elite customers. At the same time, however, it would demonstrate the remarkable capacity of the wool entrepreneurs to adapt to the new conditions of the textile markets and also their belief that the most beautiful woollen fabrics could match the splendour and appeal of the symbol textiles of the Renaissance.

Bibliography

Becattini, Ilaria. *L'economia aretina nei primi decenni del Quattrocento. Manifattura, industria e commercio attraverso lo spoglio del Catasto fiorentino del 1427.* PhD Dissertation: University of Siena, 2013.

Bianchi, Silvana, A. 'Il lanificio veronese fra XIII e XIV secolo: strutture organizzative, tecniche, prodotti'. In *Tessuti nel Veneto. Venezia e la Terraferma,* edited by Giuliana Ericani and Paola Frattaroli, 57–85. Verona: Banca popolare di Verona, 1993.

Bowden, Peter J. 'Wool supply and the Woollen Industry'. *The Economic History Review* 9 (1956): 44–58.

Bratchel, Michael E. *Lucca 1430–1494. The Reconstruction of an Italian City-Republic.* Oxford: Clarendon, 1995.

92 For the details, see Hoshino, 'La tintura di grana nel basso Medioevo', 31–35.

93 *Libro d'inventario dei beni di Lorenzo il Magnifico,* edited by Marco Spallanzani and Giovanna Gaeta Bertelà (Florence: Associazione Amici del Bargello, 1992), 74, 87, 123; Giovanni di Pagolo Rucellai, *Zibaldone,* edited by Gabriella Battista (Florence: Sismel-Edizioni del Galluzzo, 2013), 113; Maria Giuseppina Muzzarelli, *Guardaroba medievale. Vesti e società dal XIII al XVI secolo* (Bologna: Il Mulino, 1999), 100.

94 Hoshino, 'La tintura di grana nel basso Medioevo', 32–34.

95 On this, see Bruno Dini, 'L'industria serica in Italia. Secc. XIII–XV' (1995), republished in Dini, *Saggi su una economia-mondo,* 51–85; Sergio Tognetti, 'I drappi di seta', in *Il Rinascimento italiano e l'Europa,* vol. IV, *Commercio e cultura mercantile,* 143–170; Franceschi, « … *E seremo tutti ricchi*», 53–68; Luca Molà, 'The Italian Silk Industry during the Renaissance', in this volume.

Cardon, Dominique. 'Echantillons de draps de laine des Archives Datini (fin XIVe siècle, début XVe siècle). Analyses techniques, importance historique'. *Mélanges de l'Ecole Française de Rome. Moyen Age* 103/1 (1991): 359–372.

Cardon, Dominique. *La draperie au Moyen Âge. Essor d'une grande industrie européenne.* Paris: CNRS Editions, 1999.

Castagneto, Pierluigi. *L'arte della lana a Pisa nel Duecento e nei primi decenni del Trecento. Commercio, industria, istituzioni.* Pisa: GISEM-Edizioni ETS, 1996.

Ceppari, Maria and Turrini, Patrizia. 'Documenti: il commercio delle stoffe; l'abbigliamento e le provvisioni sul lusso; arredi sacri e profani'. In *Drappi, velluti, taffettà. Antichi tessuti a Siena e nel suo territorio, Catalogo della Mostra (Siena, 31 maggio–31 luglio 1994)*, edited by Marco Ciatti, 245–259. Siena: Nuova Immagine, 1994.

Chorley, Patrick. 'The Volume of Cloth Production in Florence, 1500–1600: An Assessment of the Evidence'. In *Wool: Products and Markets (13th-20th Century)*, edited by Giovanni L. Fontana and Gérard Gayot, 105–141. Padua: Cleup, 2004.

Collier Frick, Carole. *Dressing Renaissance Florence: Families, Fortunes and Fine Clothing.* Baltimore: Johns Hopkins University Press, 2002.

Collodo, Silvana. 'Signore e mercanti: storia di un'alleanza'. Republished in Collodo, *Una società in trasformazione. Padova tra XI e XV secolo*, 329–403. Padua: Antenore, 1990.

Collodo, Silvana. 'La produzione tessile nel Veneto medievale'. Republished in Collodo, *Società e istituzioni in area veneta: itinerari di ricerca (secoli XII-XV)*, 69–92. Florence: Nardini, 1999.

De Roover, Raymond. *The Rise and Decline of the Medici Bank: 1397–1494.* New York: Norton, 1966.

Demo, Edoardo. *L'«anima della città». L'industria tessile a Verona e Vicenza (1400–1550).* Milan: Unicopli, 2001.

Demo, Edoardo. 'Lane, lanaioli e mercanti nella manifattura vicentina (secc. XIV–XVI)'. In *Wool: Products and Markets 13th-20th Century*, edited by Giovanni L. Fontana and Gérard Gayot, 381–410. Padua: Cleup, 2004.

Dini, Bruno. *Le origini del capitalismo.* Florence: Le Monnier, 1979.

Dini, Bruno. 'Gli orizzonti economici'. In *Storia della società italiana*, edited by Giovanni Cherubini et al., vol. VII, *La crisi del sistema comunale*, 39–98. Milan: Teti, 1982.

Dini, Bruno. *Arezzo intorno al 1400. Produzioni e mercato.* Arezzo: Grafiche Badiali, 1984.

Dini, Bruno. 'L'industria tessile italiana nel tardo Medioevo'. Republished in Dini, *Saggi su una economia-mondo. Firenze e l'Italia fra Mediterraneo ed Europa (secc. XIII–XVI)*, 13–49. Pisa: Pacini, 1995.

Dini, Bruno. 'L'industria serica in Italia. Secc. XIII–XV'. Republished in Dini, *Saggi su una economia-mondo. Firenze e l'Italia fra Mediterraneo ed Europa (secc. XIII–XVI)*, 51–85. Pisa: Pacini, 1995.

Doren, Alfred. *Studien aus der Florentiner Wirtschaftsgeschichte, vol. I: Die Florentiner Wollentuchindustrie vom l4. bis zum 16. Jahrhundert. Ein Beitrag zur geschichte des modernen Kapitalismus.* Stuttgart: Cotta, 1901.

Edler De Roover, Florence. 'Andrea Banchi, Florentine Silk Manufacturer and Merchant in the Fifteenth Century'. *Studies in Medieval and Renaissance History* 3 (1966): 221–285.

Epstein, Stephen R. *Freedom and Growth, Markets and States in Europe, 1300–1750.* London: Routledge, 2000.

Fano, Nella. 'Ricerche sull'arte della lana a Venezia nel XIII e XIV secolo'. *Archivio veneto* ser. V, XVIII (1936): 73–213.

Filippi, Giovanni. *L'arte dei mercanti di Calimala in Firenze ed il suo più antico statuto.* Turin: Fratelli Bocca, 1889.

Fontana, Giovanni L. 'La Lana'. In *Storia d'Italia. Annali*, vol. 19, *La moda*, edited by Carlo M. Belfanti and Fabio Giusberti, 319–361. Turin: Einaudi, 2003.

Franceschi, Franco. *Oltre il «Tumulto». I lavoratori fiorentini dell'Arte della Lana fra Tre e Quattrocento.* Florence: Olschki, 1993.

Franceschi, Franco. 'L'impresa mercantile-industriale nella Toscana dei secoli XIV–XVI'. In *La storia dell'impresa nella lunga durata: continuità e discontinuità, Atti del Seminario di studi (Venezia, 22–23 Novembre 2002). Annali di Storia dell'impresa* XIV (2003): 229–249.

Franceschi, Franco. 'Lane permesse e lane proibite nella Toscana fiorentina dei secoli XIV–XV: logiche economiche e scelte "politiche"'. In *La pastorizia mediterranea. Storia e diritto (secoli XI-XX), Atti del Convegno Internazionale (Alghero, 8–11 novembre 2006)*, edited by Antonello Mattone and Pinuccia F. Simbula, 878–889. Rome: Carocci, 2011.

Franceschi, Franco. « ... *E seremo tutti ricchi». Lavoro, mobilità sociale e conflitti nelle città dell'Italia medievale.* Pisa: Pacini, 2012.

Franceschi, Franco and Molà, Luca. 'Regional States and Economic Development'. In *The Italian Renaissance State*, edited by Andrea Gamberini and Isabella Lazzarini, 444–466. Cambridge: Cambridge University Press, 2012.

Frangioni, Luciana. 'I tessuti di lana e di cotone'. In *Artigianato lombardo*, 5 vols, vol. III, *L'opera tessile*, 13–37. Milan: Cassa di risparmio delle provincie lombarde, 1977–1981.

Frangioni, Luciana. *Milano fine Trecento. Il carteggio milanese dell'Archivio Datini*, 2 vols. Florence: Opus Libri, 1994.

Goldthwaite, Richard. A. *The Economy of Renaissance Florence.* Baltimore: The Johns Hopkins University Press, 2009.

Goldthwaite, Richard. A. 'The Florentine Wool Industry in the Late Sixteenth Century: A Case Study'. *The Journal of European Economic History* 32/3 (2003): 527–554.

Grillo, Paolo. '*«Vicus Lanificio Insignis»*. Industria laniera e strutture sociali del borgo lariano di Torno nel XV secolo'. *Studi di Storia Medioevale e di Diplomatica* 14 (1993): 91–110.

Grillo, Paolo. *Milano in età comunale (1183–1276). Istituzioni, società, economia.* Spoleto: Cisam, 2001.

Guarducci, Piero. *Un tintore senese del Trecento. Landoccio di Cecco d'Orso.* Siena: Protagon, 1988.

Guerzoni, Guido. 'Novità, innovazione e imitazione: i sintomi della modernità'. In *Il Rinascimento italiano e l'Europa*, vol. III, *Produzione e tecniche*, edited by Philippe Braunstein and Luca Molà, 59–87. Treviso-Costabissara: Fondazione Cassamarca-Angelo Colla, 2007.

Hoshino, Hidetoshi. *L'arte della lana in Firenze nel basso Medioevo. Il commercio della lana e il mercato dei panni fiorentini nei secoli XIII–XV.* Florence: Olschki, 1980.

Hoshino, Hidetoshi. 'The Rise of the Florentine Woollen Industry in the Fourteenth Century'. In *Cloth and Clothing in Medieval Europe. Essays in Memory of Professor E. M. Carus-Wilson*, edited by Negley B. Harte and Kenneth G. Ponting, 184–204. London: Heinemann, 1983.

Hoshino, Hidetoshi. 'La tintura di grana nel basso Medioevo'. Republished in Hoshino, *Industria tessile e commercio internazionale nella Firenze del tardo Medioevo*, edited by Franco Franceschi and Sergio Tognetti, 23–39. Florence: Olschki, 2001.

Hoshino, Hidetoshi. 'Il commercio fiorentino nell'Impero ottomano: costi e profitti negli anni 1484–1488'. Republished in Hoshino, *Industria tessile e commercio internazionale nella Firenze del tardo Medioevo*, edited by Franco Franceschi and Sergio Tognetti, 113–123. Florence: Olschki, 2001.

La Mariegola dell'arte della lana di Venezia (1244–1595), edited by Andrea Mozzato, 2 vols. Venice: Il Comitato editore, 2002.

Laurent, Henri. *Un grand commerce d'exportation au Moyen Age: la draperie des Pays-Bas en France et dans les pays méditerranéens (XIIe–XVe siècle).* Paris: Droz, 1935.

Liber datii mercantie Communis Mediolani. Registro del secolo XV, edited by Antonio Noto. Milan: Università L. Bocconi, 1950.

Libro d'inventario dei beni di Lorenzo il Magnifico, edited by Marco Spallanzani and Giovanna Gaeta Bertelà. Florence: Associazione Amici del Bargello, 1992.

Mainoni, Patrizia. 'Il mercato della lana a Milano dal XIV al XV secolo. Prime indagini'. *Archivio storico lombardo* CX (1984): 20–43.

Mainoni, Patrizia. *Economia e politica nella Lombardia medievale. Da Bergamo a Milano fra XIII e XV secolo.* Cavallermaggiore: Gribaudo, 1994.

Mainoni, Patrizia. 'La seta in Italia fra XII e XIII secolo. Migrazioni artigiane e tipologie seriche'. In *La seta in Italia dal Medioevo al Seicento. Dal baco al drappo*, edited by Luca Molà et al., 365–399. Venice: Marsilio, 2000.

Mainoni, Patrizia. 'La fisionomia economica delle città lombarde dalla fine del Duecento alla prima metà del Trecento. Materiali per un confronto'. In *Le città del Mediterraneo all'apogeo dello sviluppo medievale. Aspetti economici e sociali, Atti del XVIII Convegno internazionale di Studi (Pistoia, 18–21 maggio 2001)*, 141–221. Pistoia: Centro italiano di studi di storia e d'arte, 2003.

Melis, Federigo. *Aspetti della vita economica medievale. Studi nell'Archivio Datini di Prato.* Siena: Monte dei Paschi di Siena, 1962.

Melis, Federigo. 'Pistoia nei secoli d'oro della sua economia'. Republished in Melis, *Industria e commercio nella Toscana medievale*, edited by Bruno Dini, 157–174. Florence: Le Monnier, 1989.

Melis, Federigo. 'La lana della Spagna mediterranea e della Barberia occidentale nei secoli XIV-XV'. Republished in Melis, *I mercanti italiani nell'Europa medievale e rinascimentale*, edited by Luciana Frangioni, 233–250. Florence: Le Monnier, 1990.

Monnas, Lisa. 'Some Medieval Colour Terms for Textiles', *Medieval Clothing and Textiles* 10 (2014): 25–57.

Morelli, Giovanni di Pagolo. *Ricordi.* In *Mercanti scrittori. Ricordi nella Firenze tra Medioevo e Rinascimento*, edited by Vittore Branca, 101–339. Milan: Mondadori, 1986.

Mozzato, Andrea. *L'arte della lana a Venezia nel basso Medioevo. Materia prima, produzione e produttori.* PhD Dissertation, University of Milan, 2003.

Mozzato, Andrea. 'Il mercato dei panni di lana a Venezia all'inizio del XV secolo'. In *Wool: Products and Markets 13th–20th Century*, edited by Giovanni L. Fontana and Gérard Gayot, 1035–1066. Padua: Cleup, 2004.

Mozzato, Andrea. 'The Production of Woollens in Fifteenth and Sixteenth-Century Venice'. In *At the Centre of the Old World. Trade and Manufacturing in Venice and the Venetian Mainland, 1400–1800*, edited by Paola Lanaro, 73–107. Toronto: Centre for Reformation and Renaissance Studies, 2006.

Munro, John H. 'The Medieval Scarlet and Economics of Sartorial Splendour'. In *Cloth and Clothing in Medieval Europe. Essays in Memory of Professor E. M. Carus-Wilson*, edited by Negley B. Harte and Kenneth G. Ponting, 13–70. London: Heinemann, 1983.

Munro, John H. 'The West European Woollen Industries and their Struggles for International Markets, c.1000–1500'. In *The Cambridge History of Western Textiles*,

edited by David Jenkins, 2 vols, vol. I, 228–324. Cambridge and New York: Cambridge University Press, 2003.
Munro, John H. 'I panni di lana'. In *Il Rinascimento italiano e l'Europa*, vol. IV, *Commercio e cultura mercantile*, edited by Franco Franceschi et al., 105–141. Treviso-Costabissara: Fondazione Cassamarca-Angelo Colla editore, 2007.
Muzzarelli, Maria Giuseppina. *Guardaroba medievale. Vesti e società dal XIII al XVI secolo*. Bologna: Il Mulino, 1999.
Pitti, Bonaccorso. *Ricordi*, in *Mercanti scrittori. Ricordi nella Firenze tra Medioevo e Rinascimento*, edited by Vittore Branca, 341–503. Milan: Mondadori, 1986.
Poloni, Alma. *Lucca nel Duecento. Uno studio sul cambiamento sociale*. Pisa: Plus-Pisa University Press, 2009.
Rebora, Giovanni. 'Materia prima e costi di trasformazione nel promemoria di una lanaiolo veneto della fine del Quattrocento'. *Rivista storica italiana* LXXXIII (1971): 144–164.
Rossini, Egidio and Mazzaoui, Maureen F. 'Società e tecnica nel Medioevo (La produzione dei panni di lana a Verona nei secoli XIII-XIV-XV)'. *Atti e Memorie dell'Accademia d'agricoltura scienze e lettere di Verona* VI, XXI (1969–1970): 571–624.
Rucellai, Giovanni di Pagolo. *Zibaldone*, edited by Gabriella Battista. Florence: Sismel-Edizioni del Galluzzo, 2013.
Statuta artis lanae terrae Fabriani. Rome: Dario Giuseppe Rossi, 1880
Sapori, Armando. *Una compagnia di Calimala ai primi del Trecento*. Florence: Olschki, 1932.
Tognetti, Sergio. 'I drappi di seta'. In *Il Rinascimento italiano e l'Europa*, vol. IV, *Commercio e cultura mercantile*, edited by Franco Franceschi et al., 143–170. Treviso-Costabissara: Fondazione Cassamarca-Angelo Colla editore, 2007.
Tortoli, Sandra. 'Per la storia della produzione laniera a Siena nel Trecento e nei primi anni del Quattrocento'. *Bullettino senese di storia patria* LXXXII–LXXXIII, (1975–1976): 220–238.
Trattato dell'Arte della Lana. In Alfred Doren. *Studien aus der Florentiner Wirtschaftsgeschichte*, vol. I, *Die Florentiner Wollentuchindustrie vom l4. bis zum 16. Jahrhundert. Ein Beitrag zur geschichte des modernen Kapitalismus*, 484–493. Stuttgart: Cotta, 1901.
Villani, Giovanni. *Nuova Cronica*. Edited by Giuseppe Porta, 3 vols. Parma: Guanda, 1990–1991.
Zanazzo, Battista. *L'arte della lana in Vicenza (secoli XIII–XV)*. Venice: R. Deputazione veneta di storia patria, 1914.

9

A Luxury Industry: The Production of Italian Silks 1400–1600

Luca Molà

For over two millennia, silk was one of the most important commodities in the world economy. As early as the first century BC, in the form of trade goods, gifts or homage, precious silk fabrics were sent from the Chinese Empire to Rome and throughout a good part of Asia. Used for a considerable length of time in calligraphy, painting and the rituals of Buddhism, monks, pilgrims and merchants would take silk with them on their travels across Central Asia. From the eighth century onwards, the regions that had converted to Islam began to use it to make fabrics and these production techniques were soon transferred to Muslim Spain. Meanwhile, from the sixth century onwards, the Byzantine Empire had also acquired the tools necessary for the production of silk fabrics, of which extremely refined samples dyed with purple and reserved for the Imperial court were produced in the state workshops of Constantinople, or manufactured by independent artisans and entrepreneurs in Thebes and Corinth for a much vaster market. Between the late Middle Ages and the early modern period, every year endless caravans would carry tonnes of silk from Persia to the Ottoman Empire and the regions ruled by the Mamlucks, and an even greater quantity would travel to the south-east, towards India, a trade that under the Safavid dynasty was controlled by Armenian businessmen. With the arrival of European ships in East Asia in the sixteenth century, the Portuguese began to supply Japan with Chinese silk via the trade-posts of Macao and Nagasaki, while by the end of the century the silver from the American mines of Potosi and Zacatecas was being transported by the Spanish to their new colonies in the Philippines where it was then traded for the fabrics that had been brought there by a populous colony of Chinese merchants. Once a year the King of Spain sent a galleon from Manila to sail the Pacific and transport Chinese silk to the Peruvian and Mexican markets where, however, the silk industry had already developed thanks to the emigration of Spanish experts in Mexico City and Puebla de los Angeles. However, in the seventeenth and eighteenth centuries it was the great East India Companies of Holland, England and France that were in charge of the distribution of silk from Asia in Europe, and they even participated in the flourishing silk market of Bengal. Silk can therefore rightly claim to have been one of the principle goods in the history of the early development of economic globalisation.[1]

Italy played a key role in these long and fascinating histories. Starting its development in the city of Lucca from the twelfth century onwards, probably thanks to Jewish or Greek craftsmen, the silk industry soon spread to Venice, and during the early modern period it took roots in both towns and cities throughout the peninsula. From the thirteenth to the seventeenth century the silk fabrics and thread produced by the Italian industries completely dominated the European markets, supplying both the elite and the middle classes all over the continent, from Portugal to the Grand Duchy of Moscow, with myriad diverse fabrics that were used for clothing, furnishings and religious functions. Furthermore, from the fifteenth century onwards, the industries in Italian cities began to export their products to the Middle East, thus overturning a long-standing technical supremacy. The knowledge and capital accumulated by Italian merchants and businessmen were undoubtedly at the basis of this success, as they knew how to mobilise their commercial networks to start an industry that focused on the employment of a highly specialised human capital. With few exceptions, it was these very entrepreneurs who established the new industrial enterprise in Italian urban centres in the early modern period, with the active support of the governments of the various states.[2]

---

1 Unfortunately, in the field of *global history* there has not yet been a detailed study on silk covering the entire period. For some general overviews or studies on individual areas see: Liu Xinru, 'Silks and Religions in Eurasia, c. A.D. 600–1200', *Journal of World History* 6 (1995): 25–48; Thomas Ertl, 'Silkworms, Capital, and Merchant Ships: European Silk Industry in the Medieval World Economy', *The Medieval History Journal* 9 (2006): 243–270; Shelagh Vainker, *Chinese Silk. A Cultural History* (New Brunswick: Rutgers University Press, 2004); Robert S. Lopez, 'Silk Industry in the Byzantine Empire', *Speculum* 20 (1945): 1–42; David Jacoby, 'Silk Economics and Cross-Cultural Artistic Interaction: Byzantium, the Muslim World, and Christian West', *Dumbarton Oaks Papers* 58 (2004): 197–240; Linda K. Steinmann, 'Shah 'Abbas and the Royal Silk Trade 1599–1629', *Bulletin of the British Society for Middle Eastern Studies* 14 (1987): 68–74; Rudolph P. Matthee, *The Politics of Trade in Safavid Iran. Silk for Silver 1600–1730* (Cambridge: Cambridge University Press, 1999); Willem Floor e Patrick Clawson, 'Safavid's Iran Search for Silver and Gold', *International Journal of Middle East Studies* 32 (2000): 345–368; Ronald W. Ferrier, 'The Armenians and the East India Company in the Seventeenth and Early Eighteenth Century', *The Economic History Review* 26 (1973): 38–62; Michael Cooper, 'The Mechanics of the Macao–Nagasaki Silk Trade', *Monumenta Nipponica* 27 (1972): 423–433; Woodrow Borah, *Silk Raising in Colonial Mexico* (Berkeley: University of California Press, 1943); Sushil Chaudhury, 'International Trade in Bengal Silk and the Comparative Role of Asians and Europeans, ca. 1700–1757', *Modern Asian Studies* 29 (1995): 373–386.

2 See: Bruno Dini, 'L'industria serica in Italia. Secc. XIII–XV', in *La seta in Europa, secc. XIII–XX*, ed. by Simonetta Cavaciocchi (Florence 1993), 91–123; Luca Molà, Reinhold C.

During the fourteenth century, Venice, Bologna, Florence and Genoa received considerable support from numerous families of artisans and merchants from Lucca who had fled their homeland following the political upheavals that started in 1314 and continued until well into the middle of the century, in a movement that continued spontaneously for decades, although they were encouraged in various ways by the cities that welcomed them.[3] In the fifteenth century, however, it was the direct agreements between city authorities and individual operators that prevailed, and the latter took it upon themselves to start the production of silk fabrics in exchange for commercial and fiscal advantages. The names of some 'founders' of the industry who introduced the production in new cities at a precise date have therefore gone down in history: Nello di Francesco in Siena in 1438, the Florentine Pietro di Bartolo in Milan in 1442, Bartolomeo Gregori in Perugia in 1459, the Genoese Urbano Trincherio in Ferrara in 1462, and the Florentine Francesco di Nerone in Naples in 1474. In some cases the businessmen in charge of these projects for industrial development were contacted and persuaded to accept the post from government boards that had been appointed for the very purpose of enriching their city with silk production, thus following an economic policy that was increasingly widespread in Italy as the advantages the silk industry offered became clearer and clearer. A fundamental aspect of this policy was the support of wealthy financiers, belonging both to the local ruling class and the international merchant and banking elites, who promised to cover the costs of starting up the business, which was no small sum. According to the calculation a Venetian expert presented the King of Naples in 1465, at least 10,000 ducats were needed if a gold-silk fabric production was to be started successfully, and this figure is not at all surprising if one considers the cost of the raw materials, silk in particular, but also valuable dyes and spun gold and silver. In addition, further money was made available by the local governments or princes to finance the initial development of the business: 100 florins a year for eight years were promised in Siena, 70 florins a month for ten years were stipulated in Milan, and an annual sum of 300 ducats for ten years was agreed upon in Naples. This also included a general reduction in excise tax and the total fiscal exemption for the trade of the materials needed for production.[4]

Mueller and C. Zanier, ed., *Dal baco al drappo. La seta in Italia dal Medioevo al Seicento* (Venice: Fondazione Giorgio Cini, 2000).

3 Luca Molà, *La comunità dei lucchesi a Venezia. Immigrazione e industria della seta nel tardo Medioevo* (Venice: Istituto veneto di scienze, 1994), 21–72.

4 Luciano Banchi, *L'Arte della seta in Siena nei secoli XV e XVI. Statuti e documenti* (Siena: Tipografia sordo-muti di L. Lazzeri, 1881), appendix, docs. I–II; Paolo Grillo, 'Le origini della manifattura serica in Milano (1400–1450)', *Studi Storici* 35 (1994): 903–906; Rita Staccini, *Le arti perugine della bambagia e della seta* (Spoleto: Centro italiano di studi sull'alto medioevo, 1994), 19–20; Luigi Napoleone Cittadella, *Notizie relative a Ferrara per la maggior parte inedite*, (Ferrara, 1864), 502–503; Raffaele Pescione, 'Gli statuti dell'Arte della seta in Napoli in rapporto al privilegio di giurisdizione', *Archivio Storico per le Provincie Napoletane* 5

We must bear in mind that alongside this intense activity regarding the preparation at an institutional and financial level, there was also another aspect that was just as arduous, which was finding the workmen and equipment to be moved, at times over long or middle distances. In cities where the silk industry was already flourishing, skilled craftsmen were hired (especially weavers) by promising them generous rewards and greater independence from corporative controls, that were originally inexistent in the new locations. In turn, since they had an intimate knowledge of local manpower in this field, these craftsmen would promise to find the workers – men and women – they needed in their workshops and take them with them, as well as purchasing or commissioning the manufacture of the equipment they needed. All of this was done with the utmost secrecy and involved a certain element of risk, since from the fifteenth century onwards, aware of increasing international competition, silk cities had forbidden the emigration of their human and technological capital, comparing it to industrial espionage. For example, Genoa and Florence went as far as promising impunity to anyone who killed a silk craftsman who had moved and was working for a competitor in the field. It is therefore not at all surprising that the emigrates asked to be granted the privilege of bearing arms when they were drawing up a contract with the public authorities, making specific mention of the danger they were exposing themselves to by moving to a new location.[5]

The proliferation of silk workshops throughout Italy had to meet a demand for silk fabrics that had increased with remarkable speed from the fourteenth century onwards. While during the Early and High Middle Ages it had been almost exclusively the nobility and high-ranking clergyman who had been able to afford silk fabrics from Asia and the Byzantine Empire, from the fourteenth century onwards it was the Italian and European urban elite who began demanding silk products of the highest quality and variety, as a result of their growing wealth. As the introduction to this volume demonstrated, a frenetic increase in consumption became a source of worry to moralists, men of the church and public authorities who, although they supported the silk industry, also wanted to stop its products from spreading among the local population, in an attempt to save their citizens' patrimony from being squandered on luxury goods. This resulted in an increase in sumptuary laws in both Italy and throughout Europe, which reached its peak in the sixteenth and seventeenth centuries, when the consumption of luxury goods seemed to have spiralled out of control. Venice alone issued 100 orders in the attempt to hit particular fashions, fabrics and dyes, or with the intention of regulating

(1919):160–166; Pescione, *Il tribunale dell'Arte della Seta in Napoli (da documenti inediti)* (Naples, 1923): 95–105; Luca Molà, 'Oltre i confini della città: gli artigiani e gli imprenditori della seta fiorentini all'estero', in *Arti fiorentine. La grande storia dell'artigianato. Vol. II: il Quattrocento*, ed. F. Franceschi et al. (Florence: Giunti, 1999), 93–98.

5 Luca Molà, *The Silk Industry of Renaissance Venice* (Baltimore–London: John Hopkins University Press, 2000), 29–51.

the entire system of clothing in the city. However, all these attempts met with little success and proved impotent in the face of this 'hunger' for silk that became a fundamental characteristic of the mentality of individuals and families during the Later Middle Ages and early modern period.[6]

Commerce and Production of Silk

The raw silk used in Italian industries was of various origins. The variety in the areas of supply depended partly on the intrinsic characteristics of the raw material, which was different according to the race of the silkworms it was produced from, their diet, how they were bred and, in particular, the quality of cocoon reeling in their place of origin. Another factor was the need to make sure they were not dependent on just one commercial trade channel, since it might be subject to frequent, short-term fluctuations. During the thirteenth century and until the 1320s, the industry in Lucca used considerable shipments of Chinese silk, brought to Tuscany via the port of Genoa and its merchants. However, it is difficult to know whether this *cattuia* silk – which came from Cathay, the name of the Chinese Empire at that time – that can often be found in the notarial registers from the second half of the thirteenth century onwards, was purchased directly on the markets of the Far East by the Italian businessmen who traded there thanks to the establishment of the *pax mongolica* (Mongol Peace), or whether it was brought to Italy via Tabriz, Urgenc, the ports of the Black Sea and the Middle East, where it had been taken by Mongol and Arabian merchants. Contrary to what one might believe, it was not of the highest quality. Raw materials of different origins cost more, perhaps because during the long journey involving all kinds of transport across the roads of Central Asia – going from one region to another it was loaded on horses, river boats, donkeys, camels and oxen-pulled carts – the packaging would be ruined and by the time the Chinese silk had reached its destination it was frayed, that is, worn (at least this is the warning Francesco Pegolotti gives purchasers in his famous *Pratica di mercatura*). At any rate, with the collapse of the Yuan dynasty and the advent of the Ming, contacts between China and Europe were interrupted for centuries and, as a consequence, Chinese silk disappears from the Italian documentation.[7]

---

6 For more on Italian sumptuary laws see: Maria G. Muzzarelli, *Gli inganni delle apparenze. Disciplina di vesti e ornamenti alla fine del Medioevo* (Turin: Scriptorium, 1996); Maria G. Muzzarelli, *Guardaroba medievale. Vesti e società dal XIII al XVI secolo* (Bologna: Il Mulino, 1999); Maria G. Muzzarelli, ed., *Disciplinare il lusso: la legislazione suntuaria in Italia e in Europa tra Medioevo ed età moderna* (Rome: Carocci 2003).

7 Robert S. Lopez, 'Nuove luci sugli italiani in Estremo Oriente prima di Colombo', in, *Su e giù per la storia di Genova*, ed. Robert S. Lopez. (Genoa: Università di Genova, 1975), 95–104; Robert-Henri Bautier, 'Les relations économiques des occidentaux avec les pays d'Orient, au Moyen Age. Points de vue et documents', in *Société et compagnies de commerce en Orient et dans l'Océan Indien. Actes du Huitième Colloque International d'Histoire Maritime*

From the thirteenth century, the most commonly used silk came from Persia, especially from the areas around the Caspian Sea, and had a variety of names, depending on the region in which it was produced. The most sought-after qualities were the *leggi, talani* and *stravai,* but the *gangia, ghella, ardassa, canari, mamodea* and *tracazi* were also frequently mentioned.[8] From the fourteenth century onwards, alongside the Persian threads those from the Iberian peninsula are mentioned more and more frequently, in particular those from Southern Spain.[9] It is instead Venetian sources that provide most information about silk from the Balkans, mainland Greece (the *coronella* and *fior di morea* silks were particularly valuable) and the Greek islands, from Syria and Palestine.[10] Each kind of silk reached the Italian industries in a different form and thus required a certain amount of experience on the part of the merchants, since they had to be able to identify it and assess its quality. A *Treatise* on silk manufacturing written in Florence during the second half of the fifteenth century lists a great number of them, including the characteristics of the external packaging, such as bags or bundles (the weight varied between approximately 150 and 300 pounds), the internal division of the skeins tied together, whether in bundles or *scagne* (weighing between a pound and a half to ten pounds, the Spanish ones with 'small strips of paper attached at the top with Arabic writing'), the length of the individual skeins, colour, brightness, thickness, strength, the presence of impurities (*brocchi),* the loss of weight and the main use they could be put to for cloth weaving (as warp, weft, or pile for various fabrics).[11]

The quantity of silk traded in Italy during the Later Middle Ages and the early modern period is staggering, growing over the centuries until it reached several million pounds a year, thus bearing witness to the considerable quantitative level the vanguard sector reached in the Italian manufacturing production. Venice imported raw silk from various areas of the Mediterranean and Persia, usually transported on the state galleys that regularly sailed between Venice, the East and Spain. According to the shipments aboard these convoys, between the fourteenth and fifteenth century hundreds of silk bales were carried each year on vessels that called in the Black Sea, at Constantinople, Negroponte, Modone and Corfu, for a total value of several

(Beyrouth 5–10 Septembre 1966), ed. M. Mollat, (Paris 1970), 288–292; Ignazio Del Punta, 'Lucca e il commercio della seta nel Duecento', in *Per Marco Tangheroni. Studi su Pisa e sul Mediterraneo medievale offerti dai suoi ultimi allievi,* ed. Cecilia Iannella (Pisa: Edizioni ETS, 2005), 111–115.

8 Del Punta, 'Lucca e il commercio', 105–111; Pierre Racine, 'Le marché gênois de la soie en 1288', *Revue des études sud–est europeennes* 8 (1970): 403–415.

9 Miguel A. Ladero Quesada, 'La producción de seda en la España medieval. Siglos XIII–XVI', in *La seta in Europa,* 125–139.

10 Molà, *The Silk Industry,* 55–72.

11 Girolamo Gargiolli, *L'industria della seta in Firenze: trattato del secolo XV* (Florence, 1868), 102–108.

hundreds of thousands of ducats.[12] But imports had grown exponentially two centuries later, when an average of around 1,500 bales of Persian and Syrian silk arrived in Venice each year via the city of Aleppo, with a peak of 2,400 bales, therefore between 350,000 and 750,000 pounds (if one calculates that each bolt weighed between 250 and 300 pounds).[13] The silk of Asian origin was also imported in large quantities by Genoese and Florentine merchants, who had established the centre of their Eastern trade in Bursa, in the Ottoman Empire, between the fifteenth and sixteenth centuries.[14]

However, during the Later Middle Ages and early modern period the Italian silk industry progressively increased its use of locally produced raw materials. At the end of the sixteenth century Calabria was exporting 700–800,000 pounds a year, and the contract on the silk excise duties yielded the noble family of the Sanseverino's of Bisignano, who had its monopoly until 1483, the incredible sum of over 50,000 ducats a year.[15] In Sicily almost the entire silk production was concentrated around the port of Messina to facilitate its purchase and transport for the merchants; around the mid sixteenth century approximately 1,200 bales, weighing 250 pounds each, left the island each year, for a total weight of 300,000 pounds, which grew to 2,400 bales, for a total of 600,000 pounds, in the last decade of the century.[16] Between the second half of the sixteenth and the beginning of the seventeenth century, an amount ranging from 300,000 to 500,000 pounds of silk was produced in the Veneto and Lombard districts of the Venetian state, while the Milanese territory yielded 300,000 pounds, Florence 90,000, Mantua 70,000 and Ferrara 50,000.[17]

---

12 Eliyahu Ashtor, 'Il commercio italiano col Levante e il suo impatto sull'economia tardomedievale', in *'Aspetti della vita economica medievale'. Atti del Convegno di Studi nel X Anniversario della morte di Federigo Melis, Firenze–Pisa–Prato, 10–14 marzo 1984,* Federigo Melis. (Florence: Monte dei Paschi di Diena, 1985), 23 (Table I), 35 (Table II), 54 (appendix I).

13 Domenico Sella, *Commerci e industrie a Venezia nel secolo XVII* (Venice–Rome: Istituto per la Collaborazione Culturale, 1961), 111–112.

14 Halil Inalcik, 'The Ottoman State: Economy and Society, 1300–1600', in *An Economic and Social History of the Ottoman Empire, 1300–1914,* ed. Halil Inalcik et al. (Cambridge: Cambridge University Press, 1994), 218–252.

15 Giuseppe Galasso, *Economia e società nella Calabria del Cinquecento* (Milan: Guida Editori, 1980), 147–148; Tedora Iorio, *Produzione e commercio della seta in Calabria nel secolo XVI* (Naples: Arte tipografica, 1988).

16 Giuseppe, Galasso, 'Seta e commercio del ferro nell'economia napoletana del tardo Cinquecento', *Rivista Storica Italiana* 75 (1963): 615–640, Maurice Aymard, 'Commerce et production de la soie sicilienne aux XVIe–XVIIe siècles', *Mélanges d'archéologie et d'histoire de l'Ecole Française de Rome* 77 (1965): 622.

17 Molà, *The Silk Industry,* 232–236; Alberto Cova, 'Interessi economici e impegni istituzionali delle corporazioni milanesi nel Seicento', in *Economia e corporazioni. Il governo degli interessi nella storia d'Italia dal Medioevo all'età contemporanea,* ed. C. Mozzarelli. (Milan: Giuffrè 1988), 126; Francesco Battistini, 'La gelsibachicoltura e la trattura della seta in Toscana', in *La seta in Europa,* 297–298; Domenico Sella, *Crisis and Continuity. The Economy of Spanish Lombardy in the Seventeenth Century* (Harvard, Harvard University Press, 1979), 20; Giuseppe Coniglio, 'Agricoltura ed artigianato mantovano nel sec. XVI', in *Studi in onore di Amintore Fanfani, IV. Evo Moderno,* ed. Amintore Fanfani (Milan: Giuffrè, 1962), 340; Franco Cazzola, 'Polemiche e contrasti per l'istituzione dell'Arte della seta a Ferrara (1595–1620)', *Economia e Storia* 14 (1967): 297–298.

While these data are by no means exhaustive, since they do not include the silk production of regions of primary importance for which, unfortunately, we do not have complete information (Piedmont, Emilia, Romagna, Marche, Abruzzi), it is nevertheless testimony to Italy's transformation into one of the most important regions worldwide in the production of raw silk, with mulberry trees becoming a common feature in the country landscape.

Indeed, a unique characteristic of silkworm farming is its inextricable link with the cultivation of mulberry trees, the leaves of which are their only source of nourishment. By following the diffusion of mulberry tree plantations in Italy from the Middle Ages to the early modern period, it is therefore possible to outline a map of the production areas of raw silk in Italy. The Italian regions with the most ancient traditions in the field of sericulture were in eastern Sicily and the hilly coastal area of Calabria, where mulberry trees were planted by Arabs and Byzantines as early as the tenth and eleventh centuries. For centuries in south Italy the black mulberry tree (*Morus nigra*) was cultivated almost exclusively, while in 1434 a businessman introduced the white mulberry (*Morus alba*) in Tuscany, which adapted to different terrain more easily and thus became the predominant plant in sericulture in the central and northern areas of the country. In some of these regions mention is made of the presence of mulberries as early as the mid thirteenth century, but the decisive moment for their diffusion was in the fifteenth and sixteenth centuries, when the trees rapidly became widespread throughout nearly the whole of Italy, so much so that several historians have even spoken of a sixteenth-century 'mulberry-mania'. These new cultivations were often actively supported by the state authorities who made it obligatory for land owners to plant a certain number of mulberry trees in the territory under their jurisdiction to favour silk production. From 1327 on, the local government of Modena demanded that at least three mulberry trees be planted for every fenced-in lot of land, followed in 1441 by Florence (five mulberry trees for every *pertica*) and in 1470 by Milan (one mulberry tree for every twenty *pertiche*), a regulation that was imitated elsewhere during the sixteenth century. In the meantime, the decision was taken to grow mulberry trees in public areas, in particular along the city walls, rivers and streets, and princely nurseries were created, such as the one in the Duchies of Mantua and Milan after the middle of the fifteenth century or that of the Duchy of Savoy in the sixteenth century, which had to supply the trees to anyone interested in cultivating them, buying the young plants in the areas with the most ancient traditions. This was by no means always a simple operation and at times it required considerable diplomacy, since the central governments mistrusted the diffusion of sericulture in nearby states that then could go on to become formidable competitors in the production of raw silk. For this reason the trees were often stolen or smuggled from one state to another, a problem felt particularly in Vicenza, where there is record of numerous mulberry trees being stolen and taken towards the lands of the Este, Lombardy and Piedmont from the 1480s onwards.[18]

Once the mulberry trees had been cultivated, the next step was the breeding of silkworms (*Bombyx mori*), the name of which varied considerably in Italy, from *vermicelli* to *cavalieri*, *bigatti*, *bruche*, *bargelli*, *mignatti*, or *bombici*. Breeding was done almost exclusively in the countryside by peasant families who saw silk production as an excellent way to increase their scanty income and involved the whole family in the activity, including the children, the elderly and in particular the women, who played a preponderant role in the various operations involved in sericulture. Bound to the landowners by a sharecropping contract in most cases, the farmers were allowed to keep some of the cocoons they produced and resell them to either traders combing the country, or at the town markets specialising in this commodity, most widespread in Emilia under the name of *pavaglioni*. The diffusion of sericulture in Italy in the fifteenth and sixteenth centuries led to the writing of numerous texts or treatises in which writers of various origins – often humanists but also polygraphs – devoted themselves to giving breeders advice to maximise their silk production. It is hard to imagine a peasant family in Italy during the Later Middle Ages and early modern period carefully studying these writings while looking after the silkworms, but we cannot ignore the fact that some landowners, who had a certain amount of learning, transmitted this knowledge to their sharecroppers. In any case, the literature on sericulture is of great interest because it was nearly always based on the direct observation of agricultural practice at that time, and it can give us an insight into what was considered the best strategy to obtain a good silk harvest. One of the oldest texts, which is anonymous, goes back to 1461, and although it is preserved in the archives of Siena, the language in which it is written clearly shows a northern Italian influence. During the following century two interesting treatises were written by Levantio Guidiciolo in 1564 and Giovan Andrea Corsuccio in 1581, while other useful information can be gleaned from the section dedicated to silk in the *Specchio di scientia universale* (Mirror of universal science) by the Bolognese physician Leonardo Fioravanti, published in 1572.

The silkworm cocoon, varying in colour between white, yellow and light green, was made of a single, extremely thin, uninterrupted thread that could be up to several hundred metres long, and this was then unravelled in the silk-reeling process. This working activity was performed almost everywhere in the countryside by highly specialised women, the silk-reeling 'mistresses' (*maestre*). It involved immersing the cocoons in metal bowls filled with water

---

18 Francesco Battistini, 'La diffusione delle gelsibachicoltura nell'Italia centrosettentrionale: un tentativo di ricostruzione', *Società e Storia* 56 (1992): 393–400; Francesco Battistini, *L'industria della seta in Italia nell'età moderna* (Bologna: Il Mulino, 2003), 32–37; Molà, *The Silk Industry*, 217–232.

and held over a stove so that the *sericin*, the natural glue in silk thread that guarantees its solidity, would soften. Once the end of the thread had been found with the aid of a small brush, the ends of a variable number of cocoons were joined and they were unravelled together to make the thread stronger, passing it around a reel to form the skein of silk. The combination of the bowl, stove and reel, which were present in considerable numbers in the silk-reeling centres and often run by true rural entrepreneurs, was given a variety of names in Italy: in the north it was called *fornello* (stove), in the centre *caldaia* (boiler) and in the south *mangano* (mangle), and they varied in both dimensions and specific techniques depending on the latitude. The preparation of the raw silk thread could involve up to four women at the same time: one to identify the end of the cocoons; another, the real expert, who unravelled them in the water and joined them together, paying great attention that the thickness of the thread always remained the same; a third, usually younger, who stoked the fire under the basin with wood; and a fourth who would turn the handle of the reel.

The quality of the raw silk obviously depended a great deal on the skill of these workers, so much so that an expert entrepreneur could tell at a glance in which region it had been reeled. Indeed, Corsuccio does not hesitate in advising producers to 'find good mistresses who reel the silk, and who are no novices to the work, since as soon as the silk is in the merchants' hands, they immediately know where it came from'.[19] The diameter and hence also the fineness of the thread of raw silk depended mainly on the number of cocoons – usually between eight and twenty – that had been joined together by the workers. However, this was not only a result of their expertise but was often also the result of a market choice, since the thread could be used as warp for valuable fabrics or as weft for cheaper and heavier cloth, depending on its thickness. For example, since they were supplying the urban industries involved in the weaving of velvets and satins, in the sixteenth century the sericulture districts of Vicenza and Tuscany concentrated on producing very fine thread, while the area around Verona had connections with the German and Flemish markets that used most of the silk for the production of tapestries and haberdashery, and therefore it concentrated on the production of a heavier, coarser semi-finished silk thread. Another decisive element in the quality and regularity of the raw silk was the number of skeins that were wrapped around the reel and, as a result, the number of strands that the reeler and her assistants had to follow at the same time in a single bowl. Once again, in this case it was possible to create a product of inferior quality but at a more competitive price, sacrificing quality for quantity.[20]

---

19 Corsuccio, *Il vermicello*, 60.
20 Battistini, *L'industria*, 71–92.

Industries in the Cities

Once reeling had been completed, the raw silk was tightly bound in skeins and sent to cities or towns where it underwent further kinds of treatment until it was finally transformed into cloth. Indeed, until the end of the sixteenth century these processes took place almost exclusively in urban centres, since for a long time government authorities and artisan guilds ensured that the cities had an unyielding monopoly on the more specialised stages of silk production, so that it was easier for them to control the quality of the finished product and make sure handsome returns went to their local merchants and workers. The second stage in the process of transforming the silk thread consisted in the rigid succession of silk throwing, dying and weaving. It was interspersed and supported by other processes that were equally important such as winding, doubling and warping. While the latter were performed by female workers who had no clear professional status, the others were of more importance and were usually entrusted to men with considerable technical skills. From the thirteenth and the fourteenth century onwards, in an attempt to protect their own interests, these more specialised craftsmen set about founding artisan guilds, even though they were not always recognised by the public authorities. From the thirteenth century onwards there was a guild of dyers and one of weavers of plain fabrics in Venice, but the throwsters had to wait until 1488 before the government allowed them to found their own corporative organisation; and while the weavers of Milan founded their own guild in 1461, the more than 150 throwsters in the city were still without one at the beginning of the seventeenth century.[21]

Since it was made of one uninterrupted strand, the raw silk obtained from top quality cocoons did not need to be beaten, carded and spun as did the other textile fibres – in particular wool, cotton and linen – that were worked in Italy during the Later Middle Ages and early modern period. However, silk thread obtained by reeling alone does not yet have the characteristics and resistance necessary to be used straight away in the weaving of high quality fabrics. It therefore had to undergo a certain degree of twisting, both to make it more robust and elastic – so it would be more able to resist the stress on the loom – and to obtain a particular and variable kind of shine. For this reason it had to undergo throwing, which in the thirteenth century was done by hand thanks to the spinning wheel, on which a single thread was wrapped around a spindle and then became a skein. Not only did this process require a great deal of time, but the two operations of rolling up the thread were not coordinated, with the final result of having a thrown silk of heterogeneous quality. These problems were overcome thanks to the creation of the mechanical silk mill, one of the most brilliant Italian technical inventions of the Middle Ages and

[21] Ettore Verga, *Il Comune di Milano e l'Arte della seta dal secolo decimoquinto al decimottavo* (Milan, 1917), xiii–xv, xxxv–xxxvi.

early modern period. Over two metres in diameter and the same in height, with hundreds of spools on spindles that turned simultaneously supplying a corresponding number of reels where the skeins were formed with twisted thread, the mechanical silk mill was a machine of considerable dimensions and complexity. Its structure could become even more imposing by putting up to five machines (each called *valico*) on top of each other, so as to employ a single central engine that could reach over 13 metres in height and could occupy several floors in the same building.

The advantage of the silk-throwing mill lay in its ability to process numerous threads at the same time with very little manpower (sometimes just two people), by mechanically combining the turning of the spools on the spindles with that of the reels that gathered the thread once it had been thrown. Its efficiency was therefore immensely higher if compared with manual twisting, and the quality of the thread was much better. With the mechanical throwing mill it was also possible to twist the silk both to the right and to the left, but by using machines that turned specifically in one direction or the other. The twist to the right was called 'Z' or '*di filato*', while that to the left was called 'S' or '*di torto*'. The most valuable silk thread produced in Italy thanks to the use of the throwing mill was the *orsoglio,* also called *organzino,* and it was mainly used for the warp of the finest fabrics. The process was highly complex: first two threads of silk were processed separately with the Z twist, then they were doubled manually and went through the mill a second time with an S twist. Furthermore, by modifying the regulation of the rotating mechanism of the reels it was possible to vary the number of twist points per metre of silk, thus obtaining different light effects of the thread surface.[22]

Unfortunately, little is still known about the origins of this highly complex and versatile machine. While we certainly have to put aside the long-standing historiographical myth that its origins go back to 1272, there is no doubt that the silk mill was designed – or at least perfected on the basis of a model that might even have been of eastern origin – in Lucca between the end of the thirteenth century and the early decades of the fourteenth century. When the registers of the Lucchese notaries mention it for the first time in the 1340s, it appears that the mill had already become a highly refined machine. Mention is also made in the same decade in the sources of Bologna and Venice, and in both cases it is linked to the silk experts who emigrated from Lucca, probably taking the secret of its construction with them.[23] The mills were soon divided into two great families: mills driven manually, and those driven hydraulically.

[22] Flavio Crippa, 'Il torcitoio circolare da seta: evoluzione, macchine superstiti, restauri', *Quaderni Storici* 25 (1990): 169–212; Flavio Crippa, 'Dal baco al filo', in *La seta in Italia* ed., Luca Molà et al. 15–31; Carlo Poni, 'The Circular Silk Mill. A Factory Before the Industrial Revolution in Early Modern Europe', *History of Technology* 21 (1999): 65–85.

[23] Florence Edler De Roover, *Le sete lucchesi* (Lucca, 1993), 47–53; Louis Green, *Lucca Under Many Masters. A Fourteenth Century Italian Commune in Crisis (1328–1342)* (Florence; L.S. Olschki, 1995), 277–279; Luca Molà, *La comunità dei lucchesi,* 139–144.

In most Italian cities it was the simpler model that dominated, operated by a particularly robust man who made the central axis of the mechanism rotate from the inside of the mill. In other city centres, and in particular in the countryside of northern Italy from the seventeenth century onwards, the mills that were instead driven by a wheel put in motion by water from a river or a canal, and they were generally known as *mulini da seta*.[24]

Thanks to the construction of a complex system of underground canals that allowed the capillary distribution of the water from the two rivers that flowed through the city, Bologna was at the avant-garde of this technology for centuries. The Bolognese authorities guarded the construction techniques of their silk mills jealously, as they were more advanced than those that were driven manually.[25] It would appear that the ban on silk mill constructors and expert throwsters was respected throughout most of the fourteenth and fifteenth centuries, but from the sixteenth century onwards the expansion of the industry and its growing popularity in many Italian regions proved too strong an attraction for some craftsmen. Thus, in 1510 a group of Bolognese throwsters who had stolen the techniques of the silk mill construction and taken it to nearby Modena were sentenced to death and excommunicated. In Modena the public authorities then gave instructions to place armed guards around the mill, as emissaries from the Bolognese government had threatened to set fire to it and destroy it. In 1538 other workers emigrated and managed to build a hydraulic mill in Trento, and this flow of knowledge continued from Bologna in the following decades, forcing the Bolognese authorities to imprison the guilty technicians or, if they could not put their hands on them, to have the effigies of them hanged by a foot painted on the walls of Communal Palace.[26]

Closely linked to silk throwing and an indispensable aspect of its function was the work of thousands of women who wound and doubled the silk, threading it more than once from the bobbins to the skeins or intersecting more than one thread together so that it could be twisted more to make it more resistant. Winding was a relatively simple operation and consisted in the manipulation of a spindle with a bobbin on it, holding it in place with the little finger and ring finger of the right hand and making it turn with the thumb and index finger, while the left hand followed the silk thread.[27] For this

---

24 Francesco Battistini, 'Le principali tappe della diffusione del torcitoio circolare per seta nell'Italia del centro-nord (sec. XIV–XVIII)', *Società e Storia* 69 (1995): 631–640.

25 Alberto Guenzi and Carlo Poni, 'Sinergia di due innovazioni: chiaviche e mulini da seta a Bologna', *Quaderni Storici* 64 (1987): 111–127, Alberto Guenzi and Carlo Poni, 'Un "network" plurisecolare: acqua e industria a Bologna', *Studi Storici* 30 (1990): 359–377.

26 Pasquino Fiorenzi, *Le arti a Modena (storia delle corporazioni d'arti e mestieri)* (Modena: Mucchi, 1962), 111–112; Carlo Poni, 'All'origine del sistema di fabbrica: tecnologia e organizzazione produttiva dei mulini da seta nell'Italia settentrionale (sec. XVII–XVIII)', *Rivista Storica Italiana* 88 (1976): 455; Giorgio Tabarroni, 'I filatoi idraulici di Bologna', *Il Carrobbio* 2 (1976): 391.

27 Gargiolli, *L'industria*, 5–7.

reason silk winding was carried out by unspecialised female workers from the lower classes, who thus had an indispensable source of additional income for their meagre family earnings or, in the case of single women, could avoid being dependent on charity. Indeed, it was usually the wives, daughters or widows of crasftsmen or simple workers who were involved in this phase of the silk production process, and there were thousands of them in every Italian city where the production of silk fabrics was of importance.[28]

The throwsters (spinners) gave the winders the raw silk partially twisted in modest quantities – usually just a few pounds – and in instalments, to make sure there was a constant supply for the machines. However, owing to the high overall value of the raw material, it was also possible that some of it was taken away from the spinners and then easily sold secretly to craftsmen, silk weavers, haberdashers or others who had no scruples about accepting the stolen silk. For many female workers this was a temptation that was impossible to resist, in particular when they were in financial straits. One extremely common ruse used by the winders was to immerse the wooden bobbins they were winding the silk around in water, taking advantage of the difference in weight to reduce the quantity of silk yarn they returned to the throwster (this was such a widespread practice that in the second half of the sixteenth century metal-covered bobbins were invented to obviate this fraud).[29] As a result, for centuries the silk industries suffered from a structural problem that was hard to resolve, and which meant the entrepreneurs had to bear the additional costs resulting from the monitoring of their workers, the pursuing of offenders with the guild authorities or, in many cases, the simple loss of the raw material owing to theft.[30] In Genoa a series of attempts were made to put an end to this phenomenon. In 1511 the Consuls of the Silk Guild decided to inspect their workers' homes to retrieve the stolen silk but the results were not particularly good, since they were 'insulted and beaten with serious wounds and left almost half dead', while in 1527 the guild was given permission by the government to create a 'women's jail' only for winders.[31]

Once the silk skeins had finally left the winders' hands and the twisters' workshops, they had to be dyed. This was a particularly delicate part of the production process and began with the so-called 'cooking' (*cocitura*) of the

---

28 Luca Molà, 'Le donne nell'industria serica veneziana del Rinascimento', in *La seta in Italia,* ed. Luca Molà et al, 423–431.

29 Carlo Poni, 'Piccole innovazioni e filatoi a mano: Venezia (1550–1600)', in *Studi in memoria di Luigi Dal Pane* (Bologna: CLUEB, 1982), 380–384; R. Berveglieri and Carlo Poni, 'L'innovazione nel settore serico: i brevetti industriali della Repubblica di Venezia fra XVI e XVII secolo', in *La seta in Italia,* 486; Molà, *Le donne,* 429–430.

30 The same occurred in the silk industry of Lyon in the eighteenth century, see: Daryl M. Hafter, 'Women in the Underground Business of Eighteenth-Century Lyon', *Enterprise and Society* 2 (2001):11–40.

31 Paola Massa, 'L'Arte genovese della seta nella normativa del XV e XVI secolo', *Atti della Società Ligure di Storia Patria* 10 (1970):175–181; Carola Ghiara, 'Filatoi e filatori a Genova tra XV e XVIII secolo', *Quaderni Storici* 52 (1983), 155.

thread, immersing it in hot soapy water to eliminate all the sericin, which had been useful until then to facilitate the treatment of the fibre but that would have made the colours opaque if left in the silk. At first, the silk cookers were independent craftsmen who had their own workshops, but from the fifteenth century onwards it became more and more common for the dyers to do this operation themselves. The technique these latter craftsmen used to treat the silk varied depending on which dye was being used; as a result, during the Later Middle Ages and early modern period specific kinds of specialisations developed within the dyers' guilds, some of whom devoted themselves to working with just one raw material. The utmost silence reigned regarding production stages and modes, with the secrets either being handed down from father to son together with the management of the workshop or passed on to trustworthy apprentices.

Some of these collections of instructions have survived, the most famous of which was written in Venice in the second half of the fifteenth century by an anonymous craftsman who describes with precision the techniques used to obtain a vast range of colours, persistently repeating, however, the need for his readers to keep the contents of his treatise secret. This veil of secrecy was openly contrasted by the Venetian Giovanventura Rosetti in the following century, when he published a vast collection of recipes entitled *Plichto de l'arte de tentori*, describing everything he had been able to learn – probably in exchange for good sums – from artisan masters from various cities in Italy on his patient searches over the years.[32] However, for centuries the profession of dyer remained shrouded in what was almost a magical haze, probably also due to the limited understanding of the main chemical reactions that took place in their cauldrons. As a consequence, particular attention was paid to the possibility of fraud, which was difficult to discover for those who were not experts in the field. If the brilliance and resistance of the colours was to be guaranteed, it was important to make sure that only materials of the best quality were used, considering the value of the silk fabrics and the hope to guarantee they would last for a long time. For this reason all silk guilds issued severe regulations to avoid falsifications, forbidding absolutely any mixing of more valuable dyes with materials of a lower quality.

Many of the dyes used in the workshops of Italian craftsmen of either vegetable or animal origins (in this case, it was usually dried insects with a high colouring power) came from the East and were mainly imported by Venetian and Genoese merchants. Of Asian origin was indigo, used for the most valuable blue, as well as crimson, lake and brazilwood (*verzino*), dyes that were used to obtain various shades of red and of decreasing value. For red gradations, materials of less exotic origins were also used, such as madder,

32 Giovanni Rebora, *Un manuale di tintoria del Quattrocento* (Milan: Giuffrè, 1970); Giovanventura Rosetti, *Plichto de l'arte de tentori che insegna tenger panni telle banbasi et sede sì per l'arte magiore come per la comune* (Venice, 1548).

orchil and grain (*grana*), the latter being collected across the Mediterranean basin, from Greece to the Iberian peninsula, while Italian or Spanish saffron was commonly used for the yellow. The arrival of new types of dyes from the American continent in the sixteenth century was of particular importance and their quality was questioned for a long time by the silk guilds and local governments, who were suspicious of any pigment without a centuries-old tradition behind them and which could therefore harm the fame of the country's renowned silk goods. The greatest apprehension was caused by Mexican cochineal, which was obtained from the parasites of a particular species of cactus and was brought to Italy via Spain at the beginning of the 1540s. The first to sell this dye were the merchants of Burgos operating in Tuscany, and it was not long before the Florentine family firm of the Botti bought several lots and began experimenting with it on silk thread to see how it compared.[33] From Florence, cochineal spread to Venice, where it was first introduced in 1543, and then to several other cities, always provoking considerable discussion as to whether it should be used in industrial production or not. The dispute was not resolved until the middle of the sixteenth century, when silk weavers and dyers everywhere realised that it was a worthy substitute for crimson or grain in red dyes.[34]

The final and most decisive stages of the silk production process consisted in warping and weaving. The first was mainly carried out by women, often from weavers' families, while during the Later Middle Ages and early modern period the production of silk fabrics became almost exclusively male territory. In the main production centres, which in the fifteenth and sixteenth centuries included Venice, Genoa, Milan, Bologna, Lucca, Florence and Naples, several thousand weavers were working on the production of a vast range of fabrics. Italian workshops produced both goods of high value, such as brocades with gold thread, velvets with various heights of pile, damasks or satins, and fabrics that were lighter and less expensive, such as taffeta, *ormesini* (or *ermisini*, as they were called in Florence) and *sendal*. From the thirteenth century onwards, it was common practice not to concentrate on just the highest segment of the market, even if it constituted the lion's share, especially in the export sector. Preference was given to flexibility and to the production of goods aimed at customers from various social ranks, a clientele that expanded rapidly over the centuries.

During the sixteenth century, with the appearance of products that were to meet the most varied needs, the typology of the new fabrics invented in Italy underwent remarkable development. Of particular importance was the start of fabric weaving that coupled a warp of pure silk with a weft made up of less

---

33 Angela Orlandi, 'Zucchero e cocciniglia dal Nuovo Mondo, due esempi di precoce diffusione', in *Prodotti e tecniche d'Oltremare nelle economie europee, secc. XIII–XVIII*, ed. Simonetta Cavaciocchi (Florence: Mondadori Education, 1998), 485–487.

34 For more on silk dying in the Renaissance, see: Molà, *The Silk Industry*, 107–137.

valuable materials such as left over silk (*floss* or *tow*), wool, linen or cotton. The result was a myriad of fabrics of which historians of the textile industry still know very little, and which are clearly represented by the list of the tens of thousands of silk cloth ells from all over Italy that were illegally deposited (since the laws prohibited the importation of foreign fabric) in the shops of Venetian mercers at the end of the XVI century: *buratti, canevazze, cataluffi, cusachi, dimiti, dobloni, felpe, ferandine, franzadi, manti, pagiete, sagiete, telette*, etc., with various internal variations and with a wide range of colours.[35] Alongside the products prepared by male weavers there was also a less important production that was generally entrusted to female workers who did not belong to the guilds: for example, silk veils, which also had a great variety of names, and for which Bologna was particularly famous but that were also produced in the thousands in Venice. Other articles included braids, ribbons and bands, trimming, drawstring, veils and belts and other haberdashery, which were produced in large quantities in the seventeenth century, and particularly in Padua.[36]

It was common practice among silk artisans and entrepreneurs to imitate the goods of other cities that proved successful on the international market. Even though these imitations were facilitated by the considerable mobility of the workers specialised in all kinds of cloth, who could offer their know-how to other centres of industry, very often the competitors merely analysed the fabric to be copied very carefully and tried to reproduce it as accurately as they could, reproducing its weave, dimensions, colours and even its characteristic elements such as the selvedges, which made it immediately recognisable by customers throughout Europe and the East. The search for innovative products led to imitations that varied over the years and in the kinds of fabrics, resulting in a kaleidoscopic circulation of textile goods between one centre and another. Thus, while in 1487 in Genoa the decision was taken to produce camocati Venetian style (*camocati ad Venetum modum*), in the sixteenth century the Venetian silk weavers asked their government for permission to weave black velvets Genoese style (*a la Zenoina*).[37] Florentine merchants active in Germany in the first decades of the sixteenth century exported large lots of 'damasks Venetian style' and 'Lucchese style',[38] and when Duke Cosimo de' Medici began silk production in Pisa in the middle of the century he concentrated on the production of '*ermisini* Lucchese style'

35 Molà, *The Silk Industry*, 89–185.

36 Carlo Poni, 'Per la storia del distretto industriale serico di Bologna (secoli XVI–XIX)', *Quaderni Storici* 73 (1990): 93–167; Molà, *Le donne*, Andrea Caracausi, *Nastri, nastrini, cordelle. L'Industria serica nel Padovano, secc. XVII–XIX* (Padua: CLEUP, 2004).

37 Molà, *The Silk Industry*, 159–160; Franco Franceschi, 'La grande manifattura tessile', in *La trasmissione dei saperi nel Medioevo (secoli XII–XV)* (Pistoia: Centro italiano di studi di storia e d'arte, 2005), 383–386.

38 Marco Spallanzani, 'Tessuti di seta per il mercato di Norimberga intorno al 1520', in *Studi in memoria di Giovanni Cassandro*, vol. 3 (Rome: Ministero per i beni culturali e ambientali, Ufficio centrale per i beni archivistici, 1991), 995–1016.

and satin 'Bolognese' and 'Genoese style', with the precise aim of connecting the new industry with trade channels that had already been consolidated.[39] At times, the comparative advantage a city had was mainly due to its greater technical knowledge in a particular segment of the production process. Between the second half of the fifteenth century and the beginning of the sixteenth century the Venetians had managed to develop a crimson and purple crimson colour that was of better quality than that of any other Italian industry. This meant that foreign traders came to buy the threads dyed in those colours in the city and then took them to Genoa, Ferrara, Bologna and Florence where, also thanks to Venetian weavers who had emigrated, they could then produce fabrics that were identical to the original goods and pass them off as Venetian.[40]

Both the old and new centres of silk weaving wanted to have the monopoly over their competitors, reserving their internal market for the local industry alone, at least for the fabrics with a sufficiently developed production. As a consequence, a great number of laws and edicts appeared over the centuries, prohibiting the importation of nearly all silk fabrics from abroad. The Genoese government issued the first decree on the matter in 1423, the year in which the silk guild was officially founded, allowing, however, the sale of the goods of their own colonies in the East – including the centre of Caffa on the Black Sea, where Armenian, Georgian and Tartar artisans worked – as well as sendals, *dimiti*, samites and taffeta, the production of which was not widespread among the Genoese artisans.[41] In 1457 Duke Francesco Sforza promised the merchants and weavers who were launching the silk industry in Milan that as soon as there were at least 80 looms in activity he would close the doors to any foreign goods, a promise he kept in 1460, when he allowed the importation of silk fabrics only for the making of garments for private individuals.[42] Siena too, in 1480, prohibited the import of silk fabrics,[43] and during the sixteenth century there were countless other such acts.

Venice was particularly aware of the problem. From 1366 on, the Senate made sure that customs officials, who controlled and recorded all the bales and parcels of goods that arrived in the city from the mainland, prohibited the import of any foreign velvet or silk and gold fabrics. As time went by, the punishment meted out to offenders – that usually entailed the confiscation of the bolts and their public destruction in the market square at the Rialto (first cut in length and then burnt) – became harsher. However, the effectiveness of these deterrents was limited. As the Senate complained in 1423, the Venetian citizens even managed to have foreign silk goods arrive in one of the cities

---

39 Roberta Morelli, *La seta fiorentina nel Cinquecento* (Milan: Giuffrè, 1976), 12 note 46.
40 ASV, *Arte della Seta*, b. 682, reg. 1, fol. 106v, 14 May 1515.
41 Massa, *L'arte genovese*, 82–84.
42 Verga, *Il Comune di Milano*, xii.
43 Marco Ciatti, 'Note sulla storia dei tessuti a Siena', in *Drappi, velluti, taffetà et altre cose. Antichi tessuti a Siena e nel suo territorio* (Siena: Nuova Immagine Ed, 1994), 18.

close to the capital where they had them transformed into clothes that could then be worn legally in Venice. A broad range of light fabrics (*sindoni, zendadini,* taffeta, veils) were excluded from Venetian fourteenth-century laws against the smuggling of silk goods, and most of these fabrics came from Bologna, since Venetian artisans paid little attention to them at the time. In 1421 there was still the possibility of not only transporting these less valuable products to Venice, but also of loading them on the state galleys that were setting sail for lands under Venetian rule in the Aegean, the Levant, Flanders and London. Even the importation of traditional goods from the Middle East was allowed; they had been redistributed throughout Europe for a long time thanks to the Venetian market, and their quality was still unrivalled in the fourteenth and fifteenth centuries. It was not until 1490 that a decree was issued forbidding the importation of *atalassi, melidari, tabini, ormesini* and satin from the Levant, with the proud declaration that while these fabrics had not been produced by Venetians in the past, luckily they were now doing so in abundance, and the quality and price equalled the originals.[44]

A fundamental element in the success of Italian fabric production was the high quality of the patterns the weavers reproduced on the fabric, which was the fruit of Renaissance artistic creativity. In the more luxurious kinds, the pomegranate prevailed and was portrayed countless times in the paintings of the fifteenth and sixteenth-century artists.[45] However, very little is still known about the figures of those who designed the motifs for silk fabrics, although there is no doubt that there were artisan-artists who specialised in this field, and that their profession was regarded with a certain amount of prestige. Furthermore, their work was avidly sought after by the main silk workshops. In Florence the guild statutes called them *maestri levatori d'opere,* or used other Latin wordings such as *pictores sive levatores drapporum* and *pictores operarum drapporum*. We know the names of some of these Florentines, one of whom was Jacopo dello Sciorina, who is praised by Benvenuto Cellini in his autobiography as an ingenious and pleasant person, who was on familiar terms with Pope Clement VII. In 1418 the Silk Guild of Florence strived to protect these craftsmen's inventions by prohibiting any entrepreneur or weaver from copying the fabric patterns without the explicit permission – granted in exchange of payment – of the artisan or workshop that had commissioned them.[46] For those merchant-entrepreneurs who wanted to put fabrics with new designs on the market these patterns were

44 For archive references on the countless Venetian laws that prohibited the importation of foreign fabrics from the second half of the fourteenth century to the sixteenth century, see Molà, *The Silk Industry*, 262–263, 393–394.

45 Rosalia Bonito Fanelli, 'The Pomegranate Motif in Italian Renaissance Silks: A Semiological Interpretation of Pattern and Color', in *La seta in Europa*, 507–530.

46 Franco Franceschi, 'Un'industria "nuova" e prestigiosa: la seta', in *Arti fiorentine. La grande storia dell'artigianato. Vol. II*, 183–185; Umberto Dorini, ed. *Statuti dell'Arte di Por Santa Maria del tempo della Repubblica* (Florence 1934), 451–452.

no small investment. Around 1430 a businessman from Lucca, Castruccio di Poggio, resident in Venice, had come to an agreement with the brother of a renowned Venetian fabric designer, Bartolomeo Rugerio, who had just died, to buy all the deceased's 'designs for silk and gold fabrics' for the considerable sum of 70 ducats (approximately the equivalent of the yearly earnings of a high-ranking craftsman or the cost of buying two slaves). In the agreement di Poggio had stipulated that he was to have all the rights to these patterns, and that they were not to be made available to any competitors, but when he began to study the sheets, presumably with great curiosity, he realised – according to the evidence he gave in court – that he had been given the most inferior ones, the leftovers that other workshops had refused, while the more original drawings he had seen earlier were missing. It was his belief that they had been sold on the side for a considerable sum to another producer of gold and silk fabrics.[47] In the light of the lack of information we have about these designers, this episode is therefore of particular interest and shows an industrial environment that had to pay considerable attention to any development in design, since entrepreneurs tried to renew the demand for fabrics by constantly developing the models on offer, in order to stimulate even further a market that was already expanding rapidly.

Finally, the production of luxury silk fabric relied on the work of artisans who smelted gold and silver and then beat it into very fine leaves, which were then cut in long tiny strips and patiently wound around a thread of silk by female workers. The production of gold and silk thread developed very quickly from the thirteenth century onwards, hand in hand with the growth of the silk industry. During that century and the one that followed, three centres that were closely linked to fabric production or the trade of raw silk dominated the scene: Lucca, Genoa and Venice. In the archives of the Tuscan city the first apprenticeship contract for goldbeating goes back to 1251, and there are more and more documents regarding this profession over the following decades. During that period the goldbeaters of Lucca founded a '*Universitas*', which had at least 40 members in 1279. In that year they met in a church to discuss the problem of trading bovine intestines, which was both an indispensable part of beating gold and silver and acted as a separating membrane between the silk thread and spun gold. The high number of goldbeaters working in Lucca at that time probably made it difficult to have sufficient supplies of these intestines and as a result, in 1288, two entrepreneurs sent a couple of artisans they employed to Lyon to work 'oxen's and calves' intestines'.[48] In Genoa the *battifolli* [leaf beaters] founded a guild with its own statute in 1248, and thanks to the vast amount of documentation in the local notarial archives various agreements for the profession of beating precious metals and

47 ASV, *Giudici di Petizion, Sentenze a Giustizia*, reg. 48, fols. 116v–117r, 31 July 1430.

48 Luigi Brenni, *L'arte del battiloro e i filati d'oro e d'argento* (Milan: Brenni, 1930), 44–45 and appendix 1.

its spinning have been preserved from the 1220s onwards.[49] A decree issued in Venice in 1248 mentions the tax levied on artisans 'who make gold cloth', who certainly supplied themselves with metal thread produced in the local workshops; and in 1268, on the occasion of the celebrations for the election of Doge Jacopo Tiepolo, the silk and gold cloth weavers paraded through the city with other guilds flaunting their rich fabrics, which even the servants following them were wearing.[50]

For a long time the supremacy of Lucca, Genoa and Venice in the production and trade of gold and silk thread was unrivalled in Italy. It is true that during the fourteenth century and throughout the whole of the fifteenth century the Italian silk industries also received abundant supplies of spun gold and silver from Cyprus and Cologne, the only two production centres outside Italy that managed to distribute these goods throughout Europe and the Mediterranean basin. In 1373 Cologne even sent instructions to Venice on how to recognise the authenticity of Cologne spun gold, which the 1376 statutes of the Merchants' Court of Lucca allowed in the production of certain kinds of high quality brocades, whereas any other kind of material produced abroad was forbidden.[51] However, it was not until the 1430s that other two Italian cities that were rapidly developing their silk manufacturing, Florence and Milan, managed to establish an independent production of gold thread that could supply their own industries without being dependent on imports from competing centres. Thanks to the initiative of three Florentine entrepreneurs and the open support they received from the local silk guild (the *Arte di Por Santa Maria*), in 1420 numerous male and female craftsmen expert in gold beating and spinning were persuaded to leave Genoa and Venice and move to Florence. The operation was a success, to the point that in 1423 the Florentine government granted a reduction in export duties on the gold thread produced by the three supporters of the new industry. Their success finds further confirmation in the registration of two workshops of goldbeaters in the city cadastre of 1427, which grew to four in 1451, seven in 1460, 10 in 1461, 15 in 1464, 17 in 1472 and 19 in 1489.[52] Milan took steps in this direction only after it had developed the production of orichalc thread (*oro de bacile*), an alloy that was similar to brass and looked like gold. Once again, it was the attraction to Milan of foreign craftsmen in 1452 that laid the foundations of the art, which

---

49 Brenni, *L'arte del battiloro*, 35–41.

50 *Deliberazioni del Maggior Consiglio di Venezia*, vol. II, ed. Roberto Cessi. (Bologna: Forni, 1931), 306; M. Da Canale, 'La cronaca dei veneziani', *Archivio Storico Italiano*, 8 (1845): 614–616.

51 Margret Wensky, 'Women's Guilds in Cologne in the Later Middle Ages', *Journal of European Economic History* 11 (1982): 635–638.

52 Florence Edler De Roover, *L'arte della seta a Firenze nei secoli XIV e XV* (Florence: Sergio Tognetti, 1999), 87–88, Franco Franceschi, 'I forestieri e l'industria della seta fiorentina fra Medioevo e Rinascimento', in *La seta in Italia*, 410–412; Bruno Dini, 'I battilori fiorentini nel Quattrocento', in Bruno Dini, *Manifattura, commercio e banca nella Firenze medievale* (Florence: Nardini, 2001), 45–65.

therefore required official support from the Ducal authorities, as had been the case a decade earlier with the agreement signed between the Florentine silk entrepreneur Pietro di Bartolo and Filippo Maria Visconti for the weaving of silk fabrics.[53] During the sixteenth century it was this new production from Florence and Milan that had the upper hand over its older rivals, who were undergoing a period of relative decline.

Setaioli and Merchant-entrepreneurs

In the cities the entire production process was dominated by an entrepreneur, the *setaiolo*. He possessed a discrete capital that was often offered by wealthy merchants, who financed the business and took their part of the profits, in many cases also participating in the management of the firm. The *setaiolo* would purchase the valuable raw materials from international importers or local suppliers and would coordinate the various production stages using a huge amount of manpower and craftsmen whom he paid by the job. Finally, he would sell the fabrics on the local markets or abroad. He had a small group of employees in his workshop to carry out the administration and control the quality of the threads and fabrics during the various stages of production. The operation he was running was therefore far-reaching and a source of considerable profit. In every city these businessmen founded the Silk Guild (*Arte della Seta*), a corporative organisation that brought together silk entrepreneurs throughout Italy and whose statutes regulated most of the production and the relations with the workers. Ideally, the *setaioli* wanted to maintain their monopoly over the production and trade of the fabrics, therefore forbidding the wealthier craftsmen, who could afford to buy the raw silk themselves, from any independent trade of twisted or dyed thread or of fabrics. However, in some cases they had to come to a compromise, for example by allowing the weavers to produce and sell some of their production on their own. In cases where this was forbidden there could be real rebellions, such as the one experienced by the entrepreneurs of Lucca in 1532, when the weavers of the Tuscan city rose up against the new prohibition of using at least one loom independently, and with the so-called Revolution of the *Straccioni* threatened the political stability of the small republic.[54]

Thanks to the survival of several series of account books and inventories, we are able to reconstruct the entrepreneurial biographies of some Italian *setaioli* in the Renaissance in various details. Florence is a particularly good

[53] Maria Paola Zanoboni, ''De suo labore et mercede me adiuvavit': la manodopera femminile a Milano nell'età sforzesca', *Nuova Rivista Storica* 78 (1994): 108–109; Patrizia Mainoni, 'La seta a Milano nel XV secolo: aspetti economici e istituzionali', *Studi Storici* 35 (1994): 892–893.

[54] Marino Berengo, *Nobili e mercanti nella Lucca del Cinquecento* (Turin: Giulio Einaudi, 1965), 117–146.

source for this, since hundreds of administrative books from the workshops of Florentine silk merchant-entrepreneurs have been preserved for the fifteenth and sixteenth centuries. Many of these records are to be found in the Archives of the *Ospedale degli Innocenti,* a charity institution for foundlings supported by the local silk guild.[55] The first silk trader to emerge clearly from these sources is Andrea Banchi, well known to silk historians because the detailed study of his business, which was carried out by an American researcher, has served as a comparison for any kind of microanalysis of the sector for a long time now. Banchi's career spanned no less than seven decades in the fifteenth century, from 1401, the year in which the 29-year-old enrolled in the guild of silk producers, to his death in 1462. Owner of a shop for the production of fabrics that he then sold at retail in Florence, Banchi acted almost exclusively in partnership with other entrepreneurs, always investing a considerable amount of capital – between around 4,000 and 5,000 florins – in his businesses. The raw materials he used, and which cost him up to 9,000 florins a year, came mainly from Persia and Spain, but he also imported considerable lots of raw Italian silk (from the Florentine Romagna, Marche, Abruzzi and Calabria) as well as from the island of Chios in the Aegean. The silk thread was then processed in Florence by a vast number of workers of both sexes, numbering a total of somewhere around 100 people, 7 of whom were employed in the main workshop as clerks, or receiving, controlling and packaging silk and fabrics. Approximately 30 looms worked non-stop for Banchi and were able to produce between 130 and 140 bolts a year, most of which were valuable fabrics such as brocades, velvets and satins. The cloth was then sold in the workshop in Florence (two thirds) or exported, in particular to Mantua and Geneva, the latter being one of the most important European banking centres of those times. However, Banchi had considerable difficulty in selling his products at the courts of Milan and Naples, in Rome and in the cities of northern Europe, Paris and Bruges in particular, where he was penalised by competition from other Italian silk traders and the lack of permanent representatives who knew the taste of the local clientele. Although his career was brilliant, he did not reach the heights of his profession and other Florentine *setaioli* could boast much greater wealth than his. Nevertheless, Andrea Banchi's tax declaration in 1427 was for a patrimony of 7,441 florins, which went up to around 18,000 florins (without counting his properties in the city and countryside which he had purchased in the meantime) at the beginning of the 1460s, a sum that made him one of the ten most heavily taxed figures in Florence.[56]

---

55 Bruno Dini, 'La ricchezza documentaria per l'Arte della seta e l'economia fiorentina nel Quattrocento', in *Gli Innocenti e Firenze nei secoli. Un ospedale, un archivio, una città,* ed. Lucia Sandri. (Florence: Studio per Edizioni Scelte, 1996), 153–178.

56 Florence Edler De Roover, 'Andrea Banchi, Florentine Silk Manufacturer and Merchant in the Fifteenth Century', *Studies in Medieval and Renaissance History* 3 (1966): 223–285.

Tommaso Spinelli, a fellow citizen of Andrea Banchi, started out differently. Born at the beginning of the fifteenth century, for most of his life Spinelli's existence focused around the Papal Curia. In 1419 he was in the service of the Alberti company in Rome, but his career really took off in 1433 when he opened a bank there, together with members of the wealthy Milanese family of the Borromeo. His financial activity made him Depository General of the Church in 1444 and he had close financial and personal ties with the various succession of Popes until his death in 1471. From 1454 on, Spinelli decided to invest some of the wealth he had accumulated in Rome in a company for the production of silk fabrics in Florence which, also thanks to the financial support of other partners, boasted an initial capital of 6,000 florins and was almost regularly renewed every three years. The operational details of this silk workshop are not all that different from Banchi's business. The same raw materials, mainly Persian and Spanish silk, with a considerable amount of Italian silk, predominated in Spinelli's company. The same can be said for the number of craftsmen and staff he employed: from 30 to 40 weavers, 35 female winders, 32 'mistresses of boiled silk', 3 throwsters, 3 to 4 dyers, making a total of around 100–110 people with around an additional dozen people employed in the *setaiolo's* workshop in Via di Por Santa Maria. Once again, the production was aimed at the highest segment of the market. In the accounts we find gold and silk brocades, velvets with various heights of pile and patterned velvets, damasks and satins, in particular in the colours crimson and black. The annual profit rate of the Spinelli business was extremely high, going from 20 to 29%, compared with the mere 8% of Andrea Banchi's workshop. There is no doubt that the contacts with ecclesiastic circles he had developed during his banking career guaranteed such success, since they secured him an exclusive clientele whom he had already been supplying with fabrics since the 1440s, before he actually began producing them. This was basically the same trade policy the Medici business had followed in their silk workshop during the fifteenth century.[57] Bishops, archbishops, cardinals and various figures belonging to the Apostolic Chamber were supplied with silk goods from Spinelli's workshop, and in addition to them were the aristocrats and wealthy bourgeois who bought his fabrics throughout Europe, from Milan to Geneva and even as far as Lübeck.[58]

A final example of a Florentine merchant-banking business active in the silk sector is that of the Serristori. Founded by Antonio di Salvestro Serristori's children, the firm was mainly family run and active from the middle of the fifteenth century to the beginning of the sixteenth century, with a capital that managed to exceed 20,000 florins and with a profit margin that

57 Raymond De Roover, *Il Banco Medici dalle origini al declino (1397–1492)* (Florence: La nuova Italia, 1970).

58 William Caferro, 'The silk business of Tommaso Spinelli, fifteenth-century Florentine merchant and papal banker', *Renaissance Studies* 10 (1996): 417–439.

reached astronomical heights, on average varying from 45% to 68% and even reaching 83% in the 1470s and 1480s. The Serristori's area of operation was huge – their fabrics were not only traded in the main Italian centres, but also in Bruges, London, Lyon, Nuremberg, Antwerp and Constantinople. Among errand boys and clerks his workshop employed 24 people, who received from and consigned to the local workforce the inevitable Persian silk and also vast amounts of Calabrese silk thread, a novelty linked to the explosion of sericulture in southern Italy.[59]

For more detailed information about individual silk entrepreneurs in other Italian cities we have to move into the sixteenth century, since outside of Florence the account books of earlier centuries are nearly all lost. For Genoa, one of the main European cities for silk production, we are informed about the operations by Vincenzo Usodimare di Rovereto between 1537 and 1542. An independent entrepreneur with a capital of average size for the local industry, equivalent to around 13,000 Genoese lire, Rovereto decided to specialise in a limited number of medium quality fabrics – velvets with a single height of pile, satins and taffeta, prevalently red or black – which were sold almost exclusively in the markets of Lyon and Antwerp. Unlike the Florentine *setaioli* in the fifteenth century, 75% of the raw material that Rovereto used was from Italy, in particular silk from Messina for satins and Calabrese silk for velvets.[60] Over twenty years later, in 1563, the post-mortem inventory of the workshop belonging to another *setaiolo* from Genoa, Bartolomeo di San Michele, shows a similar trend. With an operative capital of 12,000 lire, when he died the businessman was producing 13 bolts of fabric through the same number of weavers – in each case it was 'ordinary' one pile velvet, and most of it was black.[61] By contrast, we find a kaleidoscopic variety of fabrics listed in the inventory drawn up at the request of the Milanese *setaiolo* Giovan Antonio Orombelli's widow in 1554, which mentions goods ranging from luxury cloth woven with gold and silver thread – we must not forget that at that time Milan had become one of the two Italian capitals for the spinning of precious metals – to more modestly priced light textiles such as *ormesini* and *cendal*. Orombelli's clientele belonged to the highest circles of Milanese society, including names such as the family of Don Ferrante Gonzaga, governor of Milan in the name of the Hapsburgs, the clan of Spanish administrators such as the de Lunas and Toledo Osorios, as well as hundreds of other nobles, magistrates, professionals and members of the middle class of the Lombard capital. In his double role

---

59 Sergio Tognetti, *Un'industria di lusso al servizio del grande commercio. Il mercato dei drappi serici e della seta nella Firenze del Quattrocento* (Florence, 2002), 43–105. For more on the Serristori business in general see: Sergio Tognetti, *Da Figline a Firenze. Ascesa economica e politica della famiglia Serristori (secoli XIV–XVI)* (Florence: Opus libri, 2003).

60 Paola Massa, *Un'impresa serica genovese della prima metà del Cinquecento* (Milan: Giuffrè, 1974).

61 Paola Massa, 'La liquidazione della "volta da seta" di Bartolomeo di San Michele: aspetti tecnici ed economici', *Atti della Società Ligure di Storia Patria* 19 (1979): 149–206.

as entrepreneur – when he died he was employing five spinners, two dyers and no less than 71 weavers – and distributor of fabrics produced by other Milanese workshops, in the storerooms of his company he had almost 18,000 *braccia* of silks, which, at the ratio of 0.564 metres for every Milanese *braccio*, is the equivalent of around 10,150 metres of precious fabric, the production of which had required a higher quantity of raw silk than the amount used each year in the entire silk industry of Mantua during the same period. It is therefore no surprise that Orombelli's patrimony, consisting in land, houses, workshops, clothes, furniture and furnishings, came to the majestic sum of no less than 50,000 *scudi*, which clearly shows how in the sixteenth century the production and commerce of silk fabrics allowed entrepreneurs to make a true fortune in a very short time.[62]

Conclusion

In conclusion, for Italy the silk industry was a sector of primary importance from the economic point of view. The breeding of silkworms and silk reeling were a fundamental source of income both for peasant families and landowners, becoming one of the main sectors in the agricultural production of the peninsula from the sixteenth century onwards. The successive processes of throwing, winding, doubling, dying, warping and weaving, with the connected professions of gold beaters and fabric designers, offered jobs to a good part of the population in both small and large cities where the silk industry had been developed. At the beginning of the seventeenth century a demographic census carried out in Bologna counted almost 24,900 people employed in the silk sector or dependent on it – either full-time or part-time workers and members of their families – in a population that totalled around 60,000 inhabitants, in other words, over 40%.[63] In the other main centres of production similar employment figures were given, ranging from 20,000 to 30,000 people during the sixteenth century. At that time, a variable percentage of between 20% and 35% of all the imports of the Kingdom of France and the Netherlands consisted of fabrics and silk thread produced in Italy. The success of this industry in Italy continued for a long time, even though later it concentrated in particular on the production of semi-finished goods. During the 1890s, 30% of the value of Italian exports was made of silk, and during the 1920s Italy still dominated a third of its trade worldwide.[64] It was therefore

---

62 Aldo De Maddalena, '"Excolere vitam per artes". Giovanni Antonio Orombelli mercante auroserico milanese del Cinquecento', in *Fatti e idee di storia economica nei secoli XII–XX. Studi dedicati a Franco Borlandi* (Bologna: Società editrice il Mulino, 1977), 339–363.

63 Poni, *Per la storia*, 95–96.

64 Molà, *The Silk Industry*, xv, 14–19.

thanks to silk that for centuries Italy played a key role in the progressive expansion of economic globalisation.

Bibliography

Manuscript Sources

Venice, Archivio di Stato
Arte della Seta, b. 682, reg. 1.
Giudici di Petizion, Sentenze a Giustizia, reg. 48.

Published Sources

Ashtor, Eliyahu. 'Il commercio italiano col Levante e il suo impatto sull'economia tardomedievale'. In *'Aspetti della vita economica medievale'. Atti del Convegno di Studi nel X Anniversario della morte di Federigo Melis, Firenze–Pisa–Prato, 10–14 marzo 1984*, edited by Federigo Melis, 23 (Table I), 35 (Table II), 54 (appendix I). Florence: Monte dei Paschi di Diena, 1985.
Aymard, Maurice. 'Commerce et production de la soie sicilienne aux XVIe–XVIIe siècles'. *Mélanges d'archéologie et d'histoire de l'Ecole Française de Rome* 77 (1965): 622.
Banchi, Luciano. *L'Arte della seta in Siena nei secoli XV e XVI. Statuti e documenti*. Siena: Tipografia sordo-muti di L. Lazzeri, 1881.
Battistini, Francesco. 'La diffusione delle gelsibachicoltura nell'Italia centrosettentrionale: un tentativo di ricostruzione'. *Società e Storia* 56 (1992): 393–400.
Battistini, Francesco. 'La gelsibachicoltura e la trattura della seta in Toscana'. In *La seta in Europa, secc. XIII–XX*, edited by Simonetta Cavaciocchi, 297–298. Florence, 1993.
Battistini, Francesco. 'Le principali tappe della diffusione del torcitoio circolare per seta nell'Italia del centro-nord (sec. XIV–XVIII)'. *Società e Storia* 69 (1995): 631–640.
Battistini, Francesco. *L'industria della seta in Italia nell'età moderna*. Bologna: Il Mulino, 2003.
Bautier, Robert-Henri. 'Les relations économiques des occidentaux avec les pays d'Orient, au Moyen Age. Points de vue et documents'. In *Société et compagnies de commerce en Orient et dans l'Océan Indien. Actes du Huitième Colloque International d'Histoire Maritime (Beyrouth – 5–10 Septembre 1966)*, edited by M. Mollat, 288–292. Paris, 1970.
Berengo, Marino. *Nobili e mercanti nella Lucca del Cinquecento*. Turin: Giulio Einaudi, 1965.
Borah, Woodrow. *Silk Raising in Colonial Mexico*. Berkeley: University of California Press, 1943.
Brenni, Luigi. *L'arte del battiloro e i filati d'oro e d'argento*. Milan: Brenni, 1930.
Caferro, William. 'The silk business of Tommaso Spinelli, fifteenth-century Florentine merchant and papal banker', *Renaissance Studies* 10 (1996): 417–439.
Caracausi, Andrea. *Nastri, nastrini, cordelle. L'Industria serica nel Padovano, secc. XVII–XIX*. Padua: CLEUP, 2004.
Cazzola, Franco. 'Polemiche e contrasti per l'istituzione dell'Arte della seta a Ferrara (1595–1620)'. *Economia e Storia* 14 (1967): 297–298.
Chaudhury, Sushil. 'International Trade in Bengal Silk and the Comparative Role of Asians and Europeans, ca. 1700–1757'. *Modern Asian Studies* 29 (1995): 373–386.

Cittadella, Luigi Napoleone. *Notizie relative a Ferrara per la maggior parte inedited.* Ferrara, 1864.
Cooper, Michael. 'The Mechanics of the Macao–Nagasaki Silk Trade'. *Monumenta Nipponica* 27 (1972): 423–433.
Coniglio, Giuseppe. 'Agricoltura ed artigianato mantovano nel sec. XVI'. In *Studi in onore di Amintore Fanfani, IV. Evo Moderno,* edited by Amintore Fanfani, 321–392. Milan: Giuffrè, 1962.
Cova, Alberto. 'Interessi economici e impegni istituzionali delle corporazioni milanesi nel Seicento'. In *Economia e corporazioni. Il governo degli interessi nella storia d'Italia dal Medioevo all'età contemporanea,* edited by C. Mozzarelli, 109–132. Milan: Giuffrè 1988.
Crippa, Flavio. 'Il torcitoio circolare da seta: evoluzione, macchine superstiti, restauri'. *Quaderni Storici* 25 (1990):169–212.
De Maddalena, Also. '"Excolere vitam per artes". Giovanni Antonio Orombelli mercante auroserico milanese del Cinquecento', in *Fatti e idee di storia economica nei secoli XII–XX. Studi dedicati a Franco Borlandi* (Bologna: Società editrice il Mulino, 1977), 339–363.
De Roover, Florence Edler. 'Andrea Banchi, Florentine Silk Manufacturer and Merchant in the Fifteenth Century'. *Studies in Medieval and Renaissance History* 3 (1966): 223–285.
De Roover, Florence Edler. *Le sete lucchesi.* Lucca, 1993.
De Roover, Florence Edler. *L'arte della seta a Firenze nei secoli XIVe XV.* Florence: Sergio Tognetti, 1999.
De Roover, Raymond. *Il Banco Medici dalle origini al declino (1397–1492).* Florence: La nuova Italia, 1970.
Del Punta, Ignazio. 'Lucca e il commercio della seta nel Duecento'. In *Per Marco Tangheroni. Studi su Pisa e sul Mediterraneo medievale offerti dai suoi ultimi allievi,* edited by Cecilia Iannella, 111–115. Pisa: Edizioni ETS, 2005.
Dini, Bruno. 'L'industria serica in Italia. Secc. XIII–XV'. In *La seta in Europa, secc. XIII–XX,* edited by Simonetta Cavaciocchi, 91–123. Florence, 1993.
Ertl, Thomas. 'Silkworms, Capital, and Merchant Ships: European Silk Industry in the Medieval World Economy'. *The Medieval History Journal* 9 (2006): 243–270.
Fanelli, Rosalia Bonito. 'The Pomegranate Motif in Italian Renaissance Silks: A Semiological Interpretation of Pattern and Color', in *La seta in Europa, secc. XIII–XX,* edited by Simonetta Cavaciocchi, 507–530. Florence, 1993.
Ferrier, Ronald W. 'The Armenians and the East India Company in the Seventeenth and Early Eighteenth Century'. *The Economic History Review* 26 (1973): 38–62.
Fiorenzi, Pasquino. *Le arti a Modena (storia delle corporazioni d'arti e mestieri).* Modena: Mucchi, 1962.
Floor, Willem and Clawson, Patrick. 'Safavid's Iran Search for Silver and Gold'. *International Journal of Middle East Studies* 32 (2000): 345–368.
Franceschi, Franco. 'La grande manifattura tessile'. In *La trasmissione dei saperi nel Medioevo (secoli XII–XV).* 383–386. Pistoia: Centro italiano di studi di storia e d'arte, 2005.
Franco Franceschi, 'Un'industria "nuova" e prestigiosa: la seta', in *Arti fiorentine. La grande storia dell'artigianato. Vol. II,* 183–185.
Galasso, Giuseppe. 'Seta e commercio del ferro nell'economia napoletana del tardo Cinquecento'. *Rivista Storica Italiana* 75 (1963): 615–640.
Galasso, Giuseppe. *Economia e società nella Calabria del Cinquecento.* Milan: Guida Editori, 1992.

Gargiolli, Girolamo. *L'industria della seta in Firenze: trattato del secolo XV*. Florence, 1868.

Ghiara, Carola. 'Filatoi e filatori a Genova tra XV e XVIII secolo'. *Quaderni Storici* 52 (1983).

Green, Louis. *Lucca Under Many Masters. A Fourteenth Century Italian Commune in Crisis (1328–1342)*. Florence: L.S. Olschki, 1995.

Grillo, Paolo. 'Le origini della manifattura serica in Milano (1400–1450)'. *Studi Storici* 35 (1994): 903–906.

Guenzi Alberto and Poni, Carlo. 'Sinergia di due innovazioni: chiaviche e mulini da seta a Bologna'. *Quaderni Storici* 64 (1987): 111–127.

Guenzi, Alberto and Poni, Carlo. 'Un "network" plurisecolare: acqua e industria a Bologna'. *Studi Storici* 30 (1990): 359–377.

Hafter, Daryl. 'Women in the Underground Business of Eighteenth-Century Lyon'. *Enterprise and Society* 2 (2001): 11–40.

Inalcik, Halil. 'The Ottoman State: Economy and Society, 1300–1600'. In *An Economic and Social History of the Ottoman Empire, 1300–1914*, edited by Halil Inalcik, 218–252. Cambridge: Cambridge University Press, 1994.

Iorio, Tedora. *Produzione e commercio della seta in Calabria nel secolo XVI*. Naples: Arte tipografica, 1988.

Jacoby, David. 'Silk Economics and Cross-Cultural Artistic Interaction: Byzantium, the Muslim World, and Christian West'. *Dumbarton Oaks Papers* 58 (2004): 197–240.

Ladero Quesada, Miguel A. 'La producción de seda en la España medieval. Siglos XIII–XVI'. In *La seta in Europa, secc. XIII–XX*, edited by Simonetta Cavaciocchi, 125–139. Florence, 1993.

Lopez, Robert S. 'Silk Industry in the Byzantine Empire'. *Speculum*, 20 (1945): 1–42.

Lopez, Robert S. 'Nuove luci sugli italiani in Estremo Oriente prima di Colombo'. In, *Su e giù per la storia di Genova*, edited by Robert S. Lopez, 95–104. Genoa: Università di Genova, 1975.

Mainoni, Patrizia. 'La seta a Milano nel XV secolo: aspetti economici e istituzionali', *Studi Storici* 35 (1994): 892–893.

Massa, Paola. 'L'Arte genovese della seta nella normativa del XV e XVI secolo'. *Atti della Società Ligure di Storia Patria* 10 (1970): 175–181.

Massa, Paola. *Un'impresa serica genovese della prima metà del Cinquecento*. Milan: Giuffrè, 1974.

Massa, Paola. 'La liquidazione della "volta da seta" di Bartolomeo di San Michele: aspetti tecnici ed economici'. *Atti della Società Ligure di Storia Patria* 19 (1979): 149–206.

Matthee, Rudolph P. *The Politics of Trade in Safavid Iran. Silk for Silver 1600–1730*. Cambridge: Cambridge University Press, 1999.

Molà, Luca. *La comunità dei lucchesi a Venezia. Immigrazione e industria della seta nel tardo Medioevo*. Venice: Istituto veneto di scienze, 1994.

Molà, Luca. 'Oltre i confini della città: gli artigiani e gli imprenditori della seta fiorentini all'estero', In *Arti fiorentine. La grande storia dell'artigianato. Vol. II: il Quattrocento*, edited by F. Franceschi, 93–98. Florence: Giunti, 1999.

Molà, Luca, Mueller, Reinhold C. and Zanier, C. *Dal baco al drappo. La seta in Italia dal Medioevo al Seicento* Venice: Fondazione Giorgio Cini, 2000.

Molà, Luca. *The Silk Industry of Renaissance Venice*. Baltimore–London: John Hopkins University Press, 2000.

Morelli, Roberta. *La seta fiorentina nel Cinquecento*. Milan: Giuffrè, 1976.

Muzzarelli, Maria G. *Gli inganni delle apparenze. Disciplina di vesti e ornamenti alla fine del Medioevo*. Turin: Scriptorium, 1996.

Muzzarelli, Maria G. *Guardaroba medievale. Vesti e società dal XIII al XVI secolo*. Bologna: Il Mulino, 1999.
Muzzarelli, Maria G. ed., *Disciplinare il lusso: la legislazione suntuaria in Italia e in Europa tra Medioevo ed età moderna*. Rome: Carocci, 2003.
Orlandi, Angela. 'Zucchero e coccíniglia dal Nuovo Mondo, due esempi di precoce diffusione'. In *Prodotti e tecniche d'Oltremare nelle economie europee, secc. XIII–XVIII*, edited by Simonetta Cavaciocchi, 477–487. Florence: Mondadori Education, 1998.
Pescione, Raffaele. 'Gli statuti dell'Arte della seta in Napoli in rapporto al privilegio di giurisdizione'. *Archivio Storico per le Provincie Napoletane* 5 (1919):160–166.
Poni, Carlo. 'All'origine del sistema di fabbrica: tecnologia e organizzazione produttiva dei mulini da seta nell'Italia settentrionale (sec. XVII–XVIII)'. *Rivista Storica Italiana* 88 (1976): 444–497.
Poni, Carlo. 'Per la storia del distretto industriale serico di Bologna (secoli XVI–XIX)'. *Quaderni Storici* 73 (1990): 93–167.
Poni, Carlo. 'The Circular Silk Mill. A Factory Before the Industrial Revolution in Early Modern Europe', *History of Technology* 21 (1999): 65–85.
Racine, Pierre. 'Le marché gênois de la soie en 1288'. *Revue des études sud-est européennes* 8 (1970): 403–415.
Rebora, Giovanni. *Un manuale di tintoria del Quattrocento*. Milan: Giuffrè, 1970.
Rosetti, Giovanventura. *Plichto de l'arte de tentori che insegna tenger panni telle banbasi et sede sì per l'arte magiore come per la commune*. Venice, 1548.
Sella, Domenico. *Commerci e industrie a Venezia nel secolo XVII*. Venice–Rome: Istituto per la Collaborazione Culturale, 1961.
Sella, Domenico. *Crisis and Continuity. The Economy of Spanish Lombardy in the Seventeenth Century*. Harvard: Harvard University Press, 1979.
Staccini, Rita. *Le arti perugine della bambagia e della seta*. Spoleto: Centro italiano di studi sull'alto medioevo, 1994).
Steinmann, Linda K. 'Shah 'Abbas and the Royal Silk Trade 1599–1629'. *Bulletin of the British Society for Middle Eastern Studies* 14 (1987): 68–74.
Tabarroni, Giorgio. 'I filatoi idraulici di Bologna'. *Il Carrobbio* 2 (1976): 381–400.
Tognetti, Sergio. *Un'industria di lusso al servizio del grande commercio. Il mercato dei drappi serici e della seta nella Firenze del Quattrocento*. Florence, 2002.
Tognetti, Sergio. *Da Figline a Firenze. Ascesa economica e politica della famiglia Serristori (secoli XIV–XVI)*. Florence: Opus libri, 2003.
Vainker, Shelagh. *Chinese Silk. A Cultural History*. New Brunswick: Rutgers University Press, 2004.
Verga, Ettore. *Il Comune di Milano e l'Arte della seta dal secolo decimoquinto al decimottavo*. Milan, 1917.
Wensky, Margaret. 'Women's Guilds in Cologne in the Later Middle Ages', *Journal of European Economic History* 11 (1982): 635–638.
Xinru, Liu. 'Silks and Religions in Eurasia, c. A.D. 600–1200'. *Journal of World History* 6 (1995): 25–48.
Zanoboni, Maria Paola. ''De suo labore et mercede me adiuvavit': la manodopera femminile a Milano nell'età sforzesca', *Nuova Rivista Storica* 78 (1994): 108–109.

Centres, Peripheries and the Performative Textile: By Way of Conclusion

Graeme Small

In exploring the consumption, commercialisation and production (in that revealing order) of luxury textiles in the late medieval and early modern periods, this volume has emphatically underlined the central importance of Italy and the Low Countries within a wider European context. Not, of course, that these were the only regions where luxury textiles were made or owned in significant quantities; nor that the silk from Italy and tapestry from the Low Countries were the sole luxury textiles in demand. But only the finest woollens made in a few other parts of Europe came close to matching the high prices commanded by silk and half-silk used in the most expensive items of clothing. And until the fashion for wainscoting and panelling took hold in later times, it was tapestry – used for hangings or furnishings, sometimes incorporating gold and silk threads – which was most widely prized in the interior decoration of high-status residences.

In the case of Italy, as Luca Molà has shown here, it was the extensive trade networks in the east, built up in the central Middle Ages by merchants of the major northern and central Italian cities, that were crucial in the early development of the industry, at least until high-quality raw materials from southern Italy could be had in sufficient quantities. In the Low Countries, as Peter Stabel reminded us, luxury textiles gradually supplanted the mass production of woollen cloth that had boosted the growth of the great Flemish cities in the thirteenth century. Although these centres of luxury textile production were quite different in key respects, trading links between the two consolidated the pre-eminence of each. The Low Countries served as the central locus of the Italian luxury textile trade in northern Europe, whence the redistribution of silk from Bruges or Antwerp to 'peripheral' destinations such as London, France or the Baltic was arranged. In the reverse, Italian merchants played a key role in the import of woollen cloth and tapestry products to their home markets, as illustrated here by Christina Antenhofer in her analysis of the purchases of the Gonzaga court. Italian commercial expertise therefore dominated in both the northern and southern European networks throughout our period. It was not until the sixteenth century that Antwerp merchants, such as Pieter Van der Molen, studied here by Jeroen Puttevils, would begin to make their mark in international trade in luxury textiles. With the exception of periods of intense warfare that affected Italy in the early sixteenth century, the 'balance of trade' between the two centres was thus heavily weighted in favour of the south. However, the deficit was compensated for to some extent by a surplus in trade between the Low Countries and the other parts of Europe which, at least in terms of the luxury textile trade, constituted its periphery (Puttevils).

This volume also indicates some of the reasons why the centrality of Italy and the Low Countries was so enduring. The availability of raw materials and specialised labour in each region enabled effective response to changes in demand. In Italy, the planting and protection of mulberry trees, the leaves of which fed the silkworm and allowed the harvest of its all-important cocoon, became highly regulated by watchful municipal authorities (Molà). Flemish markets gave access to the many different grades of wool, silk and thread of precious metal, not to mention the dyes and fixing agents which enabled the production of a wide range of woven hangings and furnishings to suit varying tastes for tapestry products, at the centre of the industry and in the main markets of Spain, France and England. In both Italy and the Low Countries, large-scale specialisation in luxury textile production became a marked feature of the life of urban dwellers – at Lucca or Oudenaarde, for example, where silk and tapestry respectively provided a livelihood for thousands. As Peter Stabel demonstrates, the manufacture of luxury textiles in Mechelen encouraged the development of smaller, more flexible units of production when compared with the large-scale, proletarianised manufacturing processes of earlier times. This feature of luxury textile production may explain the ability to innovate and imitate, another key characteristic that emerges in both regions. As Franco Franceschi notes, high quality woollens came to be produced in 'the Brussels way' and 'the Douai way' on Italian looms, at first using English wool, then indigenous raw materials. Conversely, by the sixteenth century, notably in Antwerp, silk and satin, previously only imported from Italy, had become a significant feature of textile production in the Low Countries, as Jeroen Puttevils has observed. Entrepreneurs from 'peripheral' regions could not easily break into markets dominated by these flexible industries, unless by meeting the considerable start-up costs associated with production, and by attracting skilled workers from established rivals. That is not to say other centres failed to emerge: as Katherine Wilson reminds us, silks and imitation silks were beginning to be produced at Tours and Lyon in our period, and Dijon itself saw small-scale tapestry production by the sixteenth century.

Political upheaval could displace skilled labour from established centres of production, as happened at Lucca in the first half of the fourteenth century, or in the course of the Dutch Revolt in the sixteenth, discussed here by Bart Lambert and Jeroen Puttevils respectively. But as we saw in Luca Molà's chapter, local authorities were prepared to go to drastic lengths to discourage the emigration of their workforce. And looking at the Florentine merchants who found their way to the peripheral market of Nuremburg in the fifteenth and sixteenth centuries, Francesco Guidi-Bruscoli finds it was mainly newcomers and the less well-established members of the main family networks who were drawn to the challenging commercial environment of central Europe. Capital and labour might move *within* centres of production, broadly defined as the cities of the Low Countries or northern Italy; but it was a difficult and slow process for either to move into peripheral regions and flourish.

These were not the only political and social changes which accrued from the success of luxury textile production in the Low Countries and Italy. As Peter Stabel explains here, the 'move to quality cloth' and the associated rise of the 'small commodity middle-class producer' changed the political culture of Mechelen (and doubtless several other towns in the Low Countries) in profound ways, not only in terms of the composition of the town's governing bodies, but also in terms of civic ideology and identity. Further up the social scale, there emerged entrepreneurs with the ability to mobilise capital and develop the contacts that gave access to courts and cities across Europe: men such as the tapestry entrepreneurs Joris Vezelaer and Peter van der Walle in the Low Countries, discussed here by Jeroen Puttevils, or the Italian *setaioli* Andrea Banchi or Tommaso Spinelli, discussed here by Luca Molà. At this rarefied level, as we have also seen in preceding pages, the luxury textile sector shaded into the world of high finance and politics. Flemish tapestry, like plate of precious metal or jewels, had sufficient value beyond the point of purchase to serve as surety for loans for hard-pressed Italian dynasts, as Christina Antenhofer reveals. The Italian silk trade in northern Europe produced the most remarkable and sustained mechanisms for lending money, however. The Lucchese, as Bart Lambert explains, were the early experts in the field, using idle capital to fund complex buy and sell-back operations which initially helped Flemish municipalities bolster their finances in the later fourteenth century, especially Bruges. Thereafter, however, these same techniques were increasingly used by the Burgundian dynasty in the Low Countries to borrow large sums and extend its hold over the very same towns and cities. The textile entrepreneurs behind these operations were among the best connected and most influential figures in their day, uniquely placed to understand the threats and opportunities that lay before them: men such as Dino Rapondi, supplier of silks to the court of Philip the Bold Duke of Burgundy, and to all intents and purposes the duke's personal banker. In different ways, then, our contributors have shown how luxury textile production might bring about significant social and political change within cities, and a changing relationship between cities and the emerging state.

It would be easy to think the 'hunger for silk' and the demand for tapestry products that fuelled these changes was located almost exclusively among the ranks of the ruling elites, their propensity for conspicuous consumption intensified by the availability of growing fiscal revenues of government. As some of our contributors rightly remind us, however, ownership of luxury textiles extended further down the social ladder. Of over 2,000 items of clothing mentioned in around 100 probate inventories studied by Jeroen Puttevils, for example, over 18% were of silk. Katherine Wilson finds good evidence of demand for luxury textile products in similar documents from Dijon. Do data of this nature support Herman Van der Wee's contention that by the sixteenth century, demand for luxury goods came primarily 'from below', specifically from the urban middle classes? The ability of producers to cater for wider markets by producing off-the-peg tapestry furnishings such as door hangings, table or bench covers, smaller and cheaper than the great 'chambres' and series of wall hangings commissioned for the Burgundian or Gonzaga courts, would lend support to the thesis. Moreover, as Francesco Guidi-Bruscoli notes, the high aristocracy were not always the best payers, with the result that the luxury textile sector could only really flourish through sustained demand 'from below'. But from how far below, one might ask? Françoise Piponnier found 'doctors, apothecaries, clerks and artisans' among the owners of silk products. The last of these categories of owners is perhaps the most interesting, although the term 'artisan' could of course cover a broad spectrum of social realities. In this volume, Katherine Wilson's evidence of bourgeois ownership of luxury textiles in Dijon includes references to merchants, spicers, goldsmiths, mercers and tailors – people who might not necessarily be described as part of the ruling elite, certainly, but who could have owned luxury textiles because of their profession (mercers, tailors), or because they supplied the ducal court with other valuable commodities (goldsmiths, spicers). If, as Jeroen Puttevils points out, the decision made at Charles V's court to use woollen mourning cloth for a state funeral could bring about a sharp fall in the value of silk, then we may indeed suspect that the market for silk was relatively small, and that the ruling elite constituted a disproportionately large part of it. It is ultimately very difficult to weigh up the relative importance of demand 'from below' and demand from an 'elite'. It is probably safer to conclude that despite the prescriptions of sumptuary legislation, there was no sharp divide between 'court' and 'city', and that we should understand the success and durability of luxury textile industries as the result of interactions in a broad market encapsulating both, but which also included the church (as Laura Weigert reminds us), the rural aristocracy and better-off guildsmen.

Broad demand for luxury textiles cannot simply be reduced to the economic circumstances of certain sectors of the population or the ability of producers to create products for a wide range of markets. Silk was a desirable textile quite simply because of the enduring appeal of its exotic qualities, as Katherine Wilson reminds us here. The evidence occasionally allows us to discern a contemporary's aesthetic appreciation of luxury textiles, as is the case with the remarkable observations of the Venetian ambassador Michele Suriano on the beauty and craftsmanship of Flemish tapestry, cited by Jeroen Puttevils: weavers worked 'like mosaic makers with their small coloured stones ... [imitating] the most diverse of colours but ... also [simulating] shadow and light to put figures in relief, with all the nuances produced by the most skilled painter'. Here, as elsewhere in this volume, we grasp the performative quality of the luxury textile and the possibilities it presented to its owner: its ability to interact with the immediate circumstances of its display – not just light and shade, but also time of day or season of the year, the architectural features and movable furnishings surrounding it, the clothing and actions of people in the room – to produce different kinds of space, to make different kinds of statement. The colossal choir tapestries of the monastery of Saint Remi represent a 'woven performance' of the life of Saint Remigius, the significance of which only really becomes apparent when we follow, with Laura Weigert, how the work interacted with veneration of the saint's relics and performance of the mystery play of the saint's life in the city of Reims. In the Italian Renaissance palace, that most 'highly performative' of places, luxury textiles could be used in a great variety of ways to send different messages to different audiences – to the petitioner, the servant, the visiting dignitary. And as Christina Antenhofer also reminds us, 'everybody was involved in textile display ... on different scales and on different occasions'. It was not just the cost or the cachet of the luxury textile that ensured its appeal, then; it was also its remarkable ability to fashion identities.

Index

Abruzzo 182, 187, 197, 198, 227
Acciaioli family 109, 113
  Acciaioli, Agnolo 125
  Acciaioli, Bernardo 109, 126
Aegean 223
Affaitadi family 146
Agli family 109
Alberti family 183, 228
Aix, cathedral of 71
Alberti, Leon Battista 37
Aldobrandi, Benvenuto di Daddo 109
Aleppo 211
Alerdot, Hugenot 22, 23, 24, 25
Alexander the Great 71
Alexandria 28
America 220
Amiens 77
Amsterdam 126
Ancona 142
Angers Apocalypse 70
Angers, church of Saint-Maurille 72
Antenhofer, Christina 30
Antinori family 109, 117, 124
  Antinori, Alessandro 110
Antwerp 97, 98, 113, 126, 131–51, 165–6, 167, 229, 236
  Dominicans' Pand 148
  Tapestry Pand 148, 150
Arendt, Martha Sue 39, 61–2
Arezzo 186, 194
Aristotle 2
Armagnacs 101–2
Armenians 205
Arnemuiden 142
Arnolfini, Giovanni di Arrigo 95, 98–9, 103
Arras 17, 72
Artois 21, 162
Auxerre, cathedral of 76
Avalon 21

Baillet, Jean 76
Bakre, Chrétien le 99
Bakre, Louis le 99
Balkans 210
Baltic 136, 236
Banchi, Andrea 227, 237
Bandelli, Eleonora 40
baptism, textiles for 29
Barducci, Lorenzo 146
barter 119–21, 143
Bartolini family 119
  Bartolini, Gherardo 110, 120, 123, 125
Bartolo, Pietro di 207, 226
Belozerskaya, Marina 2
Beaune, Monnot de 21
Beeringhen, Hendrik van 148
Bene, Jacopo del 192
Bengal 206

Benino, Stefano del 120
Bercusson, Sarah 39, 62
Berg, Maxine 28
Bergamo 182
Bergen op Zoom 133, 141, 143
Berkshire 184
Bern, cathedral of 71–2
Bernardus of Clairvaux 2
Bernart, Ami 17
Bernart, Jean 17
Berthout family
  Berthout, Gillis 168
  Berthout, Jan 166
  Berthout, Wouter 167
Bettini, Bartolomeo 92–7
Bettoni, Iacopo 110, 126
Bini, Francesco 126
Bladelin, Pieter 99
Bohemia 117, 125
Boinebroke, Jehan 167
Bologna 120, 142, 182, 188, 207, 216, 217, 220, 221, 223, 230
Bombergen, Cornelis Van 141
Bonsi family 109, 123, 124
Boone, Marc 100
Borromeo family 228
Botti family 220
Bourguignons 101–2
Brabant 103, 133, 139, 159–60, 183, 185, 191, 193–4
Brabant, duke of 166
Bragadini, Martino 142
Brassart, Wolfgang 4
Bratislava 125
Brecht, Hans Van 147
Brescia 142, 182
Breuseghem, Gillis van 143
Brown, Clifford 51, 60
Bruges 1, 72, 92, 94, 95, 97, 98, 101, 103, 133, 137, 139, 142, 163, 227, 229
Brussels 43, 72, 76, 133, 134, 135–6, 146, 147, 148, 183, 192
Bueri, Gherardo 109
Buckingham, duke of 134
Burgos 220
Burgundy, dukes of 91–2
  Charles the Bold 71, 99, 100
  John the Fearless 20, 92, 94, 95, 97, 101–2
  Philip the Bold 14–15, 17, 19, 20, 21, 27, 92, 93, 94, 95, 101, 237
  Philip the Good 17, 93, 95, 97, 98, 100, 163
Burgundy, duchesses of
  Isabella of Portugal 98
  Margaret of Flanders 19
  Margaret of York 71, 100
Burlamacchi, Paulo 143
  Bursa 211

Caffa 222
Calabria 111–12, 211, 212, 227
Cambi, Bernardo 99
Cambrai 137
Cambrai, Peace of 134
Campes, Gauthier de 75
Camogli, Camilla 97
Canart, Jean 76
Canterbury, Christ Church 71
Capilupi, Nicolo 40
Carletti family 109, 119
  Carletti, Francesco 110, 114, 120, 123, 126
Carmignano 189
Catalonia 185
Cavalcanti, Filippo 126
Cavalli, Marino 137
Cavete de Estrella, Juan Cristobal 57
Cellini, Benvenuto 223
Cenami family
  Cenami, Bartolomeo 143
  Cenami, Giovanna 95
Cerremonde, Valentin de 24
Chaise-Dieu, abbey of, 73
Chalon-sur-Saône 17, 183
Chambellan, Etienne 17

Champagne 183, 185
Chancey, Richard du 25, 26, 28
Charles V, Holy Roman Emperor 51, 61, 131, 145, 150, 163, 238
Charles VI of France 101
Chastellain, Georges 99
Chastellan, Thierry 25–6
Chaucer, Geoffrey 2
Chevalier, Regnault 11, 17, 19, 23, 24, 27, 29
Childs, Wendy 12
China 205, 209
Chios 142, 227
Chorley, Patrick 186
Christian III of Denmark 145
Clement VII 223
Clovis 77–8
Coecke van Aalst, Pieter 136, 146
Coggeshall cloth 138
Cohen, Elizabeth and Thomas 36, 60
Cohn, Samuel 3
Colla, Giovanni 41
Collodo, Silvana 188
Cologne 124, 225
Commynes, Philippe de 99–100
Como 146, 182, 188, 189
Constantinople 189, 205, 210, 229
Corfu 210
correspondence 38–9
Corinth 205
Corsuccio, Giovan Andrea 213
Cosenza 110, 121
Cotswolds 184
Courbeton, Jean de 17
Courtrai 97, 137, 140
Cremona 182
Cristoforo, *familaro* of Gonzaga family 46–7
Croix, Jean de la 22, 23
Cyprus 225

Damascus 28
Datini, Francesco 186, 192, 197, 199
Davizani family 142
Delmarcel, Guy 61
Demo, Edoardo 196
Desrey, Pierre 74–5
Diest 135
Dijon 11–31, 237, 238
  Bourg 17
  Notre Dame, church of 17, 21
  Ouche river 22
  Proudhon road 17
  Saint-Jean, square of 17
  Saint-Etienne, cemetery of 17
  Saint-Michel, church of 17
  Sainte Chapelle 97
Domaschi, Urbano 95
Donato, Federico 52
Douai 164, 183, 192
Dubois, Henri 14, 15, 20
Dutch Revolt 139, 237
Dutour, Thierry 14, 15, 18, 20, 22
Dyer, Christopher 1, 5, 14, 15

East India Companies 206
Edingen 135
Eger, Elizabeth 28
Eleanor of France 144
Emilia 213
Erfurt 125
Este family 213
  Este Alfonso d' 61
  Este, Ippolito d' 48, 61

Fabriano 193
Faille, Della family 144
Farr, James 15
Fava, Ludovico della 146
Fava, Parente 93–7
Federico of Naples 61
female workers 163, 174, 195, 218, 220
Féré, Pierot 72
Ferrara 44, 142, 146, 207, 211, 221
Ferrari, Daniela 39, 41, 42
Fioravanti, Leonardo 213

Firmian, Nikolaus 56
Flanders 42, 159–60, 183, 185, 191, 193–4, 223
Flodoard 78
Florence 44, 107–27, 182, 183–6, 187, 189, 190, 191–200, 207, 208, 210, 211, 212, 220, 221, 223, 225–6, 227
  Oltrarno 186
  San Martino 186, 196
  San Pancrazio 186
  San Piero Scheraggio 186
Formento, Francesco 146
Foscari, Marco 186
Francesco, Nello di 207
Francis I of France
Frankfurt 108, 109, 113, 125

Geneva 227, 228
Genoa 119, 126, 131, 142, 182, 183, 184, 207, 208, 209, 218, 220, 221, 224, 225, 229
Geoffroy, Pierre 14, 15
Ghent 163, 167, 174, 183
Gideon 71
Gigli, Carlo 97–8
Giocondo, Paolo del 110
Giocondo, Amadio del 110
Giovanna of Austria 62
Giret, Nicholas 23, 30
Gloucestershire 184
Golden Fleece, Order of 21, 71
Goldthwaite, Richard 196
Gonzaga family 12, 35–63, 238
  Balzo, Antonia del 62
  Barbara of Brandenburg 49–50, 53, 57–9
  Caterina d'Austria 52
  Este, Isabella d' 37–8, 41, 60
  Farnese, Margherita 52
  Gonzaga, Anna Caterina 59
  Gonzaga, Barbara 39, 53
  Gonzaga, Cesare 51
  Gonzaga, Chiara, 53
  Gonzaga, Ercole 35–6, 40, 48, 51, 52, 60–61, 63, 146
  Gonzaga, Federico II 37, 40, 41, 44, 46, 51, 57–8, 59, 61–2
  Gonzaga, Ferrante 57, 61, 229
  Gonzaga, Francesco III 52
  Gonzaga, Gianfrancesco 62
  Gonzaga, Guglielmo, 51
  Gonzaga, Ludovico II 37, 39, 49–50, 53, 59
  Gonzaga, Paula 39, 44–7, 53–6, 57–9
  Gonzaga, Vincenzo 51, 52–3, 59
  Margareta of Bayern-München 53, 59
  Medici, Eleonora de 52–3
  Paleologa, Margherita 39, 40, 41, 61–2
Görz 56
grain 192–3
Grant Val, Girart de 22
Grasse 183
Gravelines 99–100
Greece 210, 220
Gregori, Bartolomeo 207
Groebner, Valentin 57
Guazzalotti family 187
Guicciardini, Lodovico 137
Guidiccioni, Marco 93–7, 98
Guidiciolo, Levantio 213
Guinigi family 102
  Guinigi, Paolo 102

Haarlem 141
Hainaut 103
Halle 125
hautelice 28–9
Henry III of France 51
Henry VIII of England 61
Herefordshire 184
Herentals 135–6
Hincmar 78
Holland 103, 141, 142
Hondschoote 142, 143

Hoshino, Hidetoshi 186, 200
Hume, David 3
Hungary 113, 117, 123, 125, 126

Iconoclasm 139
import substitution 140
India 205
Inecke, Henricks van 141
Innsbruck 59
inventories 11–31, 39–47, 149
Isabella of Portugal, Holy Roman Empress 144

Jadart, Henri 76
Japan 205
Jason 70
John IV of Brabant 93

Karcher, Nicola 44
Klapisch-Zuber, Christiane 58
Knesselare 97
Koopmans, Jelle 76–8, 83

Labors of Hercules 70
Lalaing, Philippe de 148
Lamoral of Egmont 150
Languedoc 185
L'Aquila 110, 121, 182
Lapi family 109
Lebevrier, Julienne 23, 24, 28, 30
Leenere, Gabriel de 134
Lefebvre, Henri 25
Leghorn 119
Leipzig 108, 109, 113, 124, 125
Lemoutardier, Jehannote 23
Leonhard of Görz 46, 57–9, 62
Leproux, Guy-Michel 75
Lernoncourt, Robert 69, 76, 82, 84
Levant 107, 113, 126, 191, 192, 223
Lévi-Strauss, Claude 53
Liénart 79–80, 82
Lienz 44, 58
Lille 137, 140
Limburg 103
Lincolnshire 184
Lindsey 184
Lis, Catharina 159–60
Lisbon 126
Lombardy 181–2, 187, 188, 213
London 97, 103, 113, 126, 136, 142, 223, 229, 236
Lorenzoni, Anna 51
Louis of Male 92
Louis of Orléans 101–2
Louis XI of France 71, 99
Lübeck 125, 228
Luca, Pazzino 199
Lucca 92, 102, 143, 182, 187, 200, 206, 209, 216, 220, 223, 224, 225, 226, 236, 237
lucchesino 200
Luxemburg 103
Lyon 12, 113, 119–20, 126, 224, 229, 237

Macao 205
Macci family 109
Maghreb 182
Magistro Bernardo 45–6
Maistre, Henri 22, 23, 26
Maître de Montmorency 75
Majorca 197–8, 199
Mamlucks 205
Mandeville, Bernard 3
Manelli family 187
Manila 205
Mantegna, Andrea 37, 49, 61
Mantua 37–63, 142, 146, 182, 190, 197, 211, 212, 227, 230
  Castello San Giorgio 49–51, 53
  Dome 51
  Palazzo Vescovile 52
Marchant, Etienne 11, 18, 23
Marche 227
Margaret of Austria 132
Marseille 119
Martin, Jacquot 11

Martin, Jean 22, 23, 24, 29
Mary of Austria 150
Mary of Hungary 61, 131, 144, 148
Maul Meu, Jean 18
Maximilian of Austria, Holy Roman Emperor 56–7
Mayolino, Nicolo 44
Mechelen 137, 159–76, 192, 236, 237
  cloth hall 164
  Nekkerspoel, suburb of 171
  Nieuwland, suburb of 171
  Saint Rumbold, church of 171, 172
Medici family 99–101, 111, 200, 228
  Medici, Cosimo de 100, 221
  Medici, Francesco I de 62
  Medici, Lorenzo de 100–101
Meliani, Paolo 97–8
Menorca 196, 197, 198
Messina 111, 142, 211, 229
Mexico City 206
Meyer, Anke De 161
Michiel, Marcantonio 61
Milan 44, 57, 126, 182, 188, 189, 197, 207, 211, 212, 215, 220, 222, 225–6, 227, 228
Ming dynasty 209
Modena 217
Modone 210
Molen, Van der family 131, 141–50
Molen, Cornelis Van der 141–2
  Molen, Daniel Van der 142
  Molen, Gijsbrecht Van der 141–2
  Molen, Pieter Van der 131, 141–2, 236
  Molen, Frederick Van der 141–2
Monferrato 40
Mongol Peace 209
Montauban, collegiate church of Saint-Martin 75
Mont d'Or 82
Monza 182
Morelli, Giovanni 195
Morelli, Roberta 111
Morande, Dyago de 94
Morando, Bernardo 142
Moscow, Grand Duchy of 206
Mulla, Giovanni da 51
Muthesius, Anna 30

Nagasaki 205
Namur 103
Naples 110, 121, 207, 220, 227
Nassieu-Maupas, Audrey 75
Negroponte 210
Nerazzi, Tizio 189
Nerone, Francesco di 207
Neve, Frans de 148
Niccolo, Agnolo di 186
Nicopolis 20
Nobili family 109
  Nobili, Piero Antonio de' 124
North Africa 182–3
Nuremberg 107–26, 229, 237
Nuyts, Jan 139

Olgiato Baldassare 146
Olivieri family 108–9, 111–12, 115, 117, 118, 121, 123, 124
  Olivieri, Alessandro di Paolo 110, 121
  Olivieri, Giovanni di Piero 110
  Olivieri, Michele di Paolo 110, 121
  Orley, Bernaert van 136
  Orombelli, Giovan Antonio 229–30
  Orvieto 182, 183
  Ottoman Empire 145, 185, 205, 211
  Oudenaarde 133, 135–6, 147, 148, 236
  Oxfordshire 184

Padua 118, 189, 190, 221
Palermo 119, 142
Palestine 210
Pannemakere, Willem de 136
Paolo, Piero di 199
Paris 12, 17, 72, 92, 101–2, 103, 183, 227

Paris, Jean de 18
Parma 182
Parma, Filipo da 44, 46
Pavia 182
Peeters, Jean-Paul 164, 169
Pegolotti, Francesco 209
Pera 120
Persia 205, 210, 227
Perugia 182, 188, 207
Pheasant, Feast of the 70
Philip the Fair 140
Philip II of Spain 57, 61, 145
Philippines 205
Pia, Bernardino 35
Piacenza 182
Piedmont 213
Pipe, Henrick 147
Piperario, Geronimo 146
Piponnier, Françoise 12–13, 18–19, 23–7, 238
Pisa 182, 187, 189, 221
Pistoia 182, 184, 187
Pitti family
  Pitti, Bonaccorso 192
  Pitti, Cione 192
  Pitti, Neri 192
Poggio, Castruccio di 223
Poissenot, Jean 21–2, 29
Poland 107
Portinari, Tommaso 100–101, 103
Portugal 206–
Potosi 205
Pourcelot, Jean 24
Prato 182, 186
Predis, Giovanni Ambrogio di 57
Provins 183
Pucci, Giannozzo 126
Puebla de los Angeles 206

Rabatta, Forese de 99
Rais, Pieter de 142
Rapondi family 92, 102
  Rapondi, Filippo 92–7, 102
  Rapondi, Dino 20, 92–7, 99, 100, 237
  Rapondi, Giovanna 93
  Rapondi, Jacopo 93
Rapp Buri, Anna 71
Reggio Emilia 182
Reformation 110
Reims 77–8
Renouard, Yves 103
Rhine 55
Riario, Girolamo 56
Rinucci family 191
Romagna 227
Romano, Giulio 37
Rome 35, 48, 62, 117, 142, 146, 189, 205, 227, 228
Roover, Raymond De 103
Rolampont, Demoingin 18
Rosetti, Giovanventura 219
Rovereto, Vincenzo Usodimare di 229
Rucellai, Cardinale 126
Rugerio, Bartolomeo 224

Safavid dynasty 205
Saint-Remi, monastery of 69–70, 76, 82, 84, 239
Saint Martin 75
Saint Maurice, cathedral of 70
Saint Remigius 78–9
Saint Remigius play 76
Saint Theodoric 82
Salins, church of Saint-Anathoile 72
Saliti family 108–9, 113, 118
  Saliti, Piero 110, 113, 114, 115, 117, 120, 123, 124, 125
  Saliti, Zanobi 109, 126
Salvatico, Francesco 101
Sancenot, Pierre 23, 24, 27, 29–30
San Giorgio, Teodoro di 51
Sankt Gallen 55
San Matteo 197–8, 199
San Michele, Bartolomeo di 229
Sanseverino 211
sarrasnoise 28

Sauvegrain family 20, 25–6
Sauvegrain, Jean 20–21, 23, 25–6, 28–30
Savoy 212
Saxony 117
Schets, Erasmus 145
Schivenoglia, Andrea 59
Schuurman, Anton 2
Sciorina, Jacopo della 223
Senati, Giovanni 142
Serristori family
Serristori, Antonio di Salvestro 228–9
Sforza family
Sforza, Bianca Maria 56–7, 59
Sforza, Francesco 222
Sforza, Galeazzo Maria 101
Shropshire 184
Sicily 187, 211, 212
Siena 182, 187, 207, 213, 222
Silesia 117
Sint-Geertruiden 141
Sint-Truiden 133, 135–6
Sluys 97
Smith, Adam 3
Soly, Hugo 159–60
Spain 113
Spinelli, Tommaso 228, 237
Spiritellus, Ambrosius 139
Stabel, Peter 4
Stoppa family 196
Straubing 125
Strozzi family, 119–20, 200
Stucky-Schürer Monica 71
Suger 3
Suivard, Jean 25
sumptuary laws 131–2, 208–9
Suriano, Michele 148, 239
Syria

Tabriz 209
Tafur, Pero 1
Talani family 109
Talani, Alessandro 119, 125
Tani, Agnolo 100
Tedesco, Iacopo di 113
Thebes 205
Thijs, Alfons 138
Tiepolo, Jacopo 225
Tolomei, Piero 118
Torre, Stefano de la 139
Torrigiani family 109, 110, 115, 119, 124
Torrigiani, Raffaello 110
Torrigiani, Ridolfo 110
Torno 188
Toulouse 77
Tournai 17, 133, 135, 137, 140
Tournai, cathedral of 72, 73
Tours 12, 237
Trincherio, Urbano 207
Troyes, Margot de 22
Troyes Passion play 75
Troyes, royal collegiate church of Saint-Urbain 74
Trento

Uberto, Domenico di 196
Udine 189, 193
Umbria 182
Urgenc 209

Valenciennes 137
Vaughan, Richard 100
Vecchietti, Raffaello di Iacopo 126
Venice 42, 44, 126, 141, 142, 146, 147, 182, 189, 190, 193, 194, 196, 207, 208, 210, 215, 216, 219, 220, 221, 222–3, 224–5
Rialto 222
Veneto 182, 188, 189, 190, 197, 198, 211
Verona 141, 182, 184, 189, 190, 196, 197–8, 214
Vezeleer, Joris 145, 237
Vicenza 182, 189, 190, 196, 197, 212, 214

Vienna 108 , 125
Villain, Jean 20–21, 24, 27–30
Villani, Giovanni 185
Villani family 109
  Villani, Lorenzo di Giovanni 109, 114, 118, 124, 126
Visconti family 187
  Visconti, Filippo Maria 226
Vivaldis, Jeronimo Azeretto di 131, 142, 143
Voragine, Jacobus de 78
Vries, Jan de 1–2

Walle, Peter van der 145, 237
Wee, Herman Van der 133, 138, 145, 149, 238
Weissen, Kurt 108
Welch, Evelyn 56
Welsh Marches 184
Wervik 97
William of Cleves, Julich and Guelders 145
Worcestershire 184

Ypres 164, 165, 183, 184
Yuan dynasty 209

Zacatecas 205
Zanchi family
  Zanchi, Bernardo di 141
  Zanchi, Joan Battista di 147
Zeeland 103
Zerchiari, Martino 142, 146

For Product Safety Concerns and Information please contact our
EU representative GPSR@taylorandfrancis.com Taylor & Francis
Verlag GmbH, Kaufingerstraße 24, 80331 München, Germany